PRENTICE HALL
WRITER'S COMPANION
■■■■ MIDDLE GRADES ■■■

Prentice Hall
Upper Saddle River, New Jersey
Needham, Massachusetts
Glenview, Illinois

ACKNOWLEDGMENTS

Art credits begin on page 457.

Editorial, design, and production coordination by McClanahan & Company, Inc.

Grateful acknowledgment is made to the following for permission to reprint copyrighted material:

Acton, Dystel, Leone and Jaffe, Inc.
From "The Scribe" by Kristin Hunter. Copyright © 1972 by Kristin Hunter. To be reprinted by permission.

Margaret Walker Alexander
"Lineage" from *For My People* by Margaret Walker Alexander. Reprinted by permission of the author.

Arizona Quarterly
From "The Circuit" by Francisco Jimenez. Copyright © 1973. Reprinted by permission of *Arizona Quarterly.*

Bantam Doubleday Dell Publishing Group, Inc.
From "Eleanor Roosevelt, an introduction to *Anne Frank: The Diary of a Young Girl.*" Copyright © 1952 by Otto H. Frank. Copyright © 1967 by Doubleday, a division of Bantam Doubleday Dell Publishing Group, Inc. Reprinted by permission.

Jamie Beard
Excerpt from "The Mercer Motel Murders" by Jamie Beard. Reprinted by permission of Jamie Beard. (An unpublished work.)

Susan Bergholz Literary Services
From *Woman Hollering Creek.* Copyright © 1991 by Sandra Cisneros. Published in the United States by Vintage Books, a division of Random House, Inc., New York and simultaneously in Canada by Random House of Canada Limited, Toronto. Originally published in hard cover by Random House, Inc., New York. Reprinted by permission of Susan Bergholz Literary Services, New York.

Brandt & Brandt Literary Agency
Excerpt from *The Secret Language of Snow* by Terry T. Williams and Ted Major. Reprinted by permission of Brandt & Brandt Literary Agency.

Children's Art Foundation
Excerpt from "Campfire" by Elisa Smith from the Sept./Oct. 1993 issue of *Stone Soup.* Reprinted with permission of *Stone Soup*, the magazine by children. Copyright © 1993 by Children's Art Foundation.

Cobblestone Publishing, Inc.
Excerpt from essay, "The Right to Rap" by Adrienne Larke, from Cobblestone's February, 1992 issue, *African American*

Inventors. © 1992, Cobblestone Publishing, Inc., 7 School St., Peterborough, NH 03458. Reprinted by permission of the publisher.

Consumer's Union of U.S., Inc.
"Testing Mini Chocolate Chips." Copyright © 1994 by Consumers Union of U.S., Inc., Yonkers, NY 10703-1057. Adapted with permission from *Zillions*, December 1993/January 1994. Although this material originally appeared in *Zillions*, the selective adaptation and resulting conclusions presented are those of the author(s) and are not sanctioned or endorsed in any way by Consumer Union, the publishers of *Zillions.*

Contemporary Books, Inc.
Reprinted from *Growing Up* by Russell Baker, Copyright © 1982. Used with permission of Congdon & Weed, Inc. and Contemporary Books, Inc., Chicago.

Curtis Brown, Ltd.
Excerpt from *No Chinese Stranger* by Jade Snow Wong. Copyright © 1975 by Jade Snow Wong. Published by Harper & Row. Used by permission of Curtis Brown Ltd. Excerpt from "An Interview with Virginia Hamilton" by Lee Bennett Hopkins. Copyright © 1972 by Lee Bennett Hopkins. Used by permission of Curtis Brown Ltd.

Eva Foster
Excerpt from "People Are Basically Good At Heart" by Eva Foster. (An unpublished work.) Reprinted by permission.

Greenwillow Books, a division of William Morrow & Company, Inc., and Laura Cecil
Excerpt from "Auntie" from *Who's Afraid and Other Strange Stories* by Philippa Pearce. Copyright © 1981, 1982, 1983, 1984, 1985, 1986 by Philippa Pearce. Reprinted by permission.

HarperCollins Publishers
Excerpt from "Breaker's Bridge" in *The Rainbow People* by Laurence Yep. Copyright © 1989 by Laurence Yep. Excerpt from *Podium Humor* by James C. Humes. Excerpt from *Banner in the Sky* by James Ramsey Ullman. Copyright © 1954 by James Ramsey Ullman. Excerpt from "Zlateh the Goat" from *Zlateh the Goat and Other Stories* by Isaac Bashevis Singer. Copyright © 1966 by Isaac Bashevis Singer. Excerpt from "The Hatchling Turtles" from *Spring Comes to the Ocean* by Jean Craighead George. Copyright © 1965 by Jean Craighead George. Selections reprinted by permission of HarperCollins Publishers, Inc.

Henry Holt & Co., Inc.
Excerpt from *Mexican Voices/American Dreams* by Marilyn P. Davis. Published by Henry Holt & Co., Inc.

Instructor Magazine
Adapted excerpt from "Different Child, Different Style" by Kathy Faggella and Janet Horowitz from *Instructor* Magazine, September 1990 issue. Reprinted by permission of Scholastic, Inc.

International Paper Company
Excerpt from "How to Read Faster" by Bill Cosby. Copyright © 1987 by International Paper Company. Excerpt from "How to Write a Personal Letter" by Garrison Keillor. Reprinted by permission of International Paper Company.

Maureen Johnson
Excerpt from Brandy Klaassen's letter to school board. (An unpublished work.) Reprinted by permission.

Bradford R. Keeler
Excerpt from "Inaugural Address of the Chief of the Cherokees" by William Wayne Keeler. Reprinted by permission of Bradford R. Keeler for the Estate of William Wayne Keeler.

Adrienne Larke
Excerpt from essay by Adrienne Larke. (An unpublished work.) Reprinted by permission.

Longman Group UK
Excerpt from "Tears of the Sea" from *Arrival of the Snake Woman and Other Stories* by Olive Senior. Copyright © Longman Group UK Limited 1989. Reprinted by permission.

Merlyn's Pen
Excerpts from Apr./May 1993 issue: "Tropical Rain Forest" by Cynthia Lin and "My Father" by Sara Orvis. Excerpt from Oct./Nov. 1993 issue: "Earthsaving" by Andrew Franklin. Excerpt from Feb./Mar. 1991 issue: "Patella, Alias the Kneecap" by Joe Talbey. These pieces first appeared in Merlyn's Pen: *The National Magazine of Student Writing.*

Chris Meyer
Excerpt from essay by Chris Meyer. (An unpublished work.) Reprinted by permission.

Elizabeth Moss
Excerpt from her letter to Crayola Marker Company. (An unpublished work.) Reprinted by permission.

Jaylene Murphy
Excerpt from her letter to Congress. (An

(Continued on page 457)

Contents

SECTION ONE The Writing Process
Developing Your Technique

SECTION TWO The Elements of Writing
Making Paragraphs, Sentences, and Words Work for You

SECTION THREE Types of Writing
How to Do Your Writing Assignments

Expressive Writing

Writing to Describe

Writing to Narrate

Creative Writing

Writing to Inform

SECTION FOUR Grammar, Usage, and Mechanics
Applying the Rules in Your Writing

Problem Solver

Alphabetized Terms and Lessons

SECTION FIVE Guide to Learning
Taking Charge of How You Learn

Research

Study Skills

Humanities

The
Writing
Process

■ ■ ■

Developing Your Technique

The Mather School, 1988, Jonathan Green
Courtesy of the artist

THE WRITING PROCESS

 How does the process of writing work?

Do you ever wonder how a writer shapes words into a story, a poem, an article, or an essay?

Writing is called a process because it goes through a series of changes or **stages.** These five stages are prewriting, drafting, revising, proofreading, and publishing. In **prewriting,** you explore an idea by using various **prewriting techniques,** such as brainstorming and questioning. In **drafting,** you work with sentences and use them to form paragraphs. Once you finish your first draft, you decide on the changes, or **revisions,** you want to make. Finally, when you are happy with your work, you **proofread** it, checking for errors in grammar, usage, and mechanics. You then make a final copy and **publish** it or share it with an audience.

You will not always progress through these stages in a straight line. You can backtrack to a previous stage or put them in a different sequence to fit your needs. To get an idea of what the writing process is like, study the following diagram. Notice that the arrows in the drafting and revising sections can lead you back to prewriting.

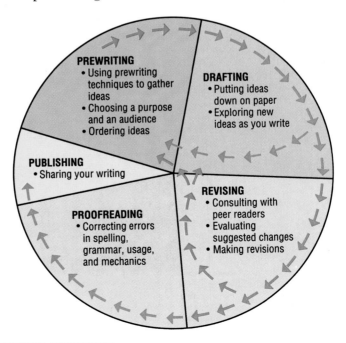

PREWRITING TECHNIQUES

How do I find and develop a writing topic?

No matter what kind of writing assignment you are given, you can use prewriting techniques to find and develop a topic. Some prewriting techniques will work better than others for certain kinds of assignments. Feel free to combine or adapt techniques.

FINDING IDEAS

During the school year, you will probably be given many writing assignments. For example, you might be asked to write a science fiction story or to tell about a personal experience that was important to you. You might be asked to describe a person, to explain a process, or to write a persuasive essay or report.

No matter what the assignment, you will probably do your best work when you can find a specific topic that matters to you. Try some of the following ways to find topics that fit your assignment and your unique personality. These methods are best for personal and persuasive essays, how-to articles, and informative reports.

TAKE A PERSONAL INTEREST INVENTORY. Your favorite activities, hobbies, and subjects can provide an inventory of writing topics for essays and reports. Begin your list with questions like the following:

- What do I want to be good at?
- What surprised me the most during the past six months?
- Where and when am I the happiest?
- What are my favorite books, magazines, movies, and TV shows?

A scene from The Cosby Show

MAKE A LIFE MAP. Creating a life map can help you think of ideas for a personal narrative or personal essay. In mapping the important events of your life, recall your thoughts and feelings about significant moments. Here's how to make a life map:

- On the far left side of your paper, write *birth*. Sketch a picture, such as a cradle, to stand for your birth.
- Draw a path from your birth to where you are now. Add words, pictures, or symbols to show important events in your life.
- To show where others have crossed your path and affected your life, draw intersecting lines. Where you took one direction instead of another, show a fork in your life path.
- Find a visual way of representing how you feel about where you are now. For example, you may feel as if you're climbing a mountain, swimming with or against the current, or crossing a level plain.
- Now write *future* on the far right side of your paper. Show where you hope to be in ten years' time.

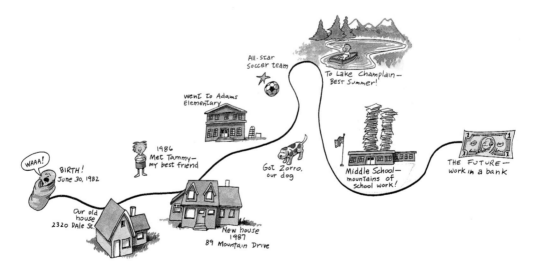

DISCOVER SOURCES OTHERS OVERLOOK. You might collect amusing cartoons and ask yourself what makes them funny or jot down striking lines from songs or jingles and think about what these lines mean to you.

KEEP A JOURNAL. A journal is a written record of your thoughts, feelings, experiences, and observations. The following tips can help you use journal writing to find topics for all kinds of writing assignments.

- Explore qualities such as *courage, honesty,* or *maturity.* What do they mean to you?

- Ask why things are the way they are. For example, why does the school week, like the work week, have five days instead of six—or four? Why don't animals keep growing all their lives, as plants do? Why are the letters of the alphabet in the order they are? Why is a ship called *she*? Explore your ideas and assumptions about these and other topics.

- Record images and words that stick in your mind: something you see on the way to school; a line from a book, a poem, or a song; the sight of a friend's face; the scent of a certain country road or city street in the rain. Explore what these mean to you.

FROM A WRITER

66 *There is nothing to write about, you say. Well then, write and let me know just this— that there is nothing to write about. . . .***99**

—Pliny the Younger (A.D. 61–105)

NARROWING YOUR TOPIC

Often your teacher will assign you a general subject such as "Inventions" and ask you to narrow it to a topic that interests you. When you narrow a broad subject, choose a topic that you can cover well in the available time and space.

For more on narrowing your topic, see p. 12.

DEVELOPING IDEAS

After finding a topic to write about, you'll want to explore and develop your ideas. You can do this on your own or with classmates. The following techniques may help you. Notice that some of them are better suited to specific types of writing.

ASK WHO, WHAT, WHEN, WHERE, WHY, AND HOW QUESTIONS. Questions that help reporters nose out the news can also help you explore a topic for an essay, article, or report. As you search for answers, you will discover information and get ideas for different approaches to your topic.

This model shows how a writer used the six questions:

For more on research techniques, see Research Report, p. 224, and Library Resources, p. 415.

M O D E L

<u>Who</u> invented the first video game?

<u>What</u> qualities do interesting video games have?

<u>When</u> did video games become popular?

<u>Where</u> are the best video arcades in my area?

<u>Why</u> might video games be harmful to me?

<u>How</u> have video games improved lately?

ASK YOURSELF SOME "WHAT IF" QUESTIONS. In addition to helping you focus on gathering information, some kinds of questions can spark a fresh approach to your topic, especially when a topic doesn't seem to "grab" you at first. Here are a few examples of stimulating questions that could lead to imaginative ways to develop your topic for any kind of writing assignment:

- For a response to literature, ask yourself, "What if I could step right into the world of my favorite book?"

- For a cause-and-effect essay, ask yourself, "What if the laws of gravity were suspended?"

- For a problem-and-solution paper or persuasive essay, ask yourself, "What if every citizen had a strict 'garbage allowance'?"

WORKING WITH OTHERS

Have you noticed that working with a friend sometimes seems to double your brain power? Exploring a topic with your classmates can be fun, and a group engaged in brainstorming can often generate more ideas than individuals who work alone.

BRAINSTORM. For any type of writing assignment, brainstorming is a great way to come up with different approaches to the same topic. Try following these brainstorming steps with your classmates:

1. Choose your topic.
2. Set a time limit, perhaps five or ten minutes.
3. Come up with as many ideas as possible.
4. Don't stop to evaluate ideas—just let them flow.

DISCUSS ISSUES. Discussing issues with your classmates is a great way to explore topics for persuasive writing because it allows you to "think out loud" before you write. Participating in a discussion forces you to put your own ideas into words and to respond to the ideas of others who may not agree with you.

INTERVIEW A CLASSMATE. Questioning a classmate can help both of you develop your topics. Here are some specific interviewing ideas that can be helpful for any type of writing assignment:

- Interview a friend who has a special skill. Find out how she or he developed that skill.

For more on interview techniques, see p. 245.

- Find an interview partner and question each other on an acceptable topic.

    Interviews can provide details for a profile, a news story, an I-Search report, or a research project.

For more on I-Search reports, see p. 234.

CREATE A GROUP STORY. Three people and plenty of paper are all you need. Then follow these steps for writing a fictional narrative:

- Brainstorm to come up with the story's opening.

- Have one person write down the opening passage and then hand the paper on to the next person.

For more on writing narratives, see p. 126.

- Have the next person read what's been written, add a sentence or paragraph, and pass the paper on.

- Develop characters, setting, action, and conflict for each addition.
- Continue to circulate the paper until the group resolves the conflict in the story.

USING GRAPHIC ORGANIZERS

DRAW OR PAINT A SUBJECT. When you need vivid details to develop a description of a person, place, or thing or to write an informative essay, you might begin by drawing or painting your subject. Some aspect of your picture may even suggest another facet of your subject to explore. Here are some other ways to experiment with your subject graphically:

- Try to place your subject against different backgrounds. What ideas do the background changes suggest about your subject?
- Try to zero in on only one part of your subject. Enlarge that part and include details.
- Try to create a portrait. Which qualities do you want to emphasize? How will you show them?

FILL IN AN OBSERVATION CHART. To come up with details to develop a piece of descriptive writing or to help you create the setting and characters for a narrative, you can fill in an observation chart. A writer created the one that follows while wondering how to describe the school cafeteria at lunch time.

Subject: cafeteria at lunch time
Senses:

See	Hear	Touch	Smell	Taste
swirl of motion	kids' voices	hot melted cheese on my chin	stuff they wash the floors with	salty chips
fluorescent lights	thuds and clunks of chairs and trays	wet plastic trays	welcoming aroma of pizza	spicy pepperoni
colors of plastic tables and chairs	scraping of chairs	cold, wet milk cartons		mild mozzarella cheese

USING WRITING AIDS

MAKE A LIST. A quick way to explore a topic is to list as many details as you can. Your list will help you see which aspects interest you most and which you can support most easily with details. A writer who wanted to write a personal narrative about experiences with an old car, for example, came up with the following list of details and decided to focus on the events leading to the decision to replace the car:

M O D E L

used to be dark blue

now faded, color looks powdery

the day the battery died in the rain

the day the horn shorted out, started honking on
   its own

coughs and smokes going uphill

back seat split and torn

the day we decided we needed a new car

DO A FOCUSED FREEWRITING. If your mind were a river, freewriting would feel like drifting downstream with the current. You simply let your mind wander and write down all your thoughts as they occur to you. Freewriting can be used either to find or develop a topic. When it is used to develop a topic, it is called focused freewriting. Follow these four steps as you use focused freewriting to develop a topic:

1. Set a time limit. (Until you get used to freewriting, write for no more than five minutes at a time.)
2. Repeat to yourself the key words of your topic, and then write whatever comes to mind about them. Don't stop; don't read or correct what you write.
3. If you get stuck, repeat a word (even the word *stuck*), or write the last word you wrote until new ideas come: you can be sure they will.
4. When the time is up, read what you wrote. Underline parts that you like best.

In the following example, a writer wanted to write a personal narrative about a first backpacking trip, but wasn't sure what to say about it. The writer's mind wandered over the experience and produced the following focused freewriting:

MODEL

Backpacking—my first time. I'm still not sure how I feel about it. What didn't I like? The pack! Ugh! I thought I was in shape. HA! What about the good stuff? All those wildflowers in the grass and the stars at night. Stars, stars, stars. What else? What else? What else? The streams, ice-blue-green and SO COLD! But we swam anyway. The rocks were warm afterward. I even remember how they smelled, sort of like clean dust. Everything smelled clean up there. So how do I feel, how do I feel now, now, now? There were times when I wished I hadn't gone backpacking. But I really miss it now. It was harder than I had expected but more beautiful, too. We were at 8,000 feet. The trees were short and twisted. Joan had trouble getting her breath. What else? What else? That freeze-dried food tasted good. I never slept so well in my life.

By the end of the freewriting, the writer had some great details to support a narrative about the rewards and challenges of backpacking.

PURPOSE AND AUDIENCE

 Why am I writing and who will read what I write?

Every piece of writing is written for an audience. Even when you write a secret in your journal, you are writing for an audience of one—yourself. To succeed at any writing task, you have to understand what your audience wants and needs to know.

> Your **purpose** is your reason for writing. Your **audience** is the people who read or listen to your writing.

Pinpointing your purpose is also essential when you write. Sometimes you write to fulfill an assignment; at other times *you* decide to whom you will write and why. For example, you might decide to write a letter to your sister about your roommates at camp. Your purpose would be to describe your roommates' looks and personalities. At another time you might write a letter to your principal about the issue of beepers. Your purpose would be to convince her to ban beepers inside your school.

DEFINING PURPOSE AND AUDIENCE

Putting information in chart form can help you define your purpose for writing and identify your audience. You will probably want to include the following questions on your chart.

COMPUTER TIP

Create a blank form for a purpose and audience chart by entering lines under each question.

- What is my topic?
- What is my purpose for writing?
- Who is my audience?
- What does my audience already know about this topic?
- What does my audience need or want to know?
- What type of language will suit my audience and purpose?

NARROWING YOUR TOPIC

How do I make sure my topic is narrow enough?

> **Narrowing your topic** means deciding what part of a subject you want to explore in a piece of writing.

"We have studied the American colonies during the Revolutionary period. Now write a two-page report on some aspect of this period that you would like to explore further. Your report is due one week from today."

Suppose that, instead of asking you to study for a test in social studies, your teacher gave you an assignment like the one above. Would you enjoy the freedom this gives you to find a topic on your own? How do you narrow a topic as broad as America during the Revolutionary period? The first thing to do is look carefully at the assignment. It contains two useful tips that can help you out—*time* and *space*. You can't cover the history of the American Revolution in one week and two pages. However, you should be able to investigate one individual's contribution to the cause of the Revolution.

HOW CAN I NARROW A BROAD TOPIC?

Note that narrowing a topic is not an exact science. It is part of the creative process of writing, which involves experimentation and leads to discovery. Following are some specific techniques you can use:

QUESTIONING Asking questions often helps you narrow your topic to fit the time and space you have available. Try asking some of the six questions that journalists use when writing news stories: *who?*, *what?*, *when?*, *where?*, *why?*, and *how?* Then, based on your answers, refocus on a narrow aspect of your topic. The following model shows how one student used this strategy:

Assignment: Two-page report

Broad Topic: America in the Revolutionary period

Question: <u>What</u> groups contributed to the patriotic cause?

Answers: Some colonists, some French soldiers, some freed or escaped slaves

Question: <u>Who</u> were the outstanding figures in each group?

Answers:

colonists—Samuel Adams, John Adams, George Washington, Benjamin Franklin

French—Marquis de Lafayette

Black heroes—Crispus Attucks

Question: <u>What</u> contribution did Crispus Attucks make to the Revolution?

Focused Topic: Crispus Attucks's small but crucial role in events leading up to the Revolutionary War

USING REFERENCE MATERIALS The reference materials you use to find information can also help you narrow a broad topic. Look up your subject in an encyclopedia or the *Readers' Guide to Periodical Literature*, or find a book, using the computer catalog at a library. Scan the resource, looking for specific, narrow topics. Sometimes a resource will be divided into sections or chapters that each deal with a specific topic.

For more on reference materials, see p. 415.

USING GRAPHIC DEVICES Another way to narrow a topic is to combine questioning with a graphic device such as a cluster or inverted pyramid. If you use an inverted pyramid, draw one in your notebook or journal, and write your broad topic across the top of the upside-down pyramid. Then, as the pyramid narrows to a point, break down your broad topic into narrower and narrower subcategories. The following graphic shows how questions can be used to do this.

Clusters and other graphic devices are explained on p. 15.

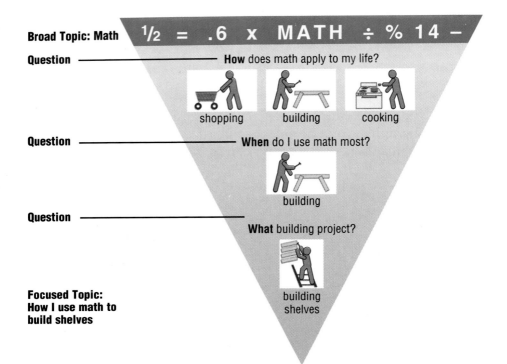

Broad Topic: Math

$\frac{1}{2}$ = .6 x MATH ÷ % 14 –

Question — How does math apply to my life?

shopping   building   cooking

Question — When do I use math most?

building

Question — What building project?

building shelves

Focused Topic:
How I use math to
build shelves

In the following excerpt from an essay on how to read faster, Bill Cosby narrows his focus as he explores a problem:

MODEL FROM LITERATURE

The writer introduces a broad subject.

The writer gives examples.

The writer begins to narrow his focus.

The writer further narrows his topic.

The problem is, there's too much to read these days, and too little time to read every word of it.

Now, mind you, I still read comic books. In addition to contracts, novels, and newspapers. Screenplays, tax returns and correspondence. Even textbooks about how people read. And which techniques help people read more in less time.

I'll let you in on a little secret. There are hundreds of techniques you could learn to help you read faster. But I know of three that are especially good. . . .

. . . The first two ways can help you get through tons of reading material—fast—*without reading every word.*

—Bill Cosby, "How to Read Faster"

GRAPHIC ORGANIZERS

 How do I organize my ideas?

Do your prewriting notes sometimes look like The Blob That Devoured Cleveland? If so, you are having trouble organizing information for your draft. One way to structure your prewriting notes is to use a **graphic organizer**—a drawing with words. Certain graphic organizers work best for certain kinds of writing. The following chart identifies some graphic organizers and the types of assignments for which they might be helpful:

GOAL	▶ GRAPHIC ORGANIZER	▶ TYPE OF WRITING
to organize related ideas	Cluster or Web (p. 16)	▪ biographical sketch ▪ scene description ▪ observation report ▪ comparison-and-contrast essay ▪ cause-and-effect essay ▪ problem-and-solution essay
to organize events in time order	Series-of-Events Chain (p. 17)	▪ story/play/personal narrative ▪ observation report ▪ research report
to outline a narrative	Story Map (p. 18)	▪ story/play/personal narrative ▪ response to literature/book report

GOAL	GRAPHIC ORGANIZER	TYPE OF WRITING
to distinguish important ideas from details	Idea-and-Details Chart (p. 19)	■ observation report ■ informative essay ■ research report ■ persuasive essay
to make a detailed plan before writing	Outline (p. 19)	■ observation report ■ business letter ■ persuasive essay ■ response to literature ■ how-to essay ■ definition ■ story/play

CLUSTER OR WEB

A cluster is useful for developing and organizing related ideas and supporting details. Begin a cluster by writing your topic in the center of a sheet of paper. Circle that topic. Then write any related ideas, circle each, and link it to the main topic with a line. Finally, write details that support each related idea, clustering these details around the ideas they support. Examine the cluster below on the topic of animal migration:

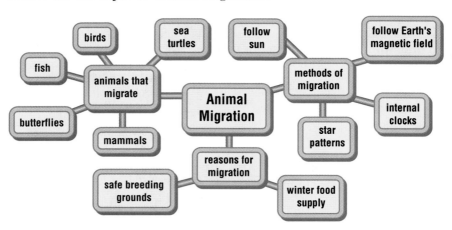

A web is similar to a cluster, except that the items are not circled. The resulting graphic, therefore, looks somewhat like a spiderweb. Either a web or a cluster may be used to explore two or more topics. Examine the following web on two different writers.

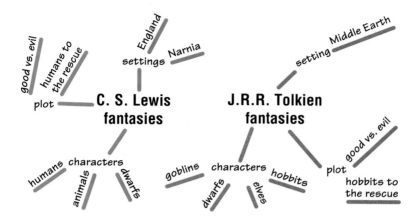

good vs. evil
humans to the rescue
plot — C. S. Lewis fantasies
England
settings — Narnia
humans characters
animals
dwarfs

setting — Middle Earth
J.R.R. Tolkien fantasies
goblins characters hobbits
dwarfs
elves
plot
good vs. evil
hobbits to the rescue

SERIES-OF-EVENTS CHAIN

A series-of-events chain can help you organize details when time order is important to your writing. Here is a series-of-events chain to organize material about the history of computers:

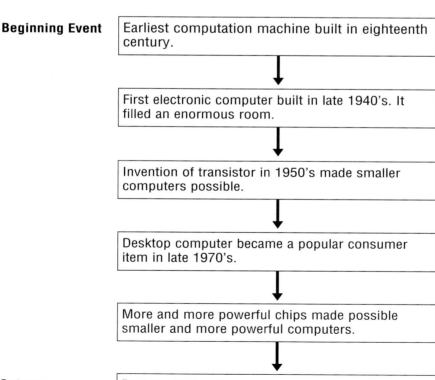

Beginning Event

Earliest computation machine built in eighteenth century.

↓

First electronic computer built in late 1940's. It filled an enormous room.

↓

Invention of transistor in 1950's made smaller computers possible.

↓

Desktop computer became a popular consumer item in late 1970's.

↓

More and more powerful chips made possible smaller and more powerful computers.

↓

Outcome

Pocket-sized computers can now do what a room-sized computer did in 1940's.

WRITING FOR SCIENCE

If you are writing a laboratory report on an experiment, a series-of-events chain can be especially useful. The chain can help you identify the steps in the experiment in the order in which you took them. It can also help you to plan your explanation of the results of each step.

STORY MAP

A story map can be useful when you are preparing and organizing material about a series of events, either real or fictional. Before you begin writing, use the map to outline the story as a whole, the personalities of the people or characters, the setting, and the events. Later, you can use the map to clarify a person's or character's reaction to an event. The story map will also help you keep the events in chronological order—order according to time.

A story map can have several different formats. Here's an example of one particular format:

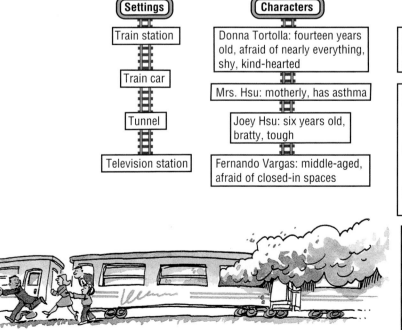

Title: Terror on a Train

Settings
- Train station
- Train car
- Tunnel
- Television station

Characters
- Donna Tortolla: fourteen years old, afraid of nearly everything, shy, kind-hearted
- Mrs. Hsu: motherly, has asthma
- Joey Hsu: six years old, bratty, tough
- Fernando Vargas: middle-aged, afraid of closed-in spaces

Plot
- Main problem: fire on a train stalled in a tunnel
- Events:
  1. Mrs. Hsu has an asthma attack.
  2. Joey burns his hands trying to open door.
  3. Mr. Vargas panics.
- Conclusion: Donna finds out how to get out, helps everyone through the tunnel, ends up on TV as a hero, is no longer afraid of things.

WRITING FOR SOCIAL STUDIES

Suppose you want to write a biographical sketch of a historical figure. You can begin by using a story map to organize details. Follow these guidelines:

1. Label the three parts of your map *People, Places,* and *Events.*

2. Under the heading *People,* list the personality traits of the person you're going to write about. You might also list personality traits of one or more people who were important in your subject's life.

3. Under *Places,* list locations that were important in your subject's life.

4. Under *Events,* list, in time order, the main events of your subject's life.

IDEA-AND-DETAILS CHART

If your writing topic divides easily into a main idea and supporting details, you can organize your work with an idea-and-details chart. Begin by thinking of as many details about your topic as you can. Then number the most important detail 1, the next most important 2, and so on. Finally, write your main idea at the bottom of your chart. An idea-and-details chart can help you formulate your main idea and decide which details support it most effectively. Remember that the order of importance of your details may vary depending upon the purpose and audience of your essay. Examine the sample chart below.

TRY THIS

To double-check the relationship between your details and your main idea, read the list to a friend and ask him or her to indicate the main idea that the details logically suggest. If this main idea differs from your original one, you may want to change your main idea or use different details.

Details

1. Automobile companies are reluctant to spend large amounts of money developing a car that might not sell.

+ **2.** The supply of oil for gasoline is limited.

+ **3.** Electric cars cause less pollution than gasoline-powered cars.

= **Main Idea** The government should pay for research into the practicality of producing electric cars.

OUTLINE

You can use an outline to organize ideas for writing projects longer than a paragraph or two. Use the guidelines on page 20 for preparing an outline.

GUIDELINES

▶ Decide whether you will use complete sentences or words and phrases in your outline. Be consistent throughout.

▶ First, state your main idea as clearly as possible.

▶ Then divide your subject into main topics. Identify each main topic with a Roman numeral.

▶ Next, divide the main topics into subtopics. Identify each subtopic with a capital letter. Indent each subtopic.

▶ If you have enough information, divide subtopics into details. Identify each detail with an Arabic numeral. Indent each detail.

▶ Begin each entry with a capital letter. If you do not write your entries as complete sentences, do not use end punctuation.

Here is an example of an outline, written in phrases:

What Makes Me Laugh

Main Idea: Cartoons, situation comedies, and amusing short stories make me laugh.

COMPUTER TIP

If your computer has a program that shows two documents on the screen at the same time, you can use your outline as a guide without printing it out. Just call up the outline into the document you are working on and revise both as needed.

I. Cartoons
   A. Comic strips that tell a story
   B. One-panel comics

II. Comedies on TV
   A. Funny characters
   B. Funny situations
      1. Mistaken identity
      2. Everyday events that get out of control
   C. Funny dialogue

III. Written stories
   A. James Thurber
   B. Shirley Jackson
   C. Paula Danziger

6

DRAFTING

Should I just begin writing, or should I follow a plan?

After you've gathered and organized ideas, you're ready to start a draft. As you make your pencil race or your word processor hum, keep in mind that at this stage, your draft is an experiment. You are trying to see what works best to express your ideas.

There are two main types of draft:

In a **quick, loose draft,** you write down your ideas as they come to you, the way an artist makes a quick sketch before beginning to paint. You can use your prewriting notes and graphic organizers, but don't consider yourself bound by them. Your aim is to work quickly and freely. This kind of draft is especially helpful for writers who get stuck or lose their train of thought if they slow down. In a quick, loose draft, remember:

1. You can revise and elaborate later.

2. Your aim is to get your ideas down on paper.

3. You can try out various structures as you work.

A **slow, structured draft** helps you keep track of ideas and details. When you draft in this way, use your prewriting tools as a basis for organization. If you are working with notes or an outline, writing a slow, structured draft will allow you to be sure you've included all the necessary information. In a slow, structured draft, remember:

1. Pay close attention to your prewriting materials.

2. Try to perfect a sentence or a paragraph at a time.

3. You can still revise and elaborate later.

Some writers find that a combination of drafting techniques works for them. You might write an introduction to a research paper in a quick draft and then turn to a slow, structured draft for the body of the paper, where the bulk of information is presented. In the conclusion, you might again draft quickly, summarizing your most important points.

FROM A WRITER

66 *The idea is to get the pencil moving quickly.* **99**

—Bernard Malamud

You can also move between drafting and prewriting. As you draft, you might find yourself pursuing ideas and details that do not appear in your prewriting. You can stop and explore these ideas in a graphic organizer and then return to drafting. Some writers consistently alternate between drafting and prewriting as they develop their work. As you write, remember to use the drafting techniques that best suit your style and your assignment.

ORGANIZATIONAL PLANS

7

How can I organize my writing?

WHY IS A PLAN IMPORTANT?

Have you ever begun a piece of writing with some terrific ideas, only to have it end up a hodgepodge? A piece of writing can be like the bicycle in the cartoon. Even though you may have all the right parts, you may fail to make them fit together because you lack a plan. In writing, an **organizational plan** is an outline or map that shows the key ideas and details that you want to include in the order that you want to include them. Following such a plan can help you structure your writing so that it makes a clearer and stronger impression on your audience.

WHAT ARE SOME PLANS I CAN USE?

Often, a piece of writing lends itself to a particular order. For instance, if you are describing a scene so readers can visualize it, spatial order may be your best option. However, if you are describing a person, you might compare and contrast the person with someone else you and your readers know, or you might reveal the person's character by describing a series of past incidents in chronological order. Following such a plan can help you structure your writing so that it makes a clearer and stronger impression on your audience.

Here are some organizational plans that you can tailor to your needs:

Chronological Order

Events or details are arranged in the order in which they occur. Words showing **chronological order** include *first, next,* and *finally.* (see p. 24)

Spatial Order

Details are given by location so that readers can visualize the scene, object, or person. Expressions showing **spatial order** include *to the right (or left), in the middle, nearby, in front of, on, beside, behind,* and *next to.* (see p. 25)

Order of Importance

Events or details are arranged from the least to the most significant, or vice versa. Expressions showing **order of importance** include *most important, above all,* and *also.* (see p. 26)

Logical Order

Each point that is made builds on previous information, and ideas are clearly linked. Expressions showing **logical order** include *it follows that, for example,* and *therefore.* (see p. 27)

CHOOSING THE MOST EFFECTIVE ORDER

CHRONOLOGICAL ORDER

The following paragraph by Isaac Bashevis Singer is an example of writing that is organized according to the sequence, or order, in which events occurred. Notice the use of words that indicate time order, such as *when*, *at first*, and *after a while*.

MODEL FROM LITERATURE

The sun was shining **when** Aaron left the village. **Suddenly** the weather changed. A large black cloud with a bluish center appeared in the east and spread itself rapidly over the sky. A cold wind blew in with it. The crows flew low, croaking. **At first** it looked as if it would rain, but instead it began to hail as in summer. It was **early in the day**, but it became dark as dusk. **After a while** the hail turned to snow.

—Isaac Bashevis Singer, "Zlateh the Goat"

The writer describes a storm as a sequence of events.

Words and phrases in bold type indicate time sequence, or the order in which events happen.

Chronological order is often used to narrate a story or a personal account. Biographies, histories, and how-to essays also rely heavily on chronological order. When you use this organizational plan, be sure the sequence of events is clear. If you vary the sequence, do so for a reason. You might, for example, write a story in which you describe a horrifying accident and then describe the events leading up to it in chronological order.

SPATIAL ORDER

When describing the position of objects in space, you can start anywhere and move in any direction—left to right, top to bottom, foreground to background, from the center outward, and so on. Notice how the expressions in bold type in the following model focus your attention on different objects in the scene and draw you into the setting.

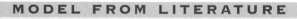

MODEL FROM LITERATURE

The road twisted suddenly **to the left** when it **came to a deep** river gorge. **On the other side** of the gorge, the many trees of the palace looked like a dark-green sea. The yellow-tiled roofs looked like golden rafts floating **on its top.** Dark mountains, their tops **capped** with snow all year round, loomed **behind** the palace like monstrous guards.

—Laurence Yep, "Breaker's Bridge"

The writer moves from right to left, then downward.

The writer creates a three-dimensional scene, sweeping upward to the mountain tops.

In this description, Yep wishes to emphasize the deepness of the gorge and the wildness of the setting. He therefore swoops down into the gorge and then ends with the snow-capped mountains in the distance. When you describe a scene, object, or person, choose a spatial order that strengthens the main impression you are trying to create.

ORDER OF IMPORTANCE

Sometimes, you may want to begin a piece of writing with your most important fact or idea to startle readers or to motivate them to read on. At other times, you may begin with less important details, saving the most powerful idea until the end so it will have a lasting impact on readers, as in the model that follows. The phrases in bold type emphasize this organization.

 MODEL FROM LITERATURE

The writer introduces the topic.

The writer lists less important Native American contributions.

The writer skips over even less important or less tangible contributions in order to move on to the most important contribution.

The writer presents the most important contribution last.

The Europeans who developed into the Americans took over from the Indians many things besides their continent. Look at **a few**: tobacco, corn, potatoes, beans (kidney, string and lima and therefore succotash), tomatoes, sweet potatoes, squash, popcorn and peanuts, chocolate, pineapples, hominy, Jerusalem artichokes, maple sugar. Moccasins, snowshoes, toboggans, hammocks. . . .

A list of **familiar but less important** plants, foods and implements would run to several hundred items. **Another long list** would be needed to enumerate less tangible Indian contributions to our culture, such as arts, crafts, designs, ideas, beliefs. . . . But there is something **far more familiar**, something that is **always at hand** and is used daily by every American and Canadian without awareness that it is Indian: a large vocabulary.

—Bernard DeVoto, "The Indian All Around Us"

In using order of importance, select the pattern that will influence your audience most. If you are writing a poster advertising your school play, put the most important facts first. If you are writing a book review, save your most important point for last. The one thing you do not want to do is bury your most important point in the middle of your writing.

LOGICAL ORDER

Notice in this model using logical order how each part of the explanation refers to the previous sentence. Each new point or piece of information builds on the last. The words in bold type help the reader to follow the complex explanation of a concept.

MODEL FROM LITERATURE

Now let's consider another kind of series of integers. Let's think of the even numbers: 2, 4, 6, 8, and so on. How many even numbers are there?

One way of arguing this question would be to say: Well, the integers can be divided into odd numbers and even numbers alternately, **so that** in the first ten numbers there are five odds and five evens, in the first hundred numbers there are fifty odds and fifty evens, and so on. **This sort of thing** would go on no matter how many integers are taken. **Therefore**, the total number of even integers is half the total number of all integers.

But this is not so. The number of integers is infinite, and one cannot talk of "a half of infinity."

—Isaac Asimov, "Endlessness"

The writer presents an idea.

The writer asks a question about the idea and begins the answer.

An example illustrates a concept.

The writer offers a "logical" assumption.

The writer points out an error in the logic of what he has just presented.

In longer pieces of writing, you often may use all these organizational plans. Your task as a writer is to select the plan or plans that will make your meaning clear to your readers.

8

INTRODUCTIONS

How do I open my paper?

Have you ever introduced two people by just saying names and then heard nothing but silence? If, however, you tell something about each person, you help draw them together.

Like a good social introduction, an effective written introduction draws your readers into your paper and interests them in your subject. The way you introduce your paper will depend on the goal you want to achieve and the type of writing you are doing. Here are some possibilities.

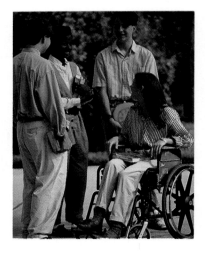

GOAL	▶ TYPE OF INTRODUCTION	▶ COULD BE USED FOR
be clear and direct	a statement of the main point (p. 29)	■ an informative paper ■ a research report ■ an editorial
appeal to readers' senses	a vivid description (p. 29)	■ a description of a scene ■ an observation report ■ a character sketch
get readers' attention	a startling fact or statistic (p. 30)	■ an informative paper ■ a persuasive essay ■ a research report
lure readers into the story quickly	dialogue	■ a story ■ a personal narrative
make readers wonder	a question	■ an informative paper ■ a persuasive essay ■ a research report
give your writing authority	a quotation	■ a persuasive essay ■ an informative paper ■ a research report ■ a book review or report

Once you know which type of introduction to use, you can begin drafting. Here are some writing tips and models.

STATING THE MAIN POINT

When your main idea is arresting or original, you may choose to state it directly in your introduction.

The writer states his main point at the beginning:

 MODEL FROM LITERATURE

Anyone thinking about numbers must come to the conclusion that there are a great many of them, and feel at a loss to express just how many. In poetry, one could make use of some simile: "as many as the sands of the sea"; "as numerous as the stars that shine and twinkle in the Milky Way."

—Isaac Asimov, "Endlessness"

The endlessness of numbers is difficult to express except with similes, comparisons using like *or* as.

For more on topic sentences, see p. 57.

WRITING A VIVID DESCRIPTION

To create a strong image in your readers' minds, use specific adjectives and revealing comparisons, as in this vivid description.

MODEL

There are few things fiercer than a polar bear. When you see one at a zoo, its whitish-yellowish fur, pigeon-toed walk, and large black nose might make you think of an old teddy bear. This couldn't be further from the truth. A 990-pound bear would come out the winner in a fight against almost any other animal in the world. Its sharp teeth are perfect for ripping and tearing, its claws are long and curved, and though it seems slow and lumbering in a zoo, on ice or snow it can move faster than you would believe.

After stating the main point—that a polar bear is very fierce—the writer uses adjectives such as "pigeon-toed" to compare a polar bear's looks to those of a teddy bear. Then, to show that, unlike a teddy, a polar bear is ferocious, the bear's teeth are described as "perfect for ripping and tearing."

For more on writing to describe, see p. 117.

USING A STARTLING FACT OR STATISTIC

If you begin with a startling fact or statistic, make sure it is accurate and helps make your main point. If, for instance, you want to make a case against using drift nets for fishing, you may begin as follows:

MODEL FROM JOURNALISM

This startling fact about the length of drift nets is emphasized by a striking image: "large enough to catch Manhattan Island."

For more on facts and statistics, see p. 33.

Drift nets, often used by commercial fishing companies, can be as much as 40 miles long, or large enough to catch Manhattan Island. On that scale, the Empire State Building would be the size of the letter *i* in this sentence. The Center for Marine Conservation estimates that 200,000 mammals die in these nets each year.

—"The World's Oceans Are Sending an S.O.S,"
The New York Times, May 3, 1992

WRITING FOR SCIENCE

If you are writing a science paper about animal behavior, such as bird migration or hibernation, starting with an unusual fact will draw your readers in. You might tell your readers, for example, the farthest a bird has ever migrated, or you might describe what happens to a bear's body temperature when it hibernates. A good source for these facts is the chapter "The Living World" in the *Guinness Book of World Records*, published annually by Bantam Books, or *Grzimek's Animal Life Encyclopedia*, published by Van Nostrand Reinhold.

ELABORATION

9

How can my idea become a whole composition?

Sometimes what you write seems to be only the seed of a composition. In order to get that seed to blossom, you must add the right details. This procedure is called **elaboration.**

> **Elaboration** is the process of adding details to a piece of writing.

WHAT ARE SOME TYPES OF ELABORATION?

Here is a chart showing the many types of elaboration you can use and what each is used for.

TYPE OF ELABORATION ▷	USED FOR	
facts and statistics (see p. 33 for an example)	essays news stories feature articles business letters	advertisements reviews research reports
sensory details (see p. 33)	observations poems personal essays advertisements	stories plays descriptions

TYPE OF ELABORATION	USED FOR	
anecdotes (see p. 33)	journal entries personal letters news stories	personal essays feature articles
examples (see p. 34)	essays news stories business letters editorials advertisements poems	responses to literature book reports research reports feature articles reviews
quotations (see p. 34)	news stories feature articles essays	responses to literature book reports
personal feelings (see p. 34)	journal entries personal letters personal essays poems	editorials reviews responses to literature
memories (see p. 35)	journal entries personal letters personal essays poems	descriptions observations stories
observations (see p. 35)	journal entries personal letters personal essays descriptions news stories editorials	reviews feature articles stories poems plays
reasons (see p. 35)	essays business letters advertisements research reports essays news stories personal essays business letters	editorials advertisements reviews responses to literature book reports research reports feature articles

Certain types of elaboration are more effective for certain forms of writing, but there are no hard-and-fast rules about which type of elaboration to use. You can use facts and statistics in a poem if you want to!

FACTS AND STATISTICS **Facts** are statements that can be proved true. **Statistics** are facts that you express as numbers.

Rain forests are densely populated with plants and animals. These forests take up only two percent of the world's surface area—six percent of the land—yet they are home to more than half the plants and animals in the world.

—Cynthia Lin, Lexington, Massachusetts

In this research report, facts and statistics tell more about rain forests and elaborate on the topic sentence.

SENSORY DETAILS **Sensory details** are details that appeal to the five senses—sight, hearing, smell, touch, and taste.

Mother and son ~~both looked very different. They~~ had nothing in common but their black color. Even that was different, because Debbie's fur was matted and dusty, ~~both had black fur, but that was all they had in~~ but Buster's sleek coat glimmered when the sun shone on it. Debbie ~~common.~~ was skinny and underfed, but Buster's muscles rippled through his healthy coat.

—Brady Tabor, Edmond, Oklahoma

In this description, sensory details let us "see" the difference between mother and son.

ANECDOTES An **anecdote** is a short account of a funny or interesting incident.

MODEL FROM LITERATURE

My sister Doris, though two years younger than I, had enough gumption for a dozen people. . . . When she was only seven she could carry a piece of short-weighted cheese back to the A&P, threaten the manager with legal action, and come back triumphantly with the full quarter-pound we'd paid for and a few ounces thrown in for forgiveness.

—Russell Baker, *Growing Up*

Instead of simply stating that Doris was unusual, Baker uses an anecdote in this personal essay to illustrate Doris's personality.

EXAMPLES An **example** is an instance of something.

This student elaborates on her point by giving an example of a specific weakness in her school's physical education program.

. . . Every school that I have attended has been weak in making sure that students take physical education seriously and try their hardest to be in good shape. For example, students in my school can run (or should I say walk?) the mile in 12:00 and still receive a passing grade.

—Jaylene Murphy, Victorville, California

QUOTATIONS A **quotation** is someone's words—often those of an expert or public figure.

This quotation from a great American author elaborates on the writer's statement by adding a voice of authority.

We all hope that when the time to be courageous comes we will be able to act in a courageous way. As Ralph Waldo Emerson said, "A hero is no braver than an ordinary man, but he is brave five minutes longer."

—Luke Newman, Bernardsville, New Jersey

PERSONAL FEELINGS **Personal feelings** are thoughts and emotions that are yours alone.

In this editorial, the writer expresses her personal feelings about freedom of speech, making her statement more specific.

The First Amendment, which is part of the Bill of Rights, guarantees freedom of speech. I feel that everyone ~~I am thankful for that guarantee.~~ should be able to say what he or she feels. Sometimes people don't agree with what we say or write, but they should not be allowed to stop us from expressing our thoughts.

—Adrienne Larke, Martinez, Georgia

MEMORIES **Memories** are recollections of your past. This writer elaborates on her memories, making her writing vivid.

I suppose I could say that he was a good father, better than most I know, anyway. He always had a ready smile, a kind word, and advice that could turn even the worst of times around. When I was little, he'd take me fishing, or to the park, and to all the places you go as a child.

—Sarah Orvis, Bristol, New Hampshire

In this description, the writer recalls specific things her father did that show he was a good parent.

OBSERVATIONS **Observations** are things you have seen or noticed firsthand.

I have learned that p⌐
Practice is one of the most important things if you want to become good at something. You can't be excellent at something without practicing.

—Nancy Yearling, Ridgewood, New Jersey

Because this student says "I have learned," we know that her own experience has taught her the importance of practice.

REASONS **Reasons** are explanations of why something is true.

There are many reasons why ⌐. First, I think it is stupid to waste my
ˆI don't use drugs ~~and I'm proud of that.~~
life going to jail and not participating in school activities. Second, I want a good job and I want to live a good life instead of spending time in prison.

—John Pempek, Wrangell, Alaska

This student's editorial is more convincing because he gives reasons for not using drugs.

HOW DO I USE TYPES OF ELABORATION?

This model shows how different types of elaboration can be used in the same essay.

The writer uses a quotation to elaborate on the topic sentence.

Two anecdotes illustrate the times when Lamont broke rules on purpose.

The writer gives Lamont's main reason for breaking rules.

An expert is quoted to show why kids in general break rules.

MODEL

My seven-year-old cousin Lamont thinks rules are for breaking, not for following. Our grandmother says, "A fence is nothin' to a child but an invitation to climb." When she says that, she must be thinking of Lamont. Once he saw a "Keep Off the Grass" sign outside the science museum, and he sat down on the grass right next to the sign until I dragged him away. Another time, when my aunt brought out a plate of cookies and said we could have two each, he grabbed five right in front of her.

If you ask Lamont why he breaks rules, the reason he gives most often is that he likes keeping other people on their toes. Child behaviorist Dr. Ramon Chuya puts it another way: "Children test rules constantly to find out their limits. They want to know that there are consequences for their behavior, and they need to find out just what those consequences are."

CONCLUSIONS

How do I end my paper?

Have you ever been left hanging by the ending of an essay, story, movie, or speech? The experience can be very upsetting. A really satisfying conclusion gives you a sense of *closure*—a feeling that the writer has finished the story or explored the subject completely. You will want to give your readers that same feeling when you conclude your writing.

CHOOSING THE RIGHT CONCLUSION

The type of conclusion you will use depends on your subject and on your purpose. Here are five ways to end a paper effectively, with suggestions on what type of writing might best suit each type of conclusion. These aren't the only possibilities. As you write more and more, you might come up with many other ways to write conclusions.

SUMMARIZE YOUR MAIN POINTS. Review the most important ideas you have discussed and what you've said about them. Instead of just listing them, try to present them in a creative way. This will help readers remember your key ideas.

This is a great way to conclude

- an observation report.
- a personal essay.
- a research report.
- an informative essay.
- a comparison-and-contrast essay.

MODEL FROM LITERATURE

The writer adds spice to his summary by comparing words to people and their families.

If all you know about a word is its meaning, you don't know the half of it. As a matter of fact, you don't know the most interesting half of it. You don't know who its parents are, who its relatives are, what country it was born in, or what picture may be hidden somewhere within it.

—Maxwell Nurnberg, "The Mystery and Wonder of Words"

RESOLVE CONFLICTS AND PROBLEMS. Did the main character survive the battle? Did the enemies become friends? Satisfy your readers by giving them the answers they want.

This is especially important to do when you're writing

- a personal narrative or autobiographical incident.
- a story or fable.
- a play.

MODEL FROM LITERATURE

This conclusion shows how a girl's brave fight to save her brother contributed to her people's victory in two battles.

The battle was still young. Not many men had been killed on either side, but the white general was thinking, "If their women fight like this, what will their warriors be like? Even if I win, I will lose half my men." And so General Crook retreated a hundred miles or so. He was to have joined up with Custer, Old Yellow Hair, but when Custer had to fight the same Cheyennes and Sioux again a week later, Crook was far away and Custer's army was wiped out. So Buffalo Calf Road Woman in a way contributed to the winning of that famous battle too.

—Rachel Strange Owl, "Where the Girl Saved her Brother"

RECOMMEND AN ACTION OR SOLUTION. You've presented your readers with an issue or problem. Now tell them what they can do about it. This will enable them to do something constructive after reading.

This is a great way to conclude

- a persuasive essay.
- a letter to the editor.
- a problem-and-solution essay.

Therefore, if you agree that orcas should live in the wild and not be imprisoned in theme parks, I urge you to write to Earth Island Institute in San Francisco, California.

OFFER A FINAL COMMENT OR ASK A QUESTION. Talk directly to your readers. You can do this by sharing your personal feelings, asking questions, or both. This will make your readers feel more involved.

This is a great way to conclude

- a personal letter.
- a persuasive essay.
- a response to literature.
- a review.

Few people can doubt that Steven Spielberg is truly talented. Is there another director alive who can bring us such different, but equally believable, characters as E.T., Indiana Jones, Peter Pan, and Celie of The Color Purple?

Here the writer uses a question that challenges readers to disagree with her opinion of Spielberg.

MAKE A PREDICTION. Does the information in your paper point to a future event? If so, spell it out for your readers. You will be helping them prepare for things to come!

This is a great way to conclude

- a persuasive essay.
- an editorial.
- a news story.

MODEL FROM LITERATURE

These writers use facts and statistics to convince us of their predictions.

    The forests' future does not look bright. Those that are still standing in 2001, except for some expanses in Brazil and Africa, are likely to disappear or be severely damaged within the following 25 years. If nothing is done to check world population growth and control tropical deforestation, there may be only 20,000 square miles of rain forest left on the globe by 2050, nothing by 2100.

—Will Steger and John Bowermaster, *Saving the Earth*

REVISING A CONCLUSION

    Suppose you've written a conclusion using one of the five techniques just illustrated, but it sounds stiff and unnatural. How can you breathe life into it? Writers face this problem all the time. It's especially hard to summarize points in a fresh way. After all, you've already made your points once.

    The student writer of the model that follows revised a summary in order to liven it up. Notice how she combined sentences and added some wordplay involving the word *world*.

STUDENT MODEL

    You can do many things help to preserve the earth. You can write to the president; urging Tell him to abolish styrofoam and aerosol sprays. You can recycle cans and other products. You can and tell others to recycle, too. You can By become ing an activist, Remember, if you do your part to save the world, you'll be helping a world of people.

—Leslie Randolph, Shelbyville, Indiana

11

PEER RESPONSE

 How can my classmates help me to improve my writing?

Do your friends laugh at every joke you tell them? They probably don't. If your friends think your joke isn't funny, they will let you know why. In the same way that you can test out a joke on your friends, you can test out your writing on your fellow students—your **peers.**

The way your peers respond can often help you look at something from a new angle or see a problem you may not have noticed before. There is no better way to find out how your audience will respond to your writing than to ask another person to read your work and give you his or her responses.

The following guidelines will help you get the most out of participating in peer response either as a writer or as a reader.

FROM A WRITER

> **❝**I usually know what I want to say. When other people read my writing, I find out how well I've said it. **❞**
>
> —Sarah Stukenberg, student, Corpus Christi, Texas

GUIDELINES FOR PEER RESPONSE

When you're the writer:

1. Be specific about what you need to know. The more information you give your peer readers about what you need to know, the more precise their comments will be. For example, you may be

- working on a first draft, wondering whether the topic needs to be narrowed.
- midway through a second draft, trying to make your organization clear and your conclusion convincing.
- beginning the final revision, wanting to be sure your word choice is as effective as possible.

2. Listen silently to your peer's comments. Don't ask questions or offer explanations until your reader has finished responding.

3. Think about whether you need more specific responses. When your peer reader has finished telling you his or her reactions, then you can ask questions. To avoid *yes* or *no* answers, start questions with words such as *what, how, where,* and *which.*

Ask peer readers to write responses to questions that you create. You might include questions like these:
• Where does my writing seem most vivid?
• What main ideas come through to you?
• Which parts of my writing seem vague or incomplete?
• Which sentences did you have to reread before you understood them?

When you're the reader:

1. Ask what you should focus on. The writer may want a response to the paper as a whole, or he or she may ask you to focus on certain concerns, such as the effectiveness of the introduction or of the supporting details.

2. Concentrate. Read the draft at least twice and think carefully about what the writer is saying. As you read, jot down your reactions.

3. Be positive. Begin your responses by pointing out the parts that you like best and explaining why they appeal to you.

4. Be specific. Comment on specific words, sentences, and paragraphs. Instead of saying, for example, "It seems confusing," say "I'm not sure what this sentence means."

REVISING WITH PEER RESPONSES

Take some time to think about peer comments and suggestions. The following chart shows some of the ways you can respond to a peer reader's comments.

IF YOUR PEER READER . . .	YOU CAN . . .
had trouble understanding some of the sentences,	• break an overly long sentence into two shorter ones. • add transitions to emphasize connections between ideas. • make sure that you clearly state your main idea.
didn't get your main idea,	• make sure that your main idea appears at the beginning of your essay.

Remember that the final decisions about revising are up to you. You may, for example, choose to follow a peer's suggestions for rewording an unclear sentence—or you may, instead, come up with your own way of making your meaning clear.

Read the peer response to the writing model that follows. It is a restaurant review that a food critic might write for a newspaper. Then read the revision of the model. Notice how the writer has responded to the reader's underlines and comments.

MODEL

First Draft

If you want to eat out in Oakville, you can't beat the Grant's Ferry Inn. <u>The atmosphere is super.</u> The food, of course, is the main attraction. <u>The Grant's Ferry Inn doesn't have fancy French cuisine or anything like that.</u> It just has normal food, like steak, chicken, and fish, served with vegetables, salad, bread, and dessert. It's all <u>cooked perfectly,</u> and there's plenty of it.

PEER COMMENTS:
What makes the atmosphere "super"?

I like this sentence. It sounds like you!

What do you mean by "cooked perfectly"?

Revision
~~First Draft~~

If you want to eat out in Oakville, ~~you can't~~ be sure to try
~~beat~~ the Grant's Ferry Inn. The atmosphere is at the Inn
~~super.~~ peaceful. The food, of course, is the main attraction.
The Grant's Ferry Inn doesn't have fancy French
cuisine or anything like that. It just has normal
food~~,~~ s like steak, chicken, and fish, ~~served with~~ but these dishes are cooked to order,
tender and juicy. Vegetables are lightly steamed and bread is homemade.
~~vegetables, salad, bread, and dessert.~~ It's all
cooked perfectly, and there's plenty of it.

The Inn is right next to the river, where the old ferry dock
used to be. Through the windows, you see huge old willows
hanging over the water. Ducks and other water birds glide by.
At night you hear bullfrogs croaking and see fireflies flickering.

More details
about the food
help to explain
what was meant
by the phrase
"cooked perfectly."

The statement
about atmosphere
becomes the topic
sentence of a new
paragraph explain-
ing what is "super."

CHECKPOINTS FOR PEER RESPONSE

When you write:

▶ Ask peers to read your work and respond to it.

▶ After getting peer responses, ask yourself how you can change
your writing to make it clear and memorable.

When you read:

▶ Respond to others' work thoughtfully. Notice
and record your reactions.

▶ Make your suggestions to the writer courteous and specific. Begin your comments
with words such as "What if you
tried . . ." and "Do you think it might be
clearer if . . ."

REVISING

12

My draft looks all right. How do I know what to change?

When you've included all your ideas and finished your first draft, you're finally ready to revise it. Few writers produce perfect drafts the first time around. You can almost always improve your paper by reworking it. Here are some hints to help you revise your work.

TAKE A BREAK. Don't begin to revise right after you finish the draft. In a few hours or days you'll be better able to see the strengths and weaknesses of your work.

LOOK IT OVER. When you reread your draft, look for ways to improve it. Use a pencil to mark places where an idea is unclear or the writing is jumpy or disjointed. Also, don't forget to let yourself know when you've written an effective image or provided a useful example. Write "Good!" next to the parts that work well.

M O D E L

I was trying to be helpful. Only, I wasn't. I
didn't mean to ruin their stuff. I didn't know not
to put bleach in dark clothes. My best sweatshirt
now looks like it has some weird skin disease.
When my mom saw that I'd bleached her new wool
skirt, she was really upset.

Sentences choppy.

What stuff? Unclear.

Nice image.

Writing jumps from idea to idea.

READ ALOUD. Your ear is a wonderful editor. Read your work aloud and listen for dull, unnecessary, or awkward parts that you didn't notice when you read your work silently. Are there any passages that you stumble over as you read aloud? Try different wordings and then read them aloud with expression, emphasizing certain words. Listen for which wording sounds best.

"I was trying to be helpful. Only, I wasn't."

This sounds boring.

"Oops! I was only trying to help."

This is a catchier beginning.

SHARE YOUR WORK. Don't be embarrassed. Your friends can help you by telling how your work affects them. Ask them whether your ideas are clear. What is interesting? What is boring? Note how one writer made a revision in response to a comment.

For more on peer reviewing, see p. 41.

MODEL

PEER COMMENT:
How did you know she was upset?

When my mom saw that I'd bleached her new
wool skirt, she ~~was really upset~~. *had tears in her eyes*

HOW TO REVISE YOUR WORK

When it's time to revise a draft, many writers are tempted just to correct a few spelling mistakes and combine a sentence or two. Eliminating surface errors, however, is only a small part of revising. After all, what good is a neat and perfectly spelled paper that doesn't make sense or prove your point?

The word *revise* means "to see again" or "to see from a new perspective." In order to revise your work, you need to rethink your basic ideas.

Step 1. REVISING BY RETHINKING

Taking a close look at the ideas in your draft is the most important part of revising. Rethinking doesn't necessarily mean tossing your paper into the wastebasket. Usually, however, you will spot some "idea" problems. When you do, it's time to get to work. Here are some strategies to help you rethink your draft.

First Draft

PROBLEM	► STRATEGY	► REVISION
My topic is boring.	Look for topics that are too general or vague, such as "My Typical Day" or "What I Did on My Summer Vacation."	Select a specific focus. If you're writing "What I Did on My Summer Vacation," focus on one event, such as "My Flop in the Diving Contest."
My opening puts me to sleep.	Look for openings that state the obvious, such as "I am going to tell you about sailing."	Begin with an inter-esting anecdote, fact, or question.
The focus of my draft is unclear.	Read your introduc-tion and your conclusion. If they seem unrelated, your main idea may be unclear.	• Add an introductory sentence to present the main idea. • Reorder your para-graphs to develop the main idea or story in a logical way. • Make sure your con-clusion sums up your main idea.
I have left out key points, ideas, or events that my read-ers need to know.	Pretend that you know nothing about your topic and then reread your draft.	Whenever your read-ers might ask *who, what, where, when, how,* or *why,* add a sentence or paragraph to your draft to tell the answer. Make sure you put the new infor-mation in logical order.
Relationships among ideas or events in my narrative are unclear.	Look for sections of the text you have to reread in order to get the meaning.	• Use a graphic device such as a chart or story map to rethink the flow of ideas. • Use transition words such as *because, therefore, next,* and *finally* to show the connections between ideas.

For more on transitional words, see p. 64.

Step 2: REVISING BY ELABORATING

When you're sure your ideas are clear and in order, it's time to elaborate on them. **Elaborating** means developing and expanding ideas by adding the right details. It's a little like painting a picture. You wouldn't just outline the figures and then put the painting away. Instead, you'd add details and choose colors you liked. Similarly, when elaborating on your draft, it's important to add the right details to develop your ideas in clear and interesting ways. You might choose any of the following:

For more on elaboration, see p. 31.

TYPES OF DETAILS	USES
facts and statistics	to illustrate a statement; to support a point
sensory details	to help readers picture what you mean; to bring a description to life
incidents	to illustrate an idea; to help tell a story; to support a point
examples	to show the meaning of a general statement; to support a point
quotations	to express an idea in a unique way; to support a point

The Model that follows is an example of a fully elaborated paragraph:

MODEL FROM LITERATURE

Statistics support the main idea of the paragraph.

At the same time the volcano began giving off huge flows of pumice and ash. The material was very hot, with temperatures of about 1,000 degrees Fahrenheit, and it traveled down the mountain at speeds of 100 miles an hour. The flows went on until 5:30 in the afternoon. They formed a wedge-shaped plain of pumice on the side of the mountain. Two weeks later, temperatures in the pumice were still 780 degrees.

—Patricia Lauber, *Volcano*

Notice how Patricia Lauber uses facts and statistics to describe the volcanic eruption that occurred in March 1990 at Mount St. Helens, Washington. By itself, the first sentence doesn't convey a full picture. With the added facts and statistics, however, readers can envision what happened.

Step 3: REVISING BY REDUCING

Just as you usually need to add specific details when you revise your draft, you sometimes need to get rid of material that is unnecessary.

Cut, compress, delete, drop, eliminate, remove, sharpen, streamline, tighten, trim. . . . There's no shortage of words to remind you that eliminating unnecessary material is part of revising. Removing unneeded words and passages will brighten and sharpen your writing.

The following chart shows you how to solve revision problems by removing unneeded words:

PROBLEM	REVISION ACTIVITY
Certain information or details in paragraphs do not develop the topic or move the story along.	Drop them.
Certain words or sentences repeat what has been said.	Drop them.
Certain sentences focus on uninteresting details.	Drop them.
Adjectives and adverbs clutter the writing.	Drop them and use a thesaurus to strengthen the nouns and verbs.
The material is filled with words that don't say much.	Omit inflated language.
Wordy: The entire group shared the same identical opinion.	***Concise:*** We all agreed.

Step 4: REVISING BY REWORDING

Choosing the right words is essential to good writing. As a final step in revising, improve your choice of words. At times a better word will spring to mind. At other times use a thesaurus to find words. As you reword your draft, you'll reveal your own style.

The following chart will help you find the right word.

Problem: I'm not sure my words say what I mean.
Revision Activity: Check questionable words in a dictionary.

Problem: Have I used the most effective word possible?
Revision Activities:

- Choose specific nouns.
  GENERAL: I wish I had some *food.*
  SPECIFIC: I wish I had some *pizza.*

- Avoid the verb *to be.*
  GENERAL: My horse *is* a good jumper.
  SPECIFIC: My horse easily *jumps* four feet.

- Choose active, colorful verbs.
  GENERAL: The sick man *walked* to his bed.
  SPECIFIC: The sick man *hobbled* to his bed.

- Choose the active voice.
  PASSIVE: Chocolate *should never be fed* to dogs, for it can poison them.
  ACTIVE: Never *feed* dogs chocolate, for it can poison them.

13

PROOFREADING

How can I be sure my paper has no errors?

Proofreading is the process of finding and correcting errors in grammar, usage, and mechanics. When you've finished drafting and revising your paper, here's how to proofread your work.

GENERAL TIPS

- Look first for mistakes that you typically make.
- Proofread for one type of error at a time.
- Read your work aloud word for word.
- When in doubt, use the Problem Solver in this text or other reference sources.
- Swap papers with a friend and proofread each other's work.

COMPUTER TIP

A spell checker on a word processor can help you, but there's a catch: Words that are spelled correctly but used incorrectly won't be picked up as errors, for example, sound-alikes such as *their* and *there* or *hear* and *here*.

When you proofread, cross out the incorrect letters or words and write the correct letters or words above them. The following proofreader's marks may also help you make corrections.

∧   Add letters or words here.

∿   Switch the order of two letters or words.

¶   Start a paragraph.

⌒   Link inserted material.

Here is how one writer corrected spelling, grammar, and punctuation mistakes.

MODEL

¶There are many theroies about which europeans or asians first explored the Americas. The Viking seafarer Lief Ericson offen gets credit for being first, but someone else could of been more earlier. Some who have been sugested for the Honor include the Phenicians, the Chinese, the Irish, and the Welsh.

Here are some proofreading strategies that may help you:

SPECIFIC TASKS	STRATEGY
Check Your Grammar ☐ Have you written any run-on sentences or fragments?	Check that each sentence has a subject and a verb. Use a comma before *and, but,* and *or* if they connect two main clauses.
☐ Do your subjects and verbs agree?	Make sure that each singular subject has a singular verb and each plural subject has a plural verb.
Check Your Usage ☐ Have you used the past forms of irregular verbs correctly?	Watch for irregular verb forms such as *seen, done, gone,* and *taken,* which are used only with the helping verbs *has, have,* or *had.*
☐ Have you used subject and object pronouns correctly?	Check that the pronouns *me, him, her, us,* and *them* are used only after verbs or prepositions.
Check Your Punctuation ☐ Have you closed each sentence with the correct end mark?	Look for inverted word order that may signal a question.
☐ Have you used apostrophes in nouns, but not in pronouns, to show possession?	Use a phrase with *of* to check for possession.
☐ Have you avoided plagiarism by using quotation marks around any words from another source?	Check your note cards to be sure.
Check Your Capitalization ☐ Did you begin each sentence or direct quotation with a capital letter?	Look for an end mark and then check the next letter.
☐ Have you capitalized proper nouns?	Look for the names of specific people and places.
Check Your Spelling ☐ Did you leave a letter out of a word?	Use a dictionary but know the spelling demons that usually trip you up.

For more on plagiarism, see p. 231.

PUBLISHING OPTIONS

How can I share my writing?

Once you've finished a piece of writing that pleases you, you may want to share it with others. What you have to say might be important or meaningful to someone else.

Here are some ways you can publish your writing—that is, bring it to the public eye.

HOW TO PUBLISH

1. Submit your work to a school newspaper or magazine.

2. Have a public reading of your work. Perform it

- over the school P.A. or radio system.

- in a school assembly or talent show.

- in a group in which members take turns reading their work.

- at your local library or community center.

3. If your work is a play or skit, have a group of classmates or the drama club present it.

4. Work with classmates to put together a class collection of written work. You can have it copied and bound at a copy shop.

5. Enter a writing contest. *Market Guide for Young Writers* by Kathy Henderson lists contests with their rules and prizes.

6. Send your writing to a local newspaper or area magazine.

7. You can publish your own work and the writings of classmates using a computer with a desktop publishing or word-processing program.

REFLECTING ON YOUR WRITING

 What can I learn from my writing?

Your writing can inform, persuade, or entertain others. It can also help you learn about your subject or the writing process—or even yourself. Once you have completed a writing assignment, sit back and think about the experience for a few minutes.

The Thinker, 1880,
Auguste Rodin,
The Rodin Museum,
Philadelphia

Ask yourself questions such as the following. If you write down your answers or record them in a computer file, you can look back on them before you begin a new assignment. This can help you decide what aspect of your writing to concentrate on.

1. What did I learn about my subject through my writing?

2. Did I experiment with writing techniques or forms? If so, were my experiments successful? If not, what held me back?

3. Am I pleased with what I wrote? Why or why not?

4. Did I have difficulty with any part of the writing process? If so, which part gave me trouble? What strategies did I use to overcome my difficulties?

KEEPING A PORTFOLIO

Sometimes a writing assignment will result in an especially meaningful piece. You may wish to keep this kind of writing in a **portfolio**—a notebook or computer file for important writing projects. Your teacher may require you to keep a portfolio to assess your progress. If that is the case, you can see for yourself how your writing changes and improves. When selecting works, follow your teacher's guidelines. Consider writing that does the following:

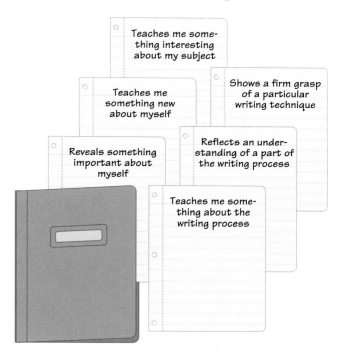

Teaches me something interesting about my subject

Teaches me something new about myself

Shows a firm grasp of a particular writing technique

Reveals something important about myself

Reflects an understanding of a part of the writing process

Teaches me something about the writing process

Choose writing you like, writing that instructs or reveals, or even writing you dislike as long as you understand why you don't like it. Place it in your portfolio after you have completed a first draft. You can go back to it later and make changes, or you can keep your final, revised copy in your portfolio. Then it will be available to look at when you need to solve a writing problem, find an idea, or simply read something good that you have written. The work you place in your portfolio can be useful in the following ways:

1. It can serve as a springboard for other writing projects.

2. It can remind you of successful strategies to use in your writing.

3. It can help you learn more about yourself.

The
Elements
of Writing

■ ■ ■

Making Paragraphs, Sentences, and Words
Work for You

E, 1915, Marsden Hartley, oil on canvas
The University of Iowa Museum of Art, Mark Ranney Memorial Fund

PARAGRAPHS

What is a paragraph?

It's not hard to recognize a paragraph on a page. Usually the first word is indented. What makes a group of sentences a paragraph, however, is not only the way the sentences look but also the relationship among them. All the sentences in a paragraph support the main idea.

> A **paragraph** is a group of sentences that all relate closely to a single main idea or central point.

A paragraph may have any number of sentences, but most of those you write will probably have at least four to six. These will include a **topic sentence** that presents the **main idea,** **supporting sentences** that reinforce it, and a **concluding sentence** that points back to the topic sentence. No matter how many sentences you include, you must relate them to the main idea.

THE PARTS OF A PARAGRAPH

All good paragraphs have several different parts. These parts work together to present an idea clearly.

THE TOPIC SENTENCE The topic sentence is the most important part of a paragraph because it indicates what the paragraph is about. Often this sentence begins the paragraph.

In the following model, the topic sentence is underlined.

MODEL FROM LITERATURE

Some of civilization's more unfortunate effects on the environment are also evident from orbit. Oil slicks glisten on the surface of the Persian Gulf, patches of pollution-damaged trees dot the forests of central Europe. Some cities look out of focus, and their color muted, when viewed through a pollutant haze. Not surprisingly, the effects are more noticeable now than they were a decade ago. An astronaut who has flown in both *Skylab* and the space shuttle reported that the horizon didn't seem quite as sharp, or the colors quite as bright, in 1983 as they had in 1973.

—Sally Ride, "Single Room, Earth View"

Here are some problems many writers face when drafting a topic sentence:

Problem: I have a topic sentence, but it seems dull to me. How can I improve it?

Strategy A: Liven up your sentence with strong, concrete nouns and verbs.

Strategy B: Write your topic sentence as a question.

DULL TOPIC SENTENCE: Chemical dumping is bad for our oceans, but the overdevelopment of seacoasts is worse.

CONCRETE WORDS: Chemical dumping threatens sea life, but the erosion of our seacoasts through overdevelopment presents a greater danger.

QUESTION: Did you know that the overdevelopment of our seacoasts is a more serious threat to ocean life than chemical dumping?

Problem: My topic sentence is too broad. How can I narrow it?

Strategy A: List aspects of your topic, and focus on one of them.

Strategy B: Use a web to focus on one aspect of your topic.

TOO BROAD: Homelessness is a terrible problem.

FOCUSED: In our city alone, there are more than 10,000 families without homes.

Problem: My topic sentence presents an interesting subject, but it doesn't show a point of view. How do I develop a point of view?

Strategy A: Use a cluster diagram to find an aspect of your topic that stirs you. For more on graphic organizers, see p. 15.

Strategy B: Ask yourself how you feel about your topic. Use your topic sentence to express your feelings.

STATING A TOPIC: Department stores often use Muzak to influence customers to buy more.

EXPRESSING AN IDEA ABOUT A TOPIC: Using Muzak in department stores to boost sales is unfair to customers.

THE IMPLIED TOPIC SENTENCE A paragraph, especially in a narrative or a description, may have no topic sentence. Instead, the paragraph is unified by its focus on a series of related events or a single scene or character. The topic sentence is suggested rather than stated outright.

MODEL FROM LITERATURE

The baker's shop, like everything else, was in ruins. No one was there. At first she saw nothing but the mass of crumpled earthen walls. But then she remembered that the oven was just inside the door, and the door frame still stood erect, supporting one end of the roof. She stood in this frame, and, running her hands in underneath the fallen roof inside, she felt the wooden cover of the iron cauldron. Under this there might be steamed bread. She worked her arm delicately and carefully in. It took quite a long time, but even so, clouds of lime and dust almost choked her. Nevertheless she was right. She squeezed her hand under the cover and felt the first smooth skin of the big steamed bread rolls, and one by one she drew out four.

—Pearl S. Buck, "The Old Demon"

This paragraph focuses on a series of related events. The suggested main idea is that the woman is looking for food.

THE SUPPORTING SENTENCES Sentences that add information or details about the main idea in a paragraph are called supporting sentences. The supporting sentences of the paragraph are like the strongest members of a tumbling team. They support the idea expressed in the topic sentence just as team members support the top tumbler in their pyramid. The paragraph that follows shows a topic sentence and the sentences that reinforce it.

MODEL FROM LITERATURE

Many types of animal behavior are designed to re-duce heat loss. Birds fluff their feathers, enlarging the "dead air" space around their bodies. Quails roost in compact circles, in the same manner as musk oxen, to keep warmth in and cold out. Grouse and ptarmigan dive into the snow, using it as an insulating blanket.

—Terry Tempest Williams and Ted Major, *The Secret Language of Snow*

The first sentence is the topic sentence.

The rest are supporting sentences.

The kinds of supporting details you use will depend on your purpose for writing. For example, if you are telling a story in a narrative paragraph, you can use events as supporting details. If you are giving directions in a how-to paragraph, present the steps in the process as the supporting details. If you are writing a description, you can use sensory details; and if you are writing a persuasive piece, use examples, reasons, and comparisons to support the main idea.

THE CONCLUDING SENTENCE A concluding sentence draws together the ideas in a paragraph, giving it a sense of completeness. Here are four techniques for ending a paragraph on preserving our natural environment:

1. Restate the main idea:

In these ways, we can all help to protect our planet.

2. State a decision:

Tomorrow won't be soon enough; I plan to start recycling today.

3. Offer an opinion:

I think we need an international agency to protect the planet Earth.

4. Use a transitional word that signals an ending:

Finally, we can refuse to contaminate the world we live in.

POSITIONING THE PARTS OF A PARAGRAPH

Not all paragraphs have to follow exactly the same pattern. For example, here are some different ways to position a topic sentence:

Beginning with the topic sentence tells readers right away what your paragraph is about.

<u>Most people have no idea how much water they waste.</u> Letting water run while you brush your teeth wastes five gallons. A shower uses five gallons a minute. A dripping faucet wastes almost ten gallons a day.

Letting water run while you brush your teeth wastes five gallons. A shower uses five gallons a minute. A dripping faucet wastes almost ten gallons a day. <u>Most people have no idea how much water they waste.</u>

Putting supporting sentences before your topic sentence can increase its impact.

Letting water run while you brush your teeth can waste five gallons of water. A shower uses five gallons a minute. <u>Most people have no idea how much water they waste.</u> They would be shocked to learn that a dripping faucet wastes almost ten gallons a day.

Placing the topic sentence in the middle allows you to support your main idea before and after you state it.

WRITING FOR SOCIAL STUDIES

You may be asked to write a paragraph as an answer to a test question. Your paragraph will be stronger if you write a clear topic sentence. Often you can use the wording of an assignment or a test question in framing your topic sentence.

Assignment: Tell one way in which an aspect of Native American life *influenced the development of the U.S. Constitution.*

Topic Sentence: The Iroquois League had a system of government that strongly *influenced the development of the U.S. Constitution.*

Follow the topic sentence with supporting sentences that include the information you have learned while studying the subject. Here is an example:

Sample Supporting Sentence: As each tribe in the League retained its own identity but sent a representative to a common council, so each state has its own government but sends representatives to Congress.

Conclude your essay response with a sentence that summarizes your ideas.

17 UNITY, COHERENCE, AND TRANSITIONS

 How can I write well-organized paragraphs and essays?

Unity means "one-ness." A paragraph has unity when all its sentences relate to the topic sentence. An essay has unity when each paragraph relates to the main idea.

Unity is essential in a paragraph. It helps readers understand the main idea you are trying to convey. To prevent yourself from wandering off the topic, refer often to your topic sentence as you draft. Be sure that each point you make is related to your topic. When you revise each paragraph, unify it by deleting any sentences or details that do not support the main idea. Notice how the unity of the following paragraph is increased by the elimination of an irrelevant idea:

MODEL

When the hunting season starts in the countryside, everything changes. We can't go outside without putting on something bright—an orange vest, a red scarf, a purple hat. We can't let our dogs out. A constant parade of strangers marches across our lawn, ignoring the "No Trespassing" signs on our property. ~~Most of these hunters are from the city.~~ After dark, we don't dare go outside.

This sentence, which does not support the main idea, has been deleted.

UNITY IN ESSAYS

Just as a paragraph has a topic sentence and supporting sentences, an essay has a main idea and several supporting ideas. In an essay, the first paragraph usually introduces the main idea, and each paragraph that follows develops a new supporting idea.

When you revise an essay, make sure each paragraph develops one supporting idea. The following is part of an essay about a remarkable woman and her sister. Notice that the writer begins a new paragraph to discuss a new idea: the sister's career.

The Delany sisters in 1993

Dr. Annie Elizabeth Delany co-authored her first book, <u>Having Our Say</u>, at the age of 102, and it promptly made the bestseller lists. ~~Few other important people in history lived to be more than 100.~~ This accomplishment was no more remarkable than the rest of her life. The daughter of a former slave, Dr. Delany earned a degree in dentistry from Columbia University in 1923. She became one of only two black female dentists in New York City at the time. Her practice thrived until her retirement twenty-seven years later.¶Her sister, Sarah Louise Delany, co-author of <u>Having Our Say</u>, also earned a graduate degree from Columbia. After receiving her M.A., Sarah Delany became the first black home-economics teacher in a New York City high school. She retired after thirty successful years. In <u>Having Our Say</u>, Sarah Delany, like her sister, reflects on the lives of African Americans in society today.

The writer deletes a statement that does not relate to the main idea of the paragraph.

This symbol signals a new paragraph: ¶.

PARAGRAPH BREAKS WITH DIALOGUE

In a story or a personal narrative, keep a speaker's words together or unified by beginning a new paragraph each time a different character begins to talk. Paragraph breaks will make it easier for your readers to know who is speaking without your having to keep repeating the names of the speakers.

Coherence means the orderly arrangement of ideas. A paragraph is coherent when the topic sentences and supporting details are organized in an easy-to-follow way. An essay is coherent when the paragraphs that develop supporting ideas follow a plan.

HOW DO I FOLLOW AN ORDERLY PLAN?

You can create coherence in a paragraph by ordering the sentences. There are different ways to do this, depending upon your purpose and your subject. You can use time order, spatial order, general to the particular, particular to the general, familiar to the unfamiliar, unfamiliar to the familiar, or order of importance.

Another feature of a coherent paragraph is the use of **transitional words** that tie the ideas in the paragraph together and carry readers' attention smoothly forward. These transitional words show relationships among ideas. For example, the transition *because* signals a cause-and-effect relationship. Other transitions signal relationships of time, place, comparison, importance, and example.

See the chart below for examples of different types of transitional words.

RELATIONSHIPS	TRANSITIONAL WORDS	
Time	first	at the same time
	next	as soon as
	suddenly	the following
	when	finally
	after	as
	before	then
	soon	after a while
Place	beside	on the left
	here	on top of
	near	around
	there	opposite
	above	next to
	below	behind

RELATIONSHIPS	TRANSITIONAL WORDS	
Importance	second better best first last	more important most important most of all least last but not least
Cause/Effect	therefore for that reason because due to thus	as a result consequently so since for
Comparison/ Contrast	similarly in contrast different from like unlike same as	on the other hand in the same way nevertheless likewise by contrast conversely
Examples STORM ↓ TORNADO	that is such as for example like in other words	along with as follows for instance as namely

Notice the transitional words and revisions for coherence in the following model:

M O D E L

The best way to recycle effectively is to organize a recycling center in your home. The <u>first</u> thing you should do is buy as many trash cans as you'll need—one for paper, one for aluminum, one for glass, one for compost, and so on. Place the cans in an area where you'll be sure to use them. If you hide them in the basement, you'll forget to recycle. <u>Next</u>, label each can. <u>Finally</u>, use the cans; believing in recycling doesn't mean anything unless you actually do it.

Transitional words—like first, next, and finally—show the sequence of steps.

The writer moves this step to its logical position in the sequence.

Here is an example of a unified and coherent paragraph:

The opening sentence expresses the main idea in question form.

The main idea is supported with three facts.

The transitional phrase *even worse* relates this idea to earlier ideas.

The concluding sentence gives an opinion and answers the question in the first sentence.

Why is there such a fuss over burning fossil fuels? When fossil fuels, like gasoline and coal, are burned, they release noxious fumes into the air. It isn't just the air we breathe that the fumes affect; they rise up and contaminate the clouds, polluting the precipitation that comes back down. Even worse, fossil fuels contribute to the <u>greenhouse effect</u>, an unnatural, irreversible, and potentially devastating warming of our planet. For these reasons, anyone who breathes, drinks Earth's water, or eats food grown on Earth should make a fuss over burning fossil fuels.

—Andrew Franklin, Ardmore, Oklahoma

COHERENCE IN ESSAYS

Keep related ideas together in an essay by organizing them according to a plan. Use the chart that follows to identify common problems with coherence and find strategies for fixing them:

PROBLEM	STRATEGY	EXAMPLE
It's not clear how some of my sentences relate to the main idea of my essay.	Repeat a key word or phrase to show how each sentence relates to the main idea. Be careful, though; too much repetition can weaken your writing. In the paragraph, notice where the key word *two* is repeated.	It took *two* to conquer Mount Everest. Tenzing Norgay of Nepal and Edmund Hillary of New Zealand were the first to climb the world's highest mountain. They inched their way up the sheer rock face and along the icy ridges. At last, the *two* stood atop the peak.

PROBLEM	STRATEGY	EXAMPLE
I need to link ideas, but I've already repeated the same word too many times. 	Use *synonyms,* words whose meanings are similar. You can find synonyms in a thesaurus, or after entry words in some dictionaries. Be sure to choose synonyms your readers will understand. Notice how the italicized synonyms give coherence and variety to the paragraph.	No one knows who first sewed sleeves on an undershirt and created the *T-shirt.* This simple *garment,* however, has become one of the world's most popular items of clothing. These soft, comfortable *knits* appear everywhere. There is almost no place *T's* don't go.
I've used the same few nouns over and over to connect my ideas. 	Use pronouns in place of nouns or other pronouns. Be sure each pronoun clearly refers to a specific noun or to another pronoun. Notice how the italicized pronouns in the paragraph allow the writer to keep referring to the same persons and things without repeating the same words.	The American Revolution was not popular with all of the colonists. While *most* supported the struggle for independence, or at least did not actively oppose *it, others* sided with England. *These* were the Tories, or Loyalists. *Many* fled to Canada, where *they* found sympathy for *their* beliefs.

◆ WHEN YOU WRITE ◆

When you revise a piece of writing, ask a partner to read your work aloud to you.

■ Listen to be sure your ideas run together smoothly and in the right order.

■ Listen for names and other words that are repeated in each paragraph.

■ Consider choosing synonyms or pronouns to replace some of the repeated words.

On the following page is a model revised to increase coherence.

The writer replaces repetitive words with synonyms and pronouns.

The writer moves this idea because it fits better below.

The writer moves this sentence because it works better as a conclusion.

The writer repeats the word *problems* to emphasize the main idea.

The writer uses a synonym in place of the word *things.*

A lot of my friends say tagging is no big deal. ~~My friends say~~ They point out that ~~tagging~~ it doesn't ~~do~~ create major ~~damage.~~ problems. I just keep wondering about the ~~people who do the tagging.~~ taggers themselves. ~~Don't~~ Can't they ~~have~~ think of anything more fun ~~to do~~ than spray-ing paint? ~~Tagging~~ It offers harmless excitement, my friends ~~say~~ maintain. I have to admit that it is sort of funny to see people's nicknames pop up overnight in unlikely places such as on highway signs and bus benches. ¶

I guess it isn't so much the ~~trouble~~ problems tagging creates that bothers me. It's ~~more a thing~~ the problems that tagging reveals. ~~I mean,~~ Why aren't ~~the people who do the tagging~~ they out playing sports, working on ~~things,~~ projects, playing music, dancing, going to games or movies or concerts, or earning money for ~~things they want?~~ treats? Is it possible that none of those ~~things~~ activities interest them? That possibility ~~says~~ makes a sad ~~thing~~ statement about the quality of ~~those people's~~ their lives.

TRANSITIONAL WORDS IN ESSAYS

HOW CAN I SHOW THE LINKS AMONG IDEAS?

Just as transitional words (see chart, pages 64–65) link ideas within a paragraph, they can also link ideas in an essay. Notice how this student used transitions (underlined) to link events in her eyewitness account of a tornado.

This transition signals time order or sequence.

When relates the times of two events.

<u>Sometime in the afternoon when</u> the sun was still bright, the air became completely still . . . I was playing outside. My mother called me into the house. <u>When</u> I went inside, she told me to stay

downstairs in the family room on the huge couch. Everyone else was gone except my mother. She was upstairs closing windows. So I was alone, sitting on the couch.

Suddenly it got incredibly windy outside. As I looked up at the window, I saw our huge maple tree blowing around at a strange speed. The sky was dark and murky. Thunder blasted. I screamed.

The first transition shows the time interval between events and the second relates the times of two events.

I ran upstairs to my room, jumped on my bed, and took all my twenty-three animals off the shelf on the wall. I wrapped them all in blankets or put baby doll clothes on them.

Then I opened my dresser and desk drawers and threw everything out onto the floor. Next, I put all my animals into the drawers and slammed them shut. I wanted to make sure they were perfectly safe. My mom finally found me and made me go downstairs with her. We crouched together underneath the stairs.

These transitions show time order or sequence of events.

Soon the tornado passed, but for the next week my room was a disaster area because I wouldn't allow my mom to take my animals out of the drawers. I was still worried about their being blown away.

—Jane Stockman, Burnsville, Minnesota

The first two transitions show time order, the third shows cause and effect, and the fourth shows time order.

18

SENTENCES

 What makes a sentence effective?

A **sentence** is a group of words that expresses a complete thought.

Which of the following three word groups makes the most sense?

1. The drummer boy is afraid.
2. To lead the army into war.
3. Too much suffering.

The first word group is the only one of the three that expresses a complete thought. When you write essays and reports for school, you are expected to write sentences because sentences generally make your thoughts clear to your readers.

HOW DO I RECOGNIZE A SENTENCE?

A sentence has a subject and a predicate. The **subject** tells who or what the sentence is about. The **predicate** tells what the subject is or does.

Study the following chart:

Subject	Predicate
The general	is concerned about his men.
You	must inspire the army.
A slow drumbeat	makes the soldiers slow and listless.
A steady rhythm	boosts the confidence of the troops.

QUALITIES OF AN EFFECTIVE SENTENCE

Using complete sentences is the first step toward good writing. To check that your sentences are complete, ask yourself

1. Does my sentence express a complete thought?

2. Does it name the person or thing that performs the action?

3. Does it tell what the subject is or does?

In addition to being complete, your sentences should be effective. An effective sentence says exactly what you mean and says it in a way that best communicates your meaning to readers. To write an effective sentence, consider these points:

DOES MY SENTENCE STRESS THE MAIN POINT?

In a short statement such as "I sing," the main point inevitably receives emphasis. In a longer sentence, a writer must place the main idea in a prominent position. For instance, a writer can emphasize something by putting it at the beginning.

> Some men would survive the battle, to hear the band play a victory tune.

The men's survival is the important idea in this sentence.

A writer can emphasize something by putting it at the end of a sentence.

> The drummer boy was afraid that the army would be defeated, but he was even more afraid that he himself would be killed.

The boy's fear of being killed is the most important detail.

A writer can use the beginning and the end of a sentence to emphasize a contrast.

> The general was a tough old warrior, known for his strict discipline, so why did his heart soften at the quiet weeping of a fifteen-year-old boy?

The contrast between the tough old warrior and the weeping boy makes this sentence effective.

IS MY SENTENCE CONCISE? A sentence should make its point with as few words as possible.

WORDY: The general was terribly frightened when he thought of the coming battle, which was likely to end in the army's bitter defeat because the army was greatly outnumbered.

CONCISE: Knowing that the army would be outnumbered in the coming battle, the general was afraid.

In the concise sentence, unnecessary words are left out. The word afraid is especially powerful at the end.

◆ WHEN YOU WRITE ◆

■ Use your first draft to get your thoughts on paper and to organize them. When you have decided what you want to say, turn your attention to saying it in complete sentences. As you write each sentence, decide what details you want to stress and place them where they will receive special emphasis. Make each statement as concise as possible.

19

SENTENCE PROBLEMS

How do I recognize when a sentence isn't working?

Sentences are like the infrastructure of a city—the roads, bridges, and other structures basic to a city's needs. When sentences are not in good working order, communication may grind to a halt. The following sections examine common problems in sentence structure and show how to correct these problems.

PROBLEM 1: SENTENCE FRAGMENTS

For more on sentence fragments, see p. 270.

A **sentence fragment** is a group of words that is punctuated like a sentence but does not express a complete thought. To correct a fragment, you can add the information to complete the thought or combine the fragment with a nearby sentence.

PROBLEM 2: RUN-ON SENTENCES

For more on run-on sentences, see p. 269.

For more on main clauses, see p. 304.

A **run-on sentence** has two or more main clauses incorrectly punctuated in a single sentence. To correct a run-on, you can divide the main clauses into separate sentences, separate the clauses with a semicolon, or use a comma and a coordinating conjunction (such as *and, but,* or *or*) between the clauses.

PROBLEM 3: STRINGY SENTENCES

A **stringy sentence** contains too many ideas connected by *and, so, then, and so,* or *and then.* Stringy sentences are dull to read and may be hard to follow because the relationships between ideas are not clear. When you recognize a stringy sentence, ask yourself how the ideas are connected. Is there a cause-and-effect relationship? Can the ideas be compared or contrasted? Are the ideas related in time?

Problem Passage: Stringy Sentence

The great white is one of the large meat-eating sharks, **and** this shark is greatly feared, **and** its attacks have been devastating, **and** it visits American coastal waters, **and then** many beachgoers are placed in danger.

To correct a stringy sentence, first decide if the ideas are closely related. When the ideas are not closely related, place them in separate sentences. When they are closely related, leave them in one sentence, but connect ideas with words that make the relationship clear. Words such as *after, before, since, until,* and *while* show how ideas are related in time. *Although, but,* and *neither . . . nor* show contrasts between ideas. *And* and *or* show how ideas are similar. *Because, since, when,* and *as a result* show cause and effect.

Revision

The great white is one of the large meat-eating sharks. **This** shark is greatly feared **because** its attacks have been devastating. **When** it visits American coastal waters, many beachgoers are placed in danger.

PROBLEM 4: CHOPPY SENTENCES

Choppy sentences are a series of short sentences that create an abrupt, jerking rhythm. Choppy sentences often fail to make their points clear because every idea is given equal emphasis and the relationships between ideas are not shown.

Problem Passage: Choppy Sentences

Lions and grizzly bears get hungry. They may attack people. Sharks are not more vicious. They can be more dangerous. They swim underwater. Unsuspecting swimmers often don't see them. Then it's too late.

To correct choppy sentences, combine closely related ideas by using a conjunction that makes the relationship clear. Words such as *after, as, before, until, while, because, since, when, but, like,* and *unlike* show relationships of time, cause and effect, and comparison and contrast.

For more on conjunctions, see p. 323.

Revision

When lions and grizzly bears get hungry, **they** may attack people. Sharks are not more vicious, **but** they can be more dangerous. **Since** they swim underwater, unsuspecting swimmers don't see them **until** it's too late.

PROBLEM 5: WORDY SENTENCES

A **wordy sentence** contains words that are unnecessary because they do not add meaning. These extra words slow the reader and create clutter that may make the message unclear. To correct the problem, replace the wordy expression with something shorter, or drop it. The following chart illustrates and corrects common examples of wordiness:

WORDY SENTENCE	REVISION
Sharks are hunted **in spite of the fact that** many are dangerous.	Sharks are hunted **even though** [or **although** or **though**] many are dangerous.
Shark-liver oil is sought **because of the fact that** it is rich in vitamin A.	Shark-liver oil is sought **because** [or **since**] it is rich in vitamin A.
Shark skin is sought **on account of the fact that** it makes a tough leather.	Shark skin is sought **because** [or **since**] it makes a tough leather.
The reason why shark meat is often renamed **is that** eating shark seems unappetizing.	Shark meat is often renamed **because** [or **since**] eating shark seems unappetizing.
Flake, **which is** a popular dish in Australia, is really shark meat.	Flake, a popular dish in Australia, is really shark meat.
Mr. Mendez, **who is** my neighbor, fishes for sharks.	Mr. Mendez, my neighbor, fishes for sharks.
He **is a man who** [or **is someone who**] catches sharks for a living.	He catches sharks for a living.
Shark hunters must work **in a** careful **manner.**	Shark hunters must work carefully.
What I want to say is that these scallops are really shark meat.	These scallops are really shark meat.
What I mean is they are sold as scallops, but they are shark meat.	They are sold as scallops, but they are shark meat.
What I ordered **was** scallops, but **what** I got **was** shark meat.	I ordered scallops, but I got shark meat.

PROBLEM 6: EMPTY SENTENCES

An **empty sentence** provides too little information either because it repeats an idea or because it makes a statement without supporting it with facts, reasons, or other details. Correct empty sentences by eliminating repetition (and combining sentences if necessary) or by adding supporting details. The following examples show how these revision methods work.

EXAMPLE:	Most sharks that feed in the open ocean have thin, tapered bodies. They have a slender shape.
ANALYSIS:	The second sentence is empty because it repeats information; the word *slender* means the same as *thin.*
REVISION METHOD:	Eliminate repetition.
REVISION:	Most sharks that feed in the open ocean have thin, tapered bodies.
EXAMPLE:	Bottom-feeding sharks are stouter than other sharks. They have a fatter shape and coarser teeth for crushing shellfish.
ANALYSIS:	The first part of the second sentence is empty because it repeats information; the word *fatter* means the same as *stouter.*
REVISION METHOD:	Eliminate repetition and combine sentences.
REVISION:	Bottom-feeding sharks are stouter than other sharks and have coarser teeth for crushing shellfish.

EXAMPLE:	Humans fear sharks because sharks inspire terror in many people.
ANALYSIS:	The sentence is empty because it does not provide facts to explain why humans fear sharks.
REVISION METHOD:	Supply facts to explain the general statement.
REVISION:	Humans fear sharks because sharks have attacked swimmers and surfers.

EXAMPLE:	I like the classic movie *Jaws* because it is a terrific movie about shark attacks.
ANALYSIS:	The sentence is empty because it does not provide details to explain why the writer likes *Jaws.*
REVISION METHOD:	Supply details to support an opinion.
REVISION:	I like the classic movie *Jaws* because it has vivid performances, realistic special effects, and suspenseful scenes of shark attacks.

PROBLEM 7: LACK OF PARALLEL STRUCTURE

Suppose Abraham Lincoln had spoken in his Gettysburg Address of a government "of the people, by the people, keeping the needs of the people in mind." The expression would never have echoed through the ages like his well-known "of the people, by the people, for the people." Lincoln's statement is powerful partly because it uses **parallel structure**, or **parallelism**—that is, repetition of a grammatical form— to help readers recognize similarity in content. Parallelism gives a sentence a pleasing rhythm and makes the ideas memorable.

FAULTY PARALLELISM:	Some sharks inhabit freshwater lakes, but the ocean is where most sharks live.
REVISION METHOD:	Use the indefinite pronoun *most,* standing for *sharks,* to make the subject of the clauses the same.
REVISION:	Some sharks inhabit freshwater lakes, but most live in the ocean.

FAULTY PARALLELISM:	The great white shark has menaced the shores of California and New Jersey and also Maine's shore.
REVISION METHOD:	Use the names of the states in a series.
REVISION:	The great white shark has menaced the shores of California, New Jersey, and Maine.

FAULTY PARALLELISM:	The great white shark located its prey, circles it slowly, and attacks with lightning speed.
REVISION METHOD:	Keep verbs in the same tense.
REVISION:	The great white shark locates its prey, circles it slowly, and attacks with lightning speed.
FAULTY PARALLELISM:	Other dangerous sharks include the gray nurse, blue shark, and the tiger shark.
REVISION METHOD:	In parallel structures, use the articles *the, a,* and *an* consistently.
REVISIONS:	Other dangerous sharks include the gray nurse, the blue shark, and the tiger shark.
	Other dangerous sharks include the gray nurse, blue shark, and tiger shark.

PROBLEM 8: UNNECESSARY SHIFTS IN VERB TENSE AND PERSONAL PRONOUNS

An unnecessary change in verb tense or pronoun can confuse readers. In the following passage, verbs and pronouns are in bold type.

For more on verb tenses and unnecessary shifts in tense, see p. 273 and p. 405.

Problem Passage: Confusing Verb Tense and Pronoun Shifts

Big-game fishers **catch** large fish for sport. **They** often **seek** thresher sharks, which **feed** near the ocean's surface. **They** also **will look** for mako and mackerel sharks. **You** usually **use** a rod and reel to catch these big-game fish.

This problem passage correctly uses the present-tense verbs *catch, seek, feed,* and *use* but shifts to the future tense *will look.* Similarly, the passage correctly uses the third-person pronoun *they* to refer to *big-game fishers* but shifts to the second-person pronoun *you.* Both of these unnecessary shifts are corrected in the following revision.

For more on pronouns and unnecessary shifts in pronoun, see p. 362 and p. 275.

Revision

Big-game fishers catch large fish for sport. They often seek thresher sharks, which feed near the ocean's surface. They also **look** for mako and mackerel sharks. **They** usually use a rod and reel to catch these big-game fish.

20

SENTENCE COMBINING

 How do I avoid writing boring, choppy, or repetitive sentences?

Anyone who has heard rap music knows that sentences have rhythm. Some are short and sharp; others are long and flowing; still others rise and fall like waves. If all your sentences repeat the same rhythm, your readers' attention will start to wander, and you will eventually lose them. But when you vary sentence rhythms, you can grab your readers' attention and keep it. By experimenting with a number of sentence-combining techniques, you can learn to notice and vary your sentence rhythms and improve your writing.

USING COORDINATING CONJUNCTIONS

Short, sharp sentences have power—unless you write too many of them. To keep their power, short sentences need to be set off by longer ones. You can sometimes create longer sentences by joining short ones.

If the ideas in two short sentences are of equal importance, join the sentences with a comma and a coordinating conjunction (such as *and, but,* or *or*). Choose the coordinating conjunction that best shows the relationship between the two sentences. In order to determine the best conjunction to use, examine the following paired examples:

The coordinating conjunction *but* shows that the sentences express differing ideas.

SHORT SENTENCES:	Mitzi Bixby loves rap music. Her parents prefer rock.
JOINED:	Mitzi Bixby loves rap music, **but** her parents prefer rock.

The coordinating conjunction *and* shows that the sentences express similar ideas.

SHORT SENTENCES:	Mitzi's mother plays the oboe. Her father plays the bassoon.
JOINED:	Mitzi's mother plays the oboe, **and** her father plays the bassoon.

The coordinating conjunction *or* shows that the sentences express a choice.

SHORT SENTENCES: Are there rock arrangements for oboe and bassoon? Must the Bixbys improvise?

JOINED: Are there rock arrangements for oboe and bassoon, **or** must the Bixbys improvise?

USING SUBORDINATING CONJUNCTIONS

If the ideas in two short sentences are of unequal importance, join the sentences by placing a subordinating conjunction—a word like those in the list that follows—before the less important idea. Choose the conjunction that best shows the relationship between the two ideas.

Subordinating Conjunctions

because	before	when	where	if
since	after	whenever	wherever	although
so	as	while	until	unless

SHORT SENTENCES: Mitzi pestered her parents. They agreed to let her take sousaphone lessons.

JOINED: Mitzi pestered her parents **until** they agreed to let her take sousaphone lessons.

SHORT SENTENCES: Mitzi gave up her sousaphone lessons. They conflicted with her favorite TV show.

JOINED: Mitzi gave up her sousaphone lessons **because** they conflicted with her favorite TV show.

SHORT SENTENCES: Mitzi used earplugs. She played a tune on her sousaphone.

JOINED: Mitzi used earplugs **whenever** she played a tune on her sousaphone.

You may use a subordinating conjunction to begin a sentence. When you do, put a comma between the ideas.

SHORT SENTENCES: Mrs. Bixby was once an opera singer. She seldom performs anymore.

JOINED: **Although** Mrs. Bixby was once an opera singer, she seldom performs anymore.

SHORT SENTENCES: She practiced at home. Neighborhood dogs yowled.

JOINED: **Whenever** she practiced at home, neighborhood dogs yowled.

JOINING SENTENCE PARTS

You know that strong sentences are rich in detail. You also know that wordiness weighs sentences down. How do you include plenty of details without being wordy? Instead of joining whole sentences, try joining sentence parts. For example, you might join subjects, verbs, objects, or modifiers.

To combine sentences by joining sentence parts,

- omit repeated words.

- add *and, but,* or *or* where appropriate.

- change punctuation and capitalization as needed.

In the short sentences that follow, lines have been drawn through repeated words. Words added to the joined sentences are in bold type. You need not use a comma with *and, but,* or *or* when joining sentence parts. Notice that no commas have been added in the examples of subjects joined and verbs joined.

SHORT SENTENCES: The Bixbys live for music. Their friends ~~live for music~~.

SUBJECTS JOINED: The Bixbys **and** their friends live for music.

SHORT SENTENCES: The Bixbys want Mitzi to love all kinds of music. ~~The Bixbys want Mitzi to~~ understand ~~all kinds of music~~.

VERBS JOINED: The Bixbys want Mitzi to love **and** understand all kinds of music.

SHORT SENTENCES:	When she was a baby, they played Beethoven for her. ~~They played~~ the Beatles ~~for her. They played~~ Frank Sinatra ~~for her.~~
OBJECTS JOINED:	When she was a baby, they played Beethoven, the Beatles, **and** Frank Sinatra for her.

For more on using commas with items in a series, see, p. 280 and p. 312.

(The names B*eethoven*, *the Beatles*, and *Frank Sinatra* create a series. Commas are used to separate items in a series.)

SHORT SENTENCES:	They played the music softly. ~~They played the music~~ continually.
MODIFIERS JOINED:	They played the music softly **but** continually.
SHORT SENTENCES:	They wondered why their baby was always wrapping her head in a blanket. ~~Their baby was~~ bright. ~~Their baby was~~ charming.
MODIFIERS JOINED:	They wondered why their bright **and** charming baby was always wrapping her head in a blanket.

CHANGING WORDS

If you want to condense the ideas in your sentences, joining sentence parts can help. When you condense ideas, you may need to change the forms of some words. Notice how the words *spoke* and *loud* change in the example that follows.

ORIGINAL:	Baby Mitzi's first words were "Turn off the music." She spoke them in a loud voice.
JOINED:	Baby Mitzi's first words, **spoken loudly,** were "Turn off the music."

Three common ways to change words are to add -*ly*, -*ed*, or -*ing*.

For more on spelling changes, see p. 410.

Adding -ly

ORIGINAL:	"Why is she saying that?" her mother asked. Mrs. Bixby sounded anxious.
JOINED:	"Why is she saying that?" her mother asked **anxiously**.

Remember that sometimes you must change the spelling of a word before adding -*ly*.

ORIGINAL:	When the music stopped, Baby Mitzi sighed. She looked happy.
JOINED:	When the music stopped, Baby Mitzi sighed **happily.**

Adding -ing

ORIGINAL:	"Do you suppose she prefers live music?" asked Mr. Bixby. He began to polish his bassoon.
JOINED:	"Do you suppose she prefers live music?" asked Mr. Bixby, **polishing** his bassoon.

Remember to change the spelling of some words before adding -ing.

ORIGINAL:	Mrs. Bixby looked at her daughter's face. Mitzi wore a smile.
JOINED:	Mrs. Bixby looked at her daughter's **smiling** face.

Adding -ed

ORIGINAL:	"What a splendid idea!" Mrs. Bixby chirped. "I'll get my oboe." She was filled with delight.
JOINED:	"What a splendid idea!" Mrs. Bixby chirped, **delighted.** "I'll get my oboe."

SENTENCE VARIETY

Short sentences aren't the only kind that can get monotonous. Even in long sentences, the same rhythm used again and again gets boring. The techniques that follow offer you several ways to improve your writing by varying the rhythms of longer sentences.

VARYING SENTENCE BEGINNINGS

In most English sentences, the subject comes first, followed by the predicate and an object.

> Cousin Raphael plays his accordion in the evenings.
> He joined a jug band last year.

One easy way to vary your sentences is to start with something other than the subject.

For more on using commas with such word groups, see p. 311.

In the evenings, Cousin Raphael plays his accordion. **Last year,** he joined a jug band.

Notice that word groups at the beginnings of sentences are usually set off with commas. You might begin a sentence with an adverb, a prepositional phrase, or a participial phrase. Notice the variety of possible ways to begin the base sentence that follows.

BASE	The band practices tunes old and new.
ADVERB	**Regularly,** the band practices tunes old and new.
PREPOSITIONAL PHRASE	**Out in Cousin Raphael's garage,** the band practices tunes old and new.
PRESENT PARTICIPIAL PHRASE	**Sounding like a rusty violin,** the band practices tunes old and new.
PAST PARTICIPIAL PHRASE	**Accompanied by Mitzi on spoons,** the band practices tunes old and new.

VARYING SENTENCE STRUCTURES

Inserting word groups into longer sentences adds variety to your sentence structures. You might insert appositives, or word groups that rename something. You might also insert word groups that start with *who*, *which*, or *that*. As you practice the techniques that follow, notice how each word group that is inserted changes the rhythm of the sentence.

For more on appositives, see p. 295.

INSERTING APPOSITIVES

An **appositive** is a noun or noun phrase that renames another noun in a sentence. In the examples that follow, appositives appear in bold type.

ORIGINAL:	Cousin Raphael's band recently played at an awards ceremony at Mitzi's school. The band is known as Masked Hamsters.
JOINED:	Cousin Raphael's band, **Masked Hamsters,** recently played at an awards ceremony at Mitzi's school.

ORIGINAL:	Dell Streeter drew loud applause for his rendition of the school song. Dell Streeter is the kazoo player.
JOINED:	Dell Streeter, **the kazoo player,** drew loud applause for his rendition of the school song.

Notice that appositives are set off by commas.

INSERTING WORD GROUPS WITH <u>WHO</u>

Word groups with *who, which,* and *that* are called relative clauses. When you insert these word groups, use *who* to refer to people.

For more on using commas in such sentences, see p. 312. If a word group with *who* is not essential to the meaning of the sentence, set it off with commas. If it is essential to the meaning of the sentence, don't insert commas.

ORIGINAL:	Mitzi couldn't decide whether or not to play in the band. Mitzi is painfully shy.
JOINED:	Mitzi, **who is painfully shy,** couldn't decide whether or not to play in the band.

ORIGINAL:	Friends urged her to perform. These friends knew how long and hard she had practiced.
JOINED:	Friends **who knew how long and hard she had practiced** urged her to perform.

INSERTING WORD GROUPS WITH <u>WHICH</u> AND <u>THAT</u>

Use *which* or *that* to insert word groups referring to things. Use *which* only for word groups that are not essential to the meaning of the sentence. Set off these word groups with commas.

ORIGINAL:	Lyle LeGrand played the gutbucket. This instrument sounds a bit like a bass fiddle.
JOINED:	Lyle LeGrand played the gutbucket, **which sounds a bit like a bass fiddle.**

ORIGINAL:	Mitzi's spoons seemed to beckon her. They sparkled from a stand on the stage.
JOINED:	Mitzi's spoons, **which sparkled from a stand on the stage,** seemed to beckon her.

Use *that* only for word groups essential to the meaning of the sentence. Do not set these word groups off with commas.

ORIGINAL: Suddenly the band struck up an old Cajun tune. The tune had always been Mitzi's favorite.

JOINED: Suddenly the band struck up an old Cajun tune **that had always been Mitzi's favorite.**

ORIGINAL: Mitzi leaped onto the stage and began a performance. Her performance was long remembered by her classmates.

JOINED: Mitzi leaped onto the stage and began a performance **that was long remembered by her classmates.**

21

SENTENCE VARIETY

 How do I write interesting sentences?

Imagine that every day in your life were just like the one before—no change, no excitement. You'd probably be bored. It would be hard to look forward to starting each day because you'd know nothing interesting would happen. Sometimes writing can have the same effect. You may have read a piece in which all the sentences sounded the same. Maybe they were all short and choppy, or maybe they all started the same way. Interesting, effective writing needs variety—in sentence structure, in sentence length, and in sentence beginnings.

TYPES OF SENTENCE STRUCTURE

In order to vary the structure of your sentences, learn to recognize the three basic sentence types:

BASIC SENTENCE TYPES

A **simple sentence** has one main clause. A **main clause** contains one subject (S) and one predicate (P) and can stand alone as a sentence.

S   P
Tandra *trudged up the hill.*

A **compound sentence** has two or more main clauses linked by the words *and, but, or,* or a semicolon.

S   P   S   P
Tandra *put on her skates,* and **she** *pulled the laces tight.*

For more on clauses, see p. 304.
A **complex sentence** has one main clause and one or more subordinate clauses. A **subordinate clause** has a subject and a predicate, but it cannot stand alone as a sentence.

S   P   S   P
Tandra *sat down* until **she** *caught her breath.*

VARYING SENTENCE STRUCTURE AND LENGTH

You can add more variety and interest to your writing in two different ways:

1. You can vary the structure of your sentences. Make your writing a mix of simple, compound, and complex sentences. Use questions and exclamations as well as declarative sentences.

2. You can vary the length of your sentences. If most of your sentences are short, you can lengthen them by adding

- descriptive details.
- quotations.
- examples.
- facts and statistics.
- observations.
- reasons.

In the following paragraph, notice how the writer changed sentence structure and length:

For more on elaboration, see p. 31.

> **TRY THIS**
>
> To find out if your sentences need varying, read your writing aloud. Use a tape recorder or ask a friend to listen to the rhythm of your sentences.

> ## MODEL
>
> Tandra put on her skates. ^, and then s⌢ She stared down the chute. It looked like a concrete ribbon. ⌢, unfurling It unfurled to a bowl-shaped skating pavilion below. Tandra was filled with both delight and dread. She gulped a breath. ^before Then she started down. Trees slipped past, ^, quickly becoming Soon they were all a blur. ^her hair flying. Tandra sped downward ^with. Would t⌢ The end of the chute never seemed to come ^?
>
> The writer creates a compound sentence.
>
> The writer uses *before* to make a complex sentence.
>
> The writer makes the last sentence into a question.

VARYING SENTENCE BEGINNINGS

If you ate the same breakfast every single morning, would you get tired of it? You can put interest back in the beginning of the day by choosing a different kind of cereal or having pancakes or a toaster waffle. You can make sentences more interesting in the same way—by varying their beginnings. Here are some ways to vary the beginnings of sentences. Notice that some of these strategies also vary the length and the structure of the sentences.

1. Begin with a quotation.

"Watch me!" Tandra shouted with excitement as she zoomed down the chute.

2. Change the order of words in the sentence.

As she zoomed down the chute, Tandra shouted with excitement.

3. Begin with a subordinate clause.

When Tandra shouted with excitement, she was zooming down the chute.

4. Begin with a descriptive word or group of words.

Excited, Tandra shouted as she zoomed down the chute.

Here is the second paragraph of the story about Tandra. Notice how the writer changed the sentence beginnings.

The writer begins with a subordinate clause and adds a quotation for variety.

The writer adds a descriptive word as an opener.

MODEL

As she flashed by, o⁀   "Wow!" she shouted, but h⁀
⋀Other skaters waved ~~as she flashed by.~~ Her
                                        Finally s⁀
voice was lost in the chilly air.⋀She ~~finally~~ reached
the skating circle. She zipped around it once, then
            Gradually s⁀
again.⋀She slowed to a stop. She bent over, laughing and gasping with the thrill of her ride.

WORD CHOICE

22

How do I know which word to use?

Which of the following sentences would get your attention if you overheard them in a conversation?

He asked to get a refund.
He demanded his $100 back.

The first sentence does not create much of a picture in our minds. The second sentence commands our attention because it mentions a *specific* amount of money and because the word *demanded* suggests someone who is angry and aggressive.

In conversation, some people know how to choose words that convey the right emotion or shade of meaning. Word choice is just as important when you write. In a first draft, your concern is just to get your thoughts on paper, so you should not worry about word choice. When you revise your work, however, ask yourself two questions:

1. Do my words help fulfill my purpose of informing, persuading, or entertaining my audience?

2. Do my words convey the exact meaning I intended and paint a clear picture?

CONNOTATIONS

Connotations are the feelings or associations a word brings to the mind of a reader or listener. When you choose words, think about whether they have pleasant or unpleasant connotations. By choosing words whose connotations fit your meaning, you can make sure you will create the precise effect on your reader that you want.

A word's dictionary definition is called its **denotation**. Two or more words with similar definitions—synonyms—can have very different connotations. Think, for example, about the synonyms *stubborn* and *firm*. Both can mean "not giving in easily." However, *stubborn* has negative connotations. Mules are known as stubborn animals.

TRY THIS

To learn the connotations of synonyms, refer to a good dictionary that gives sample sentences for several synonyms under one entry. Also notice the word choices used by good writers you admire. Become aware of shades of meaning.

Firm, on the other hand, has positive connotations. Strong leaders are often described as firm.

In the following sentences, the words in italics are synonyms, but the impressions they suggest are different.

POSITIVE CONNOTATIONS: Her questions showed that she was *curious.*
NEGATIVE CONNOTATIONS: Her questions showed that she was *nosy.*

CHOOSING SPECIFIC WORDS

Specific words can appeal to readers' senses, while general or abstract terms have little or no sensory appeal. Sometimes it is appropriate to use general terms, as in the following sentence.

People in many parts of the world yearn for **freedom of expression.**

Often, however, it is better to replace general terms with words that are more specific and precise. In the following sentences, the specific words bring a scene to life.

GENERAL: She **walked** into the lions' cage.

SPECIFIC: She **strode** into the lions' cage.

GENERAL: The thirty lions **looked** at her.

SPECIFIC: The thirty lions **glared** at her.

In the first passage that follows, the words in bold type are general and abstract. Notice the differences between this passage and the model from literature, which tells about the same incident with specific, concrete words.

. . . That bike took me all over the place. My beautiful bike jumped **anything.** My beautiful bike did everything cleverer than a clever cowboy's **animal,** with me **on top of it.** And the bell, the bell **made** such a glorious **sound.**

 MODEL FROM LITERATURE

The words shown here in bold type are more specific and concrete than the words in bold type in the passage above.

. . . That bike took me all over the place. My beautiful bike jumped **every log, every rock, every fence.** My beautiful bike did everything cleverer than a clever cowboy's **horse,** with me **in the saddle.** And the bell, the bell **was** such a glorious **gong of a ring!**

—James Berry, "Becky and the Wheels-and-Brake Boys"

VARIETIES OF ENGLISH

23

How are different varieties of English used?

Although English is spoken around the world, not everyone speaks it in exactly the same way all the time. In fact, *you* probably don't speak English the same way all the time. You might speak one way if you are giving a speech or an oral report and another way if you are talking to your friends. These different ways of speaking involve using different **varieties of English.**

The most common variety of English is **standard English,** which follows the most widely accepted rules of grammar, usage, and mechanics. There are two ways of speaking and writing standard English—**formal** and **informal.** Formal English is what people usually use to do schoolwork or to speak in a formal situation. Informal English is more casual. You might use it to write letters or to talk with friends and family.

Other varieties of English are called **nonstandard** because they depart from the most widely accepted rules of grammar, usage, and mechanics. These varieties include **dialects** of English that are spoken in different regions and cultures. The following chart shows some of the varieties of English:

Standard English

Formal English	standard English that closely follows accepted rules
Informal English	casual English suitable for everyday communication. Informal English includes the following:
COLLOQUIALISMS:	informal words and phrases that are widely used and understood
SLANG:	made-up words and phrases or old words used in a new way by a particular group

Nonstandard English

DIALECTS:	versions of English usually spoken by regional or ethnic groups within a larger culture. Dialects involve differences of pronunciation, vocabulary, and even grammar.

Think of language as the clothes your ideas wear. For some occasions you need to dress up. For others you can wear casual clothes. The same applies to writing and speaking. Formal English might be called the evening attire of language. It involves a serious approach and a careful choice of words. For example, if you were speaking formally, you might use the word *perspiration* rather than *sweat*.

Informal English is simpler and more relaxed than formal English. Since it is a form of standard English, however, it still follows the rules of correct grammar, usage, and mechanics, just as formal English does.

FORMAL ENGLISH: Would you care to accompany me to the cinema?

INFORMAL ENGLISH: Do you want to go to the movies with me?

When you write, your audience and purpose influence the type of English you should use. If you are writing a paper for school or presenting a petition to the school board, you should probably use formal English—even if the head of the school board is your aunt. If you are talking with family or friends in a casual setting, however, informal English is usually more appropriate.

TYPES OF INFORMAL ENGLISH

In informal speech and writing, people often use colorful words and phrases that they know their audiences will understand. These words and phrases include colloquialisms and slang. Does someone you know *give you the creeps*? Does your baby brother *act up* sometimes? These are examples of colloquialisms. If formal English is a tuxedo or ball gown, colloquialisms are the jeans and casual clothing of the language. Most people use colloquial language in everyday conversation. Writers often use colloquial language when they wish to capture the sound of speech. Plays, for example, often contain colloquialisms. Dialogue and fiction that feature the narrator as a character do too.

The following excerpt is from a short story told from the viewpoint of a young boy:

MODEL FROM LITERATURE

He really had me there. What did I know about licenses? I'm only thirteen, after all. Suddenly I didn't feel like the big black businessman anymore. I felt like a kid who wanted to holler for his mother.

—Kristen Hunter, "The Scribe"

The first sentence and the verb holler are colloquialisms that help convey the young boy's uneasiness.

In order to find out whether an expression is colloquial, check your dictionary. Colloquial words and terms are usually designated by the abbreviation *colloq.*

If you want to tell a friend how much you like something, would you say it is *cool? Def? Trick? Groovy? Rad?* Which word might your parents use? All these terms are slang expressions. Slang is special language used within well-defined groups. It varies from one group to another and changes continuously. Different generations and people of the same age living in different parts of the country use different slang. You might compare slang expressions to clothing fads. They show that a speaker belongs to a certain group and is up to date. If you write in slang, however, you are limiting yourself to readers who know that particular slang. Also, you can be fairly sure that in the near future most of your words will seem as old-fashioned as sun bonnets.

TYPES OF NONSTANDARD ENGLISH

"Hey yo, wasup man? Y'all just chillin', ain't ya? You be goin' to the store soon?" In standard English this greeting means "Hi. What are you doing? Are you just taking it easy? Are you going to the store soon?" The greeting is an example of one kind of nonstandard English, the Black English **dialect.**

Dialect is language spoken by a group of people who share a heritage. It develops over time among people who live in the same region or who have similar social, economic, and ethnic backgrounds. Black English, for example, is a dialect spoken by certain African Americans. Most dialects follow their own rules and patterns of grammar, mechanics, and usage. (In fact, standard English is a dialect—the most widely used and accepted one.) People who speak a dialect use their language in a consistent way.

Because the various dialects of a common language may differ greatly in grammar, pronunciation, vocabulary, or all three, writing in a nonstandard dialect may limit your audience, just as slang does. Unlike slang, however, a nonstandard dialect doesn't go quickly out of fashion. Black English, for example, has been developing for centuries. Sometimes writers have characters speak in dialect in order to make them more believable. Other writers use a dialect like Black English to express pride in their culture.

WRITING FORMAL ENGLISH FOR SCHOOL

If you are writing an essay for school, you probably need to use formal English. Most essays are serious and full of information. Here's how one writer revised an essay to make sure the language stayed formal throughout.

M O D E L

The writer starts the essay in a formal and serious tone.

Kindness is an important human trait. Without kindness, the world would be a much colder and crueler place. It is not always easy to be kind, however. Sometimes people do mean things that seem to require meanness in return. It takes a big heart and strong resolve to show kindness instead.

The writer revises the slang term *dis* and the colloquialism *do right by each other* into more formal English.

In a world where people ~~dis~~ [insult] one another, kindness seems old-fashioned. However, if people tried to ~~do right by each other,~~ [respect one another,] kindness would seem normal. Violent crimes would decrease, and the world would be a nicer, safer place.

The writer changes the nonstandard grammar of the concluding sentence to standard grammar.

Kindness is like a contagious disease. Instead of returning anger with anger, one should return anger with kindness. Perhaps then the other person will catch ~~on~~ [the kindness habit.] It only takes one person to start a chain of kindness. Why ~~don't it~~ [not have it] be you?

24

FIGURATIVE LANGUAGE

How can I say things in an interesting way?

Figurative language compares one thing to another not because the two things are literally similar but because the comparison helps us see or understand the first thing more clearly. Examples of figurative language are called **figures of speech**.

> **Figurative language** is language in which one thing is compared to something else.

We use figurative language all the time in writing and speaking. For example, if someone says she is "on pins and needles" before a test, she doesn't mean that she is actually sitting on small, sharp objects. She is merely clarifying her feeling of nervous anticipation by comparing it to the feeling of being jabbed by pins and needles.

There's just one problem with the comparison "on pins and needles": It's a **cliché**, a figure of speech that has been used so often it has lost its ability to make us think or feel in a new way. Figures of speech need to be fresh and imaginative. Instead of saying she is "on pins and needles," for example, the speaker might say "I feel like a sky diver about to jump."

COMMON TYPES OF FIGURATIVE LANGUAGE

You can use figurative language to enliven your writing, to explain something unfamiliar in terms of something more familiar, to provide a concrete image that will help readers to perceive or understand something abstract, or to help readers see something in a fresh, new way. The four most common types are **similes, metaphors, personifications,** and **symbols.**

A **simile** compares two apparently different things and directly states the comparison by using the word *like* or *as*.

 MODELS FROM LITERATURE

This simile appeals to our sense of hearing and is a concrete image.

Only today I wish I didn't have only eleven years rattling inside me like pennies in a tin Band-Aid box.

—Sandra Cisneros, "Eleven"

These similes appeal to our senses of sight and touch.

The willow is sleek as a velvet-nosed calf;
The ginkgo is leathery as an old bull.

—Eve Merriam, "Simile: Willow and Gingko"

A **metaphor** compares two apparently different things but suggests the comparison instead of using *like* or *as* to state it directly. Some metaphors present a direct equation, telling us one thing *is* another thing; other metaphors simply talk about one thing as if it were another. In either case, a comparison is being made.

 MODEL FROM LITERATURE

The poet equates the moon with a ghostly galleon and the road with a ribbon.

The moon was a ghostly galleon tossed upon
    cloudy seas,
The road was a ribbon of moonlight over the
    purple moor.

—Alfred Noyes, "The Highwayman"

Personification is a type of metaphor that talks about something nonhuman as if it were human, giving it human qualities or having it engage in human activities.

MODEL FROM LITERATURE

Let the rain kiss you.
Let the rain beat upon your head with silver
     liquid drops.
Let the rain sing you a lullaby.
     —Langston Hughes, "April Rain Song"

Hughes helps us "feel" the rain by talking about it as if it were a person who could kiss us and sing to us.

A **symbol** is a person, place, event, or object that has a meaning beyond its literal meaning. A symbol usually stands for an abstract idea or a range of related ideas like loyalty and patriotism. The writer rarely states what the symbol means; instead, the reader learns several details about the symbol and from them must determine the abstract idea or ideas that the symbol stands for.

MODEL FROM LITERATURE

The sea in her imagination was something that was constantly alive, constantly changing and, though she could hear no sounds from afar, constantly roaring. But the sea she had never seen up close for once they got off the hill and into the town which was hot and sticky and crowded and noisy, they could no longer see anything but the streets. . . . More than anything else she yearned to see the sea real close, to walk on the beach, to watch the breakers surge.

     —Olive Senior, "Tears of the Sea"

The sea has a literal meaning in the story but also seems to stand for something else. The details in the first and last sentences and the contrast with the hot, crowded town all suggest that the sea stands for freedom and self-expression.

Types of Writing

■ ■ ■

How to Do Your Writing Assignments

Laurence Typing, 1952, Fairfield Porter, oil on canvas
The Parrish Art Museum, Southampton, New York
Gift of the Estate of Fairfield Porter
Photo, Noel Rowe

EXPRESSIVE WRITING: JOURNAL WRITING

25

Why is keeping a journal a good idea?

If you keep a journal, you already know some of the advantages of recording your thoughts and experiences. Among other benefits, keeping a journal will help you to do the following things:

- remember significant events
- clarify your thoughts and feelings
- outline your plans and ideas
- recall sense impressions
- play with words
- try new writing ideas
- improve your ability to write easily

Did you know that keeping a journal is one cure for "the blank-paper blues"? That's the slightly sick, slightly panicky feeling you get when you have to fill a blank sheet of paper with original writing. The cause of these blues is simple: no ideas. That's where your journal helps.

Think of your journal as a writer's idea box. Cram it full of all sorts of things, from a creative idea for making money to your thoughts about a friendship. Your entries might include items like these:

- memorable experiences
- snatches of dialogue, dialect, or song lyrics
- jokes, puns, and funny stories
- weird news stories or headlines
- interesting words and expressions
- quotations and passages from books
- thought-provoking news or information
- drawings, postcards, and photographs

> A **journal** is a private notebook, a place to write about things that matter to you.

FROM A WRITER

> **"**People who keep journals live life twice. Having written something down gives you the opportunity to go back to it over and over, to remember and relive the experience.**"**
>
> —Jessamyn West

Here is an entry from one writer's journal:

Great Blue Heron

HOW TO KEEP A JOURNAL

Keeping a journal is easy and fun, and you can select the type
that best meets your needs. You can write in a lined notebook, an
unlined artist's sketch pad, or even a computer file. You can write
to please yourself, without worrying too much about grammar or
spelling. Here are three common types of journals:

A PERSONAL JOURNAL is a record of your thoughts and
experiences.

1. Write as regularly as possible.
2. Date each journal entry.
3. Write about issues that matter to you.
4. Try expressing your thoughts in different
forms: rap lyrics, advice-column letters, concrete
poems, humorous cartoons.

A LEARNING LOG is an ongoing record of your observations
and reflections on a school subject.

1. Create separate sections for different subject
areas.
2. Record the facts or concepts you think are
most important.
3. Explore questions and confusing issues that
come up in class or in your reading.
4. Think about your learning process. How
could you improve your performance?

A DIALOGUE JOURNAL is an ongoing written conversation between two people.
1. Write with a second person, perhaps a friend or your teacher. Be sure both of you contribute to the dialogue.
2. Respond to the thoughts your partner is expressing, but feel free, as well, to express your own opinions. After all, this is called a *dialogue* journal.
3. Date and sign each entry.

FINDING IDEAS IN YOUR JOURNAL

With your journal bulging with interesting ideas, descriptions, and events, you're ready to tackle any writing assignment. To find an appropriate topic in your journal, try the following strategies:

SEARCH STRATEGIES

Type of Writing   **Look for . . .**

poem ⟶ • descriptions of intense feelings.

• vivid memories.

story ⟶ • unusual/humorous real-life events.

• accounts of conflicts with others.

essay ⟶ • nouns that name important concepts.

• issues on which you feel strongly.

Keep your journal handy and keep on writing. That way, as time goes by, you'll have more and more good writing ideas and topics stored away. The thoughts you record tonight might make the perfect topic for a personal essay next week!

26

EXPRESSIVE WRITING: PERSONAL LETTER

 How do I write a personal letter?

A **personal letter** is an informal letter in which the writer shares personal thoughts and feelings.

When was the last time you made a telephone call to a friend or relative—last night, maybe? When was the last time you wrote a personal letter? Considering the growing popularity of beepers, car phones, and mobile phones, letters may seem a pretty slow and old-fashioned way of communicating. Still, writing a letter offers some advantages that telephoning does not.

A personal letter can be more thoughtful and revealing than a telephone call. Some people find it easier to discuss their thoughts and feelings on paper than on the telephone. Letters can also provide more enduring pleasure. A letter can be read again and again, whereas an unrecorded telephone call can be heard only once. Letter writing gives you time to refine your first thoughts and allows you to decide exactly what you want to share. Because a personal letter is informal, however, you don't have to worry as much about correctness as you would in a formal letter or essay. In a personal letter, you can include

FROM A WRITER

66 *We shy persons need to write a letter now and then, or else we'll dry up and blow away.* **99**

—Garrison Keillor, "How to Write a Personal Letter"

• detailed descriptions of events in your life.

• your personal thoughts and feelings.

• questions about the other person's life and interests.

WHAT DOES A PERSONAL LETTER LOOK LIKE?

Here is a sample. (You can handwrite or type your letters.)

679 Lawrence Street   *Heading*
Winooski, VT 05404
February 27, 1994

Dear Sam,   *Salutation*

    I was really glad to get your letter. Even after four months, I still feel like a stranger in Winooski. It's such a small town. Downtown is about ten stores! There is a great music store, though.

    School is okay. I've made some friends, and I've been trying to   *Body* find some guys who are interested in jazz. I'm on the swim team, and I'm one of the best. (Just bragging!) I'm going to the Spring Fling— that's a school dance. Here's my real reason for writing. Can you come here for the dance? It's March 25. Jenna, the girl I'm meeting at the dance, has a friend who saw that picture of you and said she'd like to see you at the dance. She likes dancing as much as you do. Check it out with your mom. It could be fun.

Your friend,   *Closing*

Cole   *Signature*

STANDARD LETTER FORM

HEADING: Include your street address, city, state, ZIP Code, the month, day, and year.

SALUTATION: Capitalize the word "Dear," followed by the name of the person to whom you are writing. End with a comma.

BODY: Indent each paragraph.

CLOSING: Use an informal closing, such as
Yours truly,   Your friend,
Love,   Sincerely,
Capitalize the first word of the closing. End with a comma.

SIGNATURE: Sign your name.

HOW DO I ADDRESS THE ENVELOPE?

On your envelope, include your address in the upper left-hand corner, the address of the person to whom you are writing in the center, and a stamp in the upper right-hand corner.

Return address

Cole Quinn
679 Lawrence Street
Winooski, VT 05404

STAMP

Address

Sam Gomez
1029 North Road
Boston, MA 02107

SOME SPECIAL TYPES OF PERSONAL LETTERS

Here are some special types of personal letters and the messages they usually convey.

Express appreciation for the gift, invitation, or experience.

Tell how the gift affected you.

Thank You

Express condolences when someone loses a friend or family member.

Share any good memories of the deceased.

With Our
Condolences

E-MAIL

Electronic mail, or E-mail, is a subscription service that links your computer with others, so you can send and receive messages instantly. Just enter your message into your computer and it can be sent to any other subscriber. E-mail is quick and informal, like a phone call, but is written and can be saved like a letter.

27

EXPRESSIVE WRITING: PERSONAL ESSAY

What is a personal essay?

How do you feel about horror movies? What do you think about the multimillion-dollar salaries that some athletes get? What is life like for a teenager today? Your ideas on those subjects and many others could be the basis for a personal essay.

> A **personal essay** is a piece of writing in which you express your thoughts or feelings about a subject.

You can tackle a wide range of subjects—from the silly to the serious—in a personal essay. The chart that follows shows some examples of subjects you might discuss:

Subjects for Personal Essays		
Personal Views	**Trends**	**News**
Procrastination: the fine art of putting things off	Computer networks breaking down borders between people	Students organize to raise money for homeless shelter.
What it means to be a friend	List of endangered species growing	One-handed pitcher pitches no-hitter.
How it would feel to be an animal in a zoo	Soccer becoming popular in the United States	Libraries limit hours because of budget cuts.

When you write an essay, consider these guidelines:

GUIDELINES

A personal essay

- ▶ starts with an introduction that gets the readers' attention and makes them want to read on.
- ▶ focuses on one subject.
- ▶ reflects the writer's thoughts and feelings on the subject.
- ▶ is logically organized.
- ▶ sounds like the writer.
- ▶ leaves readers with something to think about.

HOW CAN I FIND AN IDEA?

Any subject that interests you can become a personal essay. You can begin your search for a subject in one of these ways:

LOOK THROUGH YOUR JOURNAL. The observations recorded in your journal are a good source of writing subjects. Skim through your journal, looking for names of people, places, and things that interest you or for issues that you feel strongly about. For each one, ask yourself, "What do I think about it?"

LIST YOUR INTERESTS. Ask *why?* or *how?* questions about each hobby or field. For example, if you like lacrosse, you might ask, How did this sport begin?

READ MAGAZINES OR NEWSPAPERS. Clipping stories about well-known people, the latest trends, or world events can also lead you to a writing idea.

USE A STARTER.

Lately I've noticed that more . . .
It really makes me mad when . . .
I think it's great that . . .
One thing that's always puzzled/frustrated/worried me is . . .
Why is it that . . . ?
What if . . . ?
Have you ever wondered why . . . ?

PERSONAL ESSAY OR PERSONAL NARRATIVE?

In a *personal narrative*, you tell a story about an experience that happened to you.

Last winter I went ice fishing for the first time—and last time—in my life. As we crunched across the ice toward the fishing shanty, I could feel my face getting stiff with cold, like a Halloween mask.

In a *personal essay*, you write about a subject that interests you.

What do you know about ice fishing? I never realized what a challenging sport it is until I read an article in *Outdoors* magazine. Anglers must survive below-zero gales, bore holes in thick ice, and figure out where fish will be biting.

Once you have an idea, explore it. Try to find a focus for your essay.

THINK ABOUT IT. Ask yourself, Why do I want to write about this? Who will read my essay?

TALK ABOUT IT. Talk to your friends, classmates, and family about your idea.

HOW DO I START DRAFTING?

Sometimes, even if you're not sure exactly what you want to say, it helps to start writing. Your ideas may become clearer to you as you write. In the example that follows, the writer discovers a focus while writing a first draft:

> ### MODEL
>
> I visited a zoo last week, and even though I had been to the zoo many times before, I saw it with new eyes. I wondered how the animals in the cages felt. Were they happy? Did they feel cared for? Or did they want to be free to walk around like me?
>
> I ended up feeling that we shouldn't keep animals in zoos. They need their freedom just as much as we do. They've been taken from their natural habitats, their homes, and put in prisons, our zoos.

The writer has chosen a subject based on personal observations.

The writer shares personal feelings about the subject.

While drafting, the writer discovers the intended point.

You may choose to organize your essay in the traditional way, with an introduction, a body, and a conclusion, or in any other way that expresses your point clearly. Choose the method that best suits you and your subject.

Most important, express what you think, not what someone else thinks you should think. Write in the first person, using the pronoun *I*, as if you were simply talking to friends. Remember, it's a personal essay. It reflects *your* ideas—not your teacher's, not the encyclopedia's, not even your best friend's ideas.

WRITE THE OPENING PARAGRAPH. At some point in the drafting process, you'll need to think about how you will begin your essay. You'll want to write an opening paragraph that gets your readers' attention and makes them want to read more. A good opening paragraph engages readers with lively writing and interesting ideas. The following chart shows some good strategies for beginning a personal essay:

OPENING STRATEGY	EXAMPLE
ANECDOTE:	I was riding the bus last week when an old man with a cane got on at one of the stops. All the seats were full, and students occupied most of them. Nobody, however, offered to give up a seat for the elderly bus rider.
QUESTION:	Doesn't it drive you crazy when people put empty containers back in the refrigerator? You're dying of thirst. You race to the refrigerator and reach for a carton of juice— only to find out it's empty.

STARTLING STATEMENT:	All right, I admit it. I'm a computer nerd.

END THE ESSAY. You may find that your essay comes to a natural end. You've said all you want to say, and that's it. On the other hand, you may want to conclude with a paragraph that gives your readers something to think about. Keep in mind that the end of an essay is what is likely to stay in a reader's mind. A strong finish can make that more of a possibility. You can end with a thought-provoking idea or with a quotation.

UNFINISHED FINAL PARAGRAPH:	With just a computer, a modem, and some basic software, you can hook up to an electronic network that lets you make friends with people from Moscow to Montevideo. Borders between countries and people become invisible on the computer screen.
THOUGHT-PROVOKING IDEA:	Maybe someday they'll disappear from the world as well.
FINAL QUOTATION:	As one networker said, "I live in a small town in Iowa, but my 'electronic neighborhood' is the whole world."

HOW DO I REVISE MY ESSAY?

As with any piece of writing, it's a good idea to set your essay aside for a couple of days so that you can read it again with fresh eyes. You also might want to share your draft with a friend before you begin making changes. Here are a few points to keep in mind as you revise your personal essay:

CHECKPOINTS FOR REVISING

▶ Does my introduction get my readers' attention and make them want to read more?

▶ Does my essay focus on one subject?

▶ Does my essay reflect my thoughts and feelings on the subject?

▶ Does it sound like me?

▶ Does it seem logically organized?

▶ Does it leave readers with something to think about?

Here's a final draft of a personal essay:

MODEL

How would you feel if you had to stay in your room all day and night, day after day, night after night? You probably wouldn't like it very much, but that's life for many animals in zoos.

I visited a zoo last week, and even though I had been to the zoo many times before, I saw it with

The writer begins with a question to draw readers into the essay.

The essay focuses on one subject: why animals shouldn't be kept in zoos.

Using a natural
voice, the writer
shares thoughts
and feelings on
the subject.

new eyes. I love animals and in the past I'd always enjoyed the chance to see animals I might not get to see otherwise. This time, however, I imagined myself in those cages. Would I feel like a prisoner? Would I feel homesick for my natural habitat, or would I feel lucky and cared for?

The writer uses a
traditional essay
structure with an
introduction, body,
and conclusion.

I ended up feeling that animals probably have some of the same needs we do and that we shouldn't keep them in zoos. They belong in the wild, where they can be free to live their lives.

The writer ends
with a thought-
provoking idea.

What humans can do is try to preserve wild habitats so that someday we can visit these animals in their homes—not in our prisons.

DO NOT
FEED
THE KID

28

WRITING TO DESCRIBE: BIOGRAPHICAL SKETCH

How do I capture a personality in writing?

Have you ever drawn a sketch to illustrate a point you were trying to make? A sketch is a quick drawing that captures a subject's most important features. By highlighting essential details and eliminating unimportant ones, a sketch can bring a subject into focus.

A biographical sketch is a kind of word picture. In it, words create a vivid picture of a person. The details you choose enable your readers to "see" the person as you do.

> A **biographical sketch** is a brief written description of a person's main physical and personality traits.

Karl, Andrew Wyeth
Collection of Mr. and
Mrs. Frank E. Fowler

GUIDELINES

A biographical sketch

▶ draws a picture of a person with words.

▶ describes the subject's physical appearance.

▶ describes the subject's most important personality traits.

▶ uses incidents, examples, or quotations to show the subject's personality.

▶ reveals the writer's attitude toward the subject.

HOW DO I FIND A SUBJECT?

Almost anyone can be a subject for a biographical sketch. It is easier, however, to "sketch" someone you know well or can observe easily, because you will have firsthand experience of your subject's appearance and personality.

Family Supper (detail) 1972, Ralph Fasanella

The greater the impact or effect your subject has on you personally, the more you will have to say about that person. If no one person springs immediately to mind, try one of the following strategies to get started.

- Look at family photos and videotapes. What memories of special people and events do they spark?

- Thumb through magazines. Do you notice any public figures whose lives and accomplishments have affected your life or opportunities?

- Look closely at people around you. Notice classmates, teachers, coaches, neighbors. What qualities make any one of them unique?

HOW DO I FIND DETAILS ABOUT MY SUBJECT?

You might try freewriting, listing, charting, drawing a sketch of your subject, or combining several of these methods to gather details. One writer made the following cluster diagram to get concrete ideas about why her brother Tycho was so special to her.

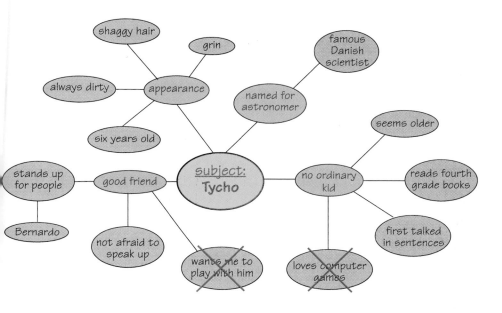

If your subject is someone close at hand, consider interviewing him or her. Decide what you would like to know, and prepare questions beforehand. Take notes, or use a tape recorder during the interview.

For more on interviewing, see p. 245.

HOW DO I ORGANIZE MY SKETCH?

Look through your details and group them in a logical way, such as into categories like Physical Details, Personality Traits, and Personal Values. Check or star the ones that reveal your subject most clearly and concentrate on those. Ask yourself, "What main impression do I want my readers to get of my subject?" Cross out any details that do not contribute to that impression.

TRY THIS

You can get off to a strong start by using dialogue, relating an incident, or describing a striking physical detail.

Next, think about how you want to organize and present your material. Here are three ways you might try:

TOPIC STATEMENT AND DETAILS Begin with a general statement on what is special or unique about your particular subject. Continue with specific examples of your subject's personality or behavior.

ORDER OF IMPRESSION What is the first detail you notice about your subject? What do you notice next? Go on from these details to build up the picture of your subject.

ORDER OF IMPORTANCE What is the most important characteristic of your subject? How do your subject's other traits support or illustrate that one essential quality?

HOW CAN I FOCUS MY SKETCH?

Whatever organizational pattern you choose, be sure that each paragraph in your sketch focuses on a single aspect of your subject. Keep these hints in mind as you draft your sketch.

ILLUSTRATE PERSONALITY TRAITS Don't just tell what your subject is like—*show* him or her doing something. People's actions give important clues to their personalities.

USE A QUOTATION TO REVEAL YOUR SUBJECT People's words can reveal their character. Find a quotation that conveys the flavor of your subject's personality.

WRITE A STRONG CONCLUSION You can conclude your biographical sketch with a paragraph that sums up your subject's special qualities and the way you feel about this person. Try to *show* your readers why your subject is important to you, rather than just *telling* them why.

Here are one one writer's thoughts on an influential person in her life.

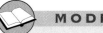 **MODEL FROM LITERATURE**

I don't think I ever saw Mrs. Flowers laugh, but she smiled often. . . . When she chose to smile on me, I always wanted to thank her. . . . She was one of the few gentlewomen I have ever known, and has remained throughout my life the measure of what a human being can be. . . .

—Maya Angelou, *I Know Why the Caged Bird Sings*

WRITING FOR SCIENCE

For a science assignment, you may be asked to write a biographical sketch of a scientist. In this type of sketch, you will have to substitute research for direct observation. Consult special reference sources such as *American Men and Women of Science*, published periodically by R. R. Bowker, or *International Encyclopedia of the Social Sciences*, published by Macmillan. Look for details on your subject's physical appearance and for revealing incidents from his or her life. Depending on when your subject lived, you may also be able to find direct quotations that show his or her ideas and personality. You may want to end your biographical sketch with an explanation of how your subject's work contributed to scientific progress.

HOW DO I REVISE MY BIOGRAPHICAL SKETCH?

As you get ready to revise your biographical sketch, keep in mind your aim of describing both physical and personality traits through a combination of vivid description, revealing incidents and examples, and dialogue.

CHECKPOINTS FOR REVISING

▶ Have I described my subject's physical appearance?

▶ Have I used incidents and examples to show my subject's unique personality?

▶ Have I shown why my subject is important to me?

▶ Is the organization of my biographical sketch logical and clear?

Here's an example of a final draft of a biographical sketch.

MODEL

My brother Tycho was named after a famous Danish astronomer. Maybe he should have been named after a meteorologist instead, because our Tycho goes through life like a hurricane. He's six years old, with a wonderful grin, shaggy hair that's always in his eyes, and a real talent for

The writer begins with a physical description that paints a vivid picture of her subject.

picking up dirt. He's always grubby, even ten minutes after his bath.

The writer uses an incident and dialogue to show one of the subject's personality traits, his brightness.

I first realized Tycho wasn't an ordinary kid when he was about two and a half. He wasn't in any hurry to talk, except for a few basic words like "Mama" and "Daddy." Then one rainy day when I was reading, he just walked up to me, pulled on my jeans, and said perfectly clearly, "Sally, will you read me Yertle the Turtle?"

Since then, he's learned to read himself. He reads—at six!—what I read in the fourth grade. And he has the sensitivity and courage of a much older person. For example, he sometimes plays with Bernardo, who is small and skinny and wears thick glasses. One day the neighborhood bully, Sam, was teasing Bernardo and snatched his glasses. Tycho saw it. He went charging out of our house and ran right up to Sam, who is about four years older and a foot taller. "Give Bernardo back his glasses, you creep!" he said. When Sam smirked, Tycho added, "My sister is inside calling the police right now!" Sam thought it over and decided not to take the chance. He gave Bernardo back his glasses.

The writer reveals the heart of the subject's personality, his courage and resourcefulness, by relating another incident and quoting her subject's words.

The writer tells how the subject has affected her life.

Tycho may look like a typical six-year-old, but his brain and his heart are much bigger than those of most kids his age. Sometimes I feel I have to live up to his standards. That can be quite a challenge, but mostly it's a challenge I'm proud to meet.

WRITING TO DESCRIBE: SCENE DESCRIPTION

29

How do I describe a scene?

When **describing a scene**, you bring a place to life for others. Most likely you describe many scenes every day, from ordinary school scenes to fantastic scenes you encounter only in dreams.

GUIDELINES

A scene description

▶ can be about a real or an imaginary place.

▶ uses sensory details (sight, sound, taste, touch, and smell) to help readers imagine the scene.

▶ is organized to guide readers easily through the scene.

▶ sets a mood.

HOW DO I START?

Choose a scene. Then explore the actual place or your mental picture of it. Here are ways to find a scene to describe:

CONSIDER THE PLACE YOU'RE IN RIGHT NOW. What colors and shapes or lights and shadows do you see? What details would you use to describe how it looks and feels?

VISIT A FAVORITE PLACE. Spend time observing any place that interests you. What sights, smells, and sounds go with the scene? What words would describe its atmosphere?

THINK ABOUT PLACES YOU'VE VISITED. What details stand out in your mind? What do you visualize at the center of the scene? What aspects of the scene give it a special mood or atmosphere?

LOOK AT PICTURES. Scan a photo album, newspaper, magazine, or book. Does any scene stir your imagination or create a mood? What details make it interesting to you?

MAKE UP SCENES. What might a scene from the age of dinosaurs be like? What if you were visiting another planet?

HOW CAN I FIND DETAILS?

Anything you can see, hear, taste, smell, or feel—physically or emotionally—can become a descriptive detail. Your job as a writer is to choose the details that will create the picture and mood you want to convey.

In order to bring a scene to life, use all your senses to observe, remember, or imagine the scene. To be sure you include a full range of details, you might divide a piece of paper into five sections, one for each of the senses. Then jot down your ideas in the appropriate sections. Here are some details observed at a city park:

Handball, 1939, Ben Shahn, Museum of Modern Art

What do I see?	asphalt, handball players, concrete wall, brick building
What do I hear?	handball bouncing, kids yelling, shoes scraping, traffic passing, wire fences rattling
What do I smell?	bus fumes, tar
What do I taste?	bubble gum
What do I feel?	handball, sun, wind

HOW CAN I SET A MOOD?

Describing a scene is more than just listing details. Before you write, think about how the scene makes you feel. What mood do you want to create? Do you want the scene to seem bleak and lonely—or lively and joyful? Once you decide on the mood, choose details and words that will create that feeling in your readers.

Notice how an eighth-grade student creates an eerie mood in this description of a motel by her careful choice of words and images.

STUDENT MODEL

The old motel was surrounded by a black iron fence cloaked in cobwebs and dark green ivy. Its windows were shattered, and countless boards were missing or dangling by a single nail.

HOW DO I SHOW INSTEAD OF TELL?

Telling is saying directly what you think or feel about something; **showing** is providing readers with details that enable them to experience a person, place, or thing for themselves. As a writer, you can get your readers to see and experience a scene as you do by choosing the details carefully. Showing usually creates more powerful descriptive writing than telling because readers must use their own imagination and, as a result, become more involved in what they are reading.

The following chart shows examples of telling and showing.

TELLING	SHOWING
There was a light breeze.	A warm breeze tugged at my sleeve and ruffled my hair.
The sun was hot and burned the earth.	The sun's rays turned the river bottom to dry, dusty clods.
The hole was really deep.	She dropped a rock down the hole but never heard it hit the bottom.

HOW CAN I ORGANIZE MY DESCRIPTION?

Imagine that you're filming a movie. If you moved the camera wildly all over the place, you would confuse the people watching the film—and maybe even make them dizzy! Just as a film director sets up shots, so you must decide how your readers will approach your scene.

For more on organizational plans, see p. 23. The following diagrams show two possible ways you can organize the details of your description to help your readers visualize a scene:

Far to **Near:**

First, describe the whole scene—the "big picture."

Then, move a little closer as if you're heading toward the scene.

Keep describing details as you see them when you move in closer and closer.

Near to **Far:**

Start by describing one item that is nearby.

Pull back and describe what surrounds the first item.

Pull back farther to describe the "big picture."

You can also describe a scene by moving from bottom to top, from left to right, or from inside to outside. You might even move in a circle, describing the scene as if you were turning slowly!

Choose any vantage point you like if you're writing a scene description that stands on its own. On the other hand, if your scene is part of a story, organize your description in a way that makes sense in the context of the plot or action. For example, in the following model, the description moves downward from the top of the crevasse, a deep fracture in the ice, to the unknown bottom. The writer is guiding your attention to a dangerous place where a struggle for survival will occur.

MODEL FROM LITERATURE

The crevasse was about six feet wide at the top and narrowed gradually as it went down. But how deep it was Rudi could not tell. After a few feet the blue walls of ice curved away at a sharp slant, and what was below the curve was hidden from sight.

—James Ramsey Ullman, *Banner in the Sky*

HOW DO I REVISE MY DESCRIPTION?

If possible, put your description aside for a few hours or even a few days. Then reread it with the following questions in mind:

CHECKPOINTS FOR REVISING

▶ Do the details I include show the scene to the reader?

▶ Have I used two or more senses to create the scene?

▶ Have I shown readers the scene rather than merely told them about it? Will they feel as if they have experienced the scene themselves?

▶ Do the details and words help set a mood? Is it the mood I want readers to feel? Do all the details help create that mood?

▶ Do I organize the details of the scene in an orderly way so that readers can follow my description?

It's a good idea to invite a friend or family member to read your draft, too. As the writer, you are already very familiar with your scene; readers' reactions and questions can help you revise your draft so that your scene will be equally vivid and clear to others.

Here is the final draft of the student's description of an abandoned motel.

The writer chooses words that immediately set the mood.

Details help the reader see the scene.

The writer leads readers into the scene, starting outside the fence, then moving closer to the motel.

The writer uses more than one sense to describe the scene.

The old motel was surrounded by a black iron fence cloaked in cobwebs and dark green ivy. Its windows were shattered, and countless boards were missing or dangling by a single nail. The porch sagged in the center. There were no steps—just a sudden drop-off to the ground. An ancient porch swing creaked as it rocked forward and back, its passenger a large black cat with yellow eyes and a thick, dirty coat. The place smelled moldy and sour.

—Jamie Beard, Birmingham, Alabama

30

WRITING TO DESCRIBE: OBSERVATION REPORT

How do I write an observation report?

What does a baby peering through the bars of a crib have in common with a scientist studying a slide through a microscope? They are both making observations. Observing involves using the senses—sight, smell, hearing, taste, and touch—to take note of things around you. An observation report incorporates descriptions of things you have observed with conclusions you have drawn from your observations.

> An **observation report** is a description of items or events you have observed and the conclusions you have drawn from your observations.

An observation report is particularly suitable for science writing, but anything that you observe and find interesting is a possible subject. For example, the construction of a building would make a good topic for a report.

GUIDELINES

An observation report

▶ includes sensory details and facts.

▶ reports only what you have observed.

▶ gives your reactions to what you have observed.

▶ states any conclusions you have drawn from your observations.

An Astrologer, 1695–1778, F. Eisen
Valenciennes, Musée des Beaux-Arts

HOW DO I BEGIN AN OBSERVATION REPORT?

Step 1: **CHOOSE WHAT YOU WANT TO OBSERVE.**

If you live near a construction site, you may be able to observe heavy equipment in operation. Then choose a machine to be the focus of your report. Your focus should reflect your purpose. For example, if you want to show how building changes the land, you might choose the bulldozer as your focus. If you want to describe how the frame of a building is put up, you might choose the crane.

Step 2: **SET THE TIME AND PLACE FOR OBSERVING.**

Often the place is set for you because you need to be where the action occurs. Several factors, however, can affect the times you observe. Consider when the event occurs, whether the event occurs in several steps or all at once, what times you are free to observe, and when your report is due.

Step 3: **DECIDE HOW TO RECORD OBSERVATIONS.**

You might want to write a list of questions to try to answer as you make your observations. Also, you may want to make drawings or take pictures. In your notes, include sensory details— sights, sounds, smells, tastes, textures, temperatures, and so on.

WHAT IS IMPORTANT TO RECORD?

Your purpose and your focus will help you determine what to record. Remember to pay close attention to the particular object, process, or event that you've chosen as your focus. Jot down answers to the questions you posed about events or processes. Come up with comparisons you can use to help explain how something looks, moves, or changes. Write down your reactions to what you see—for instance, were you surprised, excited, or amused? Draw conclusions both as you make observations and after you reread your notes.

WHAT FORMS DO OBSERVATION REPORTS TAKE?

An observation report can be part of a descriptive essay, or it can stand alone. By itself, an observation report might take the form of field notes such as you would write in science class.

 WRITING FOR SCIENCE

When you are asked to describe a natural process for science class, you are actually writing an observation report. You would usually include statistical data, measurements, and so on, to give your report credibility. For example, if you are assigned to document how a tadpole changes into a frog, you would carefully record what you see at various points in time. An observation report can also be part of a larger lab report. A lab report usually includes your hypothesis for the experiment, a description of the set-up, materials, and process you followed, and your observations and conclusions.

HOW CAN I ORGANIZE MY REPORT?

Here are some ways of organizing an observation report:

- Describe the parts of your observation chronologically.
- Describe the parts of your observations in spatial order, from top to bottom or from front to back.
- Arrange any answers to questions in a logical order.

For more on organizing your writing, see p. 23.

CHECKPOINTS FOR REVISING

▶ Is all information based on my observations?

▶ Have I reported my reactions to and thoughts on things I observed?

▶ Have I developed conclusions based on my observations?

Here is an observation report on turtles hatching that is part of a descriptive essay.

MODEL FROM LITERATURE

One morning each small turtle fought for freedom within its shell.

They hatched two feet down in the sand, all of them on the same day. As they broke out, their shells collapsed, leaving a small room of air for them to breathe. It wasn't much of a room, just big enough for them to wiggle in and move toward the sky. As they wiggled they pulled the sand down from the ceiling and crawled up on it. In this manner the buried room began to rise, slowly, inch by inch.

Within a week the whole nest chamber of little turtles was almost to the surface, as the young beasts instinctively clawed at the sand above their heads. All week they had struggled against the heavy grains a few minutes at a time. Then they would rest. In this astonishing manner they moved toward the sun.

—Jean Craighead George, "The Hatchling Turtles"

The writer uses chronological order.

The writer compares the nesting chamber of the turtles to a buried room.

The writer includes several observed details.

The writer expresses her personal reaction with the word astonishing.

31

WRITING TO NARRATE: PERSONAL NARRATIVE

 How can I write about my own experiences?

A personal narrative tells a story about something meaning-ful that happened to you.

"Wait 'til you hear what happened to me. . . ." You've probably said those words many hundreds of times. Even though you might not have known it, the stories that you told then were personal narratives.

GUIDELINES

A personal narrative

▶ is an interesting true story about the writer.

▶ is written in the first person (using the pronouns *I*, *me*, and *my*).

▶ has a beginning, a middle, and an end.

▶ presents events in a clear order.

▶ uses details to help readers see people, places, and events.

▶ shows how the writer feels about the experience and why it is meaningful to him or her.

HOW DO I FIND IDEAS?

What kinds of experiences make good personal narratives? Look for the following qualities as you search for writing ideas:

• an experience that was memorable or significant to you in some way

• an experience that you can remember in enough detail to tell about

• an experience that involved a problem or a conflict that eventually got resolved

• an experience that will be meaningful for your readers and make them think about their lives

Here are some ways to find ideas for personal narratives:

LOOK THROUGH YOUR JOURNAL. What experiences have you written about there? Look for experiences in which you faced a problem or conflict that was later resolved.

LOOK THROUGH A FAMILY PHOTO ALBUM. Is there a photograph that reminds you of a story? Perhaps there is a snapshot of the moment you were reunited with a lost pet or a picture of you on your way to your first school dance. Look for photos that evoke emotions you could share.

TRY THIS

Imagine your life as a roller coaster. What are some of the high points? What are some of the low points? Draw a picture of your roller coaster and identify the ups and downs.

WALK AROUND YOUR ROOM AT HOME. What things have you kept that have meaning for you? Does one of them remind you of an experience?

WALK AROUND YOUR NEIGHBORHOOD. Do any of the places or people you see remind you of an experience you want to write about?

TELL STORIES ALOUD. Get together with a few other students and tell stories to one another. Do any of their stories remind you of times in your own life?

MAKE LISTS OF MEMORABLE EXPERIENCES. Here are the categories one student used to help him generate ideas:

MODEL

Firsts	my first day at school my first best friend my first win at a track meet
Lasts	the last time I saw Grandmom the last time I visited my old home
Good Times	a camping trip with my scout troop my tenth birthday
Bad Times	the time I got lost when my family moved

Important Times	when I learned how much my mom cares about me when I learned to stand up for myself when I learned what it means to have a real friend

HOW DO I MAKE MY NARRATIVE INTERESTING?

A narrative that is too general will cause readers to tune you out. You need to be able to tell your story in enough detail so that your readers will feel that they are there with you, watching the action unfold. Here are some ways to come up with details about the people, the places, and the events in your story.

TRY THIS

If your dialogue doesn't sound like real speech, try listening to people talk. Jot down notes about what they say.

PEOPLE Freewrite for a few minutes about each person in your story. Think about the way each one looks, acts, and speaks. Conversation, or dialogue, is a good way to draw your readers into the action. Try to write dialogue that sounds natural— the way real people talk. To see whether your dialogue works, try reading it aloud.

Notice how the author uses dialogue in the following passage:

MODEL FROM LITERATURE

". . . Mr. Herriot, I'm so sorry to bother you today of all days. I should think you want a rest at Christmas like anybody else." But her natural politeness could not hide the distress in her voice.

"Please don't worry about that," I said. "Which one is it this time?"

"It's not one of the dogs. It's . . . Debbie."

"Debbie? She's at your house now?"

"Yes . . . but there's something wrong. Please come quickly."

—James Herriot, "Debbie"

The writer uses ellipses to show pauses in dialogue which build suspense.

PLACES Close your eyes and recall the places in your narrative. What do you see? Hear? Taste? Smell? Feel? Make a chart and jot down details for each of the five senses. Be as specific as possible. Later you can select the best details to use in your story.

EVENTS List the main events of the narrative along a timeline. Identify the conflict and how it gets resolved. Use the timeline to guide you as you write your first draft.

WRITING FOR SOCIAL STUDIES

In a social studies assignment, you may be asked to write a personal narrative from the point of view of a historical character, such as an American soldier in the Revolutionary War. To develop ideas for the narrative, ask the following questions: How old is the character? What is his or her background? What kinds of experiences would he or she have? To discover some specific details about the period, you can

- imagine yourself in a painting from that time.
- pick a subject and compare and contrast what you do now and what they did then.
- listen to music of the era.

HOW DO I ORGANIZE MY STORY?

In general, you'll want to tell your story in **chronological order**—the order in which things happened. Use transitions to guide your readers through your story. Words such as *first, later, the next day,* and *finally* help keep your readers aware of the order of events. Notice how this writer uses transitions to show chronological order in a draft of a personal narrative.

> ### MODEL
>
> I just wished the election were over.
>
> **Finally** the day of the election was here. I cast my ballot halfheartedly, thinking, "Well at least I'll get one vote."
>
> **That afternoon,** the votes were counted. I really dreaded the moment the teacher would announce the winner.

Transitions help readers understand the order of events.

At times, instead of using chronological order, you can begin your story in the middle or at the end. The chart below can help you decide where to begin your narrative:

GOAL	STRATEGY
To keep the story simple	Begin at the beginning with the first thing that happened; then continue with events in the order in which they occurred.
To draw the reader into the action	Begin in the middle of the story with an important or exciting scene; then work in the background as you tell the rest of the story.
To make the meaning of the story clear	Begin with the last thing that happened; then go back and tell the story from the beginning.

You can end your story with the last thing that happened or with your own thoughts about the meaning of the experience. Remember that you don't have to spell out the entire meaning for readers; let them discover some things for themselves.

HOW DO I REVISE MY STORY?

Remember that it is important to *show* emotions and events, not only *tell* about them. Notice how this writer revises her draft to show her anxiety:

M O D E L

The days before the election seemed to creep by.
_it_
∧ I just wished the ~~election~~ were over.

Finally the day of the election was here. I cast my ballot halfheartedly, thinking, "Well, at least I'll get one vote."

That afternoon, the votes were counted. I ~~really~~ _slumped_
further into my chair, waiting for
~~dreaded the moment~~ the teacher ~~would~~ _to_ announce the winner.

Consider these points when you revise your draft:

CHECKPOINTS FOR REVISING

▶ Is the story interesting? Does it have a clear point?

▶ Does the story have a beginning, a middle, and an end?

▶ Is the order of events clear?

▶ Do I use details to help readers see the people, places, and events in the story?

▶ Do I use dialogue to bring the people in the story to life?

▶ Do I use the first-person (I) point of view throughout?

▶ Do I show how I feel about the experience?

Here's an example of a final draft of a personal narrative:

MODEL

"Come on, you'd make a great class president," said Teresa, my best friend, as we walked home from school one night. Class elections were coming up, and even though I hadn't thought seriously about running, I kind of liked the idea.

"Think about it," Teresa insisted. "Wouldn't it be great to be <u>President</u> Angela Marquez?"

I had to admit to myself that I liked the sound of it. I was pretty popular. Why not run for president?

For the next week, Teresa and I worked hard getting a campaign committee together, making posters, and coming up with slogans. On the big day, I was so sick to my stomach that I barely made it to school at all. That afternoon, as students crowded into the auditorium to hear the speeches, I sat and watched the clock on the wall count down the minutes to my moment of doom.

The writer begins at the beginning of the story and draws the reader in with dialogue.

The writer uses the first person (I, me) throughout the story.

The writer tells how she feels about the experience.

Finally, it was my turn to speak. I got up and shakily approached the microphone. The stage lights blinded me, and my hands were sweating. I started to speak. The words seemed to fly out of my mouth. They flew faster and faster. I could hear the giggles of my classmates. I could see Teresa in the front row frantically waving her arms and mouthing, "Slow down," but I couldn't. I finished my speech in record time and slumped down into my seat. Now I knew I had lost the election. All that work would go for nothing. I had let everybody down.

The following week, I dragged myself through the halls, wishing I were invisible. Teresa tried to console me.

"It wasn't that bad," she said. "Look at it this way, at least you didn't bore everybody to death."

Finally, the day of the election was here. I cast my ballot halfheartedly, thinking, "Well, at least I'll get one vote."

That afternoon, the votes were counted. I slumped further into my chair waiting for the teacher to announce the winner. Through a fog of despair, I heard her say, "The new president of the sixth-grade class is . . . Angela Marquez!"

I had won. I hadn't ruined everything with my lightning-speed speech after all. Other students hadn't judged me on one disastrous episode. They

had faith in me, and now I realized I needed to have more faith in them—and in myself.

WRITING TO NARRATE: HUMOROUS ANECDOTE

32

How do I write a humorous anecdote?

Once, minutes before a game was to start, the legendary baseball player Babe Ruth sneaked in a couple of liverwurst-and-onion sandwiches, ate a dozen hot dogs, gulped down six bottles of cherry soda pop, and then topped off that hurried snack with an apple. Before the ninth inning he caved in with a stomachache. . . . As they carted him off

> A **humorous anecdote** is a short, entertaining account, usually of a particular event or episode.

to a hospital, the very sick and unhappy Babe moaned, "I knew I shouldna ate that apple."

Babe's comment makes readers laugh because they know, as Babe knew, that it wasn't the apple that made him sick. Many humorous anecdotes, like this one, revolve around an unexpected comment or twist that makes people laugh.

WAYS TO MAKE AN ANECDOTE HUMOROUS

An unexpected twist is one way to make an anecdote humorous. Other methods writers use to make an anecdote funny include the following:

Exaggerating wildly: The fish I caught was so big I had to hire an eighteen-wheeler truck to carry it home.

Revealing a vast difference between what the reader knows and what the characters know: Tan began his presentation to the school board not realizing that he was still wearing his pajamas.

Including unusual or unexpected details of setting or character: All in all, Jerome was a regular guy, except that he did everything while standing on his head.

Contrasting a serious tone with a ridiculous situation: The winner of the frog-jumping contest, a thoroughbred tree frog, uttered a mighty croak as she completed her record-setting jump.

As you look for anecdotes to use in your writing, you must consider more than just the element of humor. Here are some characteristics of an effective anecdote that should guide your work:

GUIDELINES

A humorous anecdote

▶ is brief.

▶ entertains readers.

▶ is often about real people.

▶ often uses dialogue.

▶ can make a point or reveal a personality trait.

HOW DO I USE A HUMOROUS ANECDOTE?

Humorous anecdotes can stand on their own or they can be used in larger pieces of writing. The following chart shows some different ways you can use your humorous anecdotes in longer works and the techniques of humor that you might choose to achieve each purpose.

PURPOSE OF ANECDOTE	TECHNIQUE OPTIONS
To enliven an introduction or conclusion	■ Use an unexpected twist. ■ Include unusual details of setting or character.
To spice up a biography or personal narrative	■ Include unusual details of setting or character. ■ Contrast a serious tone with a ridiculous situation.
To add interest to a speech or letter	■ Use exaggeration. ■ Contrast a serious tone with a ridiculous situation. ■ Use an unexpected twist.
To reveal a character's personality in a narrative, biography, or autobiography	■ Include unusual details of character. ■ Reveal a difference between what the reader knows and what the character knows.

In the model that follows, James Thurber uses a humorous anecdote to help reveal the character of an eccentric aunt.

Aunt Gracie Shoaf . . . was confident that burglars had been getting into her house every night for forty years. The fact that she never missed anything was to her no proof to the contrary. She always claimed that she scared them off before they could take anything by throwing shoes down the hallway. When she went to bed she piled, where she could get at them handily, all the shoes there were about her house.

Readers know that Aunt Gracie's fears are irrational, so her solution to her imaginary problem—pitching shoes—seems ridiculous.

—James Thurber, "The Night the Bed Fell"

ANECDOTE VS. JOKE

An anecdote is like a joke in that it entertains readers. Unlike a joke, an anecdote is often about real people, not just imaginary characters, and it sometimes may appear in a larger piece of writing to develop a complete picture of a character.

DEVELOPING HUMOROUS ANECDOTES

Sometimes it's hard to recall a real-life humorous anecdote when you need one. Try using these sources for inspiration:

YOUR JOURNAL It probably contains many humorous anecdotes about you, your friends, and family members.

FAMILY AND FRIENDS See if they recall any funny stories.

TRY THIS

One strategy that may help you develop your anecdote is to act it out as if you were a storyteller. By using gestures, movement, and dialogue, you will gain insights into what makes the anecdote funny and significant.

PHOTO OR VIDEO ALBUMS Pictures can help you remember funny stories involving people you know.

BIOGRAPHIES When you're writing about a well-known person, look for anecdotes in more than one biography. Compare different versions of the same event. Notice which biographies make you feel as if you were "behind the scenes" in the subject's life.

Once you find an anecdote you like, think about how to develop the episode. What makes it funny? If, for instance, the humor depends on dialogue, as in the Babe Ruth anecdote, be sure you build up to the comment as if it were a punch line. If the humor depends on exaggeration, you might write the account of the episode and then add exaggerated details to heighten the effect.

HOW DO I REVISE MY ANECDOTE?

Here are some points to consider when you revise your humorous anecdote.

CHECKPOINTS FOR REVISING

▶ Is it brief?

▶ Does it use one of these techniques to achieve humor: an unexpected twist; exaggeration; a contrast between a serious tone and a ridiculous event; a difference between what the reader knows and what a character knows; unusual details of character or setting?

▶ Is the dialogue appropriate to the characters?

▶ Does the anecdote serve a specific purpose?

How can I write a good story?

If someone said to you, "Listen, here's a great story" and then described a really spectacular crater on the moon, would you be satisfied? It's not likely you would be. You would want someone to show up at the crater and do something.

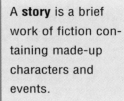

> A **story** is a brief work of fiction containing made-up characters and events.

As this example shows, a story involves characters, events, and ideas as well as a time and place.

When you develop a story, consider these guidelines:

For more on writing a personal narrative, see p. 126.

GUIDELINES

A story

- ▶ has a **plot,** or a series of events.
- ▶ focuses on a struggle, called a **conflict.**
- ▶ presents believable **characters** who speak in a natural way.
- ▶ happens in a particular time and place, called the **setting.**
- ▶ is told by a narrator from a particular **point of view.**
- ▶ contains a central message, or **theme.**

HOW DO I GET AN IDEA FOR A STORY?

Story ideas may be inspired by a colorful character, an intriguing situation, or a place you always wanted to visit.

To find story ideas, write the following questions on an index card. Repeat the questions on several cards. Then fill in as many answers as you can on each card. You should end up with a few promising characters, situations, and settings.

- WHO might be interesting to write about?
- WHAT could happen to this individual?
- WHEN and WHERE did it happen?
- HOW did it happen?
- WHY would it be interesting or worthwhile to read about?

HOW DO I EXPLORE MY STORY IDEA?

CONFLICT Most good stories involve **conflict,** which means "a problem of some kind and a struggle between opposing forces or characters." In some stories, two characters may come into conflict. For example, two friends might compete for a prize. A character can also come into conflict with an outside force, as when a lost hiker struggles through a fog. The conflict may be between a character and a social group. For example, a student might take a stand despite the ridicule of her classmates. Finally, conflict can occur within a character.

If you can't think of a conflict within your story idea, you should try a different idea that has more potential for conflict.

DETAILS OF SETTING AND CHARACTER Make your setting and characters concrete. Consider these questions:

- In what year and season does my story take place?
- Can I picture the setting and depict it in my story?
- How does the setting affect the way my characters behave?
- How old are my characters?
- How do they dress?
- How do they talk?
- What kinds of personalities do they have?

CLOTHES?

AGE?

GESTURES?

VOICE?

PERSONALITY TRAITS?

HOW DO I DEVELOP MY IDEAS INTO A STORY?

PLOT: SUSPENSE, CLIMAX, AND RESOLUTION

You have imagined your characters and setting and found a plot
with an exciting conflict at its center. Now you need to decide
how your story will begin, where it will go, and how it will end.
This information is called **plot structure.** Consider drawing a line
like the following to graph your plot structure:

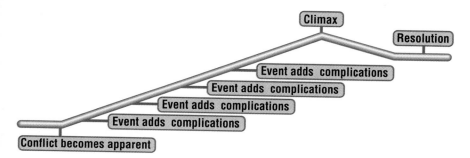

Notice that the conflict appears early in the plot. Each event
in the plot adds to the conflict, making it more intense or more
complicated. The ever-increasing tension reaches a high point at
the story's climax. Then the conflict is settled, and the story
winds down to a resolution, which explains how everything
turned out.

MAKING A STORYBOARD

You may prefer to create a **storyboard,** which details the plot
in words and pictures. It can spark new ideas for plot, character,
and setting. The following storyboard shows the first events in a
story about a student, Matt, who takes up a science teacher's challenge to name all the bones in the human body.

Matt accepts the challenge.

The class is awed.

Matt gives the right answers.

POINT OF VIEW

At this point, you should consider who will tell the story and how much or little that narrator knows about the characters' thoughts. This chart shows two types of storytellers.

POINT OF VIEW	EXAMPLE
First-person narrator relates events that happened to him or her and uses first-person pronouns such as *I, me, my,* and *we*. This is the most personal point of view, but you cannot reveal anything that this narrator wouldn't know.	"I always thought I could stomach any amusement park ride until I took on the roller coaster called the Screaming Meemie."
Third-person narrator uses third-person pronouns such as *he, she,* and *they*. Third-person narrators can know the thoughts of one or more characters. This point of view isn't as personal, but it allows you to reveal many characters' perspectives, as well as your own.	"Sam always thought he could stomach any amusement park ride until he experienced the Screaming Meemie."

Before you make a final decision, write a passage of your story from each point of view. Then ask yourself which point of view suits your particular plan or goal.

PURPOSE AND AUDIENCE

Before you begin drafting, think about your readers and what you hope to accomplish. Is your audience your best friend? Your creative writing class? The readers of a national magazine? Is your purpose to make them laugh, cry, or shiver with fright? What must you do to achieve your purpose? If, for instance, you want to frighten readers, you must build up a threatening mood.

Part of your purpose may be to communicate to your audience a feeling or belief you have about life. This intended message is called the **theme** of the story. For example, a story about two friends competing for a prize might have the theme that competition strengthens a friendship or that competition weakens a friendship—depending on how the story turns out.

For more on purpose and audience, see p. 11.

HOW DO I DRAFT MY STORY?

BEGINNING THE STORY You want your very first words to grab your readers' attention, but how? O. Henry's famous story "The Gift of the Magi" begins with the sentence fragment "One dollar and eighty-seven cents." Readers are hooked immediately. They wonder, "Why is such an exact amount of money important enough to begin this story?" and so they read on. Here are a few good ways of getting started:

1. Describe the story's most interesting character.

MODEL FROM LITERATURE

She was a large woman with a large purse that had everything in it but hammer and nails.

—Langston Hughes, "Thank You, M'am"

2. Begin with one detail of plot, setting, or character. (Remember O. Henry's "One dollar and eighty-seven cents.") Start with a specific detail, and branch out from there.

3. Hint where the story will lead.

STUDENT MODEL

Matt has never been an exceptional student, but there is one scientific term you can bet he'll never forget.

4. Begin with dialogue.

MODEL FROM LITERATURE

"We don't have much crime on Mars," said Detective Inspector Rawlings, a little sadly.

—Arthur C. Clarke, "Crime on Mars"

TELLING THE STORY As you begin to tell your story, refer to your storyboard and prewriting notes. You will create a more believable conflict if you show rather than tell about confrontations and emotions. For example, instead of explaining what a character feels, find an action that shows what he or she feels. You can also suggest what a character feels by describing the character's face and movements, allowing readers to draw conclusions.

> **Telling:** Tania felt lonely after her sister Della left for college. The room they had shared seemed so depressing.
> **Showing:** Tania sat hunched on her bed, hugging her knees. Unfinished letters to Della lay on the floor. Tania looked around the room. All her sister's stuff was gone.

WRITING DIALOGUE Using **dialogue,** or conversation between two characters, shows, rather than tells, what is going on within a character and between characters. Try to give characters their own voices. Some people are talkative; some are not. Some people are formal in their speaking style, choosing words carefully and using precise grammar and sentence structure. Some people are less formal.

FORMAL	LESS FORMAL
"Children, I want you to stop that behavior this instant!"	"Hey, kids, c'mon—cut it out!"
"This task will entail no perspiration on my part."	"No sweat!"
"We both enjoyed ourselves a great deal at your party."	"We had a lot of fun."

For more on punctuating dialogue, see quotation marks, p. 373. Listening to real people talk is a good way to develop an ear for dialogue. Be aware, however, that creative writers do not record *exactly* what people say. In actual speech, people repeat themselves, stutter, and say "uh," or "you know" far too much. The job of a story writer is to make the dialogue sound realistic.

ENDING THE STORY Be sure that you build suspense to a peak. The climax of one story could be a decisive confrontation between two characters in conflict. The climax of another story, involving physical danger, could be the most dangerous event in the story. Once you write the climax, you can end the story as dramatically or as quietly as you like.

HOW DO I REVISE MY STORY?

After you've finished your draft, put it aside for a while. Then read the draft with the following questions in mind:

CHECKPOINTS FOR REVISING

▶ Does my opening make the reader want to read on? Does it establish the point of view clearly?

▶ Do the characters act consistently? Is the dialogue natural?

▶ Can the conflict be made clearer or more gripping? Do all the events develop the conflict?

▶ Where can "showing" replace "telling"?

▶ Does the story reach a climax that resolves the conflict?

▶ Is the theme, or central message, of the story clear?

▶ Are grammar, usage, spelling, and punctuation correct?

STUDENT MODEL

Matt has never been an exceptional student, but there is one scientific term you can bet he'll never forget.

It was a cool day in the middle of May, the kind near the end of the school year that just drags on and on. The time for science had arrived. Mr. Winnekamp asked, "Would anyone like to try the bone chart today?"

All the snickering in the room turned to a dead hush when Matt said, "Yeah, Mr. Winnekamp. I'd like to take the challenge."

Anyone who could name all twenty-six bones on the chart at the back of the room would receive twenty extra credit points. You had only one chance. One mistake, one wrong word, and your chance to be the best went down the tubes.

The beginning hints at the conflict. It also establishes a third-person narrator.

Specific details establish the setting, a familiar classroom.

Dialogue introduces the conflict.

Mr. Winnekamp and Matt walked to the back of the room. After an eternity, the solemn silence was broken by Mr. Winnekamp's voice. "What is the name of this bone?" he asked, pointing to the head of the skeleton on the life-sized poster.

Matt straightened his back, looked the teacher in the eye, and answered, "That's the cranium." The class let out a huge sigh of relief.

So on they went, Matt naming each bone the teacher pointed to in a process that seemed to take hours. Finally they got to the last bone. It was the knee bone. The class fell silent.

Matt started to answer—and then his mind went blank. He couldn't remember! Then, at his lowest moment, when he was in the pit of despair, at the end of his rope, it hit him.

He straightened himself from his hunched position, grabbed hold of his overall straps, looked at the chart, and casually said, "Ah . . . I'm pretty sure that's the patella."

The whole room exploded. Everyone cheered, stood, and patted Matt on the back and hugged him.

—Joe Hasley, Cedar Rapids, Iowa

34

What is a poem?

A poem may be as short as one line or as long as an entire book. It may use sound devices like rhyme, but it doesn't have to. It may be serious or humorous, joyful, sad, or angry. It may be about something ordinary or something quite extraordinary—in fact, it may be about anything at all.

What, then, separates poetry from other writing? Poets use fewer, more carefully chosen words than most prose writers do. Poets also emphasize **images,** details that appeal to one or more of the five senses. They pay extra attention to the sounds of words and to the emotional associations that a word or image may have for readers. They also choose words carefully to create a **mood,** or feeling. Consider the words, images, sounds, and mood of the following poem.

> A **poem** expresses thoughts, feelings, and experiences in language more concentrated and imaginative than ordinary prose.

MODEL FROM LITERATURE

Lineage

My grandmothers were strong.
They followed plows and bent to toil.
They moved through fields sowing seed.
They touched earth and grain grew.
They were full of sturdiness and singing.

My grandmothers are full of memories
Smelling of soap and onions and wet clay
With veins rolling roughly over quick hands
They have many clean words to say.
My grandmothers were strong.
Why am I not as they?

—Margaret Walker

Toil is a less common word than work. It stresses the poet's appreciation for the grandmothers.

Repetition of sounds, like the s in sowing seed, helps create the poem's music.

Images of soap, onions, and wet clay appeal to the senses of smell, sight, and touch.

The last line changes the poem's mood.

There are two common kinds of poetry. A **narrative poem** tells a story. A **lyric poem**, like "Lineage," expresses the writer's or speaker's thoughts and feelings.

HOW CAN I FIND AN IDEA FOR A POEM?

Don't make the mistake of thinking that there are special "poetic" sources of inspiration. Love and nature may have inspired a host of poems, but Patricia Hubbell wrote a well-known poem about concrete mixers, and May Swenson wrote one called "Southbound on the Freeway." The truth is that absolutely anything may inspire a poem. To find your own sources of inspiration, try these strategies:

- **Sketch a scene.** Take a walk and sketch a scene that appeals to you—perhaps a face at a window or a pattern created by the blades of ice skates on a pond. Later your sketch may give you an idea for a poem.

- **Listen to popular songs.** Is there a line from one of them that you can use to begin a poem? What do you imagine seeing, hearing, and feeling as you repeat the line to yourself?

- **Play with the sounds of words.** Tap out the rhythms of familiar songs and poems, or create a rhyme chain by choosing a word that appeals to your senses and then writing down other words that rhyme with it.

    bark: *dark, spark, mark, quark, lark, shark, ark, hark, park*

- **Start with a line or two that you will repeat.** Many poems use repeated lines, called a **refrain,** to create a sense of unity. You might borrow your refrain from another poem or create one on your own. Notice the refrain in the following poem.

 MODEL FROM LITERATURE

Everybody Says

Everybody says
I look just like my mother.
Everybody says
I'm the image of my Aunt Bee.
Everybody says
My nose is like my father's,
But *I* want to look like me.

—Dorothy Aldis

HOW DO I DRAFT MY POEM?

Once something has inspired you, begin free-writing about it. Don't pause to think about or criticize what you have written. Even if what you are writing sounds foolish, keep going until you have finished describing your thought, feeling, image, or memory. One writer began with a memory of the fire at her camp last summer. She then freewrote to help her recall phrases, images, comparisons, feelings, and anything else that she associated with the campfire.

TRY THIS

Recall the smells of your favorite foods. Freewrite about your reactions to what you imagine smelling. Try to recall experiences as well as feelings and sensations.

STUDENT MODEL

singing silly songs and telling funny stories

stuck marshmallows onto sticks and cooked them over
    campfire; they became gooey

fire seemed alive, made popping and snapping noises

fire trying to move out from confining bunch of rocks

let loose puffs of smoke

throwing water on it sent up more smoke

fire powerful yet put out by the water

As you look through your freewriting, consider each detail, and decide whether it contributes to the key idea and mood that you want your poem to convey. Expand on details that do contribute, and revise or discard those that do not.

The writer describing the campfire decided that her poem's key idea would be that fire is powerful even though it can be put out by water. She also decided to create a suspenseful mood until the end. Having made these decisions, she discarded details about songs and stories and deleted the detail about marshmallows, focusing instead on sticks being burned in the campfire.

~~singing silly songs and telling funny stories~~
~~stuck marshmallows onto~~ many sticks ~~and cooked them over~~ rapidly burned up by
campfire; ~~they became gooey~~
fire seemed alive, made popping and snapping noises

HOW DO I POLISH MY LANGUAGE?

CONCISE LANGUAGE AND IMAGES Poetry is a concentrated form of writing in which every word counts. In revising and expanding your poem's details, make your language concise. In general, the fewer words you use, the better.

Also, choose precise words rather than general or vague ones, and include images that help your readers see, hear, smell, taste, and touch whatever your poem is describing. The writer followed all this advice in making the following revisions.

fire seemed alive, ~~made popping and snapping noises~~ popped and snapped
fire trying to ~~move out~~ escape from confining ~~bunch~~ circle of rocks
let loose puffs of smoke in gray clouds
throwing water on it ~~sent~~ made it sizzle and send up ~~more~~ a column of smoke

The writer changed *popped* and *snapped* to be more concise; *escape* and *circle* are more precise. The three other changes add images that appeal to the senses of sight and sound.

FIGURATIVE LANGUAGE When you use language **figuratively,** you take words beyond their usual meaning, often by comparing things that seem to be unlike. For example, you might compare a fire to a hungry person. Figurative language can make your poem more lively and memorable. The following revisions use figurative language to suggest that the fire is like a person.

For more figurative language, see p. 95.

> ### S T U D E N T   M O D E L
>
> ~~stuck marshmallows onto~~ sticks ~~and cooked them over~~ *(many)* *(rapidly burned up)* *(eaten by)*
>
> campfire; ~~they became gooey~~

CONNOTATIONS In choosing words for your poem, be alert to their **connotations,** emotional associations beyond dictionary meanings. If you choose a word with the right dictionary meaning but the wrong connotation, your readers may not get the message you want to convey. For example, *column* and *pillar* are synonyms, but *pillar* has a more positive connotation partly because of its association with the expression "pillar of society." In the following revision, the change from *column* to *pillar* suggests the idea that the quenched fire still has strength and stature.

For more on connotations, see p. 89.

> ### S T U D E N T   M O D E L
>
> *made it sizzle and send*   *pillar*
> throwing water on it ~~sent~~ up ~~more~~ smoke *(a column of)*

POETRY AND RULES In poetry you can break some of the rules of grammar, usage, and mechanics. For example, some poets use all lowercase letters; others capitalize important words. Many poets use sentence fragments to keep their language direct and concise. In the following portion of her revision, the writer turned a sentence into a two-part fragment.

> ### S T U D E N T   M O D E L
>
> *A*   *pillar*
> ~~made it~~ sizzle ~~and send~~   ~~a column~~ of
> ~~throwing water on it sent~~ up ~~more~~ smoke

HOW ELSE CAN I MAKE MY POEM APPEALING?

Like vivid images and figurative language, sound devices can make your poem more interesting and memorable. However, don't let the sound seem forced or unnatural; instead, use it to enhance the mood and meaning of your poem. Consider using some of the following sound devices.

REPETITION As illustrated in "Lineage" and "Everybody Says," the repetition of words and phrases can stress key ideas and help tie together the images of a poem.

ASSONANCE AND ALLITERATION **Assonance** is the repetition of vowel sounds; **alliteration** is the repetition of consonant sounds at the beginnings of words. Both can help enhance the mood or meaning of a poem. In the following revision, for example, the alliterated *s* sounds and repeated short *i* sounds help capture the crackling and hissing of the fire.

STUDENT MODEL

sudden
a sizzle, a pillar of smoke

ONOMATOPOEIA Onomatopoeia [än′ ə mä′ tə pē′ə] is the use of words that imitate sounds—for example, *bang, clatter, oink,* and *hush.* In the model, the word *sizzle,* used to describe the sound of the water putting out the fire, is an example of this device.

RHYTHM In English certain syllables are emphasized and others are not. When you say *water,* for instance, you stress the first syllable but not the second: WA ter. In poetry, **rhythm** refers to the arrangement of stressed syllables (marked ′) and unstressed syllables (marked ˘).

A regular pattern of stressed and unstressed syllables can help single out key words and make a poem sound musical and memorable. On the other hand, if you choose words simply to fit a particular rhythm pattern and forget what you're trying to say, your poem will sound forced. The following poem uses a rhythm pattern effectively. Notice how natural it sounds when you read it aloud.

MODEL FROM LITERATURE

Martin Luther King

Hĕ cáme ŭpón ăn áge
Bĕsét bў grief, bў ráge—

Hĭs lóve sŏ deép, sŏ wíde,
Hĕ coúld nŏt túrn ăsíde.

Hĭs pássiŏn, só prŏfoúnd,
Hĕ woúld nŏt túrn ăroúnd.

Hĕ taúght thĭs súffĕrĭng Eárth
Thĕ méasŭre ŏf Mán's wórth.

Hĕ shówed whăt Mán căn bé
Bĕfóre déath séts hĭm frée.

—Raymond Richard Patterson

The first three
stanzas, or
groups of lines,
establish a rhythm
pattern in which a
line contains three
unstressed sylla-
bles each followed
by a stressed
syllable.

In the fourth and
fifth stanzas,
breaks in the
rhythm pattern
draw attention to
the words Man's
and death. The
attention is appro-
priate since the
words indicate key
ideas in the poem.

Rev. Martin Luther King, Jr.

RHYME The device known as **rhyme** is the repetition of sounds at the ends of words: *wide/aside, suffer/tougher, singing/ringing, Earth/worth.* Often rhyme follows a pattern, as it does in "Martin Luther King," in which the two lines of each stanza rhyme. Like rhythm, rhyme can call out words that are especially im-portant and make a poem more memorable, but it can also seem forced if you choose words merely for their rhyming sounds and forget what you're trying to say.

WRITING FOR MUSIC

The lyrics, or words, of most songs use sound devices similar to those used in poetry.

- Song lyrics usually rhyme and have a regular rhythm; they also may use repetition, especially in a refrain.
- The music and the lyrics of a song work together to create a mood and express meaning.

WHAT FORM SHOULD MY POEM TAKE?

Traditional verse uses regular patterns of rhythm (and often of rhyme); **free verse** does not. The poem "Martin Luther King" is traditional verse; the poem "Lineage" is free verse. Since free verse has no rhythm pattern dictating where lines should break, the poet must decide to end a line after language that best reflects the poem's mood and meaning. In her poem about the campfire, the student writer used free verse because she felt it would help capture the fire's freedom. As you read the final version, notice the decisions the student made about where to break lines.

STUDENT MODEL

Campfire

The writer breaks most lines so that each image stands on its own.

The poem's ragged edges resemble the flickering of a campfire.

Fire,
Popping, snapping, eating stick after stick.
Shooting sparks in all directions.
Leaning,
Trying to escape its confinement, a circle of rocks.
Letting loose
Puffs of smoke in gray clouds.
A sudden sizzle,
A pillar of smoke,
Water, fire's enemy, has put it out.

—Elisa Smith, Yakima, Washington

WRITING TO INFORM: EXTENDED DEFINITION

35

How do I define a term or concept?

Imagine that you're writing to a pen pal whose culture is very different from yours. You want to explain one of your favorite winter pastimes—sledding—to your new friend. In the dictionary, you find sledding defined as "the act of using a sled for sport." That's not much help. Then you find this fuller definition: "Sledding is the sport of coasting down a snowy hill on a runnered sled or toboggan. Sledding combines the hush of a snowy winter landscape with the rush of excitement that comes from speeding down a steep slope. When you go sledding, you become a part of winter." This fuller, more complete definition, called an **extended definition**, brings your subject into clear focus by providing both interesting and informative details.

> An **extended definition** is a definition elaborated with details such as statistics, vivid descriptions, comparisons, or examples.

HOW CAN I EXTEND MY DEFINITION?

The details you include in your definition depend, in part, on your purpose for writing. Is your definition part of a larger piece of writing? Are you trying to explain, inform, or persuade? Different details help to fulfill different purposes. When you are planning your extended definition, follow these suggestions:

GUIDELINES

An extended definition

▶ includes a brief statement of your subject's characteristics.

▶ elaborates this basic statement with details.

▶ includes details that best suit your writing purpose.

When you have written a brief one-sentence definition of what your subject and its characteristics are, create a word web to help you "flesh out" your ideas. The following is an example of a one-sentence definition and word web.

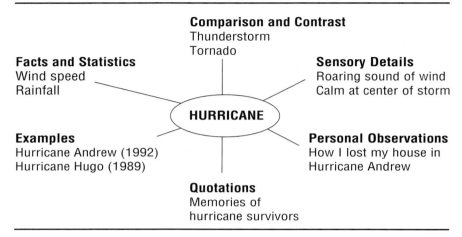

A hurricane is a huge tropical storm with high winds and heavy rains.

Comparison and Contrast
Thunderstorm
Tornado

Facts and Statistics
Wind speed
Rainfall

Sensory Details
Roaring sound of wind
Calm at center of storm

HURRICANE

Examples
Hurricane Andrew (1992)
Hurricane Hugo (1989)

Personal Observations
How I lost my house in
Hurricane Andrew

Quotations
Memories of
hurricane survivors

For more on
elaboration,
see p. 34.

After you've completed a word web, decide which details give a clearer idea of your subject. Then add details to your definition until you are satisfied that you have presented your readers with a full picture.

For example, you might start adding to the basic definition of a hurricane by giving statistics about windspeed and rainfall. You might continue by giving sensory details that suggest what it's like to be in a hurricane.

WRITING FOR SCIENCE

If you are asked in science class to explain a term or concept such as *red tide* or *bioluminescence*, you may need to write an extended definition. The following tips may be helpful.

• Many scientific terms are made up of two or more familiar words (e.g., *red tide*) or of words with a Greek or Latin root (e.g., *bioluminescence*). You can include the brief dictionary definition of these words as a starting point for your definition. Then you can extend the definition by explaining how the dictionary meaning relates to the scientific meaning of the term.

• You can find details to extend a scientific definition by using an elaboration graphic such as a cluster, web, or classification frame. In such a graphic, you explore the different parts or aspects of a subject. For instance, you might include research details about bioluminescence in insects, fish, fungi, and bacteria.

HOW DO I REVISE MY EXTENDED DEFINITION?

When you have completed an extended definition, read it over carefully. Then ask yourself these questions:

CHECKPOINTS FOR REVISING

▶ Does my definition fulfill my purpose in writing—to inform, explain, or persuade?

▶ Have I used an assortment of details to extend my definition?

▶ Do my details help give a complete, vivid picture of my subject?

Here is a finished draft of the extended definition. Note the wide variety of details that have been included.

MODEL

A hurricane is a huge tropical storm that can cut across wide areas and cause serious damage. Winds blow up to 130 miles an hour, and heavy rains fall. Sometimes more than a foot of rain can fall in a few hours! Some hurricane survivors say that the roaring winds sound like an approaching freight train. Glass, wood, and even metal can bend or break from the force of the high winds. The last big hurricane to hit the United States was Hurricane Andrew, which devastated southern Florida in 1992. I know because I was there! My family lives near Miami, and the hurricane ripped the roof off our house and knocked down the palm trees in our yard.

Statistics

Sensory details/ Memories

Vivid descriptions

Example

Personal observations

36

WRITING TO INFORM: COMPARISON-AND-CONTRAST ESSAY

 How can I show similarities and differences between items?

In a **comparison-and-contrast essay**, a writer explores both the similarities and the differences between two (or more) items.

A comparison-and-contrast essay can give you and your readers new perspectives. A key word in the definition of this type of essay is *explores*. If you write with a spirit of exploration, you will make your essay more than a boring and predictable listing of similarities and differences.

GUIDELINES

A comparison-and-contrast essay

▶ explores similarities and differences between two or more related items.

▶ reveals unexpected relationships between these items.

▶ can have one or more of the following purposes: informing, persuading, evaluating, and entertaining.

▶ uses specific examples to support its points.

▶ is organized clearly and consistently.

▶ uses transitional words and phrases—such as *but, however, on the other hand, like,* and *unlike*—to organize information.

WHAT SHOULD I COMPARE AND CONTRAST?

Make sure you choose items that are similar enough to be compared. In Lewis Carroll's poem "The Walrus and the Carpenter," the Walrus wants to talk about "shoes—and ships—and sealing wax—/ ...cabbages—and kings." This odd collection would be the worst possible material for a comparison and contrast. The items are so dissimilar that their only link is their presence in the mind of a nutty Walrus.

By applying the Walrus rule to a comparison-and-contrast essay, you will avoid comparing "cabbages—and kings."

	Do Compare	Don't Compare
Language Arts	■ the settings of two stories ■ two story plots ■ two characters from different stories	■ a setting to a plot ■ a plot to a character ■ a character to a setting
Social Studies	■ two historical figures ■ two battles ■ two key inventions	■ a historical figure to a battle ■ a battle to an invention ■ an invention to a historical figure
Science	■ two scientists ■ two theories ■ two observations	■ a scientist to a theory ■ a theory to an observation ■ an observation to a scientist

Also, be sure that the focus of your comparison is narrow enough. For example, if you enjoy the fiction of Sam Selvon and James Ramsey Ullman, you might be tempted to compare and contrast every novel and short story written by these authors. However, it would be much easier to compare and contrast two characters.

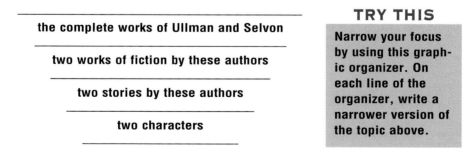

the complete works of Ullman and Selvon

two works of fiction by these authors

two stories by these authors

two characters

TRY THIS

Narrow your focus by using this graphic organizer. On each line of the organizer, write a narrower version of the topic above.

GATHERING INFORMATION FOR AN ESSAY

Try using graphic organizers to gather information. One writer used the interlinked circles of a Venn diagram to indicate the similarities and differences between the main characters of Selvon's story "The Mouth Organ" and Ullman's story "A Boy and a Man."

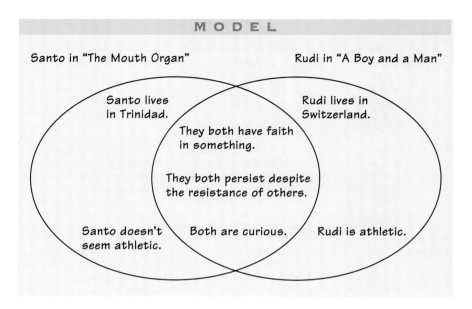

MODEL

Santo in "The Mouth Organ"

Rudi in "A Boy and a Man"

Santo lives in Trinidad.

Rudi lives in Switzerland.

They both have faith in something.

They both persist despite the resistance of others.

Santo doesn't seem athletic.

Both are curious.

Rudi is athletic.

 WRITING FOR SCIENCE

Try using a Venn diagram when you have to compare and contrast items for your science class. For example, if you were comparing and contrasting closely related animals like an otter and a platypus, you would label one of the interlinked circles *otter* and the other *platypus*. You would list the qualities that are unique to each animal in the main part of that animal's circle. Then you would put qualities that they have in common—fur and webbed feet, for example—in the area where the circles overlap.

COMPUTER TIP

Make a chart like the one below and store it in your glossary. Then you can copy it when you need to.
Item #1 _____
Item #2 _____
Similarities
_____
Differences
_____

Another way to gather information is to talk to a friend about the items you chose. As you talk, you may think of ways in which they are similar and different.

When Lee Bennett Hopkins interviewed author Virginia Hamilton (see p. 159) about the characters she had created, she explored the ways in which these characters were similar to and different from real people. Although she was not preparing to write an essay, her response could have been the starting point for a comparison and contrast. You can gather information in the same way, thinking aloud and coming up with new similarities and differences between your items.

I asked Virginia if any of her characters are based on real people she knows or knew. She commented: "Oh, I'd say that Uncle Ross in *Zeely* is somewhat similar to my Uncle Lee who was a collector of antiques and stray cats; Geeder and Toeboy talk and act and sleep outside in much the same way my brother and I did. I don't really base any of my characters on real people. I do take the atmosphere of known people, their emotions, and give them to my characters. . . . I think I'd have to say my characters are for the most part based on me. If you'll notice, every lead character is something of a loner, imaginative and contemplative, from Zeely up through Thomas Small in *The House of Dies Drear* to Junior Brown.

—Lee Bennett Hopkins, *Virginia Hamilton*

HOW DO I DRAFT MY ESSAY?

Your essay will consist of three parts: an introduction, a body, and a conclusion; however, you do not have to write these in the order they appear. For example, you can begin drafting the body of your essay and then write the introduction.

THE INTRODUCTION Use your introductory paragraph to capture readers' attention and to summarize the similarities and differences between the items you are discussing.

MODEL

What could a teenage boy living in the mountains of Switzerland have in common with a boy growing up in tropical Trinidad? Rudi in James Ramsey Ullman's "A Boy and a Man" and Santo in Sam Selvon's "The Mouth Organ" do come from very different places and have different interests and abilities. However, they both are faithful to their dreams.

The first sentence captures readers' attention by asking a question. The next two sentences briefly summarize the boys' similarities and differences.

This paragraph makes it clear that the writer's purpose is to inform readers.

THE BODY You can organize the body of your essay in two different ways. One approach is to discuss the features of the first item you are comparing, then discuss the features of the second. An alternative is to compare and contrast the items feature by feature. Before writing about the characters Rudi and Santo, a writer created an outline for each of these two approaches.

MODEL

First One Item, Then Another	Feature by Feature
Para. 1: Introduction	Para. 1: Introduction
Para. 2: Santo	Para. 2: Feature—Background
Where he lives	and Abilities (Contrasts
His personality and abilities	between Rudi and Santo)
His curiosity and faith	
Para. 3: Rudi	Para. 3: Feature—Faith and
Where he lives	Curiosity (Similarities
His personality and abilities	between Rudi and Santo)
His curiosity and faith	
Para. 4: Conclusion	Para. 4: Conclusion

THE CONCLUSION When you draft your concluding paragraph, you will lose your readers' attention if you simply repeat the summary from your introduction. Instead, show them how the comparison and contrast has been a process of discovery for you. Give them something to think about long after they have finished reading.

HOW DO I REVISE MY ESSAY?

As you revise your essay, be sure that you have used transitional words to help readers understand the relationships among your ideas. Following are some transitional words you can include as you revise your essay:

Comparison Words: like; similarly; in the same way; also; as; likewise; just as

Contrast Words: unlike; on the other hand; in contrast with; however; but; instead; rather than

Unlike Rudi,
^Santo comes from a Caribbean island and has
in contrast with Rudi,
never seen snow. Also,^Santo seems to be a
thoughtful boy with no special interest in sports
or athletics.

The writer has inserted contrast words to clarify the differences between the two boys.

As you revise your comparison-and-contrast essay, ask yourself the following questions:

CHECKPOINTS FOR REVISING

▶ Have I explored the similarities and differences between two or more related items?

▶ Have I learned something new and communicated it to readers?

▶ Have I fulfilled one or more of the following purposes—informing, persuading, evaluating, entertaining?

▶ Have I used specific examples to support my points?

▶ Have I organized the essay clearly and consistently?

▶ Have I used transitional words and phrases?

Here are the body and conclusion of the same essay on Rudi and Santo.

The contrasts between the two characters are
obvious. Rudi is a rugged boy from the mountains
of Switzerland. He shows courage and resourcefulness when he rescues Captain Winter from the
crevasse into which he has fallen. This rescue is

This is a feature-by-feature comparison, so the writer con-trasts the background and personality of each character.

not completely surprising, because Rudi has been brought up in a tradition of mountaineering. His father, killed in a climbing accident, was one of the greatest mountain guides in Switzerland. Unlike Rudi, Santo comes from a Caribbean island and has never seen snow. Also, in contrast with Rudi, Santo seems uninterested in athletics. He helps his father work in the fields, but he does not seem to be especially fond of exercise.

On a deeper level, however, the two boys are very similar. Rudi's most important traits are his curiosity about mountaineering and his faithfulness to his dream of climbing the Citadel. Although his mother and uncle try to keep him from climbing, he disobeys their rules and still hopes to conquer the mountain on which his father died. Like Rudi, Santo is alert and curious. When he hears about Father Christmas, he wants to know more. He learns more and begins to dream about receiving a gift from this magical man. Just as Rudi resists his family's commands, Santo holds on to his dream and ignores the discouraging words of his sister and mother.

Despite obvious differences, both boys share an important quality—faith. Rudi believes that he can climb a mountain that has never been conquered. In the same way, Santo believes that Father Christmas will bring him a gift. This underlying similarity of two very different boys shows that we are all more alike than we know.

The writer uses transitional words—unlike, in contrast with—to contrast the two boys.

The writer compares the boys, showing how they are similar.

The writer uses comparison words—like, just as—to point out the similarities between the boys.

The conclusion does not simply repeat the summary in the introduction; it stresses the importance of similarities in this comparison and contrast.

How do I write a "how-to" essay?

How do you build a campfire or care for a new puppy? One way of discovering how to do both of these things is to read about how to do them.

> A **how-to essay** is an essay that explains how to do something.

Written instructions come in many forms. Some, such as instructions on how to do a particular physical exercise, are nothing more than a list of steps. Others, such as instructions on how to use word processing software, include explanatory paragraphs between the steps. Still others, such as instructions on how to care for a pet or appreciate a work of art, come in essay form.

GUIDELINES

A how-to essay

► clearly explains the steps involved in doing or making something.

► presents the steps in chronological order; that is, in the sequence in which they should be performed.

► uses transitional words and phrases, such as *then*, *next*, and *so that*, to guide readers through the steps.

► sometimes tells readers about possible problems and how to correct or avoid them.

► conveys the author's perspective on the activity.

► has an interesting introduction and a strong conclusion.

HOW CAN I FIND A TOPIC?

Next time you're at the library, do a title search for books whose titles begin with the phrase *How to*. Look at the number of how-to books listed. Almost anything can be the subject of a how-to book. The important thing is to find a topic that interests you. If you spend some time thinking about your interests and activities and those of your friends, you may discover that many of them would make good topics for a how-to essay. To find a topic to write about, try asking yourself these questions.

1. *What things do I like to do?*

Do you like to bake? Skateboard? Play soccer? Maybe you are a good drummer or a smart bargain shopper. Other people might not know how to do these things at all. You have expert advice to share because you have knowledge and experience.

2. *What special things can my friends do?*

Maybe you have a friend who can style hair, throw a great curve ball, draw portraits, or fix a leaky faucet. Interviewing and observing your friend at work can give you the information you need to write a how-to essay.

3. *What would my friends and I like to know how to do?*

Brainstorm topics for a how-to essay with friends. Maybe you and they would like to know how to earn extra money, how to write a computer program, or how to study for a test.

HOW DO I ORGANIZE MY ESSAY?

Clear organization is essential in a how-to essay. Readers must be able to follow your instructions step by step, so be sure to present the steps in the exact order or sequence in which they should be performed.

Making a numbered list of the steps is a good way to start organizing your draft. One student listed the following steps in chronological order for an essay about how to get on a horse.

STUDENT MODEL

1. Stand on the left side of the horse.
2. Hold the reins in your left hand.
3. Hold some of the mane in your left hand, too.
4. Hold the back of the saddle in your right hand.
5. Put your left foot into the stirrup.
6. Pull yourself up.
7. Stand up straight on your left leg.
8. Swing your right leg over the horse's back.
9. Sit down in the saddle.

WHERE DO TRANSITIONS FIT INTO MY ESSAY?

Transitions are words and phrases such as *before, after, while, next, meanwhile, in order to,* and *then.* They guide readers from one step to the next and link the different parts of the process you are presenting. To get a good idea of how transitions work, read a chapter from a how-to book and see how the transitions help readers proceed from step to step.

When you have outlined the steps in the process you are explaining, read them aloud and see what transitional words would make the sequence clearer or easier to follow. Here is how one student revised part of her instructions on how to mount a horse. She added transitions and information to clarify the instructions.

For more on chronological order, see p. 24.

> ### STUDENT MODEL
>
> First, approach the horse on its left side. Then gather
> ~~Stand on the left side of the horse. Hold~~ the
> and hold them firmly along with a
> clump of the horse's mane. Next, h⁀
> reins ~~and mane~~ in your left hand. ʌ Hold the back of
> the saddle in your right hand.

This revision is more specific. Transitions such as *first, then,* and *next* help readers follow along.

◆ WHEN YOU WRITE ◆

■ Include extra suggestions to help readers avoid making mistakes even if they're following the steps one by one. The "don'ts" are sometimes as important as the "do's"!

HOW DO I START AND FINISH MY ESSAY?

A how-to essay should inspire confidence in a learner. One way to do this is to present your steps in chronological order, use language that is precise, and develop a friendly tone that will encourage the learner. Introductions and conclusions play an important part in this process. Introductions can put learners at ease and at the same time spark their interest. Conclusions can help them to see the advantages of what they have learned. The following are some examples of effective introductions and conclusions:

STRATEGIES FOR INTRODUCTIONS	EXAMPLES
Identify a problem.	"Most beginners suffer cuts and bruises when skateboarding. By following these simple steps, you. . . ."
Ask a question.	"Have you ever wanted to bake a chocolate layer cake but thought it would be too complicated?"
Use an anecdote.	"My turtle wouldn't eat. In fact, it wouldn't come out of its shell. Then I found a surefire way to tempt it."

STRATEGIES FOR CONCLUSIONS	EXAMPLES
Point out what readers have learned.	"Now you'll be able to do amazing math problems in your head."
Suggest a "next step."	"Now that you've got a good group of friends, see if you can help out another shy person."
Use humor.	"Keep practicing, and you'll never get a -49 on a test again!"

For more on introductions and conclusions, see p. 28 and p. 37.

HOW CAN I REVISE MY ESSAY?

Keep these points in mind as you revise your essay.

CHECKPOINTS FOR REVISING

▶ Do I explain each step, using words my readers can understand?

▶ Are the steps in chronological order?

▶ Do I use appropriate transitions to link the steps?

▶ Do I warn readers, when necessary, about potential problems and suggest ways to deal with them?

▶ Does my introduction tell readers what they will learn from my essay and why they should learn it?

▶ Does my conclusion reinforce the importance of what they've learned?

▶ Is my essay engaging? Will it keep readers' interest? Does it reflect my feelings about the activity?

Here is how the student revised the rest of her essay on how to get on a horse.

Riding a horse isn't just galloping into the sunset. The riding process starts while you're still on the ground. ~~Here's how to get on a horse:~~
You can't go anywhere until you get on the horse safely.

First, approach the horse on its left side. Then gather the reins in your left hand and hold them firmly along with a clump of the horse's mane. Next, hold the back of the saddle in your right hand.

Now put your left foot into the stirrup. Be careful not to ~~Don't~~ kick the horse in the side because it may move forward. If you do. If this happens, stop the horse by pulling gently on the reins in ~~with~~ your left hand. Then p⌒ ~~Pull~~ yourself up with both arms. It's perfectly all right to ~~You can~~ bounce a few times on the ground with your right leg to give yourself an extra push. ~~to get more push.~~

As soon as you are up, ~~Now~~ stand up straight on your left leg. Then s⌒ ~~Swing~~ your right leg over the horse's back while sliding your right hand forward in the saddle. ~~but don't drag~~ Finally, ~~it. Then,~~ sit down gently in the saddle.

[Don't drag your leg—make sure you clear the saddle and the horse.]

¶ Now that you can get on a horse gracefully and safely, you'll be ready to go—as soon as you learn how not to fall off!

—Chris Meyer, Seattle, Washington

The student engages her audience with a humorous first line based on a cliché from old westerns. She then adds a reason for learning how to get on a horse.

The student's firm, confident tone makes it clear that she has plenty of experience with mounting and riding horses.

She revises her instructions to make them more precise and to inspire confidence in the learner.

She adds a humorous conclusion that reminds readers of the advantages of learning how to get on a horse.

WRITING FOR MATH

Did you know that when you explain how to work a math problem like the following, you are really writing a how-to essay?

Sachi is making hand-dipped candles to sell at a craft fair.

She worked $3\frac{1}{4}$ hours one weekend and $2\frac{1}{2}$ hours the next weekend.

How much time in all did she spend making candles?

In your explanation, you would want to explain the sequence of steps you took to solve the problem. To make the sequence clear, use transitional words such as *first, next,* and *then.* Be sure to define mathematical terms such as the *numerator* or the *denominator.* Finally, tell what the answer represents. For instance, if the answer is 12, does it refer to 12 dogs or 12 miles per hour? The following paragraph tells how to solve the math problem above.

The transitional word *First* tells readers how to begin working the problem.

Math terms are defined.

The answer tells that the number refers to *hours.*

First, write an addition sentence using the numbers that tell how many hours Sachi worked:

$$3\frac{1}{4} + 2\frac{1}{2} = X.$$

Next, change the denominators, which are the bottom numbers in each fraction, so that they are the same. You now have a sentence that reads

$$3\frac{1}{4} + 2\frac{2}{4} = X.$$

Next, add the whole numbers and add the numerators, or the top numbers in each fraction. The denominators remain the same. The answer is $5\frac{3}{4}$ hours.

WRITING TO INFORM: CAUSE-AND-EFFECT ESSAY

38

How do I explain why things happen?

When you were young, did you ask a lot of *why?* or *what if?* questions? Maybe you still do. Why are there so many brush fires in southern California? What if cars could run on water instead of gasoline? What if the British had won the Revolutionary War? These questions make you think about causes and speculate about effects. Therefore, they would make good topics for cause-and-effect essays. Writing such essays helps you explore not only *what* happens but also *why* it happens.

> A **cause** is an event, condition, or situation that makes something happen. An **effect** is the result of a particular event, condition, or situation. In a **cause-and-effect essay**, a writer explores the connections between causes and effects.

GUIDELINES

A cause-and-effect essay

▶ explores the causes and effects of an event or situation.

▶ provides facts and other evidence to support its points.

▶ follows a clear, logical sequence.

▶ clarifies cause-and-effect connections with words like *because, so that, therefore,* and *thus.*

▶ has one or more of the following purposes—informing, persuading, evaluating, and entertaining.

WHAT SHOULD I WRITE ABOUT?

When you select a topic for a cause-and-effect essay, try to find a subject that you genuinely want to explore. After all, a paper explaining why your finger hurts after you burn it would be pretty dull reading. To find an idea that requires creative thinking, use one of these prewriting techniques:

LOOK THROUGH YOUR LEARNING LOG. Skim the science section of your log for a natural event that you would like to know more about, such as an eclipse of the moon. Ask some *why?* questions about it, such as "Why does the moon disappear?"

EXPLORE YOUR OWN THEORIES. Do you have a pet theory about why something happens or why people behave in a certain way? What are some of the reasons or evidence you have to support your theory? Brainstorm and jot down your ideas.

USE A STARTER. *Why?* questions ask you to look for causes, and *what if?* questions ask you to predict effects. Use a starter question like the following to find a topic:

- I wonder why . . .
- What might happen if . . .
- Why does _____ happen?

WRITING FOR SCIENCE

Science assignments often explore *what if?* questions such as "What if the ozone layer disappeared?" A good way to explore the possible effects of such an event is to make a prediction chart. Write your *what if?* question at the top of a piece of paper, and list as many possible effects as you can. After you have suggested several possibilities, choose the ones you think are most likely to occur, and investigate them.

PREDICTION CHART

What if the ozone layer disappeared?
  Harmful UV rays would no longer be blocked.
  People would develop skin cancer.
  People would have eye damage.
  Plants could be damaged or die off.
  Animals that eat the plants could get sick or go hungry.

HOW DO I EXPLORE CAUSES AND EFFECTS?

The techniques you use to explore causes and effects will vary depending on your topic. If you are dealing with a scientific topic such as an eclipse of the moon, consult a nonfiction book. If you want to know the effects of smog on a particular kind of plant, conduct some experiments. As you gather information, watch out for these pitfalls:

UNDERSTANDING CAUSE AND EFFECT

- **Do not assume that the first cause you find is the only cause.**
  A single event may have many causes.

Cause 1: wet streets

Effect: bad accident

Cause 2: speeding

Cause 3: poor visibility

When researching and writing, be careful not to oversimplify the causes of a complicated situation.

- **Do not assume that a single event had only one result.**

Effect 1: bad traffic accidents

Cause: heavy rain

Effect 2: flooding in low-lying areas

Effect 3: dam overflow

Be sure not to oversimplify the effects of an event or condition.

- **Do not fall into the false cause-effect trap.** The fact that event A happened *before* event B does not mean that A *caused* B .
  (The storm did not *cause* you to get the flu. You caught the flu because you were exposed to the flu virus.)

- **Be alert for cause-effect chains.** In these chains, one cause creates an effect, which in turn becomes a cause for another effect. The following graphic explains why rain falls:

In such chains, a series of related events occur over a period of time. To explain these events, you must not only know their sequence but also understand their causal relations.

Explanations of cause-effect chains are often part of cause-and-effect essays, as you can see in the model at the end of this lesson.

HOW DO I DEVELOP MY ESSAY?

A cause-and-effect essay focuses on the relationships between causes and effects. For some subjects, it is best to begin your essay by discussing the causes and then to move on to the effects. Another approach is to begin by describing the effects and then to explore the causes. This approach helps to interest readers by posing the question *why*? In the following excerpt, Jade Snow Wong, a writer and pottery maker, uses this approach.

From the first, the local Chinese were not Jade Snow's patrons. The thinness and whiteness of porcelains imported from China and ornate decorations which came into vogue during the late Ching Dynasty satisfied their tastes. They could not understand why "silly Americans" paid dollars for a hand-thrown bowl utilizing crude California colored clays, not much different from the in-expensive peasant ware of China. That the Jade Snow Wong bowl went back to an older tradition of under-stated beauty was not apparent. They could see only that she wouldn't apply a dragon or a hundred flowers.

—Jade Snow Wong, "A Time of Beginnings"

The first sentence states the effect.

Cause 1: The local Chinese preferred thin, white, ornate porcelain.

Cause 2: Wong's pottery reminded them of "peasant ware."

Cause 3: They were unaware of an earlier pottery tradition.

If your topic deals with a cause-effect chain, the best ap-proach would be to present the events in chronological order. You would present the first cause and its effect and then show how those effects caused another event or situation to occur and so on.

HOW DO I PROVIDE SUPPORTING DETAIL?

In a cause-and-effect paper, you explain why or how one event or condition led to another. Your explanations will be more convincing if you provide specific evidence or proof. Suppose a writer is explaining the causes and effects of the shrinking of the Everglades in southern Florida. He or she might choose any of the following types of evidence to explain these relationships:

TYPES OF EVIDENCE

1. Facts are statements that can be proved true. **Statistics** are facts that involve numbers. You can back up facts by making ob-servations, doing an experiment, or consulting a reference.

FACT: The Everglades extend from Lake Okeechobee to the Bay of Florida.

STATISTICS: One hundred years ago, the Everglades spread over **four million acres**. Massive development has cut down this figure to **two million acres.**

Note how statistics show that the Everglades are shrinking.

2. Incidents are events or occurrences. For example, an incident illustrating that the Everglades are shrinking might be an eyewitness account of a water moccasin dying from lack of water.

3. Examples are instances of something. An alligator is an *example* of an Everglades reptile. To back up the statement that many creatures in the Everglades are going hungry, you might write:

EXAMPLE:　　　Creatures from **freshwater fish** to **white ibis** to **alligators** have suffered losses in their food.

4. Expert opinion is the point of view of an expert whose views are respected by other authorities. Use a quotation to support your explanation or to serve as a strong opening or closing.

HOW DO I REVISE MY ESSAY?

Make sure your readers understand the links between causes and effects. Draw attention to the links by using **transitions**, words and phrases that clarify relationships among ideas. Transitions include words like *because, due to, consequently,* and *therefore.*

M O D E L

Consequently signals that the presence of chemicals caused the grass to die.

Due to introduces an effect.

Chemicals such as phosphorus are present in water runoff from sugar and vegetable farms. Consequently, the native saw grass has died in many areas of the Everglades, and cattails have taken the place of the native grass. Due to these changes in vegetation, the algae that nourish fish have lost oxygen and died off.

As you review your draft, consider these questions:

CHECKPOINTS FOR REVISING

▶ Did I stick to my topic?

▶ Did I explain the links between causes and effects?

▶ Did I include specific evidence to support my explanation?

▶ Did I present the causes and effects in logical order?

▶ Did I use transitions to make the relationships clear?

In addition, consider the following recommendation:

ACTIVE VOICE Use the active voice to make cause-and-effect relationships explicit and clear. The passive voice blurs relationships because it downplays or omits the cause of an event.

PASSIVE: This figure has been cut down by massive development.

ACTIVE: Massive development has cut down this figure.

Here is the final draft of the model on the Everglades:

M O D E L

Take a walk in the Florida Everglades and look around you. If you are observant, you will see signs everywhere of a dying environment. One hundred years ago, the Everglades spread over four million acres. Massive development has cut down this figure to two million acres.

The most serious threat to the animals, plants, and birds of the Everglades comes from human interference with the water supply. People did not realize until recently that the Everglades is not a swamp. It is actually one vast river system, about fifty miles wide. This shallow river extends from Lake Okeechobee to the Bay of Florida. Because scientists did not understand the true nature of the Everglades, developers easily succeeded in taking over large areas for farmland. As a result, dams and drainage projects have changed the volume, routes, and quality of water in this part of Florida. Water that used to support vegetation and wildlife now goes for plumbing and irrigation.

The writer grabs readers' attention with a command.

The writer states the cause-and-effect relationship.

This paragraph explains a series of causes and effects.

The writer uses transitions to link causes and effects: Because and As a result.

The changes in water quality are especially serious. Chemicals such as phosphorus are present in
water runoff from sugar and vegetable farms.
Consequently, the native saw grass has died in
many areas of the Everglades, and cattails have
taken the place of the native grass. Due to these
changes in the vegetation, the algae that nourish
fish have lost oxygen and died off. As a result,
creatures from freshwater fish to white ibis to alligators have suffered losses in their food supply.

Water shortages and pollution have combined to
create a crisis in the Everglades. In August 1992,
the area experienced additional damage from
Hurricane Andrew. Due to human invasion and
occasional forces of nature, a unique piece of our
national heritage is in danger. As Dick Ring, the
superintendent of the Everglades National Park,
said: "What's at stake is the biological future of
the Everglades and the Florida Bay."

An alligator in the Everglades

WRITING TO INFORM: PROBLEM-AND-SOLUTION ESSAY

39

How do I describe problems and solutions?

> A **problem-and-solution essay** focuses on a problem and proposes possible solutions to that problem.

In a problem-and-solution essay, you must not only analyze a problem; you must also offer concrete solutions and show readers that your solution or solutions represent the best possible course of action.

We all face problems, big and small, every day. Maybe you've wondered how you can stop your little brother from tagging along with you all the time. Perhaps you've noticed a noise problem in your neighborhood that you think could be solved if people worked together. A problem-and-solution essay is one way to present a problem and to propose solutions that can make a practical difference.

The following chart lists the characteristics of a problem-and-solution essay.

GUIDELINES

A problem-and-solution essay

- ▶ clearly states a problem.
- ▶ explains why the problem is worth considering.
- ▶ presents one or more solutions and shows how each one would work.
- ▶ presents the practical benefits of the solution(s).
- ▶ ends with a strong conclusion.

WHAT PROBLEMS SHOULD I WRITE ABOUT?

The supply of problems is nearly limitless. You might choose to write about personal concerns or about local issues such as problems at school or in your community. You could also choose larger issues such as state, national, or world problems. Coming up with problems is easy, but selecting one to write about requires careful thought. As you try to select a problem, consider the following points:

CHOOSE A PROBLEM THAT AFFECTS OTHERS. For example, few people are likely to care if your school prevents you from bringing your pet guinea pig to class. However, people might care if the city planned to build a highway next to your school.

CHOOSE A PROBLEM THAT CAN BE SOLVED. The problem of homelessness, for example, is complex and controversial. A discussion of its causes and cures would probably require a book-length analysis, and so it would not be a good idea to deal with this particular issue in a short essay.

TRY THIS

Draw a large insect on chart paper and label it "The What-Bugs-You Bug." Get permission to hang the paper somewhere in your school. Tie a pencil to a string and attach the string to the drawing. Write a headline that invites people to stop and jot down what bugs them about the school, the community, or the world.

HOW DO I FIND IDEAS?

Imagine that you had a magic wand. What would you fix? Get ideas on what is bothering you and others in any of the following ways:

CHECK YOUR JOURNAL. If something has bothered you, you probably have written about it in your journal. Look to your journal for problems you would like to explore further. Scan for key words such as *problem*, *trouble*, *worry*, *concerned*, or slang expressions such as *ticked off*.

TALK TO YOUR FRIENDS. Trade ideas. What problems bother them the most? Which of these problems also bother you? Do you have any opinions on how to solve them?

TAKE AN OPINION POLL. What do most of your classmates consider to be their "number one problem"?

HOW DO I EXPLORE THE PROBLEM?

Writing about a problem is not simply complaining about how bad things are. After stating the problem, you must explain its causes and discuss what can be done to solve it. To do this, you must gather as much information as you can and come up with at least one workable solution. If you can think of more than one solution, explore all the options. The following chart suggests ways you might go about gathering facts and exploring solutions.

TO GATHER INFORMATION	TO EXPLORE SOLUTIONS
■ Have people affected by the problem hold a group discussion.	■ Use a cluster diagram showing several possible solutions radiating from the problem written in the center.
■ Research the topic in a library.	
■ Interview experts on the subject.	■ Invite experts to hold a brainstorming session.
■ Write to organizations with experience working on similar problems and ask for information.	■ Compare the problem to similar problems that have already been solved, and see if any solutions can be borrowed and adapted.

Examining a problem doesn't stop when you list solutions to it. You must still determine which solution is best. Every solution is going to have favorable and unfavorable points, or pros and cons. By using the process described in the following chart, you can weigh the pros and cons to select the best solution. The following example focuses on the problem of rising dropout rates among schoolchildren. Notice how various solutions to the problem are evaluated and a particular solution is selected for specific reasons.

PROBLEM	CAUSES
Too many kids are dropping out of school.	**1.** lack of self-confidence
	2. failing grades
	3. home and family problems
	4. inadequate counseling services

SOLUTIONS	PROS (+) AND CONS (-)
Start peer tutoring programs in school.	+ Kids like being tutored by someone their own age. − It's hard to recruit volunteers.
Set up peer counseling groups.	+ Kids can explore problems with trained peers. − Kids would have to be trained as counselors.
Improve school administration and teacher training.	+ There are not as many dropouts from schools that are well run and have high teacher morale. − It would be an expensive and slow process.

MY SOLUTION	REASONS
Set up peer tutoring and counseling.	1. It has immediate results. 2. It involves students in solving their own problems. 3. It is not expensive; it relies largely on volunteer time and effort.

HOW DO I ORGANIZE MY ESSAY?

Most problem-and-solution essays follow this general organization:

INTRODUCE THE PROBLEM. Catch your readers' attention. You might start with a personal anecdote, an example of the problem, a vivid description, or some striking statistics.

TELL ABOUT THE PROBLEM. State the problem in a sentence or two. Explain its causes and its effects. Then explain how the problem negatively affects your readers' lives, using facts, statistics, examples, personal anecdotes, and other details.

TELL ABOUT YOUR SOLUTION. State your solution in a sentence or two. Give practical suggestions for carrying it out. Then explain why the solution will work. Answer any objections your readers might have to your solution.

CONCLUDE YOUR ESSAY. End with a strong conclusion that restates the main idea or urges readers to take action.

HOW DO I REVISE MY ESSAY?

Here are some points to keep in mind as you revise your problem-and-solution essay:

CHECKPOINTS FOR REVISING

▶ Have I stated the problem clearly?

▶ Do I make it clear why my readers should be concerned?

▶ Do I propose a workable solution?

▶ Do I end my essay with a strong conclusion?

Here's a final draft of a student's problem-and-solution essay:

STUDENT MODEL

Members of the School Board:

In recent years, dropout rates in schools across the nation have been steadily increasing. My fellow students and I are very concerned about this problem. Although there is no one way to stop the trend, there are some practical, inexpensive measures we can introduce right here that will help keep more students in school. To begin with, we need to look at the reasons why kids drop out.

The writer introduces the problem and tells why it is important.

First, many students drop out because they feel they are not smart enough to pass and never will be. Their grades are dropping, and so is what little self-confidence they have. Peer tutoring can address these students' worries. Failing students don't respect their tutor less because he or she is not an adult. Instead, they are more willing to acknowledge their problems and accept help.

The writer clearly states one cause of the problem.

The writer states one solution.

The writer anticipates a possible objection and addresses it.

Many kids also drop out because they have serious problems at home. Sometimes they are under too much pressure from their families to succeed, or the family has too many other problems to care about how the teenager is doing in school. Some of these students drop out, run away, and never look back. In the long run, this creates more problems for society than just high dropout rates. Again, calling on other students to form peer counseling groups is an answer. The counselors and group members could work together to explore student alternatives and the consequences of their decisions.

I urge you to look over and consider these suggestions seriously. I feel everyone could benefit in the long run.

—Brandy Klaassen, Victorville, California

The writer states a second solution, explains how it would work, and describes its benefits.

The writer concludes by urging the School Board to take action on her solutions.

 ## WRITING FOR MATH

A math word problem has only one correct solution. To find it, you need to identify the details of the problem. These steps will help you reduce the word problem to its basic parts and find the solution:

1. Read the problem carefully to make sure you know what answer you are seeking.

2. Determine which operation (addition, subtraction, and so on) you will need to use to solve the problem. Pay special attention to key words.

3. Find the solution, then double-check it. Don't just work the numbers again. Put the answer in a sentence to be sure it makes sense.

WRITING TO INFORM: WRITTEN EVALUATION

40

How do I write an evaluation?

Have you ever been tempted to write a glowing review of a movie you loved? Have you ever had to justify your decision to purchase a certain product or attend a certain event? These different situations have something in common: They call on you to provide evaluations, or ratings. The guidelines that follow will help you understand what this type of writing requires you to do.

> A **written evaluation** is an essay stating an opinion about an item that can be judged and supporting that opinion with evidence and examples.

GUIDELINES

A written evaluation

- ▶ expresses the writer's judgment about a product, performance, book, idea, or other item.

- ▶ describes the item in as much detail as the particular audience needs, including main strengths and weaknesses.

- ▶ presents facts, reasons, examples, logical arguments, and other convincing evidence in support of the writer's judgment.

- ▶ ends with a strong restatement of the writer's judgment.

AN EVALUATION OR A PERSUASIVE ESSAY?

An **evaluation** is a form of analytical writing that has persuasive elements. Your main purpose in writing an evaluation is to inform your readers and to make a judgment. Like a persuasive essay, however, an evaluation presents an opinion and supports it.

HOW DO I PLAN AN EVALUATION?

First, become an expert on your subject and audience.

KNOW YOUR SUBJECT. Make your judgment a fair one by becoming informed in the following ways:

- • Experience the subject as fully as possible. For instance, reread the book, wear the running shoes, listen to the CD again.

- Read up on the subject; go to the library if necessary.
- Seek opinions from people who know about the subject.

KNOW YOUR AUDIENCE. You also need a clear idea of your readers' background and needs. Ask yourself these questions:

- Am I writing mainly for myself? (You may be trying to make a decision about a new bike or a summer job.)
- Am I writing for a small audience I know well (family or classmates) or a large, unknown audience (the whole school, the community, the readers of a particular magazine)?
- How much does my audience already know about my topic?
- What information do they need from me?

MAKE YOUR JUDGMENT CALL. Once you have done your homework about your subject and audience, it's time to form your view. Note the strengths and weaknesses of what you are evaluating. Decide whether the pros (plusses) outweigh the cons (minuses), or vice versa. Then write your judgment in a clear, brief statement. The rest of your writing will spring from this statement.

> *Sample Judgment:* The West Highland terrier ("Westie") demands a lot of attention, but makes a great family pet.

MARSHAL YOUR EVIDENCE. You have formed your judgment. Now, with your particular audience in mind, marshal facts, opinions, examples, and reasons to support it.

> *Opinion:* These homemade minis are a soft, moist, fresh-tasting oatmeal cookie with plenty of crunchy nuts.

> *Fact:* Bite for bite, minis have fewer calories and less fat than the full-sized cookie.

> *Example:* Almost three out of four teenaged testers ranked the homemade minis tops in taste.

> *Reason:* At 11 cents per serving, the homemade minis are a good buy.

ORGANIZE YOUR EVIDENCE. Now it's time to decide on the order in which to present your nuggets of evidence. Which points are most important and convincing? Plan to put these either first or last in your argument. Also, plan to give the most space to your strongest evidence.

Here is a sample outline for a paper evaluating West Highland terriers as family pets. The outline places the most significant points last.

TRY THIS

In organizing your evidence, consider comparing your subject to another similar one in order to show strengths and weaknesses.

M O D E L

Judgment: Westies make great family pets.

   A. Westies' likable physical appearance

      1. small (sturdy, cute, easy to handle)

      2. charming face (bright eyes, perky ears)

   B. Westies' winning personality

      1. feisty (need firm hand)

      2. intelligent (learn quickly)

      3. playful (energetic; love to fetch, run, play hide-and-seek)

      4. loving (respond enthusiastically to affection, deeply loyal)

HOW DO I WRITE MY EVALUATION?

THE BEGINNING Write a statement that will get your audience's attention and make your subject interesting to them. Then state your judgment right away.

M O D E L

A funny, vivid description leads to the writer's opinion.

Imagine an energetic white fur ball with bright, dark eyes, capering along the sidewalk. This is a Westie (West Highland terrier), a feisty little dog that demands a lot of attention, but makes a great family pet.

M O D E L

This account of a painful lesson sets up the audience for a negative evaluation of the shoes.

I thought running shoes were all alike until both my feet bubbled with blisters after a hike in my new Zippeez. My sadder but wiser feet will vote "no" on these shoes next time.

THE MIDDLE This is where you line up the facts, reasons, examples, and opinions in support of your judgment. You may also need to describe your subject in some detail, depending on how much your audience needs to know about it. If you

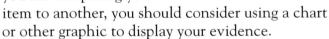

have a lot of information to present, especially if you are comparing your item to another, you should consider using a chart or other graphic to display your evidence.

TRY THIS

If you are comparing items, you might award points for various features so that you can support your judgment with comparative scores.

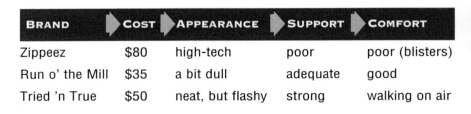

BRAND	COST	APPEARANCE	SUPPORT	COMFORT
Zippeez	$80	high-tech	poor	poor (blisters)
Run o' the Mill	$35	a bit dull	adequate	good
Tried 'n True	$50	neat, but flashy	strong	walking on air

THE CONCLUSION End your evaluation by reaffirming your judgment. If possible, leave your readers with a final, memorable twist or turn of phrase.

MODEL

Julius Erving and Bill Walton inspired an entire generation of basketball players. Who will be the next to follow in their giant footsteps?

HOW CAN I REVISE MY EVALUATION?

As you revise your first draft, look for opportunities to clarify your judgment statement and to strengthen your argument. Use the following questions:

CHECKPOINTS FOR REVISING

▶ Does my opening make readers want to know more?

▶ Did I state my judgment clearly?

▶ Is my evidence organized in the most logical order?

▶ Can I add specific details and examples to make my evidence seem even more compelling?

▶ Did I conclude with a striking or clever restatement of my judgment?

Here is a model that evaluates West Highland terriers as family pets.

MODEL

Imagine an energetic white fur ball with bright, dark eyes, capering along the sidewalk. This is a Westie (West Highland terrier), a feisty little dog that demands a lot of attention, but makes a great family pet.

Most breeders will tell you that Westies are among the most attractive small dogs around. Their bright eyes, eager manner, and perky ears give these little dogs tons of character and charm.

The writer interests readers with a lively beginning.

The writer states a judgment early and clearly.

The writer uses expert opinion to support the judgment.

The Westie's thick coat, black or white, is beautiful when well maintained, but keeping your pup dog-show clean can be difficult. These dogs love to follow their inquisitive noses into mud.

Most important is the Westie's winning personality. Like all terriers, Westies are feisty critters, and they also expect you to pay attention to them.

They are not easily impressed by huge Siberian huskies or by their own stern owners. At a training session with my dog, I ferociously roared, "Off!" to make Stixie back away from a forbidden item. I impressed the teacher. I impressed the other owners. The only one I didn't impress was Stixie, who completely ignored me.

Although Westies like Stixie require an owner with a stout heart and firm hand, the effort is worthwhile because they are so intelligent, playful, and affectionate. Once Westies understand who is boss, they can easily be trained to do tricks. (Hopping around the house on her back legs, Stixie seems to have a secret yen to join the circus.) Westies just naturally take to games like catch and hide-and-seek. Above all, they love to love their human families. They enjoy being cuddled, and they'll follow you everywhere for a scrap of affection.

As a Westie owner, I can say that a day with a Westie is not necessarily a relaxing one, but it is a day filled with laughter and love. Who could ask for anything more?

What is a news story?

Suppose your favorite basketball team played a big game last night but you weren't able to watch it on television. Where could you turn to find out about the game? One place you could look is in today's newspaper. Newspapers contain news stories about a variety of subjects, including sports. Reporters write news stories about many different events, but every reporter follows the same basic guidelines. You will want to keep these guidelines in mind when writing a news story of your own.

> A **news story** is a factual, written report about a current event.

SPORTS SECTION
January 14, 1999

Jayhawks Win
Second Straight

GUIDELINES

A news story

▶ tells about a recent event of interest and importance to its audience.

▶ provides accurate facts, not the writer's opinions.

▶ answers the following six questions: *Who* was involved? *What* happened? *When* did it happen? *Where* did it happen? *Why* did it happen? *How* did it happen? These are called "the five W's and H."

▶ may report on people's opinions, but never takes sides or makes judgments.

FROM A WRITER

66 *Get it first, but first get it right.* 99

—Seymour Berkson, journalist

WHAT IS A NEWS EVENT?

If someone asks you about your day, do you describe every part of it, no matter how small? You probably don't. You're more likely to describe a few events that you think will be of interest. In the same way, news editors and reporters make decisions about which events to cover.

What makes one event more newsworthy than another? Four features tend to make the difference.

AN EVENT IS NEWSWORTHY IF

it's unusual.

▶ "No School on Thursday" breaks the routine, and so it's news.

it affects the readers.

▶ If a fast-food chain were about to manage your school cafeteria, many students would probably like to know that.

it's local or of interest to a particular audience.

▶ A library closing is important to you if it's the one in your neighborhood.

it's recent.

▶ Last year's basketball championship might have been exciting, but yesterday's basketball game has greater current interest.

A group of students skimmed a newspaper and divided the news stories into categories based on subject. You can see the results of their research in the notebook on page 191. Which types of story do you think would be newsworthy items for your school newspaper?

SPORTS

- Stuyvesant girls' swim team wins PSAL championship.

- August Martin boys' basketball team undefeated.

LOCAL NEWS

- Medical Center needs contributions of toys and gifts for children's party.

- New post office opening in Park Slope.

ENTERTAINMENT/EVENTS

- Jazz concert series starts.

- Beginner's workshop in astronomy scheduled to start.

- Play set to open.

HOW CAN I FIND AN EVENT TO WRITE ABOUT?

You can't invent a topic for a news story—you have to go out and find one in the real world. The following are some strategies you can use.

FIVE WAYS TO LOOK FOR NEWS

- Ask people you meet whether anything interesting happened to them or to anyone they know recently.

- Watch for changes in your community such as buildings going up, stores closing, or people moving.

- Attend events, such as fairs, field trips, meetings, and sporting events that may be newsworthy.

TRY THIS

Spend a week using the five ways to look for news. Keep a list of newsworthy events you find. Pick one of these to investigate for your news story.

- Read bulletin boards, leaflets, posters, memos, local newspapers, and other public messages to find out what's going on in your area.

- Cultivate sources by introducing yourself to people in key places and then calling them regularly to see whether they have news.

HOW CAN I GATHER INFORMATION?

You are your readers' eyes and ears. Finding out "what happened" may be your main job as a news reporter. Here are four ways to train yourself to gather information:

OBSERVE. If you know a newsworthy event is about to happen, be there to witness it firsthand.

RECORD. *Always* keep a notebook handy. Jot down information that will help you answer the five W's and H: *who, what, when, where, why,* and *how.*

INTERVIEW. If a newsworthy event has already happened, find and interview people who were there. Get as many versions of the event as possible. Compare accounts to get as complete a story as you can.

READ. Background information can help you put a news story in context so that readers will understand its importance. Be prepared to use the library.

TRY THIS

Use a tape recorder when you interview an eyewitness or expert. (*Always* ask for permission before you tape anyone.) To be sure you know how to use the machine, tape an interview with a friend beforehand.

WRITING FOR SOCIAL STUDIES

For social studies, you may have to write a news story about a historical event as if you had been a reporter at the time the event occurred. As with any news story, you will have to gather information first. You may want to organize your information by creating a timeline of important events leading up to the event you are covering. This will help you see the event through the eyes of someone who lived during that time and experienced the events leading up to this one. Then make a list of people who might have witnessed the event. What might they have said about it in an interview? Remember that they would have known only what had happened up to the time of the event. For example, none of the signers of the Declaration of Independence would have used the term "the United States" because the name was not used at the time they signed the document.

Declaration of Independence, Edward Hicks, private collection

HOW CAN I DRAFT MY NEWS STORY?

The most important part of a news story is at the beginning. That's because news stories resemble an upside-down pyramid. At the top is a headline: "head" for short. The head gives the core of the story in one short phrase. Next comes the lead or first paragraph. It summarizes all the basic information. Then comes the body, which can vary in length. It gives, in decreasing order of importance, additional and more specific details about the event.

The Three Parts of a News Story

HEAD

LEAD

BODY

If you're writing
with a computer,
copy your first draft
into a new file.
Then edit the new
file. If you change
your mind about
something you've
cut, you can
retrieve it from the
original file.

Before you start to write a news story, decide which information will be in the lead, and arrange the rest of your information in descending order of importance. Reporters often try to answer as many of the six *who, what, when, where, why,* and *how* questions as possible in the lead. (A good news story usually answers at least five of the six questions.)

Then write your story from your notes, using relatively short sentences and clear, plain language. Most reporters write the lead first, the body next, and the headline last.

Talk to your sources
again to verify your
facts. You can what
one person says by
consulting another
source.

HOW CAN I REVISE MY NEWS STORY?

For many readers, your news article will be their only source of information on the topic you are discussing. They will depend on it for accuracy and completeness. Look through your news story for errors and gaps in information. Check all names, titles, dates, addresses, numbers, and direct quotations twice.

Consider these points when revising a news story:

CHECKPOINTS FOR REVISING

▶ Does my headline tell the basic story?

▶ Does my first paragraph summarize the whole event?

▶ Do I answer the questions *who, what, when, where, why,* and *how?*

▶ Have I presented details in decreasing order of importance?

▶ Have I left out anything important or interesting?

▶ Is all the information accurate?

▶ Have I used facts rather than my own judgments or opinions?

▶ Have I spelled proper names correctly?

▶ Is my language clear, concise, and direct?

Here is how one writer revised a news story.

MODEL

Wind Flattens Students' Tent
~~Windy Horror~~

Gale-force winds blew a tent belonging to two students across a field on Friday, just before midnight. The wind on the mountain may have been as fast as 50 miles per hour, according to the Weather Bureau. Two students were sleeping in the tent at the time. Joanie Kemp and Marisol Martínez were shaken up by the incident but not hurt.

It happened during San Francisco Community School's annual fall camping trip to San Bruno Mountain.

"I felt like a bowling ball," said Marisol. "I woke up and the whole tent was rolling over, crashing through bushes and stuff. It was awful."

¶ The students had neglected to tie their tent to stakes in the ground. "I didn't think it was that important," Joanie said later. "I guess I was wrong."

Earlier some students had joked that the wind might blow someone away that night.

The camping trip is an annual tradition for Community School, a public junior high school in San Francisco.

The headline now tells the basic story.

Less important information has been moved closer to the end.

The spellings of proper names have been checked.

The reporter has told *who*, *what*, and *when* but adds *where*.

The quotations help bring the story to life.

The added paragraph answers the question *why*.

WRITING TO INFORM: BUSINESS LETTER

 How do I write a business letter?

A **business letter** is a formal letter written to a person or organization for a specific, practical purpose.

You bought something, it broke, and now you want your money back. What do you do? Write to the company and state your case. Such a letter is called a business letter. People write business letters for a variety of reasons: to order products, get application forms, request information, lodge complaints, demand action, and express opinions.

STANDARD BUSINESS LETTER FORM

A standard business letter usually has six parts, as shown in the model that follows:

The Two Forms of a Business Letter

Block	Modified Block

Heading

(4 spaces)

Inside Address

(2 spaces)

Salutation
Body

(2 spaces)

(2 spaces)

(2 spaces)

Closing

(4 spaces)

Signature

Heading aligns on right with closing and your name

Inside Address

Salutation

Body

Closing

Signature

HEADING: Write your full address and the date.

INSIDE ADDRESS: Include the company name and address, and the name and title (if you know them) of the person to whom you are writing.

SALUTATION: Greet someone by name, or use *Dear Sir* or *Dear Madam,* or *To Whom It May Concern,* and end with a colon.

BODY: State your business.

CLOSING: Capitalize the first letter of your closing and end with a comma. *Yours truly* and *Sincerely* are often used.

SIGNATURE: Print or type your full name on the last line, then sign your name in the space above it.

GUIDELINES

An effective business letter

▶ follows a standard format of six parts.

▶ states its purpose clearly and directly.

▶ stays focused on the matter at hand.

▶ uses formal language and a courteous tone.

Here is how a sixth-grade student began the body of a business letter. Her changes reflect the suggestions in the margin.

STUDENT MODEL

To Whom It May Concern:

~~I've thought about this for a long time and have decided to write to you.~~ Recently I bought an eight-pack of your markers, and I was very disappointed. ~~What kind of company are you running over there, anyhow?~~ The first time I used the markers, they leaked all over me, my clothes, and my brand-new white bedspread. I tried to get the stains out, but the markers were not "washable," as claimed on your package. ~~The package looked good, I'll admit.~~ All of this has become quite costly for me. Please send me a refund.

Be direct: Get right down to the business at hand.

Be polite: Use a courteous, businesslike tone.

Stay focused: Make your wishes clear.

HOW DO I PREPARE A FINISHED COPY?

Try drafting the body of your business letter first. Once you're satisfied with it, make a clean copy and add the rest.

Before you send the letter, look at it one last time. Keep the following points in mind:

CHECKPOINTS FOR REVISING

▶ Have I included all six business letter parts and punctuated them correctly?

▶ Did I address the right person?

▶ Have I spelled all names and titles correctly?

▶ Have I spelled and punctuated both addresses correctly?

▶ Have I made the purpose of my letter clear?

▶ Is my language direct, courteous, and formal?

COMPUTER TIP

Create the shell of a business letter. Key in the heading, your favorite closing, and your name. Store this on a disk. When you want to write a business letter, simply copy this file and add the missing parts.

HOW DO I FOLD THE LETTER AND ADDRESS THE ENVELOPE?

If you have a standard business envelope, which is just a bit wider than a sheet of $8\frac{1}{2}$-by-11-inch typing paper, fold your letter in equal thirds and insert it into the envelope.

If you have a smaller envelope, fold the paper in half first. Then fold it in thirds and insert it.

A correctly addressed envelope looks like the model below.

Your return address —— Elizabeth Moss
8573 My Street
St. Louis, MO 63123

The full name and address of the person or organization to which you're writing —— Customer Service Department
Colorfast Marker Company
P.O. Box 514
New York, NY 10057

Here is an example of a business letter of complaint written by a sixth-grade student in St. Louis, Missouri.

8573 My Street
St. Louis, MO 63123
June 5, 1994

The heading lets the company know where to send the refund.

Customer Service Department
Colorfast Marker Company
P.O. Box 514
New York, NY 10057

The writer addresses her letter to the department that handles complaints.

To Whom It May Concern:

Since the writer is not addressing a particular person, she uses a general salutation.

Recently I bought an eight-pack of your markers, and I was very disappointed. The first time I used the markers, they leaked all over me, my clothes, and my brand-new white bedspread. I tried to get the stains out, but the markers were not "washable," as claimed on your package.

The writer's complaint is stated plainly but politely.

All of this has become quite costly for me. Please send me a refund. I have enclosed the sales receipts for the items that were ruined by your markers. I would like a refund for the markers as well. The total due me is $145.99.

The writer explains exactly what she wants.

Yours truly,

Elizabeth Moss

Elizabeth Moss

SOURCES FOR FINDING OR CHECKING ADDRESSES

- Yellow Pages of the telephone directory
- ZIP Code directory, available in any post office
- Various business and association directories, available at a library reference room. A book called the **Reverse Directory** gives the address for any phone number.

COMMON ABBREVIATIONS IN ADDRESSES

Avenue	Ave.	Highway	Hwy.	South	S.
Boulevard	Blvd.	Lane	Ln.	Square	Sq.
Court	Ct.	North	N.	Street	St.
Drive	Dr.	Park	Pk.	Terrace	Ter.
East	E.	Place	Pl.	West	W.
Heights	Hts.	Road	Rd.		

WRITING TO PERSUADE: LETTER TO THE EDITOR

43

What is a letter to the editor?

Have you ever read something in a magazine or newspaper that made you say, "Are you kidding?" Have you ever known a fact or statistic that the writer of an article did not know? These situations might prompt you to write a letter to the editor.

> A **letter to the editor** is a persuasive letter written for publication in a newspaper or magazine.

GUIDELINES

A letter to the editor

▶ responds to an article, letter, or editorial in a periodical.

▶ tries to persuade readers or informs them of a fact.

▶ states its opinions or facts quickly, clearly, and politely.

▶ supports opinions with evidence.

▶ is written as a business letter.

PURPOSE If your purpose is to respond to a particular article, editorial, or letter, be sure to mention its title and the date of the newspaper or magazine edition in which it appeared.

MESSAGE State your main idea directly. Don't force readers to figure it out for themselves.

EVIDENCE Effective supporting evidence may include facts, statistics, and logical reasoning as well as personal experiences.

LANGUAGE Use language appropriate for the newspaper's or magazine's usual readers, and choose examples and other details in keeping with their backgrounds and concerns.

CONCLUSION A strong conclusion usually stresses an important point or asks readers to do something.

CHECKPOINTS FOR REVISING

▶ Do I state my position or point clearly?

▶ Do I support my opinion with evidence?

▶ Is the tone of my letter polite rather than sarcastic or rude?

Here's an example of a letter to the editor of *Earth Magazine*:

M O D E L

The writer uses correct business-letter form.

4 Regent Street
Schenectady, NY 12309
October 12, 19—

Earth Magazine
21027 Crossroads Circle
Waukesha, WI 53187

The writer begins by indicating the article to which she is responding.

Dear Editor:

I enjoyed your September 1993 article "Bakker's Field Guide to Jurassic Park Dinosaurs."

The writer states her basic message and backs up this opinion with examples and personal experience.

Unfortunately, the scientific research upon which the film was based is seriously under-funded. As someone who enjoys visiting dinosaur displays, I was shocked at the run-down condition of our local natural history museum. Museum field trips that gather dinosaur fossils also need more funds. I hope everybody who enjoyed the movie Jurassic Park will give what he or she can to projects that add to our knowledge about dinosaurs.

The writer concludes with a call to action.

Cordially,

Maura Davis

Maura Davis

WRITING TO PERSUADE: PERSUASIVE ESSAY

44

How can I express my opinion in a convincing way?

Have your friends ever disagreed with you over an important issue, even though you knew that you were right? One good way to get others to agree with you is to write a persuasive essay. Although a persuasive essay may not be appropriate to convince your friends to go to the movies with you, it can be a useful way to present your opinion on a more serious subject. The guidelines that follow list the characteristics of a persuasive essay:

> A **persuasive essay** is written to **persuade,** or convince, an audience to think in a certain way or to take a certain kind of action.

GUIDELINES

A persuasive essay

- ▶ states a narrowly focused opinion on a matter that can be debated or discussed.

- ▶ offers facts, statistics, examples, reasons, or other evidence that will grab readers' attention and support the opinion.

- ▶ presents information logically.

- ▶ uses transitions between ideas.

- ▶ ends by urging readers to think differently or take action.

WHAT ISSUE SHOULD I CHOOSE?

Some of the issues you care about may not be good choices for a persuasive essay. Choose an issue that can be argued "for" and "against" and supported in various ways.

Also, keep in mind that it's easier to be persuasive when you are writing about an issue that is important to you. Issues you care about may fall into some of these categories:

School Issues	Personal Issues	Local Issues	Global Issues
• homework	• popularity	• jobs	• development
• grades	• peer pressure	• crime	• pollution
• leadership	• prejudice	• housing	• war

HOW CAN I EXPLORE MY ISSUE?

STATE YOUR OPINION CLEARLY. A good way to focus your thinking is to write a statement that sets forth your view. You need to think about your main point in order to gather information that will support your opinion and persuade your readers. Make sure that this statement is narrowly focused. If your topic is too broad, it will be difficult to persuade your readers.

TOO BROAD: Bill Cosby is the best comedian of all time.

MORE FOCUSED: Families could learn a lot about getting along together from Bill Cosby's humor.

THINK ABOUT YOUR AUDIENCE. How much do your readers know about the subject you plan to discuss? How likely are they to agree with you? Try to imagine their reactions and the questions they will have. Give them reasons to *want* to do what you ask. For example, will they be happier or better informed or safer if they do what you ask? They are more likely to agree with you if they expect to get benefits.

THINK ABOUT OTHER VIEWPOINTS. If you present just one side of a question, readers will notice that. It's better to admit that there is an opposite point of view and then explain why your viewpoint is the better one.

TRY THIS

A pro-and-con chart can be useful when you write a persuasive essay. On a piece of paper make two columns. In the first column, list all the "pro" evidence. In the second column, list all the "con" evidence. Let your audience know if the pros outweigh the cons. If the cons outweigh the pros, you might change your topic.

WRITING FOR SCIENCE

What do you think of high-density television or the telecommunications highway? Do you think either will revolutionize communications? Writing a persuasive essay can be a good way to present your opinion about the development of a technology. Be sure to define any technical terms you use and describe the technology. Because the impact of a new technology has not yet been measured, you will be more persuasive if you support your views with expert scientific opinions.

HOW SHOULD I ORGANIZE MY ESSAY?

Your **introduction** should include your topic sentence, the issue you will consider, and your opinion.

The **body** of your essay should present your "evidence," the various kinds of support you have gathered. The foundation of persuasive writing is the information you present to support your opinion. You might want to begin with the most persuasive piece of evidence, or you might save that piece for last. Use whatever order you think will have a stronger impact on your readers. Here are five possible ways you can support your opinion:

Facts: statements that can be proved true

Statistics: facts expressed in numbers

Instances: real-life things or events

Reasons: explanations of why your opinion is valid

Expert Opinions: opinions of people who know

The following chart shows several examples of support you can use:

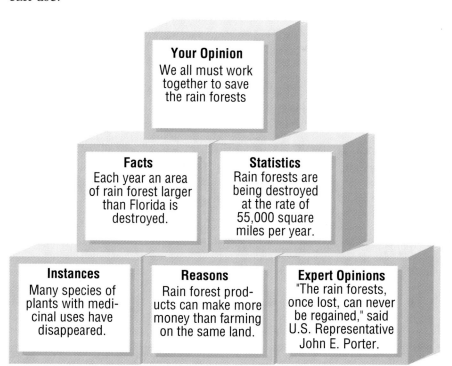

Your Opinion
We all must work together to save the rain forests

Facts
Each year an area of rain forest larger than Florida is destroyed.

Statistics
Rain forests are being destroyed at the rate of 55,000 square miles per year.

Instances
Many species of plants with medicinal uses have disappeared.

Reasons
Rain forest products can make more money than farming on the same land.

Expert Opinions
"The rain forests, once lost, can never be regained," said U.S. Representative John E. Porter.

Since the purpose of your essay is to persuade, the conclusion should be forceful. You might want to ask your audience to make a specific response or you may want to restate your strongest argument.

HOW SHOULD I REVISE MY ESSAY?

GUIDE READERS FROM ONE POINT TO THE NEXT. Try using transitional words and phrases such as these:

To offer evidence	To state an opinion	To introduce opposing views
first, second, third	in my opinion	although
most important	I believe	on the other hand
for example	therefore	even though
for instance	for these reasons	but
according to	consequently	nevertheless
		however

CHECK YOUR REASONING. Make sure your evidence accurately supports your position. One common problem is **overgeneralization.** Don't use words such as *everyone, no one, always,* or *never* unless you can back them up. Also avoid **circular reasoning.** Don't try to support an argument by stating it again. Examine the reasoning in the following sentences.

OVERGENERALIZATION:	"*Everyone* wants to save the rain forests."
	Some people don't believe that it is important to save the rain forests. Therefore, it would be more accurate to say,
IMPROVED:	"*Many* people want to save the rain forests."
CIRCULAR REASONING:	Watch out for **circular reasoning,** the mere restatement of an argument.
	"Rain forests should be saved because it is important to preserve them."
	This statement does not explain why rain forests should be preserved. The following statement uses facts to tell why:
IMPROVED:	"Rain forests should be saved because they are home to more than half the plants and animals in the world."

These questions will help you as you revise your essay.

CHECKPOINTS FOR REVISING

▶ Do I clearly state my opinion at the beginning of the essay?

▶ Do I use evidence such as facts, statistics, examples, and reasons or cite experts' opinions to support my opinion?

▶ Do I present information in a well-organized, logical way?

▶ Do I use transitional words to guide my readers from one idea to the next?

▶ Does my essay end forcefully? Does it urge my readers to take action or react in a certain way?

Following is a model of a persuasive essay. Note how the student writer introduces, supports, and concludes her argument.

STUDENT MODEL

Rain forests take up only 2 percent of the world's surface area—6 percent of the land—yet they are home to more than half the plants and animals in the world. Rain forests are being destroyed at a rate of 55,000 square miles a year. The rain forests cover an area about the size of the continental United States, excluding Alaska. In relative terms, an area larger than Florida is being destroyed annually. Every second a football-field-sized plot of rain forest comes tumbling down. At this rate, none will be left by the year 2000. We all must work together to save the rain forests before it's too late.

The writer uses startling facts and statistics to introduce the issue.

She states her thesis.

A rain forest is a delicate, intricate balance of life. Though most of us are aware of its role in protecting the ozone layer, some people don't know that the rain forest is a world where more than ten million species thrive. Who knows if among the unexplored regions there lies a cure for cancer? Unfortunately, it may already be too late. Each year an estimated 50,000 irreplaceable species meet with extinction. This cure may have already slipped out of our reach forever.

She uses a transitional device to deal with a conflicting viewpoint and then cites facts, statistics, examples, and reasons as evidence in the body of the essay.

Although many people believe that destroying the rain forests will bring great profits, this is not the case. If they were managed wisely, these tropical treasure troves would yield a much higher, much more stable profit than farming, ranching, or logging done on the same land. For example, Brazil nuts alone can generate 5 times more income than the beef produced in the same area.

There may be as many as 3,000 varieties of fruit, but only 200 are in use. Many natural products can be taken from the rain forests and grown elsewhere commercially. There are even environmentally sound ways to get timber without disturbing the delicate balance. If we invested our time and money in these rain forests, we would definitely reap many benefits.

The writer concludes forcefully by urging readers to take action.

Think about it. If preserving the rain forests means a lot to you, then you should take action immediately. Write to your representatives, expressing your concern and urging them to protect the remaining rain forests. Buy an acre of rain forest and support preservation groups. There are a lot of us out there who want to save the rain forests, but unless each of us takes an active role, nothing will happen. Together we can—and must—do something before it's too late.

—Cynthia Lin, Lexington, Massachusetts

WRITING A PUBLIC-SERVICE AD

A public-service advertisement can involve words, visuals, and sound, depending on whether the ad appears in print or on radio or television. A good public-service ad should be aimed at people who are most likely to respond to it. A public-service ad, like a persuasive essay, needs to be convincing. Here are some things to think about when you are writing such an ad.

THE MESSAGE An ad about homelessness will be more convincing if you appeal to people's sympathy. An ad about registering to vote needs to be clear, serious, and informative.

THE AUDIENCE It's important to design your ad for the people you want to reach. Don't aim an ad about registering to vote at children because they are too young to vote.

THE MEDIUM If you're creating a print ad, your main concern will be getting the words and pictures to work together. If your ad will be broadcast on radio, you'll want to think about what the audience will hear—music, voices, and sound effects. If you're creating a TV commercial, think about whether you want your message to be spoken, sung, or shown on the screen in the form of words and pictures.

If you're creating a print ad, your main concern will be getting the words and pictures to work together.

If your ad will be broadcast on radio, you'll want to think about what the audience will hear—music, voices and sound effects.

If you're creating a TV commercial, think about whether you want your message to be spoken, sung or shown on the screen.

45

WRITING ABOUT LITERATURE: RESPONSE TO LITERATURE

How can I express my responses to a work of literature?

A **response to literature** is an essay expressing the thoughts and feelings inspired by a literary work.

Have you ever read a story or poem that made you feel sad, angry, happy, or bored? A response to literature includes *any* thoughts and feelings that a piece of writing stirs in you. Even "no reaction" is a response. When a literary work leaves you cold, it's sometimes interesting to think about why that happened and perhaps write about it.

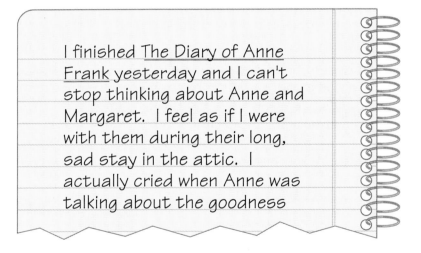

> I finished The Diary of Anne Frank yesterday and I can't stop thinking about Anne and Margaret. I feel as if I were with them during their long, sad stay in the attic. I actually cried when Anne was talking about the goodness

The purpose of writing a response to literature is to explore your own reactions and to share them with others. The following guidelines can help you write a response.

GUIDELINES

A response to literature

► briefly summarizes the work or the passage for readers.

► explains your feelings and thoughts about the work.

► analyzes why the work makes you feel or think as you do.

► uses examples from the work to show what you are responding to.

WHAT DO I DISCUSS IN MY RESPONSE?

Carefully read a literary work such as a poem, a short story, a novel, or an essay. Then note the immediate effect it has on you. Next, reread the piece or the passage. This time reflect on how it does or does not relate to your own experience. One or more of the following techniques can help you explore your reactions.

FREEWRITE. While reading, jot down any words, thoughts, feelings, or memories that come into your mind.

DISCUSS. Compare and contrast your reactions with those of other readers. Discuss how and why your responses are alike or different.

QUESTION. Ask yourself specific questions about the work like the ones in the following cluster:

TRY THIS

If you are having trouble coming up with a written response to a work, try responding in other ways first. Try ideas like these:
• Create a comic strip based on the work.
• Construct scenery for a scene from the work.
• Design an advertisement for the work.
• Create a dance that reflects the mood of the work.

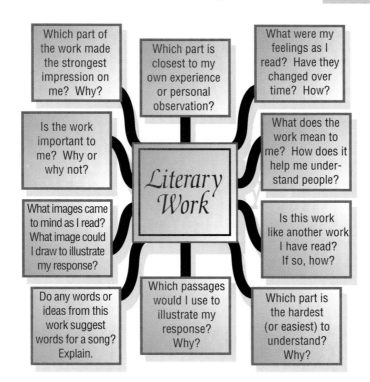

Which part of the work made the strongest impression on me? Why?

Which part is closest to my own experience or personal observation?

What were my feelings as I read? Have they changed over time? How?

Is the work important to me? Why or why not?

What does the work mean to me? How does it help me understand people?

What images came to mind as I read? What image could I draw to illustrate my response?

Literary Work

Is this work like another work I have read? If so, how?

Do any words or ideas from this work suggest words for a song? Explain.

Which passages would I use to illustrate my response? Why?

Which part is the hardest (or easiest) to understand? Why?

Here is how one student used freewriting—continuous writing without pauses for revision—to explore her ideas about the ending of the play *The Diary of Anne Frank:*

For more on freewriting, see p. 9.

Anne Frank seems very innocent and good—she really believes that <u>all</u> people are good at heart. How can she say this when she's being persecuted and may die because of Hitler? Maybe at the time, she didn't think about Hitler or know much about him, but nowadays people do know. We <u>can't</u> feel like Anne does—at least I can't. Still, I'd like to believe what she believes—maybe she's just talking about people's intentions. Do people have good intentions? Not Hitler, but maybe the Van Daans in the play do have them— maybe most people do.

HOW CAN I ORGANIZE MY RESPONSE?

Generally, our thoughts and feelings float in and out of our minds in no particular order, like seeds on the wind. Here are two organizing strategies that work for many writers: First, write down good ideas before they get away. Second, put those ideas into a logical order before you begin drafting a response. You can arrange your ideas by making a graphic organizer. Here is an outline for a response to the play *The Diary of Anne Frank:*

For more on organizational plans, see p. 23.

Anne Frank

MODEL

I. Introduction

    A. Give title of work: <u>The Diary of Anne Frank.</u>

    B. Summarize part of work being responded to.

       (Paraphrase Anne's statement about people.)

II. Body

    A. Give my personal response to Anne's statement.

    B. Relate my response to personal experience.

    C. Analyze and evaluate Anne's statement.

III. Conclusion

    A. Summarize my overall response.

Paraphrasing is putting text in different words but keeping the same meaning.

Here is an action-reaction chart for a response to the play *The Diary of Anne Frank*. In a literary work, an event or a character's action may trigger your reactions.

Paragraph 1 Introduction	**Title of literary work:** *The Diary of Anne Frank*
	Summary of what I'm responding to: Anne's statement about people
	Main idea: I think Anne is right about most people's intentions, not their actions.

	ACTIONS	**MY REACTIONS**
Paragraph 2 Body	Hitler shipped the Jews to death camps.	He's not good at heart— he's evil.
Paragraph 3 Body	Mrs. Van Daan wouldn't leave her house and furniture to save her own life.	She's frivolous and too caught up in her possessions, but she's not evil.
Paragraph 4 Body	Mr. Van Daan stole food.	He's greedy, thoughtless, and unfair to others but not evil.
Paragraph 5 Conclusion	My overall response to the work	

Once you have an organized plan, begin drafting a response. Linking your response with an observation or experience from your own life can make your essay more convincing.

Here the writer draws on her own experience and observation of people to comment on Anne Frank's point of view.

Perhaps what Anne meant was that many people who do bad things have good intentions and that they are doing what they think is best. If so, I would agree. It is my view that many people simply become so caught up in themselves that they don't realize how unfair they are being to others.

—Eva Foster, Edmond, Oklahoma

Here is a famous First Lady's response to Anne's diary.

MODEL FROM LITERATURE

Drawing on her knowledge of books about war, Eleanor Roosevelt expresses a strong personal response to Anne's diary.

This is a remarkable book. Written by a young girl—and the young are not afraid of telling the truth—it is one of the wisest and most moving commentaries on war and its impact on human beings that I have ever read. Anne Frank's account of the changes wrought upon eight people hiding out from the Nazis for two years during the occupation of Holland, living in constant fear and isolation, imprisoned not only by the terrible outward circumstances of war but inwardly by themselves, made me intimately and shockingly aware of war's greatest evil—the degradation of the human spirit. . . .

These are the thoughts and expression of a young girl living under extraordinary conditions, and for this reason her diary tells us much about ourselves and our own children. And for this reason, too, I felt how close we all are to Anne's experience, how very much involved we are in her short life and in the entire world.

—Eleanor Roosevelt, an introduction to
Anne Frank: The Diary of a Young Girl

WRITING FOR ART

For an art assignment, you may be asked to write a response to a piece of art such as a painting or sculpture. The guidelines for responding to a literary work can also be applied to an artwork. Like literature, a piece of art expresses a message, a mood, and a point of view. The main difference is that the artist uses color, shape, and texture instead of words to convey meaning or create an effect.

Here are some strategies for writing a response to art.

For more about looking at art, see p. 453.

- Include a drawing or a photocopy of the piece of art so you can ask your readers to look at the specific elements you are responding to.

- Focus on a message or an effect that the artist wants to achieve and explore your response to it.

- Use words that are suitable for a response to art; for example, *color, line,* and *composition.*

- Compare a piece of art with a literary work you have read.

HOW CAN I REVISE MY RESPONSE TO LITERATURE?

As you evaluate your response, keep the following checkpoints in mind:

CHECKPOINTS FOR REVISING

▶ Do I identify the title and the author of the work I am writing about?

▶ Does my summary of the work tell readers enough to clarify my response?

▶ Does my response say what I honestly feel about the work and why I feel this way?

▶ Do I illustrate my response with examples from the work and from my own experience?

Following is a final draft of a response to the play *The Diary of Anne Frank.* The essay was written for readers who were familiar with the work. Therefore, the introduction briefly refers to a comment Anne makes in the last scene rather than summarizing the entire play.

People Are Basically Good at Heart

The last excerpt from Anne Frank's diary given in the play <u>The Diary of Anne Frank</u> stated that despite all that had happened, Anne still felt that people were good at heart.

I do not believe that all people are good at heart. I think that most people, not <u>all</u> people, are good at heart. For instance, Adolf Hitler did not ship the Jews to death camps because he felt it was in their best interest.

I cannot completely agree with Anne. It is my view that many people simply get so caught up in themselves and their immediate needs that they don't realize how unfair or inconsiderate they are being to other people. For example, Mrs. Van Daan

is a frivolous woman who cares more about her fur coat and furniture than her own safety and the safety of others. She wouldn't leave home when she had the chance because she loved her possessions too much. Mr. Van Daan is greedy, thoughtless, and selfish, but he is not evil. He steals food because he is thinking of his <u>own</u> welfare, and not of others. Both of these people probably had the best of intentions; their good intentions were simply not carried out.

In conclusion, I would like to state that although Anne's statement was naive, all in all, she was telling the truth. Not everyone is good at heart, but most people have the <u>best of intentions.</u>

—Eva Foster, Edmond, Oklahoma

RESPONDING TO DRAMA

You can write a response to a movie, TV drama, or live play in the same way that you do for literature. Reflect on a dramatization that touched you emotionally or made you think. Then ask yourself questions similar to those on the cluster on page 211. Reword the questions to apply to a dramatization instead of a written work. For example: Change "What *images* came to mind as I read?" to "What *ideas* or *associations* came to mind as I watched?"

46

WRITING ABOUT LITERATURE: BOOK REPORT

 How do I write a book report?

> A **book report** is an essay in which the writer gives information about a book and evaluates it.

Have you read a book lately that was just too good to put down? You may even have urged friends and relatives to read it.

Evaluations of books are so useful that some people make a living writing them. Tens of thousands of books are published each year, and book reviewers can save readers time and trouble by pointing out which books are worth reading and which aren't.

Any book—old or new, good or bad—can be the subject of a book report. Consider these guidelines when you set out to write your first draft.

GUIDELINES

A book report

▶ gives some background information about the book and the author.

▶ briefly summarizes the content of the book and presents the book's **theme,** or its main idea.

▶ expresses the writer's opinion of the book.

▶ backs up the writer's opinion with examples and quotations.

▶ recommends or rejects the book and gives reasons for doing so.

"Cricket trashed it."

HOW CAN I GATHER INFORMATION?

Although the cartoon from *Cricket* (a children's magazine that reviews books for its readers) does not suggest it, there's more to writing a book report than simply saying "I loved it" or "It was awful." Readers will want to know specific information about the book so that they can decide whether to read it. Here's how to gather information for your report.

1. Keep pen and paper handy as you read the book, or use your literature response log.

2. As you read, jot down the major events and main ideas and your reactions to them.

3. Record page numbers of passages you might quote in your report to illustrate your opinion.

4. When you finish reading, respond to the book as a whole. You might want to freewrite, dramatize, or illustrate your reactions. Keep nearby any prewriting work you do so that you can refer to it as you draft your report.

TRY THIS

If you don't feel quite ready to plunge into writing your first draft, try telling somebody about the book you are reviewing and your reaction to it. This conversation may help you express your ideas about the book.

HOW CAN I BEGIN MY BOOK REPORT?

If you begin your report with a detailed summary, you may lose readers. Here are some tips for grabbing readers' attention with your first sentence:

STRATEGY	EXAMPLE
Ask a question—or several questions.	What bird dives at more than 175 miles per hour? Why do jays let ants run around in their feathers? You'll find the answers to these questions and many others in *Bird* by David Burnie.
State what the book is about, and give readers a reason for becoming involved in it.	In *Happily May I Walk,* Arlene Hirschfelder investigates the lives of Native Americans and takes readers on a journey through a world that few Americans see.

STRATEGY	EXAMPLE
Make a personal statement about your reaction to the book.	I've never wept while reading a book—but *Picture Bride* by Yoshiko Uchida moved me to tears.
Compare and contrast the book with other books.	Of all the poetry books by African American women that I've read, *Blacks* by Gwendolyn Brooks made the deepest impression on me.
Introduce the reader to a main character.	If you keep a journal, you'll identify with Julia, whose "Book of Strangenesses" helps her to figure out the world around her in *A Room Made of Windows* by Eleanor Cameron.

HOW CAN I DEVELOP MY REPORT?

After introducing the book and capturing your readers' interest, you'll want to answer the questions they might naturally ask:

Who are the main characters?

What happens to the main characters?

What is the setting?

What is the book's theme, or central message?

Is the book nonfiction?

What subject is it about?

What is the author's point of view?

Does the author present information clearly?

Is the author an authority on this subject?

When organizing your report, follow these steps:

• Attract your readers' attention.

• Introduce the book.

• Briefly discuss the book.

• Evaluate the book.

• Recommend or reject the book.

When you evaluate the book, you may want to develop a list of **criteria,** or standards, for judging the work. Suppose you were reviewing a historical novel set during the Civil War. You might develop the following list of standards to share with your readers:

Does the novel have

- accurate descriptions of historical details?
- convincing dialogue appropriate to the time period?
- believable characters?
- a historically accurate plot?
- a suspenseful central conflict?
- vivid descriptions of scenery and actions?
- a theme or message that is important in today's world?

TRY THIS

To sharpen your reviewing skills, try writing several kinds of evaluations in your journal. For example, write a review of the next movie or TV show you watch. Write an evaluation of your favorite pizza place. You can even write a review of your day at school.

HOW CAN I REVISE MY REPORT?

As you polish your first draft, remember that your readers will need to have enough information to decide whether they want to read the book. Your opinions or reactions will have little impact if you do not back them up with specific examples from the text. One effective way to support your statements is to provide quotations. Note how the reviewer uses a quotation to revise this model.

M O D E L

The writer's descriptions of life on a Virginia farm are vivid and precise. When she describes how Uncle Jed teaches Will how to make a split-rail fence, she uses words that make you see exactly what Jed is doing.∧

She says, "Will did as he was told. Then he watched while Uncle Jed tapped the sharp-bladed froe with the mallet-like wooden maul and split sections off each side of the last few lengths of locust [wood], leaving a piece with smooth, flat edges."

You might also ask yourself the questions in the following checklist while revising your report:

CHECKPOINTS FOR REVISING

► Is my introduction snappy and attention-grabbing?

► Are the title and author of the book identified early in my report?

► Is my presentation of the plot or main idea brief and accurate?

► Do I support my opinions with examples and quotations?

► Do I conclude with a recommendation and a summary of my reasons for making it?

Here is a review of a novel about the Civil War.

MODEL

The reviewer begins with an interesting, provocative question and gives a recommendation that will be backed up in the body of the paper.

The reviewer names the title and author at the beginning of the report.

What would it be like to lose your immediate family in a war? Fortunately, that's something most of us will never have to go through. If you'd like to read a compelling story of a young boy who loses everything but learns to accept the past and build a new life for himself, I'd recommend <u>Shades of Gray</u> by Carolyn Reeder.

The reviewer describes the main character, the basic plot, and the setting.

Will Page, the main character in this historical novel, is twelve years old when the story begins. Born and raised in the Shenandoah Valley, Will endures loss after loss during the Civil War. His father, a Confederate officer, is killed in battle; his older brother is shot by a Union sentry. A typhoid epidemic claims his two younger sisters, and shortly afterward his mother dies of grief. Will is angry that he must live with his aunt and uncle in the hills of central Virginia. His Uncle Jed refused to fight in the Civil War, and Will is ashamed to live with a man he thinks is a coward.

In time, though, Will comes to respect his uncle. Jed teaches Will to trap rabbits, make fence posts, and tend a garden. He also teaches Will valuable lessons about courage and self-reliance.

Reeder, a teacher and writer, knows how to make history come to life. All the characters in <u>Shades of Gray</u> seemed real to me, and the descriptions of life on a farm in Virginia are vivid.

The only thing I disliked about the book was that the theme—courage is doing what you believe in—is laid on a little too thick. The characters always seem to be saying things like "A man has to do what he believes is right" or "A person thinking you're a coward doesn't make you one."

Still, if you don't let the preaching bother you, you will enjoy this book. <u>Shades of Gray</u> shows that in war there are few heroes and villains—most people fall somewhere in between. That's as true today as it was a hundred years ago in Will Page's time.

47

REPORTS: RESEARCH REPORT

 How do I investigate a topic in depth?

> A **research report** is an examination of a topic, using information from many sources.

Read the excerpt below. Is Mr. Thurber right? Do fish indeed lack ears? You could look it up, and, before you know it, you could be on your way to writing a research report. If you haven't wondered about the hearing ability of fish, you probably have other questions you want answered.

MODEL FROM LITERATURE

Q. We have a fish with ears and wonder if it is valuable.

—Joe Wright

A. I find no trace in the standard fish books of any fish with ears. Very likely the ears do not belong to the fish, but to some mammal. They look to me like a mammal's ears. It would be pretty hard to say what species of mammal, and almost impossible to determine what particular member of that species. They may merely be hysterical ears, in which case they will go away if you can get the fin's mind on something else.

—James Thurber, "The Owl in the Attic"

GUIDELINES

A research report

► presents factual information about an interesting topic.

► states and develops a main idea.

► brings together information from a variety of sources.

► has a beginning, a middle, and an end.

► credits sources for ideas, quotations, and information presented.

The flowchart that follows maps the process one writer went through to write a research report. You may use this chart as a guide as you plan your own research procedure.

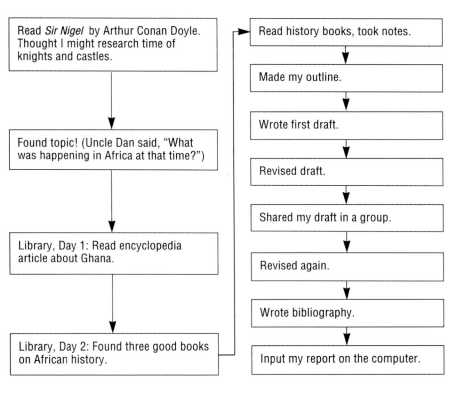

Read *Sir Nigel* by Arthur Conan Doyle. Thought I might research time of knights and castles.	Read history books, took notes.
↓	↓
Found topic! (Uncle Dan said, "What was happening in Africa at that time?")	Made my outline.
↓	↓
Library, Day 1: Read encyclopedia article about Ghana.	Wrote first draft.
↓	↓
Library, Day 2: Found three good books on African history.	Revised draft.

WHAT MAKES A GOOD TOPIC?

You will probably be assigned a research report by a language arts, social studies, or science teacher. These teachers will probably give you a general subject, such as Africa, that you will have to narrow. The key to writing a successful paper is discovering a specific and interesting topic within this broad category.

Here are two strategies for coming up with ideas for a specific topic:

- Punch in a keyword on the computer catalog and follow wherever it leads.

- Look up the call number of an interesting nonfiction book. Then go to that part of the library and look at other books on the same subject.

Here are four questions you can use to evaluate topic ideas:

- Does it interest me?
- Will it interest my readers?
- Can I find enough information about it?
- Can I cover it well in a short report?

HOW CAN I LIMIT MY TOPIC?

Consider how much time you have and how many pages you plan to write. Limit your topic to one you can cover in the amount of time and space available. Divide your topic into parts by asking questions and stay with one part. Repeat this process as shown in the diagram that follows:

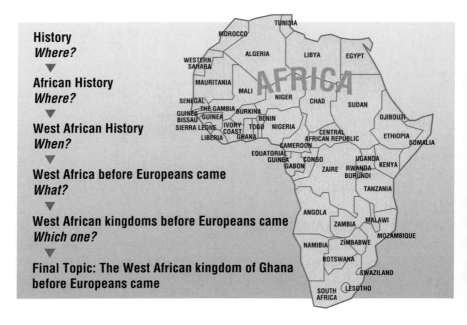

History
Where?
▼
African History
Where?
▼
West African History
When?
▼
West Africa before Europeans came
What?
▼
West African kingdoms before Europeans came
Which one?
▼
Final Topic: The West African kingdom of Ghana before Europeans came

HOW DO I FIND INFORMATION?

Gathering information for a report involves several steps.

Step 1: LIST YOUR QUESTIONS ABOUT YOUR TOPIC

A good list can guide your search and save you time. Think of it as a shopping list of items that you want to get information about from the library (and other sources). Feel free to update the list as you go along.

Step 2: READ

You'll probably find much of the information you want in print. Sources may include the following items:

- **Encyclopedias** These general reference works are a good place to start. An encyclopedia article can give you a broad overview, like an airplane flight over your topic. Once you know the terrain, you can decide where to land. Also, many encyclopedia articles list sources of further information.

- **Books** These provide information in depth. To identify books likely to be helpful, look in the card or computer catalog: Each entry has a brief description of what is in the book.

- **Magazine and Newspaper Articles** These can give detailed information about very specific aspects of a topic. Use the *Readers' Guide to Periodical Literature* to find articles that may be useful. This yearly guide lists articles published in major magazines and newspapers. A librarian will show you how to use this reference book.

For more on the Readers' Guide, see Library Resources, p. 415.

Step 3: INTERVIEW EXPERTS

An expert in this case is anyone who knows more about your topic than you do. People to interview may include one of your friends, a friend of your parents, your family doctor or school nurse, or a teacher at your school.

HOW CAN I TAKE NOTES?

Notes are a way of carrying information back to your desk. They are a written record of the research work you have done. You have taken good notes if

- you can read your own handwriting.
- you have all the information you need when you start writing.
- you can find any particular note quickly when you need it.
- you can rearrange your notes easily if they get out of order.
- you can identify the source of each note.

TRY THIS

If your library has a computerized card catalog, it probably is hooked into a database service. Access the service, and then run a search, using key words related to your topic.

COMPUTER TIP

If you have access to a computer bulletin-board service, see if people online have information about your topic or can suggest places to look for information.

Most writers make two sets of index cards for their notes. **Source cards** are for recording information about sources, such as the author, the title, the publisher, and the date of each work. **Note cards** are for jotting down information about the topic.

THREE TYPICAL SOURCE CARDS

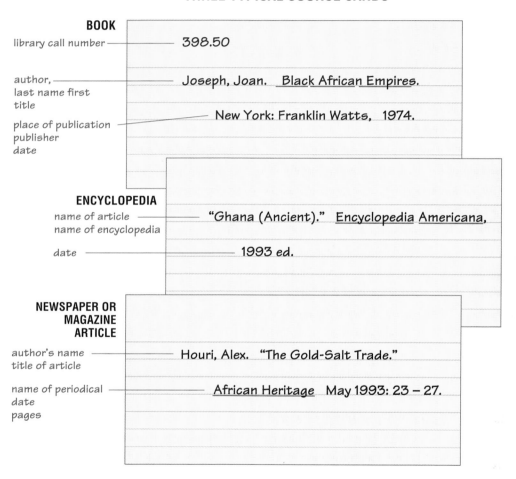

BOOK

library call number ———— 398.50

author, —————— Joseph, Joan.   Black African Empires.
last name first
title

place of publication ———— New York: Franklin Watts,   1974.
publisher
date

ENCYCLOPEDIA

name of article ———— "Ghana (Ancient)." Encyclopedia Americana,
name of encyclopedia

date ———————— 1993 ed.

NEWSPAPER OR MAGAZINE ARTICLE

author's name ———— Houri, Alex. "The Gold-Salt Trade."
title of article

name of periodical ———— African Heritage   May 1993: 23 – 27.
date
pages

WHAT SHOULD I PUT IN MY NOTES?

Your notes will eventually become the backbone of your paper. Therefore, use your own words as much as possible. Also, be exact in quoting other people's words. Here are techniques for note-taking as you do research:

PARAPHRASE INFORMATION. Make sure you record information accurately and in your own words. You may use incomplete sentences and make up your own abbreviations if you like.

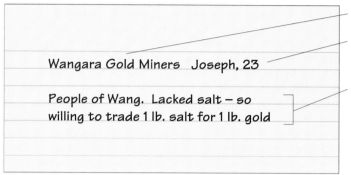

This phrase tells the topic of the note.

A key word identifies the related source card and a number indicates the page number.

The note-taker uses abbreviations and other short cuts.

The information is paraphrased — recorded in the note-taker's own words.

GET QUOTATIONS RIGHT. If you're planning to quote a writer directly, record his or her words exactly as they appear in the source, including punctuation. Always put quotation marks around someone else's exact words so that you will remember that they are direct quotations.

ORGANIZING YOUR INFORMATION

Before you start writing, develop a plan for presenting your information. The following two steps can help:

WRITE A THESIS STATEMENT. A thesis statement is a sentence about your central purpose — what you plan to "show" in your paper. You may revise it for the finished report, but at this stage, it gives you a peg to hang your ideas on. Here is a thesis statement for a paper on the ancient Kingdom of Ghana:

> Ghana was one of the strongest, richest kingdoms of its time.

MAKE AN OUTLINE. Here is where your note cards can really begin to help. If you have followed the guideline of writing only one note per card, you can now sort and rearrange your note cards until you find a satisfactory and logical order. Then present that order in outline form.

TRY THIS

Put direct quotations on index cards of a particular color so you won't mistake quotations for your own ideas.

TRY THIS

Group your note cards into piles that make sense and label each pile. Use these labels as topic headings in your outline. Regroup each pile of cards to spark ideas for subtopic headings.

For more information on outlines, see p. 20.

The model that follows shows a standard outline format:

An Ancient African Empire
I.   Introduction
II. General facts about Ghana
     A. What it was
     B. Where it was located
     C. When it existed
III. The military might of Ghana
     A. The role of iron weapons
     B. The size of armies
IV. The wealth of Ghana
     A. The gold trade with the south
     B. The salt trade with the north
V.   The fall of Ghana

TRY THIS

If you don't know
how to begin, skip
the introduction and
begin drafting with
your first major
topic. Imagine
telling a friend
about your topic;
then just write down
what you have
learned.

HOW CAN I DRAFT MY REPORT?

Incorporate as much information as possible from your note cards into your draft. Use your outline only as a guide. If you discover a new idea you would like to explore, go ahead. (The outline is always there to get you back on course.)

Make sure that your research report has a definite beginning, middle, and end.

BEGINNING A good first paragraph should "hook" your readers, introduce your topic, and hint at your main idea as well. A story, an anecdote (brief story or incident), an amazing fact, a gripping quotation—any of these can make a good introduction.

MIDDLE Use your outline as a guide to structure your writing, and remember to give credit where credit is due. Each time you include a fact or quotation, you'll need to name your source. Put the relevant key word and page number in parentheses as follows:

The Arab scholar El-Bekri wrote that "the King of Ghana can put 200,000 warriors in the field . . ." (Chu 25)

Avoid plagiarism. Plagiarism means using another writer's words or ideas as if they are yours. It is a form of stealing and is considered a serious offense. You must credit your sources.

When is credit due?

Name your source when you are

- using another writer's exact words.
- reporting an original idea that isn't yours.
- reporting a fact available from just one source.

Do not name your source when you are

- reporting common knowledge—information available from many sources, such as the location of Ghana.

END Bring your report to a satisfying conclusion either by summing up your main idea or leaving readers with a question for further thought.

HOW DO I REVISE MY REPORT?

If, by the time you're finished drafting, you have a thicket of details, cut, prune, and trim them to bring out your main idea.

CHECKPOINTS FOR REVISING

▶ Will my introduction catch my readers' attention?

▶ Does my report state and logically develop one unified idea?

▶ Are all my facts accurate?

▶ Have I used my own words, except in direct quotations?

▶ Have I named the source of each direct quotation, each idea that is not mine, and each fact that is not common knowledge?

▶ Does my report come to a satisfying conclusion?

HOW DO I CREATE MY BIBLIOGRAPHY?

A **bibliography** is a list of sources. Write your bibliography after you've finished your report. All the information you need for this list should be on your source cards. You need list only sources you have actually used. Follow these guidelines:

- List the entries in alphabetical order by authors' last names or by the first word in the title (excluding articles).
- Follow the standard form for bibliographies that follows.
- Put the bibliography at the end of your research report.

Bibliography

"Ghana (Ancient)." <u>Encyclopedia Americana</u>.
   1993 ed.

Joseph, Joan. <u>Black African Empires</u>. New York:
   Franklin Watts, 1974.

Rengko, Susan. "Lost Empires." <u>Cobblestone</u>
   Apr. 1993: 19–20.

"West African Treasures Come to Portland
   Museum." <u>The Oregonian</u> 2 May 1993:
   10–12.

Encyclopedia article

Book, one author

Magazine or newspaper article. one author

Magazine or newspaper article. unidentified author

Here's part of a research report on Ghana:

MODEL

A Glorious African Empire

The writer introduces his topic with a fact that arouses readers' interest.

The writer expresses the main idea to be developed: that ancient Ghana was a great empire.

In the days of knights and castles, people in Europe told stories about a great kingdom far away. Gold, they said, was as common as salt. The king of this place hitched his horse to a 60-pound nugget. The kingdom existed, and the stories were true. Located in West Africa between the Niger River and the Sahara, the Ghanaian empire was founded around A.D. 300 and lasted almost 800 years. It was one of the great empires of its time.

The ruling tribe of Ghana were the Soninkes. They were the first people in their region to start using iron. With their iron weapons, they were able to conquer their neighbors, who were still using weapons made of wood and bone. Thus, Ghana grew ever more powerful. In 1067, an Arab historian named El-Bekri told how "the King of Ghana can put 200,000 warriors in the field, more than 40,000 of them being armed with bow and arrow." (Chu 25)

Ghana was not just strong; it was also rich. It controlled the "gold–salt trade." (Joseph 22) The salt came from a place north of Ghana. The gold came from a mysterious place in the south known as Wangara. The people of the north wanted gold, and the people of Wangara wanted salt. Both had to go through Ghana to trade.

The writer uses a transition sentence to move the readers to a new paragraph. Strong echoes the preceding paragraph; not just . . . was also introduces a new idea.

In 1054, invaders from the north attacked and conquered the empire. Thus ended a "golden" chapter in West African history.

The writer ends with the historical facts on the fate of the empire of Ghana, touching on the main idea of a golden age again.

 ## WRITING FOR SCIENCE

As a science assignment, you may be asked to write a paper on a topic that requires research. For example, suppose you are asked to classify the plants, birds, or animals of your region. Identify sources of information, such as the U.S. Department of Fish and Wildlife, *National Wildlife* magazine, Roger Tory Peterson's birdwatching guides, or *Gray's Manual of Botany*. As you write, think of ways to display your classification graphically: that is, by using photos, drawings, or diagrams.

48

REPORTS: I-SEARCH REPORT

 What is an I-Search report?

An **I-Search report** tells about a writer's personal involvement with a topic and also conveys information about it.

Suppose you loved the game of chess. If you were to write a paper about chess, you would probably reveal something important about yourself as well as about chess. To share even more about yourself, you could discuss how you learned about chess—the many afternoons you spent indoors reading chess books, the tournaments you entered, the master players you met. Such a paper is sometimes called an I-Search report because it tells about discoveries of interest and importance to you.

GUIDELINES

An I-Search report

▶ discusses a topic of personal interest to you, the writer.

▶ describes your own experiences with the subject and the research that you have done.

▶ presents factual information about the topic that you have gathered from various sources.

▶ includes your own reactions and responses to the information that you have gathered.

HOW DO I FIND A TOPIC I CARE ABOUT?

Since an I-Search report explores something meaningful to you, the best topics are probably ones that you have already thought about. Look for ideas in your journal. Consider topics you often bring up in conversations with friends. Above all, pay attention to questions and ideas that occur to you in the course of everyday activities—while reading, watching television, or just daydreaming. Try to find a way to record these questions and ideas without interrupting what you are doing. For example, you might keep a wallet-sized notebook handy to jot down ideas, or you might record them on a hand-held tape recorder. Here are some questions that one writer recorded in a journal.

Topic Ideas	When They Occurred
How do the best basketball players of today compare with the best 25 years ago?	while watching a basketball game on TV
Why not rid the world of poisonous snakes?	while reading a nature magazine at the dentist's office
What would it be like to invent computer games for a living? How profitable is it?	when Aunt Tanya said, "You can't spend your life playing computer games."

HOW DO I GATHER INFORMATION?

Sometimes the information needed for an I-Search report is not available in the library. Here are some alternative strategies:

FRIENDLY CONVERSATIONS Much useful information may come up in informal conversations. For example, if you want to learn what games were popular twenty-five years ago, you might ask your parents what they did for fun at your age.

INTERVIEWS People in your community may have valuable information about your topic. For example, if you're writing about jobs related to computer games, talk to someone who creates or sells computer software. Get names and phone numbers of people to interview from friends, family, relatives, and teachers. Before interviewing someone, find out as much as you can about the person and the topic you plan to discuss. People will be more responsive to you if you are well-informed and ask intelligent questions.

TRY THIS

To get a conversation going, use a "conversation piece"—an object that has special meaning for the person with whom you are talking. For example, bringing an old board game from the attic may get your parents talking enthusiastically about games they used to play.

For more about interviews, see p. 245.

WRITING FOR SOCIAL STUDIES

In a social studies assignment, you may be asked to write about some event in recent history, such as the Vietnam War. Try talking to people whose lives were touched by the war. For example, you may be able to set up an interview with a veteran through the local office of the Veterans Administration. As you interview, use your subject's answer to one question to ask more focused and specific follow-up questions.

First question: What was it like to fight a ground war in a jungle environment? *(Subject complains that the heat and humidity made it difficult to track the enemy.)*

Follow-up question: How did the heat and humidity affect your ability to pursue the enemy? *(Subject dwells on the discomfort and ungainliness of wearing heavy boots in dense jungle.)*

ACTIVITIES Often you can explore a subject best through active involvement. For example, if you play chess and want to write about the world of professional chess, enter a tournament.

WRITTEN SOURCES Look beyond the library for sources of written information. For example, companies, government agencies, and other political, cultural, and scientific organizations often have up-to-date information that they will provide on request. Write a business letter to the public relations department of the appropriate organization, asking for material that relates to your topic.

HOW DO I WRITE MY I-SEARCH REPORT?

Information is important in an I-Search paper, but so is the personal dimension. As you draft your paper, try to answer the following questions (though not necessarily in this order).

• Why am I interested in this topic?

• What happened to me while I was doing the research?

• What did I find out about the topic?

• What did the information show me about myself?

Go over your first draft and circle the sentences that answer the preceding questions. If you did not include any personal information on your research process, be sure to add it to your draft.

YOU HAVE CHOICES You can structure an I-Search paper in many ways. The form you choose depends on your purpose.

PURPOSE	STRUCTURE
Share some interesting information.	Follow the main idea and supporting details structure of a traditional research report.
Tell about a dramatic change you went through.	Use a narrative structure and dialogue to tell the story of your search for information.
Get people to see why you feel or believe something.	Give an opinion and present persuasive reasons for it.

You can even weave together several approaches as long as you keep to your topic and make your transitions smooth and clear. Compare the two beginnings that follow:

**Game Designers:
Exploring a World of Work**

I was just breaking into the fifth level of Macropods when my aunt came up behind me. "Another computer game?" she said. "You can't play games all your life."

"Why not? I'll just get a job inventing them." As soon as I said the words, I wondered: Do jobs like that exist? Could I get one someday—and would I enjoy it? I decided to find out.

**Designing Computer Games:
Portrait of a Profession**

Inventing computer games sounds like a wonderful job—but is it? The question is of special interest to me because I'm good at computer games and I love playing them. It's only natural to think that someday I might look for a job in that field.

That's why I called a game publisher one day to see if I could get any information. To my surprise, they put me directly in touch with Kim Matsui.

In the first example, which has a narrative structure, the events are presented in chronological order. In the second example, the writer introduces the main topic with a question and some personal information.

HOW DO I REVISE MY I-SEARCH REPORT?

To help you revise your I-Search report, you may want to have a friend or classmate read it. Then ask questions to find out his or her response. Avoid general questions and those that can be answered with yes or no. More specific responses will be more useful in pinpointing what needs to be revised.

Here are some revisions the writer made after hearing responses from a reader:

There is a catch, of course. Game designers have to sell their games to software publishers. ~~This is pretty much what authors have to do, except that they, of course, peddle their products to book publishers.~~ Usually they get a royalty⌃ If the game sells a lot of copies they ~~make a lot of money and if it sells fewer copies they make that much less money.~~

⌃, a percentage of the profits on games sold.

get rich. If not, they starve.

Here are some points to consider when you revise your I-Search report:

CHECKPOINTS FOR REVISING

▶ Is my report interesting and informative?

▶ Does my report have a clear and effective structure?

▶ Have I shared information about my research process?

▶ Will readers know why this information is important to me?

▶ Have I written anything I'd rather not share?

Here's an example of a final draft of an I-Search report:

Designing Computer Games:

Portrait of a Job

The writer presents the main idea and explains its personal relevance.

Inventing computer games sounds like a wonderful job—but is it? The question is of special interest to me because I'm good at computer games and I love playing them. It's only natural to think that someday I might look for a job in that field.

That's why I called a game publisher one day to see if I could get any information. To my surprise, they put me directly in touch with Kim Matsui. In fact, I had a chance to meet the designer of Macropods in person. (Was I thrilled? You bet!) Kim wanted me to try out a new game he's working on and give him some feedback. That's how I learned that playing games and designing them are two sides of the same coin. As Kim puts it, "Most designers are players first. You have to know what's fun to design a good game."

The writer shares information about the research process.

Informal language reflects the writer's voice.

The writer uses a direct quotation to make his point.

Later, Kim gave me a pass to a game designers' conference at the Royal Hotel. About 100 designers were there to show off their games, and I met three of them. They told me that most game designers are freelancers: They work for themselves, at home, on their own schedule. It sounds great to me!

The writer adds supporting details about the job.

There is a catch, of course. Game designers have to sell their games to software publishers. Usually they get a royalty, a percentage of the profits on games sold. If the game is a hit, they get rich. If not, they starve.

The writer presents specific information based on research.

I'd be willing to take that chance. It's not just the work. I think I would enjoy the people I would meet — everybody in this field likes games. I just hope the profession still exists by the time I'm looking for a job — because frankly it sounds like the type of work for me.

Ending on a personal note echoes the introduction and gives the paper a balanced, finished feeling.

49

SPEAKING AND LISTENING PROJECTS: SPEECH

? *How do I compose and deliver a speech?*

> **A speech** is a talk or public address delivered to an audience on a specific occasion.

How do you feel about speaking in public? Whether you love the limelight or avoid it, you may need to deliver a speech as a class assignment, as an after-school activity, or as part of a campaign for a class office.

Speeches differ from written compositions. Your audience must grasp the main points of your speech just by hearing your words once. They cannot review what you have said as they could if they were reading. To get your message across, you must use precise words, emphasize important ideas, and write sentences with a pleasing sound and rhythm.

GUIDELINES

A speech

▶ can inform, persuade, evaluate, and entertain.

▶ uses language that suits the occasion, audience, and purpose.

▶ is clearly organized and easy for the audience to follow.

▶ uses rhythm, repetition, and variety to help keep an audience's attention.

▶ is delivered in a relaxed manner, with careful attention given to voice quality and audience reaction.

Follow these steps as you prepare a speech:

Consider purpose and audience and choose a topic. | Organize ideas. | Use speech-making strategies. | Practice your speech. | Deliver your speech.

Step 1: CONSIDER PURPOSE AND AUDIENCE AND CHOOSE A SUITABLE TOPIC

Make your speech fit the occasion and the audience. The occasion, purpose, and audience will determine your subject, your words, the organization of your ideas, and the length of your talk. If, for example, you are giving a pep talk to a team before a championship game, your speech will be brief, informal, and to the point. Your purpose will be to inspire your audience. Here are some questions that will help you plan your speech:

- Where and why am I giving this speech? What is the occasion?

- What is my purpose? Do I want my audience to laugh? To learn something?

- What age is my audience? What topic would suit them?

- What does my audience already know and not know about my subject? What information must I give them?

- How long should my speech be to maintain my audience's interest?

- What language should I choose for this occasion and this audience? Do I need to be formal or informal?

Once you have thought about these questions, you will be ready to plan, compose, and practice your speech.

Step 2: ORGANIZE IDEAS

Arrange your ideas in either chronological order or order of importance. Use chronological, or time, order to talk about a series of events or a process, as in a speech about programming a VCR. Use order of importance to analyze a topic or to present arguments in a persuasive speech.

Step 3: USE SPEECH-MAKING STRATEGIES

Use sentence variety. Make your speech interesting by varying the length and structure of your sentences.

Repeat key words and phrases. Stress key points by repeating words and phrases and by summarizing ideas.

> **FROM A WRITER**
>
> 66 *It usually takes three weeks to plan a good impromptu speech!* 99
>
> —Mark Twain

Use parallelism. The use of similar words, phrases, and clauses to express similar ideas is called **parallelism.** When you use parallel structures in a speech, listeners will remember your words more easily.

MODEL FROM LITERATURE

Note how John F. Kennedy used both repetition and parallel structure in this excerpt from his Inaugural Address.

And so, **my fellow Americans: Ask not what** your country can do for you—**ask what** you can do for your country.

My fellow citizens of the world: **Ask not what** America will do for you, **but what** together we can do for your country.

—John F. Kennedy

Another example of these techniques is the following part of a speech given by William Wayne Keeler when he was elected chief of the Cherokee nation in 1971. He stirred the pride of his people by reminding them how their ancestors survived a tragic time in Cherokee history called the Trail of Tears. In 1838 the Cherokee were ordered to leave their homeland in Tennessee because white settlers wanted their lands. They were forced to march hundreds of miles to Oklahoma. Many died along the way. Note the strategies Keeler used in referring to that tragic time.

Trail of Tears (detail), 1838, Elisabeth James, Oklahoma Historical Society

MODEL FROM LITERATURE

This is a historic moment for all Cherokees. . . . We are a dauntless people. Our fathers would **not** bow to a stronger force. **Neither** have we ever bowed to it. **Not when we were** penniless; **nor when we were** without food to fill our children's stomachs. **Not when we were** without clothing to shield us against bitter winds that howl in the forgotten hollows between these hills; **nor when** these hallowed grounds on which we stand were a place of mockery and contempt for those who had herded us onto them.

—William Wayne Keeler

Sentence Structure
The first four sentences are brief statements. The fifth, a long fragment, sets a pattern followed in the last fragment.

Repetition
Note the repetition of not.

Parallel Structure
Note the repetiton of clauses.

Step 4: PRACTICE YOUR SPEECH

Practice aloud. Rehearse your speech in front of a mirror while you time it. If possible, tape-record or videotape your speech, and ask your family and friends for advice on how to improve your performance.

Memorize the speech but outline key points on note cards. Watching someone read a speech can be boring. Therefore, outline the main points of your speech on note cards and memorize the rest. That will help you look at your audience most of the time and glance down only occasionally at your note cards to remind you of your main points.

Step 5: DELIVER YOUR SPEECH

Relax while delivering the speech. Stand up straight. Distribute your weight evenly on both feet. Do not fidget or pace. Use natural gestures and facial expressions to emphasize your points.

Look at your audience. Make brief eye contact with individuals in different parts of the room. Try to make each person think you are speaking directly to him or her. Another strategy is to find a face that inspires confidence and speak to that person.

Use your voice well. Speak so that you can be understood and heard. Otherwise, you may lose your audience's attention.

Experienced speakers often ask people to raise their hands if they cannot hear.

Pause when appropriate. Give your audience at least three or four seconds to think about an idea before you go on to the next one. Dramatic pauses help emphasize your important points.

Watch for audience cues. The expressions on your listeners' faces can tell you how they are receiving your message. The following chart lists possible trouble signs and solutions.

TROUBLE SIGN	PROBLEM	POSSIBLE SOLUTION
People are looking at their watches or fidgeting.	The audience is becoming bored.	■ Vary the pitch and tone of your voice. ■ Move on to more interesting points.
People are leaning far forward and holding their hands behind their ears.	The audience can't hear you.	■ Speak louder. ■ Pause, and ask someone in the audience to shut doors and windows to keep out noise.
People are looking at one another and seem puzzled.	The audience is confused.	■ Summarize your main ideas. ■ Give examples. ■ Ask for questions.

Use the following checkpoints to revise a speech you have drafted:

CHECKPOINTS FOR REVISING

► Have I fulfilled my purpose?

► Have I used words that suit the occasion, audience, and purpose?

► Have I organized my speech so that it is easy to follow?

► Have I used rhythm, repetition, and sentence variety?

► Have I practiced delivering my speech in a relaxed manner, paying attention to the quality of my voice?

50

SPEAKING AND LISTENING PROJECTS: INTERVIEW

▶ *How do I conduct an interview?*

Imagine having lunch with a new friend. He is a little shy, but you're curious, so you ask him about his life. "Where were you born?" you ask. "Who are your parents and what do they do?" Although you may not think of yourself as a talk-show host, you are conducting an informal interview.

> An **interview** is a focused question-and-answer conversation between two people. The interviewer usually asks the questions and the subject responds.

There are two types of interviews: informal and formal. You do an informal interview when you ask a friend questions to satisfy your curiosity. In a formal interview, on the other hand, you usually plan the questions ahead of time. You have a set purpose in asking the questions and may bring a notebook or tape recorder to record the answers.

GUIDELINES

An interview

▶ has one or more of the following purposes: informing, persuading, evaluating, and entertaining.

▶ has a clear focus.

▶ includes questions that fulfill the purpose and focus of the interview.

▶ follows either the question-and-answer or the narrative format.

▶ may be incorporated into many different types of writing, such as I-Search reports, newspaper or magazine articles, books, or oral history projects. A taped or videotaped version may also be aired publicly or kept as documentation for a project.

HOW SHOULD I PLAN MY INTERVIEW?

Imagine you are working on a social studies unit about the problems of homeless people. Your teacher suggests that you interview someone who works with homeless people in your community. Before you rush out with your notebook or tape recorder, ask yourself the following questions about your purpose and audience.

Purpose and Audience

- What is the purpose of my interview? What do I want to find out?

- Who is my audience? Will they be familiar with the person I'm interviewing?

- What is the focus of my interview? Is it my subject's life, or is it a specific part of my subject's life?

Once you've determined your purpose, audience, and focus, you're ready to get started. Research your subject. If your subject is a public figure, look up articles about him or her in a local newspaper or in the *Readers' Guide to Periodical Literature*. If you're especially interested in finding out about a special project—perhaps a restaurant for homeless people—use resources to familiarize yourself with the project.

TRY THIS

To test whether your questions lead to specific, full answers or to the dead-end "yes" or "no," role-play your interview with a classmate. Use the list of questions you have composed.

After you have done some background research, make an appointment with your subject. Politely introduce yourself, explain the purpose of your interview, and tell where you plan to publish your interview or how you plan to use the information you gather. You might even ask if your subject can give you printed information about a specific topic before the interview.

Use this and other background information to help you write out a list of questions suited to your purpose and focus. Your questions should be open-ended. In other words, avoid questions that can be answered with a simple "yes" or "no."

To create open-ended questions, avoid beginning with the words *do* or *does*. Instead, use *who, what, when, where, why,* and *how* words, as in "How did you get the idea to start a restaurant for homeless people?"

HOW DO I CONDUCT THE INTERVIEW?

Before you sit down to talk, ask permission to use your tape recorder and test it to make sure it is working properly. If you are taking notes for the interview, make sure you have enough paper. Keep these pointers in mind as you conduct your interview:

- Open with a question that is not directly related to your topic but is about something of special interest to your subject. Starting the interview in this way may help relax your subject and make it easier for the two of you to establish rapport.

- Invite your subject to express opinions and feelings, provide anecdotes, and tell stories, as well as give facts.

- Let your subject tell his or her own story. Avoid leading questions, and don't put words in your subject's mouth.

- Listen. Focus on what your subject is saying rather than worry about your next question. If you listen carefully, you'll come up with good follow-up questions.

- Don't exhaust your subject. When you have answers to all your prepared questions and have followed up on them, thank your subject politely. Remember to request permission to call back in case you need to ask an additional question or check a fact.

HOW DO I WRITE UP THE INTERVIEW?

You may want to transcribe the interview from your notes, or make a written copy from your tape. Then you must decide how to organize your material. There are two ways to present it:

THE QUESTION-AND-ANSWER FORMAT (Q-AND-A)
This is an edited version of your interview. It consists of a series of questions and answers. You may shorten it if you need to, but you must use the subject's exact words.

THE NARRATIVE ARTICLE Use the information from your interview to write an article about your topic. While most of the article will be in your words, it will also contain direct quotations.

HOW SHOULD I REVISE MY INTERVIEW?

You should plan on revising the first draft of your interview. As you revise it, ask yourself the following questions:

CHECKPOINTS FOR REVISING

▶ Do I give my audience enough background information to understand my subject and what my subject does?

▶ Does my writing have a consistent focus, whether it is broad or narrow? Do I need to sharpen the focus and delete material that isn't related?

▶ Do I include information from the interview, such as the subject's opinions, personal feelings, anecdotes, or plays on words, that help reveal my subject as a person?

▶ Do I follow a consistent format?

▶ Do I incorporate information from my interview into an appropriate written form, such as a report, newspaper or magazine article, book, or oral history project?

Here is an example of an interview in a question-and-answer format:

M O D E L

The interviewer begins with a question to set the subject at ease.

Q: Mrs. Garcia, I've heard that you love to cook. What's the favorite dish you make and how do you make it?

A: I do love to cook and other people like my cooking, too. Back when I lived in Chicago, I won second place in a citywide rib barbeque contest. My ribs are hot, spiced with Mexican spices—chili peppers, cilantro, cumin. But my favorite dish is a thick, cheesy cornbread. It goes with everything. I'm getting hungry just describing it.

After relaxing the subject, the interviewer goes on to a broad introductory question.

Q: Let me get some background information. When did you start working with homeless people?

A: I started about five years ago when I was living in Chicago. I helped run a shelter for homeless women and their children.

Q: Why did you decide to open a restaurant for homeless people here in St. Louis?

A: I had read about similar restaurants in New York City and Washington, D.C., and I decided we needed one here at home.

The interviewer doesn't offer an opinion.

Q: How does the restaurant work?

A: The homeless people are referred to the restaurant by social service agencies. People have meal tickets given to them by an agency; they don't have to pay. They are allowed to come twice a month. It's not like a soup kitchen where people come two or three times a day.

Questions are brief and to the point.

Q: What else makes your restaurant different from a soup kitchen?

A: It gives people dignity. Instead of waiting in a long line and being handed bowls of soup, they sit at a table with linens and flowers and order their own food.

This follow-up question probes more deeply.

Q: What kinds of meals do you serve?

A: We serve lunch only. Yesterday, let's see, we had a choice of Cajun chicken with rice and black-eyed peas or pork chops with fried apples. I bet that's better than what you had at school!

The interview ends on a light note.

51

MULTIMEDIA PROJECTS: ORAL HISTORY

 What is an oral history?

> An **oral history** is a personal recollection in the form of a recording or script of a recording.

Instead of just reading about events, styles, and ideas of recent times, why not interview someone who experienced them firsthand? Preparing an oral history is a way to give a personal face to the past. It can also provide key background information for a large assignment such as a project on Americans' responses to lunar landings.

GUIDELINES

An oral history

▶ contains a person's complete and detailed memories of a topic or event.

▶ provides details that answer questions raised in a larger project.

▶ is recorded or transcribed so it can be easily listened to or read.

WHOM CAN I INTERVIEW?

Everyone has a story to tell. Do you know someone who served in the Gulf War or in Somalia? Has one of your friends or neighbors lived in another country? What do your older relatives remember about the Civil Rights Movement or the space race of the 1960's? Think about people you know who have had unusual experiences or who can provide insights into a topic you are studying. Once you have located some likely candidates to interview, call or write to them, asking if they would like to participate.

John Young on moon, Apollo 16

HOW DO I PREPARE FOR MY INTERVIEW?

In many ways, the preparation for an oral history interview is like that for a regular interview. You make an appointment with your subject, devise questions that will prompt your subject to talk, and make sure your recording equipment is working.

However, there are some special requirements for an oral history interview. Usually such an interview is part of a larger research project. You will therefore want to know how the interview will support that project. For instance, you may be studying the Civil Rights Movement of the 1960's. If your subject participated in that movement, you may want him or her to reflect on its historical impact and its continuing influence. In general, the clearer you are about the purpose of your oral history, the better your interview will go.

Also, remember that an oral history consists of one long reminiscence on a broad topic. The questions you ask may therefore be more open-ended than those in a regular interview. A typical opening question might be "What were your experiences in the Civil Rights Movement?" An oral history is a person's lengthy response to one or a few questions.

For more on interviewing, see p. 245.

HOW DO I CONDUCT MY INTERVIEW?

BE SURE THE RECORDER IS SET UP PROPERLY. Check to make sure that it is recording your subject's words loudly and clearly.

BRIEFLY INTRODUCE THE INTERVIEW. Identify the date, topic, and person being interviewed. Include some background on the person if you think it will be helpful.

MAKE YOUR SUBJECT FEEL AT EASE. Encourage the subject to tell the story in his or her own way, speaking freely in dialect, slang, or whatever other language seems natural for the occasion.

ASK QUESTIONS ONLY WHEN NECESSARY. Begin with your general question, and allow your subject to respond fully. If he or she comes to a standstill, ask an additional question that you think will spark a response. Ask additional questions if you must, but try not to take over your subject's story.

HOW DO I PREPARE THE FINAL PRODUCT?

Your final version of the oral history may take one of two forms.

FINAL PRODUCT 1: AN AUDIOCASSETTE

If your final product will be an audiocassette, you might edit the original taped interview to eliminate gaps, interruptions, repetition, or sections that seem unimportant. To edit, get a blank audiocassette and either a dual-cassette or second tape deck. Using the original audiocassette as your master, transfer all its relevant portions to the new audiocassette, which will become your final product. Be sure to label it; for example: "Oral History of Toni Topaz, Gulf War Veteran, Interviewed 9/11/95."

FINAL PRODUCT 2: A WRITTEN TRANSCRIPT

Your final product may take the form of a written transcript. In that case, you will have to listen carefully to the taped interview and write down precisely what the subject said. You may edit the interview to eliminate interruptions, repetition, or unimportant sections; however, indicate deletions by inserting ellipses (. . .), and place added material in parentheses. For those sections that you *do* include, use the subject's own words.

If your oral history is part of a larger project, make sure the material you include on the audiocassette or in the transcript contributes to the goal of the project. As you listen to your edited audiotape or reread your transcript, ask yourself questions like the following.

CHECKPOINTS FOR REVISING

▶ Does my subject give lengthy and detailed recollections?
▶ Does the content of the oral history contribute effectively to the purpose of the larger project?
▶ Have I labeled and identified the oral history?
▶ Are additions to or deletions from the transcript indicated by appropriate punctuation?

The subject of the following oral history is Cesar Rosas, lead guitarist and singer for Los Lobos, a well-known band that blends rock and traditional Mexican music.

MODEL FROM LITERATURE

When I was a little kid in Mexico I remember the Saturday night dances in the ranch. People would come from different areas. I'll never forget that, my mom and dad dancing. There was no electricity, right, so they'd bring generators and hang strings of light bulbs, sockets and extension cords, and all these bright light bulbs. That was the dance area and you'd have the Norteño (Mexican music style) groups. The Norteño guys, the *bajo sexto* (a stringed instrument), and the accordion doing all these great songs of the time. I've been collecting that kind of music maybe ten or fifteen years. . . . That was actually my first influence in music. When I came to the States as a kid I really loved music and rock and roll. This was before the Beatles, before all that stuff. This was right at the time that the fifties had gone over to the sixties: Ray Charles, Chubby Checker, the Rhythm Tens! Absolutely. I have such warm memories about that music. Those were my first influences with American rock and roll. It was a big, big influence on me. The songs were fresh.

—Marilyn P. Davis, *Mexican Voices/American Dreams*

Rosas tells his story in his own words, prompted perhaps by a general question about his background.

The interviewer uses parentheses to insert brief explanations of Spanish terms.

The ellipses indicate that material has been omitted by the editor.

52

MULTIMEDIA PROJECTS: DOCUMENTARY VIDEO

 How do I shoot a documentary video?

> A **documentary video** uses moving pictures to depict a news event, a person's life, a natural process, or a social problem or trend.

The word *documentary* comes from the word *document*, meaning "evidence." A documentary video is a taped factual record of a subject. People make documentaries for many reasons: such as to explore a subject that interests them or to express an opinion about an issue. Anyone can make a documentary. All you need is a subject and a video camera with a microphone.

CHOOSING A SUBJECT

A documentary video can be about almost anything. It is important, however, to have a purpose or a goal in mind when you choose a subject. Do you think a certain issue is important? Is there a particular subject that you know a lot about or would like to explore? Who will be your audience? Asking yourself questions like these can help you choose a subject for your video.

WRITING A DOCUMENTARY OUTLINE

Once you have chosen your subject, your first step is to outline your documentary. Divide a sheet of paper in half. At the left, list the video shots you want to get. At the right, describe the audio for each shot. You may find the following terms useful:

Close-up:	a view of a subject at close range
Cut to:	changing from one scene to the next
Dub in:	adding narration, music, or other sound effects to a tape
Establishing shot:	first shot of a series; shows general location
Fade:	making an image slowly appear (fade in) or disappear (fade out)
Live sound:	sound recorded along with the original pictures
Long shot:	looking at a subject from far away
Pan:	moving the camera smoothly in one direction
VO:	voice-over (the words of an unseen narrator)
Zoom:	coming in on a subject from far to close

The model that follows shows part of a documentary outline of a school basketball game.

<table>
<tr><th colspan="2">MODEL</th></tr>
<tr><td>Video</td><td>Audio</td></tr>
<tr><td>1. Establishing shot of school gym with fans arriving for game.</td><td>VO: Identify school, date, and occasion.</td></tr>
<tr><td>2. Show home team taking practice shots.</td><td>Live Sound: Students cheering in stands</td></tr>
<tr><td>3. Show opposition team coming onto court.</td><td>VO: Comment on won-and-lost records of both teams.</td></tr>
<tr><td>4. Cut to "reporter" standing on sidelines with coach.</td><td>Live Sound: Introduce coach and start brief interview.</td></tr>
</table>

Since a documentary does not contain fictional characters or fictional dialogue, it is not usually necessary to write a complete script. Some students prefer to **ad-lib**, or make up on the spot, the voice-overs and the dialogue. Others actually write out the exact words they will use in each voice-over, interview, and so on. If you choose to write the audio before you shoot, remember to estimate the time you will give to each shot and coordinate your text to fit. The following model shows an opening voice-over for the basketball game:

MODEL

VO#1

"Washington Junior High is a busy place tonight, November 11, as parents, teachers, and fans pour into the gym to see if the Blazers will trounce their rivals, the Pine Plains Panthers."

SHOOTING THE FOOTAGE

Most video cameras now have built-in controls that adjust automatically for focus, color balance, and lighting. If possible, however, avoid shooting in the unflattering glare and shadows of the noonday sun. As you shoot, follow your outline, keeping these points in mind:

KEEP YOUR SUBJECT MOVING. Making a video is different from taking still photographs. Most of the time you will want to show your subjects in motion.

BE SENSITIVE TO SOUND. The camera microphone will pick up live sound that may make your point. For some shots, however, you may want to use the "audio dub" option on a VCR to add narration, music, or other sound effects later.

VARY YOUR SHOTS AND CAMERA ANGLES. Try for a good balance of long shots, pans, and close-ups.

KEEP THE CAMERA STEADY. When you pan, don't move the camera too quickly. If you're doing an interview, place the camera on a tripod. Avoid using the zoom lens during a shot. Instead, use it between shots to change the viewpoint. Never walk with a camera while filming. If you do, you'll end up with a jiggling, distracting sequence. Stand still and let your subjects do the moving.

EXPECT THE UNEXPECTED. Some of the best video footage results from spontaneous, unrehearsed words or actions. In this way, video is like photography. Stay alert to take advantage of the unexpected!

EDITING YOUR DOCUMENTARY VIDEO

The final stage of preparing a video program is editing. In editing, you copy sections of the original onto a fresh tape in whatever order you wish. The extent of the editing process will vary, depending on the specific features of your equipment. Whatever equipment you use, however, the following general guidelines will be helpful:

GUIDELINES

▶ Review all your footage first, jotting down notes on the best scenes.

▶ Keeping in mind your purpose for making your video, select the shots you want to keep, arranging them in order on a final list. Remember that your viewers will be influenced by what they see, and so selecting your final shots is one of the most important steps in the documentary process.

▶ Look at the footage a second time, noting the exact counter numbers on your camera or VCR for the scenes selected. Counter numbers help you track where scenes begin and end on your tape.

▶ Make a preliminary version of your documentary. Be sure to copy your shots in the correct order after you have made clean edits or deletions. Use your list of counter numbers as a guide.

▶ Decide which scenes need voice-overs or sound effects.

▶ Use your equipment to dub in additional sound.

For more information on any stage of this process, consult the following handbook written for grades 6–9: *Video Power: A Complete Guide to Writing, Planning, and Shooting Videos* by Tom Shactman and Harriet Shelare, ©1988, Henry Holt and Company.

53

MULTIMEDIA PROJECTS: MAGAZINE

How can I put together a class magazine?

Do you have a favorite magazine? Many people can name one or more magazines that they look forward to reading each week or month. There are all kinds of magazines for people with all kinds of interests, and most readers feel as though their favorite magazines are written just for them.

Did you ever stop to think of all the steps that go into the creation of a popular magazine? Creating a classroom magazine of your own is a great way to learn about this fascinating form of publishing. You and your classmates will have to divide among you the many tasks involved. The steps that follow will help you to plan your product, divide the work, and issue a magazine that's a treat for the eyes as well as the mind.

EDITOR: STEPHANIE BROWN
ART EDITOR: JIMMY RICARDO
CIRCULATION MANAGER: WAYNE WONG
ADVERTISING MANAGER: SUSAN CHANG
BOOK REVIEW EDITOR: ALI McDOWELL
ASSOCIATE EDITORS: TARA FRAMER, KRISTIN BJORNSTADTER

Step 1: FIND A FOCUS AND AN AUDIENCE

Depending on the kind of magazine you want to publish, you could ask each classmate to submit his or her favorite piece of writing for publication. It might be more fun, however, to focus each issue of your magazine on a different topic, like sports or music, or a type of writing, like fiction, poetry, or essays. Before you choose a focus, decide on an audience for your work. Will your readers be other students in your school? Family members? Teachers? Other adults in the community? Knowing your audience will help you choose the type of pieces they will enjoy.

Step 2: MAKE CONTENT AND DESIGN WORK TOGETHER

Who will decide what to publish in your magazine? Will you include drawings or photos? Will your magazine contain such features as advice columns, letters from readers, and editorials? Your decisions on these matters will depend on your focus, your audience, and the interests of your classmates.

Plan a table of contents for your magazine. Then study your favorite magazines to get ideas for designing your publication. Don't forget to choose a title.

Step 3: PUT TOGETHER A FIRST ISSUE

When the contents of the issue have been chosen, use stiff paper boards to plan the **layout,** or the arrangement of the elements on each page. Study the layout boards that appear above. They show how much space each selection, feature, and illustration will occupy. The boards also show how these elements will be positioned on each page. Your writers and artists may need to alter their work so that it will fit the available space. Remember also to leave room for a table of contents. After the writing, typing or word processing, and illustrations are completed, paste up each page as it will look in the finished version. Insert the table of contents. Photocopy the pages and assemble your magazine.

COMPUTER TIP

Desktop publishing software can help you create a professional-looking publication. You can design and lay out the magazine content onscreen, leaving space for art. Some software allows you to create or reproduce art and to use color.

Step 4: DISTRIBUTE YOUR MAGAZINE

Deliver your magazine to your readers. After they have read the first issue, ask them for comments that will help you plan future issues. Your first issue might include a form with questions like these:

- Which selections interested you most, and why?

- Which selections interested you least? What changes would have made these items more interesting?

- Which illustrations were most effective? Why?

- What hobbies or interests do you have that you would like to read about in a magazine?

- What magazines do you read regularly?

- What would you like to see included in future issues of *this* magazine?

 WRITING FOR SCIENCE

Some national magazines are directed at science-minded readers. You can slant your magazine in the same way. Decide whether to offer a broad range of general science articles or to focus, instead, on a specific area, such as astronomy. Your magazine might include some of the following kinds of writing:

- articles on experiments done in your school
- reviews of science fair entries
- articles presenting science news, and quoting and referring to information in news programs, newspapers, or magazines
- reviews of books or movies with a scientific slant
- interviews with science teachers or scientists
- photos and drawings of scientific phenomena
- write-ups of exhibits and programs at science centers or museums

MULTIMEDIA PROJECTS: MULTIMEDIA PRESENTATION

54

What is a multimedia presentation?

Someone places a lei around your neck and the room fills with the sound of guitars. On a screen flash images of erupting volcanoes, surfers, and hula dancers. Someone hands you a slice of juicy pineapple and then walks to the front of the room and says, "Images of Hawaii: Fact or Fiction? I hope my presentation will help you decide."

> A **multimedia presentation** uses two or more media, or forms of communication.

WHAT MEDIA CAN I USE?

Whatever people can look at, listen to, read, touch, smell, or taste can be used for a multimedia presentation. The media you choose will depend on the topic, the audience, and the available equipment. Possibilities include tapes, slides, art works, and artifacts.

These guidelines will help you give a good presentation:

GUIDELINES

A multimedia presentation

▶ presents information about a topic of interest.

▶ delivers information through a variety of media.

▶ appeals to different senses and different ways of learning.

▶ has a unified focus.

▶ gives accurate facts and credits others for their words or ideas.

HOW DO I CHOOSE A TOPIC?

It's best to find a topic of interest to both you and your audience. Then ask yourself whether your topic can be presented in a multimedia format. If not, why not do a traditional written report? Finally, be realistic: Choose a topic you can cover in the time available and with the equipment you have.

Following are four topics for a multimedia presentation. Suppose you decided that two of them would work better as research reports. Here is how you could classify the ideas:

BETTER FOR A MULTIMEDIA REPORT	BETTER FOR A RESEARCH REPORT
Modern-day Indian music	Asian democracies
Behind the scenes at the radio station where Mom works	Behind the scenes at the Census Bureau

HOW DO I GATHER INFORMATION?

Collecting information for a multimedia presentation can be like a scavenger hunt. What you're after is not just information but interesting ways of conveying that information to your audience. What can you give them to look at, listen to, and touch?

BEFORE YOU START GATHERING INFORMATION,
- **list the questions** you want to answer.

- **put together a multimedia resource kit,** ranging from a camera, a tape recorder, or a video camera to boxes for the objects you find. Don't forget a notebook.

TO FIND MULTIMEDIA MATERIALS,
- **visit the library.** Check books, records, and databases.

- **visit museums, historical societies, factories, and other businesses.** Look for art works, documents, and artifacts—objects that represent a people's way of life.

- **talk to people** who know about your topic.

DURING YOUR SEARCH,
- **if possible, arrange to borrow items** you want to use in your multimedia presentation.

- **research information** about any art works, documents, or artifacts you borrow so that you can give credit to the lenders as you tell your audience about the resources. Also, be sure you know when and to whom you are supposed to return each one.

HOW DO I DEVELOP A COMPLETE PLAN?

When you're putting together a multimedia presentation, you will need to develop a plan that includes a traditional outline, a diagram or a flowchart, and a script. Here is a complete strategy for planning such a presentation:

1. Make an outline, as you would for a research report. Next to each heading, indicate the multimedia resources that you will collect to show your audience.

MODEL

Outline for a Multimedia Presentation
of Indian Music

I. Classical music: Audiotape of Ali Akbar Khan;
Photograph of musicians at a traditional Hindu
wedding; slide of Kathak dancer

    A. The groups of musicians: Slides of group of 4
       musicians, group of 2

    B. The instruments: Audiotape of Vilayat Khan
       and Ali Akbar Khan playing sitar, vina,
       sarod; Uncle Vijay's tablas (drums)

II. Popular music: Videotape of scene from The
Wicked King, a contemporary Indian movie

---

2. Create a diagram or a flowchart that shows the order in which you will present your information. For some presentations you will need to show some media at the same time. In those situations, you should note on your diagram the joint use of media.

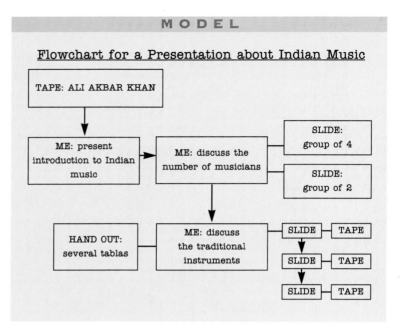

Flowchart for a Presentation about Indian Music

Some computer programs give you the ability to create flowcharts. If you have access to such a program, see whether it can help you plan your presentation.

3. Finally, create a script based on your chart—something you can refer to or even read from during your presentation.

HOW CAN I PRESENT MY MULTIMEDIA REPORT?

The success of your presentation will depend largely on your preparation. Here are some steps you may wish to follow:

BEFORE THE AUDIENCE ARRIVES

1. Prepare your equipment. Plug in and test your tape recorder, VCR, or other machines to make sure they are working. Check to see that slides are right side up and in order in their carousel.

2. Rehearse your helpers. Run through all the steps of the presentation with your helpers to make sure everyone knows what to do and when.

WHEN THE AUDIENCE ARRIVES

1. Begin your presentation on time.

2. Follow your script.

ANTICIPATE PROBLEMS

Try to devise solutions to potential problems.

PROBLEM	▶ POSSIBLE SOLUTION
"How can I show everyone my color pictures without having to make costly color slides?"	See if your school has an opaque overhead projector you can borrow for your presentation.
"How can I make sure my tapes get played in the right order?"	Edit all the sounds you plan to use onto one tape, leaving a short gap between items.
"What if I drop my script and the pages get out of order during my presentation?"	Copy your script into a notebook, or put loose pages in a three-ring binder.

CHECKPOINTS FOR REVISING

▶ Have I presented information on an interesting topic? Have I used a variety of media that appeal to different senses and different ways of learning?

▶ Does my presentation have a unified focus?

▶ Have I checked the accuracy of all the facts I have presented?

▶ Have I credited others for their words or ideas?

▶ Have I made the best use of all available technology?

Here is part of a script for a multimedia presentation:

MODEL

[TAPE: Ali Akbar Khan]

[FADE TAPE TO QUIET BACKGROUND LEVEL]

What you hear is the music of Ali Akbar Khan, a classical musician from India. My family listens to this music all the time. My parents came from India, and many of my relatives are musicians.

Today, I'll tell you a bit about Indian music. A classical Indian musical group is never large.

The directions are in capital letters so that they stand out.

The writer has written a script of the introduction, though in practice the words in the script may not be followed exactly.

Now the writer presents a new medium: slides.

[SLIDE: Group of four musicians]

Four musicians would be a large group. Often there is just a drummer and someone to play or sing the melody.

[SLIDE: Two Indian musicians]

The musicians start with a melody and then vary it again and again. This can go on for hours, and the music usually gets faster as the improvisation continues.

[TAPE: Ali Akbar Khan: faster music: middle of tape]

[TAPE: Ali Akbar Khan: fastest music: end of tape]

Perhaps you'd like to see some of the instruments used in this kind of music. This is a drum called a tabla.

[HAND TABLA TO SOMEONE IN AUDIENCE]

It belongs to my Uncle Vijay. Go ahead and hit it with your fingers. See how different each of the three rings sounds!

[SLIDE: Sitar] [TAPE: Sitar music]

Back here you see some stringed instruments. This one is called a sitar. This

[SLIDE: Sarod] [TAPE: Sarod music]

is called a sarod, and this

[SLIDE: Vina] [TAPE: Vina music]

is called a vina.

Each slide is accompanied by a sentence or two identifying the relationship of what is shown to the subject of Indian music.

When only segments of a longer tape are being used, the writer lists each separately, indicating where each appears on the tape.

The writer does not have to describe the drum in words since the audience can see and handle it.

Here two media work together: The tape lets the audience hear the instrument shown on the slide.

Grammar, Usage, and Mechanics

■ ■ ■

Applying the Rules in Your Writing

Incident in the Library I, 1983, Julian Opie
Courtesy Hal Bromm Gallery

Problem Solver

This Problem Solver gives examples of errors that student writers often make and tells you how to correct them. In each section of the Problem Solver, you will find one or more strategies to correct the error as well as sample revisions. To solve a problem quickly, use the following table of contents.

RUN-ON SENTENCES

55

A run-on sentence strings one or more main clauses together without adequate punctuation. A main clause contains a subject and a verb and can stand alone as a complete sentence.

55A PROBLEM: Two main clauses with no punctuation between them:

Error: Our class read *A Christmas Carol* last year some students suggested that we perform it as a class play.

Revision: Our class read *A Christmas Carol* last year. Some students suggested that we perform it as a class play.

> Separate the clauses with an end mark. Capitalize the next word.

Revision: Our class read *A Christmas Carol* last year; some students suggested that we perform it as a class play.

> Use a semicolon between the main clauses.

Revision: Our class read *A Christmas Carol* last year, and some students suggested that we perform it as a class play.

> Use a comma and a coordinating conjunction between the main clauses.

55B PROBLEM: Two main clauses separated only by a comma:

Error: Mr. Lopez agreed to direct, he held auditions to cast the parts.

Revision: Mr. Lopez agreed to direct. He held auditions to cast the parts.

> Create two sentences with an end mark.

Revision: Mr. Lopez agreed to direct; he held auditions to cast the parts.

> Use a semicolon between the two main clauses.

Revision: Mr. Lopez agreed to direct, so he held auditions to cast the parts.

> Add a coordinating conjunction.

56A PROBLEM: A fragment that lacks a subject:

Error: Students tried out for different roles. Wanted to play the part of Scrooge or one of the ghosts.

Add a subject to make the frag- ment a complete sentence.

Revision: Students tried out for different roles. Many wanted to play the part of Scrooge or one of the ghosts.

Combine the frag- ment with a sentence.

Revision: Students tried out for different roles, such as the part of Scrooge or one of the ghosts.

56B PROBLEM: A fragment that lacks a verb:

Error: Several of my friends chose to be on the tech crew. The group in charge of scenery, lighting, and props.

Make the frag- ment a sentence by adding a verb.

Revision: Several of my friends chose to be on the tech crew. The group is in charge of scenery, lighting, and props.

Combine the frag- ment with a sentence.

Revision: Several of my friends chose to be on the tech crew, the group in charge of scenery, lighting, and props.

Error: Auditions began after school. Classmates sit- ting eagerly in the auditorium.

Add a verb to the fragment.

Revision: Auditions began after school. Classmates were sitting eagerly in the auditorium.

56C PROBLEM: A fragment that is a subordinate clause:

Error: After everyone had read a passage. Our direc- tor announced his casting decisions.

Revision: After everyone had read a passage, our director announced his casting decisions.

Combine the fragment with another sentence.

Revision: Everyone read a passage. Our director then announced his casting decisions.

Rewrite the fragment as a sentence.

56D PROBLEM: A fragment that lacks both a subject and verb:

Error: Our schedule was going to be hectic. With only three weeks of rehearsals before the first performance.

Revision: With only three weeks of rehearsals before the first performance, our schedule was going to be hectic.

Combine the fragment with a sentence.

LACK OF SUBJECT-VERB AGREEMENT

57A PROBLEM: A subject separated from a verb by a prepositional phrase:

Error: Rehearsals of each scene is necessary.

Revision: Rehearsals of each scene are necessary.

Make the verb agree in number with its subject.

57B PROBLEM: A subject that follows the verb (inverted order):

Error: On the director depends key decisions.

Revision: On the director depend key decisions.

Make the verb agree with its subject.

Error: There is also important tasks for the stage manager.

Revision: There are also important tasks for the stage manager.

Make the verb agree with its subject.

57C PROBLEM: A compound subject joined by *and*:

Error: Khawanna and Bobby was in charge of props.

If the parts of the subject name more than one thing, use a plural verb.

Revision: Khawanna and Bobby were in charge of props.

Error: My neighbor and best friend were the lighting designer.

If the parts of the subject refer to the same thing, use a singular verb.

Revision: My neighbor and best friend was the lighting designer.

57D PROBLEM: A compound subject joined by *or* or *nor*:

Error: Neither the Lockyear twins nor Samson were ever absent from rehearsals.

Make the verb agree with the subject part closer to the verb.

Revision: Neither the Lockyear twins nor Samson was ever absent from rehearsals.

57E PROBLEM: A compound subject preceded by *many a*, *every*, or *each*:

Error: Each actor and understudy have to memorize his lines.

Use a singular verb.

Revision: Each actor and understudy has to memorize his lines.

57F PROBLEM: A subject separated from a verb by an intervening expression:

Error: Set design, as well as costume design, take time.

Make the verb agree with its subject, *design*. Ignore *as well as*, *in addition to*, and *together with*.

Revision: Set design, as well as costume design, takes time.

57G PROBLEM: A collective noun as subject:

Error: The cast rehearse often.

Revision: The cast rehearses often.

If the subject refers to a whole group, use a singular verb.

Error: The cast offers different ideas about how to interpret each role.

Revision: The cast offer different ideas about how to interpret each role.

If the subject refers to group members, use a plural verb.

57H PROBLEM: An indefinite pronoun as subject:

Error: Each of the cast members have lines to memorize.

Revision: Each of the cast members has lines to memorize.

If the subject is a singular pronoun, use a singular verb.

Error: Some of the play consist of stage directions.

Revision: Some of the play consists of stage directions.

The indefinite pronoun *some* refers to a singular noun. Use a singular verb.

Error: Some of the stage directions tells actors how to move and speak.

Revision: Some of the stage directions tell actors how to move and speak.

The indefinite pronoun *some* refers to a plural noun. Use a plural verb.

INCORRECT VERB TENSES AND SHIFTS

58

58A PROBLEM: An incorrectly formed irregular verb:

Error: We all knowed the production would be hard work.

See the list of irregular verbs on p. 403.

Revision: We all knew the production would be hard work.

58B PROBLEM: Confusion between the past form and the past participle:

Error: The technical crew had chose Felipe as special effects manager.

Use the past participle form after the helping verb.

Revision: The technical crew had chosen Felipe as special effects manager.

Error: Roberto rung a gong to signal the start of rehearsals.

The past participle cannot be the main verb. Replace it with the past form.

Revision: Roberto rang a gong to signal the start of rehearsals.

58C PROBLEM: An incorrect shift in tense:

Error: As Pam rattled a heavy chain, Roberto accidentally drops the gong.

When events occur at the same time, use the same tense.

Revision: As Pam rattled a heavy chain, Roberto accidentally dropped the gong.

58D PROBLEM: Failure to shift tense to show that one event preceded another:

Error: Since the final rehearsal went so smoothly, this opening-night catastrophe came unexpectedly.

When events occur at different times, shift tenses to show the time sequence.

Revision: Since the final rehearsal had gone so smoothly, this opening-night catastrophe came unexpectedly.

INCORRECT PRONOUN SHIFTS AND PRONOUN REFERENCE

59A PROBLEM: A singular antecedent that can be male or female:

Error: Each class member enjoyed making his contribution to the play.

Revision: Each class member enjoyed making his or her contribution to the play.

Use both a male and female pronoun.

Revision: Class members enjoyed making their contributions to the play.

Reword to make the antecedent and the pronoun plural.

Revision: Each class member enjoyed contributing to the play.

Reword to eliminate the pronoun.

59B PROBLEM: A second-person pronoun that refers to a third-person antecedent:

Error: Denzel loved playing Scrooge because you could have so much fun with the part.

Revision: Denzel loved playing Scrooge because he could have so much fun with the part.

Use the third-person pronoun.

Revision: Denzel loved playing Scrooge because a performer could have so much fun with the part.

Use a noun instead of the pronoun.

59C PROBLEM: An incorrect shift in person between two pronouns:

Error: We hated Scrooge at first, but you felt more sympathetic later.

Revision: We hated Scrooge at first, but we felt more sympathetic later.

Use a pronoun in the same person as the antecedent.

Use an antecedent in the same person as the pronoun.

Revision: You hated Scrooge at first, but you felt more sympathetic later.

Reword to avoid the second pronoun.

Revision: We hated Scrooge at first but felt more sympathetic later.

59D PROBLEM: A singular indefinite pronoun as an antecedent:

Error: Each of the ghosts had their moments on stage.

Change the personal pronoun to a singular form.

Revision: Each of the ghosts had its moments on stage.

Change the indefinite pronoun to a plural form.

Revision: All of the ghosts had their moments on stage.

Reword to avoid the indefinite pronoun.

Revision: The ghosts had their moments on stage.

59E PROBLEM: A vague or weak pronoun reference:

Error: Marley's ghost entered, which made a racket.

Reword and add a clear antecedent.

Revision: Marley's ghost entered in chains, which made a racket.

Error: The ghost scared Scrooge, and that was only the beginning.

Use an appropriate noun instead of the pronoun.

Revision: The ghost scared Scrooge, and its visit was only the beginning.

59F PROBLEM: A pronoun that could refer to more than one antecedent:

Error: When Scrooge met the Ghost of Christmas Past, he was upset.

Revision: When Scrooge met the Ghost of Christmas Past, Scrooge was upset.

Use a noun instead of the pronoun.

Revision: Meeting the Ghost of Christmas Past upset Scrooge.

Reword to eliminate the pronoun.

Revision: Scrooge was upset when he met the Ghost of Christmas Past.

Reword to clarify the antecedent.

59G PROBLEM: The use of *they* or *you* without a clear antecedent:

Error: In the class production, they had some moving performances.

Revision: The class production had some moving performances.

Reword to eliminate the pronoun.

Error: In Tiny Tim's scenes, you were often moved to tears.

Revision: In Tiny Tim's scenes, the audience was often moved to tears.

Use a noun instead of the pronoun.

MISPLACED OR DANGLING MODIFIERS

60

60A PROBLEM: Misplacing the adverb *only*:

Error: Scrooge only loved money.

Revision: Scrooge loved only money.

Place *only* before the word or phrase it modifies.

60B PROBLEM: A misplaced modifier:

Error: Bob Cratchit asked the old miser for a special request in a timid voice.

Move the modifier
closer to the term
it modifies.

Revision: In a timid voice, Bob Cratchit asked the old miser for a special request.

Error: Cratchit spoke to Scrooge, hoping for time off at Christmas.

Move the modifier
closer to the term
it modifies.

Revision: Hoping for time off at Christmas, Cratchit spoke to Scrooge.

60C PROBLEM: A dangling modifier:

Error: After working all year, a holiday had been earned.

Reword to include
the term modified.

Revision: After working all year, Bob Cratchit had earned a holiday.

Error: Refusing Cratchit's request, Christmas became another work day.

Reword to include
the term modified.

Revision: Refusing Cratchit's request, Scrooge made Christmas another work day.

MISSING OR MISPLACED POSSESSIVE APOSTROPHES

61A PROBLEM: Possessive forms of singular nouns:

Error: Scrooges coldness had made him forget Christmas meaning.

Revision: Scrooge's coldness had made him forget Christmas's meaning.

Use an apostrophe and -s to form the possessive of every singular noun.

61B PROBLEM: Possessive forms of plural nouns ending in *-s*:

Error: Scrooge almost spoiled the Cratchit's Christmas plans.

Revision: Scrooge almost spoiled the Cratchits' Christmas plans.

To form the possessive of a plural noun ending in -s, use an apostrophe after the -s.

Error: Could the ghosts visits change his outlook?

Revision: Could the ghosts' visits change his outlook?

Do not omit the apostrophe in the possessive of a plural noun that ends in -s.

61C PROBLEM: Possessive forms of plural nouns not ending in *-s*:

Error: Scrooge failed to recognize other peoples needs.

Revision: Scrooge failed to recognize other people's needs.

To form the possessive of a plural noun not ending in -s, use an apostrophe and -s.

61D PROBLEM: Incorrect possessive apostrophes in plural nouns:

Error: Could the ghost's show Scrooge his error's about life?

Revision: Could the ghosts show Scrooge his errors about life?

61E PROBLEM: Possessive forms of pronouns:

Error: Scrooge laughed scornfully at everyones Christmas spirit.

Revision: Scrooge laughed scornfully at everyone's Christmas spirit.

Error: Nevertheless, the last laugh was their's.

Revision: Nevertheless, the last laugh was theirs.

61F PROBLEM: Confusion between *its* and *it's*:

Error: *A Christmas Carol* has it's serious side.

Revision: *A Christmas Carol* has its serious side.

Error: Its also an entertaining story.

Revision: It's also an entertaining story.

Do not use an apostrophe to make a noun plural.

Use an apostrophe and -s for the possessive of a singular indefinite pronoun.

Do not use an apostrophe for the possessive of a personal pronoun.

Do not use an apostrophe in the possessive personal pronoun its.

Use an apostrophe in the contraction of it is or it has.

62 MISSING COMMAS

62A PROBLEM: Missing commas in a series:

Error: Ghosts show Scrooge the past present and future.

Revision: Ghosts show Scrooge the past, present, and future.

Error: Scrooge sees scenes from his youth from his present life and after his death.

Use commas to separate three or more words in a series. Include a comma before the conjunction.

Revision: Scrooge sees scenes from his youth, from his present life, and after his death.

Use commas to separate three or more phrases or clauses.

62B PROBLEM: Missing commas with coordinate adjectives (adjectives that modify separately and equally):

Error: *A Christmas Carol* is a warm memorable tale.

Revision: *A Christmas Carol* is a warm, memorable tale.

Use a comma to separate adjectives that can be reversed.

Error: It is a popular, family classic.

Revision: It is a popular family classic.

Do not use a comma between adjectives that cannot be reversed.

Alphabetized Terms and Lessons

The Alphabetized Terms and Lessons listed here provide definitions of grammatical elements and examples of usage. Follow the cross-references after each definition to see more detailed information on a topic and to find related sections in the Problem Solver.

63 ABBREVIATIONS

IDENTIFYING ABBREVIATIONS

> **Abbreviations** are shortened forms of words.

1. Use periods with most abbreviations:

Titles:	Mr.	Dr.	Rev.	Ph.D.
Organizations:	Inc.	Co.	Corp.	Assn.
Units of Measure:	ft.	in.	oz.	qt.
Addresses:	St.	Rd.	Ave.	Blvd.

Capitalize the following abbreviations for times and dates:

TIMES: A.M., P.M.   **DATES:** B.C., A.D.

The abbreviation B.C. (before Christ) is written after the date; the abbreviation A.D. (in the year of our Lord) is written before the date: 753 B.C.; A.D. 1995.

2. Units in the metric system are abbreviated without periods:

cm = centimeters
m = meters
km = kilometers

g = gram
kg = kilogram
L = liters

Abbreviate the names of certain organizations, companies, and government agencies by using the first letter of each word. Do not use periods:

CIA = Central Intelligence Agency
OPEC = Organization of Petroleum Exporting Countries
AMA = American Medical Association
IBM = International Business Machines

ABSTRACT NOUN: a noun that names something that cannot be perceived by any of the five senses [See **Nouns**.]

64

ACTION VERB: a verb that expresses physical or mental action [See **Verbs**.]

65

ACTIVE VOICE: any verb form indicating that the subject performs the action [See **Verbs**.]

66

ADDRESSES

67

WRITING ADDRESSES

1. When addressing envelopes, use a comma between the name of the city or town and the state or between the city or district and the country. Do not use a comma between the state or country and the ZIP or postal code.

372 Morse Avenue
Sacramento, CA 95825

120 D. P. Sasmal Road
Calcutta, India 700 033

Remember to use the correct two-letter postal abbreviations for states when you are addressing an envelope. Do not use periods.

◆ WHEN YOU WRITE ◆

Do not use postal abbreviations for states within a sentence, as in "I live in AZ."
CORRECT FORM: I live in Arizona.

2. Use numerals for both streets and avenues numbered over ten and for all house, apartment, and room numbers. Spell out both streets and avenues numbered ten or under.

324 West **79**th Street
Apartment **4B**

246 **Third** Avenue
Room **7**

1650 **Fourth** Street

3. When you write an address in a sentence, use a comma between each part of the address but not before the ZIP code.

My address is 4022 Douglas Road, Miami, Florida 33134.

68 **ADJECTIVE CLAUSE:** a subordinate clause that
modifies a noun or pronoun   [See **Clauses**.]

69 **ADJECTIVE PHRASE:** a prepositional phrase that
modifies a noun or pronoun   [See **Phrases, Prepositions**.]

70 ## ADJECTIVES

IDENTIFYING ADJECTIVES

> An **adjective** is a
> word that modifies,
> or describes, a
> noun or a pronoun.

Adjectives bring the world into sharper focus. They provide information about nouns and pronouns by answering questions such as *which?*, *what kind?*, *how many?*, or *how much?*

TYPES OF ADJECTIVES

Besides common adjectives like *tall*, *last*, and *five*, there are four special categories of adjectives: articles, proper adjectives, demonstrative adjectives, and indefinite adjectives.

Articles

SAMPLE WORDS:	*the, a, an*
EXAMPLE:	**A** world championship meet in track and field is **an** exciting event for **the** participating athletes.
EXPLANATION:	Articles restrict the meanings of nouns they modify. *The* is a **definite article** because it indicates a specific person, place, or thing. *A* and *an* are **indefinite articles** because each one indicates that the following noun refers to someone or something in general.

Hint: Use the sound of the noun's first letter to select *a* or *an*. Use *an* before a vowel sound. Use *a* before a consonant sound.

Proper Adjectives

SAMPLE WORDS:	*African, Japanese, Spanish, Californian, Greek*
EXAMPLE:	Where else can a **Kenyan** marathoner make the acquaintance of a **Californian** high jumper, a **Japanese** discus champion, or a **Norwegian** javelin thrower?

EXPLANATION:	A **proper adjective** is formed from a proper noun. Proper adjectives always begin with capital letters. All other adjectives are known as **common adjectives** and begin with small letters.

For more on proper nouns, see p. 342.

Demonstrative Adjectives

SAMPLE WORDS:	*this, that, these, those*
EXAMPLE:	The women's 200-meter race will be run on **this** side of the field. On **that** side, the men's pole vault will begin at 2:00 P.M.
EXPLANATION:	A **demonstrative adjective** points out a particular person, place, or thing. *This* and *these* point out subjects that are near. *That* and *those* point out subjects that are at a distance. *This* and *that* are used with singular nouns. *These* and *those* are used with plural nouns.

Indefinite Adjectives

SAMPLE WORDS:	*any, each, few, many, more, most, several, some*
EXAMPLE:	**Each** year **some** events attract **more** spectators than the stands can hold.
EXPLANATION:	**Indefinite adjectives,** like all adjectives, modify nouns or pronouns. When the same words are used without nouns as subjects or objects in sentences, they are indefinite pronouns taking the place of nouns or other pronouns: **Each** of the events has its loyal followers.

FORMS OF ADJECTIVES

Comparing one person, place, or thing with another is a way of describing or telling about it. Adjectives change form to show comparison.

The **comparative** form of an adjective is used for comparing two items.

A sprinter is **faster** than a discus thrower.

The **superlative** form is used for comparing more than two.

She is the **fastest** runner in the field.

The way in which the comparative and superlative are formed depends on the number of syllables the adjective has. Some add -er and -est to the adjective form, and some use *more* or *most*.

Adjective Forms

Number of Syllables	Adjective	Comparative	Superlative
all with 1 syllable:	the **high** bar	the **higher** bar	the **highest** bar
some with 2 syllables:	the **speedy** dash	the **speedier** dash	the **speediest** dash
most with 2 syllables:	the **fluid** motion	the **more fluid** motion	the **most fluid** motion
all with 3 syllables:	the **exciting** race	the **more exciting** race	the **most exciting** race

Hint: Comparative forms are used for comparing *two*. Many have the *two*-letter ending -er or begin with the word *more*, which contains an *r* sound. **Superlative** forms are used for comparing at least *three*. They have the *three*-letter ending -est or begin with *most*, which contains an *st* sound. **Negative comparisons** can be made by using *less* for the comparative and *least* for the superlative.

Some adjectives have irregular comparative and superlative forms.

Irregular Adjective Forms

Adjective	Comparative	Superlative
good	better	best
bad	worse	worst
little	less	least
much *or* many	more	most

POSITION OF ADJECTIVES

Adjectives can come before or after the words they modify. Two or more adjectives can modify one noun or pronoun.

Lenny's **smooth** follow-through, **firm** and **graceful**, helps him to excel in the discus.

A **predicate adjective** is an adjective that follows a linking verb (LV) and modifies the subject (S) of the sentence.

When Marti competes in the long jump, she seems airborne.
$$\overset{\text{S}\downarrow \qquad \text{LV}}{}$$

COMMON USAGE PROBLEMS

AVOIDING ERRORS IN COMPARISONS

Avoid **double comparisons.** Do not add -er or -est to an adjective if you have already used *more* and *most.*

Mimi and Yolanda have been **busier** than ever preparing for the 100-meter hurdles. [not *more busier*]

Dwayne is the **most able** (or **ablest**) high jumper on our track team. [not *most ablest*]

Also, be careful not to use the superlative form instead of the comparative when two are being compared.

Of the Diaz twins, Carlotta is the **faster** sprinter. [not *fastest*]

Her sister, Teresa, is the **more impressive** jumper of the two. [not *most impressive*]

AVOIDING OTHER ERRORS

Do not use the words *here* and *there* after the demonstrative adjectives *this, that, these,* and *those.*

Do you prefer **these** [not *these here*] running shoes?

Use **that** [not *that there*] jogging suit if you want to be comfortable.

DEVELOPING YOUR STYLE: ADJECTIVES

USING PRECISE ADJECTIVES

You can improve your writing style by using precise adjectives that create strong effects. Avoid vague or empty adjectives like *awful, cute, great,* or *interesting.* Examine the following revised model:

disappointed

I saw the ~~awful~~ look on Jeremy's face. He had

have the winning time.

wanted to ~~make a great track record.~~

AVOIDING THE OVERUSE OF ADJECTIVES

Although adjectives are often useful in descriptions, overusing them can make your writing strained and artificial. Often precise nouns and vivid verbs can be more effective than adjectives alone. Study this model:

intelligent

Walruses are ~~interesting~~

MODEL

A strong verb replaces a vague adjective-noun combination.

A precise noun replaces a weaker adjective-noun combination.

One vivid verb replaces six less precise words.

Mike Conley's final attempt at the triple jump

electrified

~~had an awesome effect on~~ the crowd. Conley's

determination

~~determined attitude~~ showed in the grim clench of

catapulted

his lips. He ~~made a catapult-like take-off~~ into the

air, landing an incredible 58 ft., 7 1/4 in. beyond.

71 **ADVERB CLAUSE:** a subordinate clause that modifies a verb, an adjective, or an adverb [See **Clauses.**]

ADVERB PHRASE: a prepositional phrase that modifies a verb, an adjective, or an adverb [See **Phrases, Prepositions.**]

72

ADVERBS

73

IDENTIFYING ADVERBS

Adverbs make writing more vivid and precise by answering the questions *how?*, *when?*, *where?*, and *to what extent?* about verbs and the question *to what extent?* about adjectives and other adverbs.

> An **adverb** is a word that modifies, or describes, a verb, an adjective, or another adverb.

Adverbs Modifying Verbs

How? Lucia plays video games **skillfully.**

When? **Yesterday** she visited a computer software store.

Where? She bought a new video game **there.**

To what extent? She **barely** noticed the other stores in the mall.

Adverb Modifying an Adjective

To what extent? Lucia was **quite** happy with her purchase.

Adverb Modifying Another Adverb

To what extent? Lucia plays video games **very** skillfully.

Adverbs that modify verbs can usually be placed in more than one position in a sentence without changing the sentence's meaning.

She plays video games **skillfully.** OR She **skillfully** plays video games.

Yesterday she bought a game. OR She bought a game **yesterday.**

Adverbs that modify adjectives or other adverbs usually come right before the word they modify and cannot be moved to another position.

She is **very** happy with her purchase.   She plays **rather** competitively.

ADVERBS THAT END IN -LY

You've probably noticed that many adverbs are formed by adding -ly to an adjective. Sometimes the spelling of the adjective changes, as in the second line of the following chart.

Adjective	Adverb	Adjective	Adverb
skillful + -ly =	skillfully	frequent + -ly	frequently
happy + -ly =	happily	weary + -ly	wearily

Keep in mind that words ending in -ly are not always adverbs. For example, the words *lively, lovely, lonely, friendly,* and *unfriendly* are usually used as adjectives. The word *early* is often an adverb, but it can also be used as an adjective.

ADJECTIVE: Lucia was an **early** arrival at the software store.

ADVERB: Lucia arrived **early** at the software store.

ADVERB OR PREPOSITION?

For more on prepositions, see p. 358.

Many words that show position or direction can be used as prepositions as well as adverbs. They are prepositions when they are followed by an object (a noun or pronoun).

As prepositions, they connect the object to the rest of the sentence. As adverbs, they answer the question *where?* about the verb.

ADVERB: At the software store, several shoppers walked **around.**

PREPOSITION: Several shoppers walked **around** the software store.

COMPARATIVE AND SUPERLATIVE FORMS

Like adjectives, most adverbs have comparative and superlative forms. For one-syllable adverbs and a few two-syllable adverbs, form the comparative by adding *-er* and the superlative by adding *-est*. Use *more* and *most* to form the comparative and superlative of most two-syllable adverbs and all longer adverbs.

Adverb	Comparative	Superlative
fast	faster	fastest
soon	sooner	soonest
early	earlier	earliest
sadly	more sadly	most sadly
often	more often	most often
easily	more easily	most easily

A few adverbs have irregular comparative and superlative forms.

Adverb	Comparative	Superlative
well	better	best
badly	worse	worst
far	farther [distance]	farthest [distance]
	further [degree]	furthest [degree]

If you are uncertain about which adverb form to use, check the dictionary. The dictionary will list acceptable *-er* and *-est* forms under the entry for the base form of the adverb. When such forms are not listed, use *more* and *most* to form the comparative and superlative.

For more on comparative and superlative forms, see p. 285.

COMMON USAGE PROBLEMS

ADVERB OR ADJECTIVE?

Because so many adverbs are formed from adjectives, it is easy to confuse them. Remember to use an adverb, not an adjective, to modify a verb.

INCORRECT:	A good video game player moves **quick**.
	[*Quick* is an adjective.]
CORRECT:	A good video game player moves **quickly**.

Use a predicate adjective after a linking verb, such as a form of *be*. The predicate adjective modifies the subject of the sentence, not the verb.

CORRECT: A good video game player is **quick.**

Good and *bad* are always adjectives. *Well* and *badly* are adverbs; *well* may also be used as an adjective to describe someone's health. Remember to use *good* as a predicate adjective after a linking verb when health is not involved. Also use *bad* as a predicate adjective after a linking verb.

For more on linking verbs and predicate adjectives, see p. 287.

INCORRECT:	That new Skyrocket video game looks **well**.
CORRECT:	That new Skyrocket video game looks **good.**
INCORRECT:	The Earthworms on Mars game looks **badly**.
CORRECT:	The Earthworms on Mars game looks **bad.**

Use *well* and *badly* to modify action verbs.

INCORRECT:	In video game competitions, Carlos does **good.**
CORRECT:	In video game competitions, Carlos does **well.**
INCORRECT:	His sister Martá usually plays **bad.**
CORRECT:	His sister Martá usually plays **badly.**

AVOIDING DOUBLE NEGATIVES

No, not, never, and a few other adverbs are **negative words,** or words that say "no." To express a negative idea, you need only one negative word. Avoid using a **double negative,** two negative words in the same sentence.

For more on double negatives, see p. 334.

DEVELOPING YOUR STYLE: ADVERBS

Adverbs can make your writing more vivid by helping you to describe actions clearly and to indicate precise degrees of certain qualities or conditions. They can also replace wordy phrases and make your writing more direct. In addition, like adjectives, carefully chosen adverbs can contribute to the mood of a story, a poem, or other type of writing.

Here is an example of how to improve a story with adverbs:

M O D E L

Bravely s⌐
~~She~~ climbed the stairs. They were ∧very steep. As the stairway
steadily
grew ∧smokier, she moved ~~with slow, careful steps.~~ slowly and carefully. Only f⌐ Five or
ten minutes remained. Would she ∧ever rescue the trapped
workers?

Be aware, however, of overusing adverbs when you write. A strong, precise verb is more effective than a weak verb propped up by a strong adverb.

AGREEMENT: making a subject and verb match in number and person or a pronoun and its antecedent match in number, gender, and person   [See **Pronouns, Verbs, Problem Solver #57.**]   `74`

ANTECEDENT: the noun or pronoun to which a pronoun refers   [See **Pronouns.**]   `75`

APOSTROPHE   `76`

IDENTIFYING AN APOSTROPHE

An **apostrophe** (') is a punctuation mark that shows possession and in contractions indicates the omission of letters or numbers.

FORMING POSSESSIVES WITH APOSTROPHES

1. To form the **possessive of a singular noun:** Add an apostrophe and s.

Only one egg was left, and the egg**'s** shell was cracked.
Ramon**'s** mother sent him to the store.

2. To form the **possessive of a plural noun that ends in *s* or *es*:** Add only an apostrophe.

The store owner cried, "These eggs' shells are all cracked!"

3. To form the **possessive of a plural noun that does not end in *s*:** Add an apostrophe and *s*.

"That might be the young children**'s** fault," Ramon said. "At the back of the store they are using men**'s** shoes for bats and eggs for baseballs."

4. To form the **possessive of a compound noun:** Put the last word of the noun in the possessive form.

A woman standing nearby said, "Mario and Anita are my next-door neighbors' toddlers."

5. To indicate **joint possession:** Put the last subject in the possessive form.

"It was Mario and Anita**'s** idea to play baseball with the eggs." [Mario and Anita had the same idea.]

6. To indicate **individual possession:** Give the possessive form to each subject.

"They are using Mr. Garcia**'s** and Mr. Chen**'s** shoes for bats." [Mr. Garcia and Mr. Chen own different shoes.]

7. To form the **possessive of an indefinite pronoun:** Add an apostrophe and *s*.

It is anybody**'s** guess how many home runs the toddlers hit.

8. To discuss **money or time:** Give the possessive form to amounts of money or units of time that modify a noun.

> The store owner said, "They've cracked forty dollars' worth of eggs in two hours' time!"

USING APOSTROPHES IN CONTRACTIONS

9. A **contraction** is a word created by combining two words and removing certain letters. Use an apostrophe to replace these missing letters:

For more on contractions, see p. 330.

> The next day, the store owner said to Ramon, "Were**n't** you the one who told me about that game of egg baseball? I**'d** like to thank you by giving you six free cartons of eggs."

10. Use an apostrophe to replace the first two numbers in a year when it is clear what they are:

> That was a true story! It happened in the summer of **'91.**

OTHER USES FOR AN APOSTROPHE

11. Use an apostrophe to form the plural of letters, numbers, dates, symbols, and words:

three n**'s**	two +**'s**
two 6**'s**	and**'s**
the 1700**'s**	

12. Use an apostrophe in slang or dialect when parts of words have been omitted:

> comin' round the mountain
> fixin' to set sail on the Mississippi

APPOSITIVES

IDENTIFYING AN APPOSITIVE

An **appositive** is a noun or pronoun that generally follows another noun or pronoun to identify or provide extra information about it.

My sister **Beth** is a specialist in the art of the Old West.
The word **muskrat** comes from the Algonquian word
musquash.
The American artist **George Catlin** painted scenes of Native
American life.

An **appositive phrase** is a group of words that contain an appositive (APP) and its modifiers:

APP
Fancydancing, **a Native American *art form*,** has become
very popular.
The Nez Percé tribe raised appaloosas, **the wildly spotted**
APP
***horses* of the West.**

USING COMMAS WITH APPOSITIVES

Two rules will help you decide when to use commas with appositives:

1. If the appositive adds information that is absolutely necessary to the sentence's meaning, **do not** set it off with commas.

The author **Leslie Marmon Silko** writes of the Laguna Pueblo.
The poem **"The Time We Climbed Snake Mountain"** is about
appreciating nature.

Try reading each sentence without the appositive, and you will see that the sentence doesn't convey much meaning.

2. If the appositive adds information that is not absolutely necessary to the sentence's meaning, **do** set it off with commas.

Ramona Maher, **author of *Alice Yazzie's Year,*** won the Spur
Award of the Western Writers of America.
Gilroy, **a town in California**, has long been known as the
Garlic Capital of the World.

An appositive set off with a comma or commas *can* be cut from the sentence, and the sentence will still make sense and provide information.

DEVELOPING YOUR STYLE: APPOSITIVES

Appositives enable you to combine two sentences that contain related information, as in the following example:

SEPARATE:	Frederick Remington was an American artist and sculptor.
SEPARATE:	He liked to portray the Old West.
COMBINED:	Frederick Remington, **an American artist and sculptor,** liked to portray the Old West.
SEPARATE:	*The Outlier* shows his technique.
SEPARATE:	*The Outlier* is a precise, detailed painting.
COMBINED:	*The Outlier*, **a precise, detailed painting,** shows his technique.

The Outlier, 1909, Frederic Remington, The Metropolitan Museum of Art, New York

ARTICLE: the adjective *the, a,* or *an*

78

The is called a definite article because it refers to someone or something in particular. *A* and *an* are indefinite articles because they refer to one of a group. [See **Adjectives.**]

CAPITALIZATION

79

Like punctuation, capitalization is a signpost for the reader. It tells you what's important and what's not. It also gives you clues about how to read a particular passage. When deciding whether or not to capitalize, observe the following guideline:

Capitalize **proper nouns,** that is, words that name a specific person, place, thing, or idea. Do not capitalize nouns that refer to a general type or group of things.

SPECIFIC PERSON:	Jamaica Kincaid
GENERAL TYPE:	writer

SPECIFIC WORDS

Names and Titles of People

When writing, follow these guidelines for capitalization:

1. Capitalize the pronoun *I*.

After supper **I** finished my homework.

2. Capitalize people's names and initials, and family titles used as names.

Nikki Giovanni	**U**rsula **K.** Le **G**uin	José **G**arcía **V**illa
Mom	**D**ad	**G**randfather

3. Capitalize professional and family titles that come before a person's name.

Rev. Jobson	**D**r. Sánchez	**C**aptain Selby
Ms. Chung	**K**ing George III	**P**resident Clinton
Prime **M**inister González	**A**unt Irelle	**C**ousin Rudi

A title that is used alone without a name, especially if it follows a possessive adjective such as *my, your, his, her, our,* or *their* or the words *the, a,* or *an,* is normally not capitalized.

Rudi is my **c**ousin. My **m**om and his **m**om are sisters.
Selby is a **c**aptain in the police force.
Irelle Hollifield is my **a**unt.
George III was the **k**ing of England.
Bill Clinton was elected the forty-second **p**resident.

However, do capitalize the following titles for high officials when they are used alone and they refer to the current holders of the positions.

White House

the **P**resident
the **Q**ueen of England
the **V**ice **P**resident
the **S**ecretary **G**eneral

Buckingham Palace

4. Capitalize a title when it appears without a proper name in direct address.

"Will you yield the floor, **S**enator?"

Names of Places

1. Capitalize the names of villages, cities, states, countries, and continents.

Des **M**oines   **M**ontana   **V**ietnam

2. Capitalize the names of geographic features.

Mount **E**verest   **P**acific **O**cean   **M**issouri **R**iver

3. Capitalize the names of specific streets, highways, parks, and so on.

River **R**oad   **U**nion **P**ark   **C**oastal **H**ighway

4. Capitalize the names of geographical areas.

Aunt Irelle lives in the **S**outh.
Have you ever visited the **M**idwest?

Do not capitalize *east, west, north, south,* and so on, when they indicate direction.

We drove **s**outh to reach the ocean.
She lives **n**ortheast of the airport.

5. Capitalize adjectives that come from the names of geographical areas. Do not capitalize adjectives that simply show direction.

Eastern religions   a **w**estern flight
(those from Asia)   (one going west)

Names of Things, Ideas, Groups, and Organizations

1. Capitalize the names of particular documents, buildings, landmarks, and monuments.

Declaration of Independence   the Kremlin
Emancipation Proclamation   Lincoln Memorial
Statue of Liberty   the Great Wall of China

2. Capitalize the names of specific ships, trains, planes, spacecraft, and the brand names of cars.

The *Titanic* (ship)   *Orient Express* (train)
Spirit of St. Louis (plane)   *Challenger* (spacecraft)
Chevrolet (brand of automobile)

3. Capitalize the names of languages.

Swahili   Chinese   Yiddish

4. Capitalize the titles of specific school courses. Do not capitalize the name of a general subject, except for the names of languages.

Spanish 102   homework in Spanish
Art 101   my art class

5. Capitalize the first word, the last word, and all important words in the titles of literary works, newspapers, works of art, songs and longer musical compositions, and movies.

Do not capitalize articles (*a*, *an*, *the*), short prepositions with fewer than four letters (such as *at*, *of*, *in*, *on*, *to*), or coordinating conjunctions (such as *and* and *but*).

LITERARY WORKS:	*The Pearl*
	The Monsters Are Due on Maple Street
	"Mother to Son"
	"Stopping by Woods on a Snowy Evening"
PAINTING:	*The Buffalo Trail*
MUSICAL COMPOSITION:	*Tommy, a Rock Opera*
SONG:	"America, the Beautiful"
MOVIE:	*Return of the Jedi*
NEWSPAPER:	*San Francisco Examiner*
MAGAZINE:	*Life*

6. Capitalize the names of races, nationalities, and ethnic groups.

Caucasian	Turkish	Hebrew
Native American	Polish	Korean
African American	Egyptian	Asian American

7. Capitalize adjectives formed from the names of ethnic groups and nationalities.

Swedish

Ghanaian

Japanese

8. Capitalize the names of organizations, institutions, businesses, and political parties.

Army Corps of Engineers	Girl Scouts of America
the Republican Party	a Democrat
Texas Tech University	the Senate
Chemical Bank	General Motors
Court of Appeals	United Nations

Do not capitalize nouns like *university* or *court* unless they are part of a proper noun.

> Next fall Minelo will be a freshman at the state **u**niversity.
> My neighbor had to appear in traffic **c**ourt.

9. Capitalize religious names and terms.

Buddhist temples	the **K**oran	the **H**oly **S**pirit
Hinduism	the **T**almud	**C**hristianity
the **A**lmighty	**E**aster	**Y**om **K**ippur

10. Capitalize words referring to time periods and historical events.

Days	Months	Holidays	Eras	Historical Events
Thursday	**M**arch	**P**residents' **D**ay	**B**ronze **A**ge	**C**ivil **W**ar
Saturday	**J**une	**L**abor **D**ay	**P**rohibition	**V**ietnam **W**ar

Do not capitalize the names of the seasons.

late **w**inter	the coming of **s**pring	**s**ummertime

CAPITALS TO MARK BEGINNINGS

1. Capitalize the first word of every sentence.

> **W**e took a family vacation in Yellowstone National Park.

2. Capitalize the first word of a direct quotation, unless the quotation is a fragment that cannot stand alone as a complete sentence.

> Shawna asked, "**I**s there any chance we'll see some bears?"
> *Life* magazine called Old Faithful "**t**he most famous geyser in the world."

In divided quotations, do not capitalize the first word of the second part unless this word begins a new sentence.

> "**D**o you really think," asked Lonnie, "**t**hat bears come near tents?"
> "**T**hey certainly do," Mom replied. "**L**et's be prepared."

3. Capitalize the first word in most lines of poetry.

Listen, my children, and you shall hear
Of the midnight ride of Paul Revere . . .
—Henry Wadsworth Longfellow, "Paul Revere's Ride"

Midnight Ride of Paul Revere, 1931, Grant Wood
The Metropolitan Museum of Art, New York
Arthur Hoppock Hearn Fund 1950

Some modern poets choose not to follow the traditional rules for capitalizing words, sentences, and opening lines.

4. Capitalize all the important words in the greeting of a letter.

Dear Ms. Rodríguez: Sir or Madam:
Dear Mayor Poulos: Dear Uncle Ralph,

5. In an outline, capitalize the first word in each line. Also capitalize the letters next to the major subtopics.

 I. Facts about dolphins
   A. Physical description
   B. Intelligence
   C. Methods of communication
 II. Dangers to dolphins
   A. Natural predators
   B. Commercial fishing
   C. Environmental hazards

CHOPPY SENTENCES: a series of short sentences
that create an abrupt, jerking rhythm
[See **Sentence Combining, Sentence Problems** from Section Two of
the book.]

CLAUSES

IDENTIFYING CLAUSES

A **clause** is a group
of words that con-
tains a subject and
a verb.

Some walls, like the Great Wall of China, can
stand alone, and others cannot. Similarly, some
clauses can stand alone (as sentences), and others
need support.

TYPES OF CLAUSES

Sentences contain **main clauses** and **subordinate clauses.**

Main Clause	A **main clause** can stand alone as a sentence.
EXAMPLE:	**The concert began at 9:00.**
	A sentence can contain more than one main clause.
EXAMPLE:	**The band played**, and **a mime entertained us.**
Subordinate Clause	A **subordinate clause** cannot stand alone. It must be linked to a main clause.
EXAMPLE:	**As the mime bowed**, the band played a fanfare.

Types of Subordinate Clauses

There are three kinds of subordinate clauses: **noun clauses,
adjective clauses,** and **adverb clauses.**

Noun Clause	A **noun clause** is used as a noun in a sentence.
AS SUBJECT:	**Who the mime was** didn't matter.
AS DIRECT OBJECT:	Tran says **that he loves pantomime.**
AS INDIRECT OBJECT:	Give **whoever the mime is** a round of applause!
AS PREDICATE NOUN:	A funny routine was **what the crowd wanted.**
AS OBJECT OF PREPOSITION:	They hummed along to **whatever the band played.**

Here are some words that introduce noun clauses:

that	whatever	where
which	whoever	whether
what	whose	when
who	how	why
whomever		

Adjective Clause An **adjective clause** is used as an adjective to modify a noun or pronoun in the main clause.

EXAMPLE: Donna, **who had bought the tickets,** cheered the band.

Everyone loved the music **that the band played.**

Jamal was the one **who cheered loudest.**

Vendors had set up booths **where they sold T-shirts, buttons, and caps.**

Here are some words that introduce adjective clauses:

that	where
whom	when
whose	which
who	

An adjective clause that is introduced by one of the words listed above can also be called a **relative clause.** You can sometimes omit the introductory word from this kind of clause:

They were the group [*that*] we liked best.

RESTRICTIVE OR NONRESTRICTIVE? Some adjective clauses are essential to complete the meaning of the noun or pronoun that they modify. These **restrictive** or **essential clauses** are not set off by commas from the rest of the sentence.

> The musician **who played the drums** is a friend of ours.

> I bought a hat **that advertised the concert.**

Some adjective clauses add nonessential information about the noun or pronoun they modify. These **nonrestrictive clauses** are set off by commas from the rest of the sentence.

For more on commas with clauses, see Commas, p. 309.

> The conductor, **who teaches band at Franklin Junior High,** took a bow.

> The most colorful buttons, **which were red and white,** sold out quickly.

Use *which* to introduce this type of clause when the antecedent is not a person.

TRY THIS

You can often tell if an adjective clause is restrictive or nonrestrictive by reading the sentence aloud without the adjective clause. If the meaning changes substantially, then the clause is restrictive.

Adverb Clause	An **adverb clause** is used as an adverb in a sentence.
TELLS HOW:	The lead singer howled **as if he were a wolf.**
TELLS WHEN:	**After the third set was over,** a new band came on.
TELLS WHERE:	The audience danced **wherever there was room.**

TELLS WHY:	We liked their songs **because the lyrics made sense.**
TELLS UNDER WHAT CIRCUMSTANCES:	**Although I shouldn't spend the money,** I'll buy their new record.

Here are some words that introduce adverb clauses:

after	whenever	although
as	while	unless
as soon as	where	as
before	wherever	as if
until	because	as though
when	so that	

◆ WHEN YOU WRITE ◆

When you use an adverb clause to begin a sentence, you should separate it from the main clause with a comma.

COMMON USAGE PROBLEMS

AVOIDING FAULTY SUBORDINATION

A subordinate clause is called *subordinate* because the idea it expresses is not as important as the idea in the main clause. If you mistakenly place your main idea in a subordinate clause, your sentence will have **faulty subordination.** The main clause should contain the main idea, and the subordinate clause, ideas of lesser importance. In the sentences below, the main idea is in boldface.

FAULTY:	Everyone was tired, although we had had a wonderful time.
CORRECT:	Although everyone was tired, **we had had a wonderful time.**
FAULTY:	Since they have chosen to room together at college, they are best friends.
CORRECT:	**Since they are best friends,** they have chosen to room together at college.

For more on subordinate clauses as fragments, see Problem Solver, p. 270.

To tell whether a sentence has faulty subordination, follow these steps:

1. Determine the main idea in your sentence.

2. Identify the subordinate and main clauses.

3. Make sure the main idea is expressed in the main clause. If it is not, restructure the sentence.

COMPUTER TIP

It is easy to correct faulty subordination on a word processor. Just *highlight,* or *block,* the faulty main clause. Then *move* the clause, placing it after the introductory word that begins the faulty subordinate clause. Correct the punctuation. Now your main clause has become your subordinate clause, and vice versa.

DEVELOPING YOUR STYLE: CLAUSES

You can use clauses to give your writing variety and interest. Clauses can help you do the following:

- Begin your sentences in different ways.
- Vary the length and structure of your sentences.
- Add vivid descriptions to your sentences.

Here is a passage from a story in which the writer carefully uses several different kinds of clauses.

MODEL FROM LITERATURE

The writer uses a noun clause as a direct object.

The writer uses an adverb clause, a noun clause, and an adjective clause in one sentence.

The writer combines two main clauses to create a compound sentence in the next-to-last sentence.

Suddenly he made out the shape of a hill. He wondered **what it could be.** Who had piled snow into such a huge heap? He moved toward it, dragging Zlateh after him. **When he came near it,** he realized **that it was a large haystack which the snow had blanketed.**

Aaron realized immediately that they were saved. With great effort he dug his way through the snow. **He was a village boy** and **he knew what to do.** When he reached the hay, he hollowed out a nest for himself and the goat.

—Isaac Bashevis Singer, "Zlateh the Goat"

82 **COLLECTIVE NOUN:** a noun that refers to a group
[See **Nouns.**]

USING A COLON

1. Use a colon to introduce a list, especially if the list follows words like *these*, *the following*, or *as follows*.

> Latoya will take these courses: math, music, and social studies.

Do not use a colon if the list immediately follows a verb or a preposition.

> We will need rice, beans, bananas, grapes, and oranges.

2. Use a colon after the greeting of a business letter.

> Dear Ms. Rappaport:

3. Use a colon between the hour and the minute when you use numbers to write the time of day.

> at 3:05 P.M.
> after 6:00 A.M.

> A **colon (:)** serves as a signal to expect something. It appears before a list or after the greeting in a business letter. Colons also are used in writing the time of the day in numbers.

COMMA

84

Have you ever run out of breath when reading aloud? Seeing a comma can be a friendly reminder to pause for air. More important, carefully placed commas help make your meaning clear.

Sometimes reading a sentence aloud will help you decide where to place commas. For example, two commas are missing from the following example. Can you tell where?

> A bobsled team from Jamaica a tropical island entered the Olympics.

Placing commas after the words *Jamaica* and *island* clearly separates a piece of interesting but nonessential information from the rest of the sentence.

> A **comma (,)** indicates a pause or change in thought and helps to add clarity to writing.

Reading aloud, however, won't always tell you where commas do and don't belong. You will need to learn some rules, or conventions, for using commas.

1. Put a comma before the coordinating conjunction (*and, but, or, nor, for,* and *so*) that joins the main clauses in a compound sentence.

Two sentences:

A Caribbean Olympic team was a rarity. A Jamaican bobsled team was incredible.

A combined sentence with two main clauses:

A Caribbean Olympic team was a rarity, **but** a Jamaican bobsled team was incredible.

Don't use a comma with *and, but,* or *or* when it links words or word groups that are *not* main clauses.

LINKS TWO WORDS: Athletes ***and*** spectators were dumbfounded.
Sportscasters **laughed *and* joked.**
Jamaica is **a hot *and* sunny** island.

LINKS TWO PHRASES: You can see the winter Olympics **on TV *or* in person.**

LINKS TWO VERB PHRASES: The Jamaican team **went along with the fun *but* kept on preparing for competition.**

2. Put a comma between two adjectives of equal importance. To discover whether adjectives are of equal importance, reverse their order. If the sentence still makes sense, you can use a comma instead of the word *and*.

COMMA NEEDED: Jamaica is a hot, sunny island. [You could reverse the order of the adjectives and say "a sunny, hot island," or you could say "a hot and sunny island."]

NO COMMA NEEDED: Jamaica is a small Caribbean nation about the size of Connecticut. [You could not say "a Caribbean small nation" or "a small and Caribbean nation."]

3. Put a comma after an introductory subordinate clause. You can recognize a subordinate clause because it begins with a subordinating conjunction.

For more on clauses, see p. 304.

Frequently Used Subordinating Conjunctions

after	if	whenever
although	since	where
as	unless	wherever
because	until	whether
before	when	while

When the Jamaican bobsledders arrived, the sportscasters had fun making jokes.
Because Jamaica is a tropical island, the spectators stared in disbelief.

Do not use a comma in most cases when a subordinate clause follows the main clause.

The sportscasters had fun making jokes **when the Jamaican bobsledders arrived.**

4. Put a comma after some introductory words, two or more introductory prepositional phrases, and introductory participles and participial phrases.

Actually, the bobsledders had never seen snow. [introductory word]
Living in a tropical climate, they weren't prepared for winter. [introductory participial phrase]

In Canada at the Olympics, the Jamaican bobsledders had their first experience of subzero weather. [two introductory prepositional phrases]
Nevertheless, they competed seriously despite the jokes and the cold. [introductory word]

5. Put commas before and after words that interrupt the flow of thought in a sentence or add nonessential information.

Common Interrupters

after all	in any case	moreover
by the way	in fact	nevertheless
for example	in general	of course
furthermore	in my opinion	on the other hand
however	meanwhile	therefore

The Caribbean bobsledders, **of course,** had trained in their sport.
All their practice runs, **believe it or not,** had been on bobsleds with wheels.

This interrupter is an appositive—it names the noun next to it.

The sportscasters, **an often tough and unsympathetic group,** took the bobsled team to their hearts.

For more on appositives, see p. 295.

Don't use commas to set off a **restrictive clause**—a clause that is essential to the meaning of the sentence.

The clause is essential to the meaning.

RESTRICTIVE: Bobsledders who trained in snow were amazed by the Jamaican team's skill.

The clause is an interrupter. It adds nonessential information.

NONRESTRICTIVE: Canadian bobsledders, who always train in snow, could not imagine training without snow.

6. Put commas between words and word groups in a series of three or more items.

The United States hosted the winter Olympics in **1932, 1960, and 1980.**

Athletes compete **on skis, on ice skates, on luges,** and **on bobsleds.**

All over the world people **buy tickets, schedule vacations, book flights,** and **reserve lodgings** to attend the winter games.

TRY THIS
To discover whether a clause is restrictive or nonrestrictive, omit it and see whether the sentence retains its meaning.

7. Use a comma to set off a direct quotation from the rest of the sentence.

"I like watching the winter Olympics on TV," Akiko said.

Put the comma inside the quotation mark.

"What's your favorite event**?**" Lauren asked.

Use a question mark when the direct quotation is a question.

Akiko answered**,** "I like speed skating the best."

If the speaker is identified first, a comma follows.

"Well**,**" Lauren said**,** "downhill skiing is much more exciting to watch."

Use two commas when the speaker's identification interrupts.

Denita rolled her eyes and said that bobsledding was much more exciting than either event her friends had mentioned.

Don't use a comma with an indirect quotation.

8. Use a comma to set off a **noun of direct address** — the noun that names a person being spoken to.

"**Akiko,** who do you think will win the gold in the figure skating competition?" Lauren asked.

"Beats me, **Lauren,**" Akiko replied. "I guess we'll find out on Saturday."

9. Put a comma after the greeting of a personal letter and the closing of both a personal and a business letter.

For more on punctuating quotations, see p. 373.

GREETING FOR A PERSONAL LETTER:

Dear Mom,
The bobsled races are tomorrow.
You won't believe this, but. . . .

GREETING FOR A BUSINESS LETTER:

Dear Mr. Wheeler:
I'm returning the bobsled that I ordered. The silly thing has wheels! When I opened. . . .

In a business letter, put a colon after the salutation.

CLOSING FOR A PERSONAL LETTER:	. . . I'm having fun at the Olympics, but I miss you and Dad. **Love,** Max
CLOSING FOR A BUSINESS LETTER:	. . . I just hope the next bobsled you send doesn't have propellers. **Sincerely,** Max Henderson

10. Use commas to separate the parts of an address in a sentence.

Put commas after the street name, city, and state.

Don't put a comma between the state and zip code.

Write to Wheeler Bobsleds, Inc., at **2703 Industrial Way, Cincinnati, Ohio,** for a catalog.

Write to Wheeler Bobsleds, Inc., at **2703 Industrial Way, Cincinnati, Ohio 45234,** for a catalog.

11. In a sentence, put a comma after the day and year in a date.

Use a comma to set off the day and the year.

A film about bobsledding was shown on May 18, 1994, in the school auditorium.

Don't use commas with the month and day or the month and year alone.

A film about bobsledding was shown on May 18 in the school auditorium.

A film about bobsledding was shown during May 1994 on Wednesdays and Fridays.

12. In numbers of four digits or more, put a comma before every third numeral, counting from the right.

1,000
19,383
6,038,012
349,471,476
5,684,674,275

13. Use "comma sense."
Notice how moving a comma can change meaning:

This sentence says that they were not playing a joke.

Before, we thought the Jamaicans were playing a joke.

This sentence says that they were playing a joke.

Before we thought, the Jamaicans were playing a joke.

Remember, the comma should clarify the meaning.

COMMON NOUN: a noun that does not refer to a specific person, place, thing, or idea and that usually begins with a lowercase letter   [See **Nouns.**]

COMMONLY CONFUSED OR MISUSED WORDS

The word pairs that follow often pose problems in usage. They include words that are often confused because they sound alike or look alike to many people.

accept, except   *Accept* means "to take something as a gift" or "to agree with something." *Except* means "not including."

> Mariska **accepted** the scholarship gratefully.
> Everyone **except** Christine attended the ceremony.

advice, advise   *Advice* is a noun meaning "a suggestion" or "help." *Advise* is a verb meaning "to give advice or help."

> I needed some **advice** on a party for Mariska.
> Mrs. Hansen **advised** that I make lists of everything to do.

affect, effect   *Affect,* most often used as a verb, means "to influence." *Effect,* most often used as a noun, means "result."

> Her advice will **affect** my planning.
> Careful preparation is necessary to create a festive **effect**.

all ready, already   *All ready* means "all of us are ready." *Already* means "before this" or "previously."

> We are **all ready** for the party. Where are the guests?
> We've **already** decorated the house and prepared the refreshments.

all right, alright   *All right* is two words. *Alright* is incorrect.

a lot, alot   *A lot* is two words that mean "very much." *Alot* is incorrect.

> I buried myself in **a lot** of crepe paper.

bad, badly   *Bad* is an adjective that means "not good." *Badly* is an adverb that means "poorly" or "very much."

For more on bad/badly, see Adverbs, p. 291.

I feel **bad** that Christine missed Mariska's ceremony.
So do I, but Christine **badly** needed that dental work. It couldn't be postponed any longer.

beside, besides *Beside* means "next to." *Besides* means "in addition to."

Sit **beside** me and explain what happened.
Of course, and I have something else to tell you **besides.**

bring, take *Bring* suggests motion *toward* the speaker. *Take* suggests motion *away* from the speaker.

The flowers have just arrived. Please **bring** them here.
Remember to **take** the boxes outside.

borrow, lend, loan *Borrow* means "to receive something on loan." *Lend* means "to give something temporarily." *Loan* means "a temporary gift." *Loan* is often misused as a verb meaning "to lend."

Did you **borrow** that strobe light from Pietro?
Yes, he never refuses to **lend** it to me when I have a party.
That is a generous **loan**.

choose, chose *Choose*, meaning "select," is the present tense, and *chose*, meaning "selected," is the past tense.

I **choose** to leave the flower boxes in the hall.
I **chose** the flowers yesterday.

compliment, complement *Compliment* means "praise." *Complement* means "make complete."

I want to **compliment** you on your taste.
The flowers **complement** the decorations beautifully.

desert, dessert As a noun, a *desert* (DEZ ert) is "a dry land where few plants and animals thrive." As a verb, *desert* (de ZERT) means "to abandon." *Dessert* (de SERT) is "a sweet food, often the last course in a meal."

Mariska's family plans a trip to the California **desert.**
Is she going to **desert** us for a week?
No problem; we'll have a **dessert** party when she gets back.

farther, further   *Farther* means "a greater distance." *Further*
means "additional" or "with greater depth."

How much **farther** from school is my house than yours?
I estimated it, but I'll check **further** when I have a map.

Do not use the expression "all the further," as in "that's all
the further I can go." Instead, say "as far as," as in "This is as far as
I can walk."

fewer, less   Use *fewer* with items that can be counted. Use
less with things that can't be counted, such as information.

I'm taking **fewer** classes than you are this year.
True, but I get so anxious that I may be learning **less**.

good, well   *Good* is an adjective, which modifies a noun or
pronoun. *Well* is usually used as an adverb that tells how. Use *well*
as an adjective only when referring to health.

I have really **good** science classes.
You always did **well** in science, so I'm not surprised.
Do you feel **well** enough to go on the field trip today?

For more on *good/well*,
see Adverbs, p. 292.

hear, here   *Hear* means "listen." *Here* means "in this
place."

I **hear** you've been accepted into Saint Louis University High
School.
Yes, but I can't decide whether to go there or stay **here**.

its, it's   *Its* is a possessive pronoun meaning "belonging to
it." *It's* is a contraction meaning "it is."

Saint Louis University High School has a great science
curriculum. Have you seen **its** catalog?
No, but I've sent for it, and **it's** on the way.

For more on *its/it's*, see
Possessive Forms,
p. 356.

lay, lie   *Lay* means "to put or set something down." *Lie*
means "to place [yourself] down" or "to be in a horizontal
position."

Please **lay** my science project on the desk.
I'm going to **lie** down now.

lead, led   As a noun, *lead* (LED) means "a heavy metal." As a verb, *lead* (LEED) means "to show the way." *Led* (LED) is the past tense of the verb *lead*.

This equipment is as heavy as **lead**.
Will Mr. Mukerji or Mrs. Allen **lead** this field trip?
Mr. Mukerji **led** the last one; so Mrs. Allen will go today.

learn, teach   *Learn* means "to gain knowledge." *Teach* means "to impart knowledge" or "to instruct."

Today we'll **learn** about lowland and meadow plants.
Nature will **teach** me even more than my teachers will.

leave, let   *Leave* means "to go away." *Let* means "to allow."

We should **leave** this meadow and study the boggy area next.
Don't **let** me forget my camera.

loose, lose   *Loose* means "not tight." To *lose* something is "to misplace or get rid of it."

Your field jacket is much too **loose**.
Did you **lose** weight, or are you wearing my down jacket by mistake?

like, as, as if   *Like* is a preposition and should begin a prepositional phrase, not a clause. *As* is a conjunction and should begin a clause.

> I've been taking photographs **like** a maniac.
> I've been taking photographs **as if** I were a maniac.

For more on *like/as/as if*, see Conjunctions, p. 326.

passed, past   *Passed* means "gone by." It is the past tense of the verb *to pass*. As a noun, *past* means "a former time." As a preposition, *past* means "beyond."

> We **passed** that oak about ten minutes ago, didn't we?
> I remember one in the **past**, but it wasn't this large.
> I would have remembered going **past** an oak that large.

peace, piece   *Peace* means "quiet" or "the absence of war." *Piece* means "a part."

> I feel at **peace** with nature today.
> Well, enjoy it. I'm getting a **piece** of pizza from Mrs. Allen.

principal, principle   As a noun, *principal* is "the head of a school." As an adjective, *principal* means "of chief importance." A *principle* is "a rule of behavior" or "a basic truth."

> The **principal** has approved two more field trips this month.
> No doubt the weather will be a **principal** concern.
> It's a **principle** of life that when we want sun, it will rain.

raise, rise   *Raise* means "to lift something up." *Rise* means "to go upward." *Raise* requires a direct object, whereas *rise* does not.

> **Raise** your hand if you're going on the next field trip.
> You'll have to **rise** early. We're leaving at 5:00 A.M.

real, really   *Real* is an adjective meaning "actual" or "true." *Really* is an adverb meaning "actually" or "truly."

> Its **real** point is to gain experience outside the classroom.
> I am **really** looking forward to this trip!

regardless, irregardless   *Regardless*, meaning "in spite of," is the correct form. *Irregardless* is incorrect.

> **Regardless** of which school I choose, I will study hard.

sit, set   *Sit* means "to occupy a seat." *Set* means "to place something somewhere."

Come and **sit** with me in the bus.
I'll **set** up my traveling science kit.

stationary, stationery   *Stationary* is an adjective meaning "still" or "in one place." *Stationery* is "letter paper."

Go ahead and walk around while the plane is **stationary**.
I brought some **stationery** to write letters.

than, then   *Than* is a subordinating conjunction that introduces the second part of a comparison. *Then* is an adverb that means "next" or "after that."

I thought the plane would be more crowded **than** it is.
Good! Enjoy the view for a while, and **then** we'll have lunch.

their, there, they're   *Their* is a plural possessive pronoun meaning "belonging to them." *There* is an adverb that means "in that place." *They're* is a pronoun contraction meaning "they are."

Why do people across the aisle have **their** shades down?
The sun is coming in **there**, and maybe it was too bright.
Well, they don't know what **they're** missing!

theirs, there's   *Theirs* is a possessive pronoun that stands alone. It means "belonging to them." *There's* is a contraction for "there is" or "there has."

For more on
theirs/there's, see
Possessive Forms,
p. 356.

Our seats are great, but **theirs** are not so good.
Now **there's** a beautiful landscape, off to the left!

to, two, too   *To* is a preposition meaning "toward." *Two* refers to the number *2* and may be used as a noun or as an adjective that tells how many. *Too* is an adverb that means "also" or "more than enough."

Our plane will fly **to** Akron-Canton after leaving Pittsburgh.
I wonder if those **two** flight attendants know where we are.
I'd like to know **too**. We should be over land, not water. This is **too** scary for me.

weather, whether   The noun *weather* refers to outdoor conditions such as rain, sun, or fog. *Whether* means "if" and suggests some kind of choice.

Maybe the **weather** is bad over land.

I'm not sure **whether** I like being so close to the water.

who, whom   *Who* is a subject pronoun that can either be used to ask a question or introduce a subordinate clause. *Whom* is an object pronoun that can be the object of a verb, the object of a preposition, or an indirect object.

For more on who/whom, see Pronouns, p. 366.

> **Who** would know about the landscape below?
> The navigator **who** filed the flight plan should know.
> **Whom** did the pilot just mention in that announcement?
> To **whom** was he referring?
> He gave **whom** the flight plan?

whose, who's   *Whose* is a possessive form of the pronoun *who*, meaning "belonging to whom." *Who's* is a contraction for "who is."

> **Whose** country does the landscape resemble?
> It looks a little like Ilona's, **who's** from Hungary.

your, you're   *Your* is a possessive pronoun that means "belonging to you." *You're* is a contraction for "you are."

> Why not take out **your** camera and snap a few photos from here?
> **You're** right! This landscape is too beautiful not to have a picture of it!

Landscape, 1925, Maurice de Vlaminck, Art Resource

87 **COMPARATIVE FORM:** an adjective or adverb form used to compare two things, usually created by adding *-er* to the base form or by using *more*   [See **Adjectives, Adverbs.**]

88 **COMPLETE PREDICATE:** in a sentence or clause, the verb along with its objects, its modifiers, or any predicate nouns or adjectives   [See **Sentences: Structures and Types.**]

89 **COMPLETE SUBJECT:** in a sentence or clause, the simple subject along with its modifiers
        [See **Sentences: Structures and Types.**]

90 **COMPLEX SENTENCE:** a sentence that contains one main clause and one or more subordinate clauses
        [See **Sentences: Structures and Types.**]

91 **COMPOUND-COMPLEX SENTENCE:** a sentence that contains at least two main clauses and one or more subordinate clauses   [See **Sentences: Structures and Types.**]

92 **COMPOUND NOUN:** a noun made up of more than one word   [See **Nouns.**]

93 **COMPOUND OBJECT:** two or more direct objects linked by a coordinating conjunction
        [See **Sentences: Structures and Types.**]

94 **COMPOUND PREDICATE:** two or more predicates linked by a coordinating conjunction
        [See **Sentences: Structures and Types.**]

95 **COMPOUND SENTENCE:** a sentence containing two or more main clauses linked by a coordinating conjunction or a semicolon.   [See **Sentences: Structures and Types.**]

96 **COMPOUND SUBJECT:** two or more subjects linked by a coordinating conjunction
        [See **Sentences: Structures and Types, Problem Solver #57C-E.**]

COMPOUND VERB: two or more verbs linked by a coordinating conjunction   [See **Sentences: Structures and Types, Verbs.**]

97

CONCRETE NOUN: a noun that names something that can be perceived by one or more of the five senses   [See **Nouns.**]

98

CONJUNCTIONS

99

IDENTIFYING CONJUNCTIONS

Conjunctions are hard at work in much of what you read and write. Like the metal links that join the cars of a train, conjunctions often go unnoticed, but they help hold writing together and make sure that it moves along smoothly. In the following passage, the conjunctions are in bold type.

> A **conjunction** is a word that links single words or groups of words.

📖 **MODEL FROM LITERATURE**

    I still felt a little dizzy **when** we took a break to eat lunch. It was past two o'clock **and** we sat underneath a large walnut tree. . . . **While** we ate, Papá jotted down the number of boxes we had picked. Roberto drew designs on the ground with a stick. Suddenly I noticed Papá's face turn pale **as** he looked down the road. "Here comes the school bus," he whispered loudly in alarm. Instinctively, Roberto **and** I ran **and** hid in the vineyards.

          —Francisco Jimenez, "The Circuit"

When makes the second clause subordinate to the main clause.

Here and links two main clauses.

While and as make clauses subordinate.

And links the words Roberto and I; and the words ran and hid, describing what Roberto and I did.

TYPES OF CONJUNCTIONS

Based on the way they work in a sentence, conjunctions fall into four categories: **coordinating conjunctions, correlative conjunctions, subordinating conjunctions,** and **conjunctive adverbs.**

Category	Coordinating Conjunction
COMMON EXAMPLES:	and, but, or, nor, for, yet
FUNCTION:	links words or groups of words of equal rank
SAMPLE SENTENCES:	**Kraits, pythons, *and* cobras** are deadly snakes. [links three subjects]
	Most snakes eat **rats *and* mice**. [links two direct objects]
	They may catch their tasty dinners by **night *or* day**. [links two objects of prepositions]
	The snake **ate a rat *but* wanted another.** [links two predicates]
	A mouse came by, *so* the snake took a gulp. [links two main clauses]

Category	Correlative Conjunction
COMMON EXAMPLES:	both/and, either/or, neither/nor, not only/but also, whether/or
FUNCTION:	works in pairs to link words or groups of words of equal rank
SAMPLE SENTENCES:	***Neither* my dress shoes *nor* my loafers** are in the closet. [links two subjects]
	They should be ***either* in the closet *or* under the bed.** [links two prepositional phrases]
	I have searched ***both* here *and* there.** [links adverbs]
	***Not only* am I late for the interview, *but* I'm *also* wearing sneakers.** [links two main clauses]

Category	Subordinating Conjunction
COMMON EXAMPLES:	after, although, as, as if, because, before, if, since, so that, though, unless, until, when, whether, while
FUNCTION:	makes a clause subordinate, or unable to stand alone, and links it to the rest of the sentence

SAMPLE SENTENCES:	**The robot demanded a glass of milk *before* it obeyed our commands.** [makes the second clause subordinate and links it to a main clause]
	The robot said that it would calculate square roots *if* it got a brownie. [makes the last clause subordinate and links it to a complex sentence]
	After the robot completed the job, it took a nap, and we ate the rest of the brownies. [makes the first clause subordinate and links it to a compound sentence]

Category	Conjunctive Adverb
COMMON EXAMPLES:	also, as a result, besides, for example, furthermore, however, in fact, instead, likewise, moreover, nevertheless, otherwise, similarly, still, therefore
FUNCTION:	links main clauses and clarifies their relationships; is usually preceded by a semicolon and followed by a comma
SAMPLE SENTENCES:	**She could not fit the dog in the doghouse; *as a result,* she bought a new dog.** [links two main clauses and clarifies a cause-and-effect relationship]
	She bought a new dog; *however,* she should have bought a new doghouse. [links two main clauses and clarifies a contrast]

CONJUNCTION OR PREPOSITION?

You've probably noticed that some subordinating conjunctions can also be used as prepositions. To tell what the word is, see what it introduces. The word is a **preposition (Prep)** if it introduces a prepositional phrase, which usually ends with a noun or pronoun called the **object of the preposition (OP).** The word is a **subordinating conjunction (SC)** if it introduces a subordinate clause, which contains a **subject (S)** and a **verb (V).**

                                                  PREP   OP
He didn't notice the hole in the floor **after** a few days.

                                             SC   S   V
He didn't notice the hole in the floor **after** he threw a rug over it.

 SC   S   V
After he fell in the hole, he noticed it again.

COMMON USAGE PROBLEMS

CONFUSING <u>LIKE</u> WITH <u>AS</u> OR <u>AS IF</u>

Keep in mind that *like*, meaning "similar to," is a preposition, not a subordinating conjunction. Use *like* to introduce prepositional phrases; use the subordinating conjunction *as* or *as if* to introduce subordinate clauses.

CORRECT:	The motorcycle roared **like** a locomotive.
INCORRECT:	The motorcycle roared **like** we predicted.
CORRECT:	The motorcycle roared **as** we predicted.

BEGINNING SENTENCES WITH <u>AND</u>, <u>BUT</u> OR <u>OR</u>

In the past, starting a sentence with *and, but,* or *or* was discouraged in formal writing such as newspaper articles and school reports. Today, however, many recognized writers open sentences with *and, but,* or *or* to create transitions, to produce a dramatic effect, or to make dialogue more realistic.

FOR DRAMATIC EFFECT:	She cried for help. **But** it was too late.
IN DIALOGUE:	"**But**, Mom, I need help!" she cried.
TO CREATE TRANSITIONS:	"It was too late. **And** then, suddenly, help appeared."

USING <u>SO</u>

So is often used as a coordinating conjunction in informal English, but such usage is discouraged in formal writing.

AVOID:	Toni Morrison won a Nobel Prize, **so** her book sales rose.
BETTER:	**Because** Toni Morrison won a Nobel Prize, her book sales rose.
OR:	Toni Morrison won a Nobel Prize; **as a result,** her book sales rose.

Also frowned on in formal English is the use of *so* in place of the subordinating conjunction *so that.* In general, you should replace *so* with *so that,* meaning "in order to," whenever *so that* makes sense in a sentence.

	AVOID:	We visited the bookshop **so** we could meet Toni Morrison.
	BETTER:	We visited the bookshop **so that** we could meet Toni Morrison.

AVOIDING <u>THE REASON IS BECAUSE</u>

The expression *the reason is because* is ungrammatical and repetitious. It is grammatical to use *the reason is that* instead, but this expression is wordy. The best solution is to reword the sentence so that it uses just the subordinating conjunction *because* (or *since*).

	AVOID:	**The reason** for my absence **is because** I slept late.
	BETTER:	**The reason** for my absence **is that** I slept late.
	BEST:	I was absent **because** I slept late.

DEVELOPING YOUR STYLE: CONJUNCTIONS

USING CONJUNCTIONS TO EXPRESS RELATIONSHIPS AND COMBINE SENTENCES

You can use conjunctions to express a variety of relationships among ideas. The following chart lists the most common relationships and some of the specific conjunctions that are often used to express them.

Relationship	Coordinating Conjunction	Correlative Conjunction	Subordinating Conjunction	Conjunctive Adverb
ADDITION: One idea is added to another.	and	both/and	as	also moreover furthermore
EQUALITY: The two ideas are equally important.	and	both/and	as	likewise similarly
ALTERNATIVE: The two ideas are different possibilities.	or, nor	either/or neither/nor	if, unless	otherwise

CONTRAST: One idea contrasts with another.	but, yet	not only/ but also	although though	however instead still nevertheless
CONSEQUENCE: One idea is a consequence of the other.	for, so		as, because, if, since, so that	therefore as a result
TIME: The two ideas are related in time.	and		after, when, since, until, while, before	meanwhile afterward

In the following examples, notice the way different conjunctions combine two short sentences into one longer one. Each new combined sentence has a different meaning, depending on the conjunction chosen. In the same way, you can scan your own writing for short, choppy sentences and try to combine some of them with conjunctions.

> **SHORT SENTENCES:** I blow the whistle. Play stops.
> **COMBINED SENTENCES:** **When** I blow the whistle, play stops. [time]
> Play will continue **unless** I blow the whistle. [alternative]
> Play stopped **because** I blew the whistle. [consequence]
> I blow the whistle, **and** play stops. [addition]

USING CONJUNCTIONS OTHER THAN AND

Sometimes the conjunction *and* is used too often. Replacing *and* with other conjunctions can improve the style of a piece of writing. Scan your own writing to determine whether you are using *and* too often to string together ideas. By selecting the appropriate conjunctions, you can revise a stringy sentence that does not hang together very well into two or more short clear statements. When you combine sentences in this way, your writing will sound more mature, and your meaning will be clearer to your audience.

STRINGY SENTENCE:	I woke up Luis, and we hopped on our bikes and cruised to the mad scientist's laboratory, and the service door was unlocked, and so it was easy to slip inside, and we released all the white mice.
REVISION:	**After** I woke up Luis, we hopped on our bikes and cruised to the mad scientist's laboratory. **Because** the service door was unlocked, it was easy to slip inside and release all the white mice.

See sentence errors, p. 72.

In this revision, the conjunction *after* subordinates the first idea to the second, making it unable to stand alone, and reveals the order of events. In the second sentence, the subordinating conjunction *because* establishes a cause-and-effect relationship between the unlocked service door and the rest of the sentence.

In the following paragraph, notice how a student writer has revised with conjunctions to emphasize the relationships among ideas and to improve her style.

STUDENT MODEL

Have you ever wondered what it would be like to have two heads? To me it would be ̂botĥ extraordi-

nary and wonderful, ̂; however,̂ ~~but~~ there might also be a lot of problems. Take dressing, for example. A two-headed person would have difficulty putting on an

ordinary T-shirt. ̂because î~~It~~ would be too small to pull over two heads. Of course, you could always make a special shirt for that "special" person.

—Lynn Yen, San Diego, California

The correlative conjunction *both/and* emphasizes the writer's enthusiasm.

The conjunctive adverb *however* stresses the contrast.

The subordinating conjunction *because* clarifies the cause and effect.

CONJUNCTIVE ADVERB: a word that serves both as a conjunction linking main clauses and also as an adverb in the clause it introduces   [See **Conjunctions.**]

100

IDENTIFYING CONTRACTIONS

A **contraction** is a word created by combining two words and removing letters.

The omitted letters in contractions are replaced by apostrophes. Here are some examples.

she'll = she will (*wi* in *will* is left out)

don't = do not (*o* in *not* is left out)

it's = it is (*i* in *is* is left out)

they'd = they would (*woul* in *would* is left out)

◆ WHEN YOU WRITE ◆

Be careful not to write the word *of* instead of the contraction *'ve* in sentences containing the helping verb *have.*

BASIC FORM: I **could have** caught the ball.

INCORRECT: I **could of** caught the ball.

CORRECT: I **could've** caught the ball.

Other examples of contractions that are often misspelled in this way are *might've*, *should've*, *would've*, and *must've*.

If you are combining a pronoun and a verb or helping verb to form a contraction, remove letters from the verb, not the pronoun:

We'll *(We will)* fly in a balloon someday.

He'd *(He would)* choose a red balloon.

I'm *(I am)* going to pick a striped one.

They're *(They are)* planning a trip soon.

It's *(It is)* a dream come true.

Note that certain pronoun-verb contractions can have two different meanings.

Contractions	Meaning 1	Meaning 2
it's	it is	it has
who's	who is	who has
she'd	she had	she would

If you are not sure of the meaning, read the whole sentence to determine which verb is in the contraction.

Who's there? (*Who is* there?)
Who's been drinking my soda? (*Who has* been drinking my soda?)

POSSESSIVE PRONOUN OR CONTRACTION?

Some possessive pronouns and contractions look similar and sound exactly the same. How can you tell whether to write *whose* or *who's*? *Your* or *you're*? Remember this rule: A possessive pronoun never has an apostrophe. A contraction always has one. Every time you write a pronoun with an apostrophe, the apostrophe should show where letters have been omitted from a verb. Supply the missing verb in your mind as you proofread.

Possessive Pronoun	Contraction
whose	who's = who is
Whose dog is this?	**Who's** going to claim it?
theirs	there's = there is
The dog is **theirs.**	**There's** the paper they signed.
its	it's = it is
The dog eats **its** food.	**It's** as hungry as a horse.
your	you're = you are
The dog is eating **your** shoes.	**You're** going to be barefoot.
their	they're = they are
They came to claim **their** dog.	**They're** taking it home now.

DEVELOPING YOUR STYLE: CONTRACTIONS

DECIDING WHEN TO USE CONTRACTIONS

Contractions give your writing a chatty, informal tone. This works well when you are writing a personal letter, dialogue for a story, or an informal speech. However, for some audiences and purposes you may want to create a more formal, dignified feeling in your writing. In these situations, you should avoid contractions.

MODEL

In this personal letter, contractions create the feeling that Matt is actually talking to his friend Jack.

Dear Jack,

How's everything? Guess who's the newest member of the track team? Your old buddy Jason. We're both looking forward to seeing you in May.

Your friend,

Matt

MODEL

Avoiding contractions creates a more formal, serious tone for a serious issue.

Who is going to pay the price for the damage we are causing to the environment today? How is our behavior going to affect future generations? These are questions I hope to answer for you. . . .

---

102 **COORDINATING CONJUNCTION:** a conjunction that links words or groups of words of equal rank

[See **Conjunctions**.]

103 **CORRELATIVE CONJUNCTIONS:** a pair of conjunctions that work together to link words or groups of words of equal rank

[See **Conjunctions**.]

104 **DANGLING MODIFIER:** a prepositional phrase, a verbal phrase, a subordinate clause, or another modifier that appears in a sentence without the word it modifies

[See **Phrases, Verbals, Problem Solver #60C.**]

DANGLING PARTICIPLE: a participle or participial 105
phrase that appears without the word it modifies
[See **Phrases, Verbals, Problem Solver #60C**.]

DASH 106

1. Use a dash to set off or emphasize additional information in a sentence.

> A **dash (—)** is a mark of punctuation that often indicates an abrupt change in thought or a deliberate pause. Dashes can be used singly or in pairs.

I cannot tell where it came from—perhaps from the next room, perhaps from the lawn.
—Sir Arthur Conan Doyle, "The Adventure of the Speckled Band"

The sweaters she had knitted in yellow, pink, bright orange—all the colors I hated—I put those in moth-proof boxes.
—Amy Tan, *The Joy Luck Club*

For six hours I had walked, reading signs, looking for a delicate print in the damp soil or even a hair that might have told of a red fox passing that way—but I had found nothing.
—Paul Annixter, "Last Cover"

If the additional information is less important than the rest of the sentence, use parentheses.

2. A dash can also be used to mean *namely, in other words*, or *that is* before an explanation or illustration.

We must accept all that God gives us—heat, cold, hunger, satisfaction, light, and darkness.
—Isaac Bashevis Singer, "Zlateh the Goat"

3. Use a dash in dialogue to show that the speaker has been interrupted.

"Mother—" he would begin, as he tried to tell her what he must do, but he could not go on.
—Yoshiko Uchida, "The Wise Old Woman"

DECLARATIVE SENTENCE: a sentence that 107
makes a statement and ends with a period
[See **Sentences: Structures and Types**.]

108 **DEMONSTRATIVE ADJECTIVE:** the word *this,* *that, these,* or *those* when used to modify a noun or pronoun

[See **Adjectives.**]

109 **DEMONSTRATIVE PRONOUN:** the word *this,* *that, these,* or *those* when it stands alone in place of a noun

[See **Pronouns.**]

110 **DIRECT ADDRESS:** speaking directly to someone or something

[See **Capitalization, Comma.**]

111 **DIRECT OBJECT:** a noun or pronoun that receives the action of a verb in the active voice and that answers the question *Whom?* or *What?* after the verb

[See **Sentences: Structures and Types, Verbs.**]

112 **DIRECT QUOTATION:** a restatement of someone's exact words placed within quotation marks or set off on separate lines

[See **Quotations.**]

113 **DOUBLE COMPARISON:** the **incorrect** use of both *more* and the *-er* ending to create the comparative form or of both *most* and the *-est* ending to create the superlative form of an adjective or adverb

[See **Adjectives, Adverbs.**]

114 **DOUBLE NEGATIVES**

A **double negative** is the use of two negative words when only one is needed.

Most people understand a negative message when they see or hear one. There is no need to use two negative words when one will do. In fact, doing so usually makes your message more difficult to understand. Avoid using two negative words in the same clause.

NONSTANDARD: On our vacation, we **hardly** spent **no** time outdoors.

STANDARD: On our vacation, we **hardly** spent **any** time outdoors.

NONSTANDARD:	We **never** saw **no** bears in Yellowstone Park.
STANDARD:	We **never** saw **any** bears in Yellowstone Park.
STANDARD:	We saw **no** bears in Yellowstone Park.

ELLIPSES

115

1. Use **ellipses (. . .)** to signal a pause in dialogue or an incomplete thought. Leave one space both before and after the three dots.

> "Well . . . I'm not sure about this," said Kwan.

2. Use ellipses to mark omissions from quoted material.

> In *I Know Why the Caged Bird Sings*, Maya Angelou writes, "Mrs. Bertha Flowers was the aristocrat of Black Stamps. She had the grace of control to appear warm in the coldest weather . . . and her printed voile dresses and flowered hats were as right for her as denim overalls for a farmer."

3. When the words before the ellipses form a complete sentence, end the sentence with a period and *then* add the three dots, for a total of four dots. Do not leave a space before the first period.

> "I don't think I ever heard Mrs. Flowers laugh, but she smiled often. . . . When she chose to smile on me, I always wanted to thank her."

EMPTY SENTENCE: a sentence that provides too little

116

information, either because it simply repeats an idea or because it makes a claim not supported by facts, reasoning, or other details
[See **Sentence Problems** in Section Two.]

EXCLAMATION POINT

117

USING AN EXCLAMATION POINT

1. Use an **exclamation point (!)** at the end of an exclamatory sentence to express strong emotion.

For more on exclamatory sentences, see p. 387.

> What a great singer Paula Abdul is!
> How loud this music is!

2. Also, use an exclamation point after an interjection showing strong emotion.

Wow**!** I thought we'd never get a copy of her video.
Hey**!** Isn't that Mary Beth in the front row?

◆ WHEN YOU WRITE ◆

Avoid overusing exclamation points. Used too often, they seem like continual shouting. Readers may tune you out.

118

EXCLAMATORY SENTENCE: a sentence that expresses strong emotion and ends with an exclamation point
[See **Sentences: Structures and Types.**]

119

FAULTY PARALLELISM: failure to use similar grammatical structures to express similar ideas
[See **Sentence Problems** in Section Two of the book.]

120

FIRST PERSON: the person speaking or writing, including the first-person pronouns *I, me, my, mine, myself, we, us, our, ours,* and *ourselves* [See **Pronouns, Verbs.**]

121

FRAGMENT: an incomplete thought incorrectly punctuated and capitalized as a sentence [See **Problem Solver #56.**]

122

FUTURE TENSE: a verb form showing an action or condition that has not yet occurred, formed by using the helping verbs *will* or *shall* plus the base form of the main verb [See **Verbs.**]

123 GENDER

Gender is a grammatical concept that distinguishes the sex of something named by a noun or pronoun.

1. Nouns and pronouns have three genders.

masculine *(he/him)*	human males/some animals
feminine *(she/her)*	human females/some animals
neuter *(it)*	some animals/things/ideas

2. Pronouns must agree with their antecedents in gender.

Preston rides **his** bike to school. (male)
Since **Barb** lives only two blocks from school, **she** can walk.
(female)
The **eagle** spread **its** wings as **it** soared above the trees.
(neuter)

3. Use either a masculine or a feminine pronoun to refer to
an animal whose gender is known or self-evident, including family pets.

Duke wags **his** tail when I get home from school. (masculine)
The **hen** squawked as I approached **her** chicks. (feminine)

4. When referring to people, use both the masculine and
feminine pronouns to refer to an antecedent if that antecedent
may be either masculine or feminine.

Anyone who plans to try out for the play needs to bring **his** or
her script.

If your sentence sounds awkward, try rephrasing it, either by
using the plural form or by eliminating the pronoun entirely.

All students who are going to try out need to bring **their**
scripts.
All students who are going to try out need to bring **a** script.

GERUND: a verbal that ends in *-ing* and is used as a noun
[See **Verbals**.]

`124`

GERUND PHRASE: a group of words serving as a noun
and consisting of a gerund and its object and/or modifiers
[See **Phrases, Verbals**.]

`125`

GRAMMAR: the set of rules governing the forms of words and
their arrangement in phrases, clauses, and sentences

`126`

HELPING VERB: a verb that works with the main verb in a
verb phrase
[See **Verbs**.]

`127`

IDENTIFYING A HYPHEN

A hyphen (-) links two or more words together or divides a single word into syllables.

1. Use a hyphen in certain compound nouns.

brother-in-law
jack-o'-lantern

Consult a dictionary to find out whether a compound noun is closed up (stockbroker), hyphenated, or open (press agent).

2. Use a hyphen with compound modifiers that precede the words they modify. A compound modifier consists of two or more words that function as a unit, express a single thought, and modify a noun or pronoun.

a **well-designed** computer
a **world-famous** engineer

Do not use a hyphen when a verb comes between the noun and the compound modifier.

a computer that was **well designed**

Do not use a hyphen when an adverb ending in *-ly* and an adjective or participle modify a noun or pronoun.

a **beautifully designed** computer

3. Use a hyphen in compound numbers from twenty-one through ninety-nine, in the ordinal forms of these numbers, and in fractions used as modifiers.

CARDINAL NUMBER: **thirty-eight**
ORDINAL NUMBER: **fifty-fourth**
FRACTION: **one-quarter** cup

4. Use a hyphen to join the prefixes *self*, *ex*, *all*, and *great* or the suffixes *elect* and *free* to another word.

She was his **self-appointed** spokesperson.
The **president-elect** rode in the limousine.

5. Use a hyphen to divide a word between syllables at the end of a line. Do not leave a single letter alone at either the beginning or end of a line.

A *junction* is the point at which **cross-roads** meet. Such places often mark **political** divisions and serve as town borders.

IMPERATIVE SENTENCE: a sentence that gives a command or makes a request and whose subject is always *you*, usually omitted but understood [See **Sentences: Structures and Types.**] 129

INDEFINITE ADJECTIVE: a term sometimes applied to a word used as an adjective that in other instances is used as an indefinite pronoun [See **Adjectives.**] 130

INDEFINITE PRONOUN: a pronoun that does not refer to a specific noun [See **Pronouns, Problem Solver #59D.**] 131

INDIRECT OBJECT: a noun or pronoun that answers the question *To whom? For whom? To what?* or *For what?* after an action verb [See **Sentences, Structures and Types.**] 132

INDIRECT QUESTION: a question reworded within a declarative sentence [See **Question Mark.**] 133

INDIRECT QUOTATION: a restatement of someone's words as part of a noun clause [See **Quotations.**] 134

INFINITIVE: the base form of a verb, usually preceded by *to,* used as a noun, an adjective, or an adverb [See **Verbals.**] 135

INFINITIVE PHRASE: a group of words consisting of an infinitive plus its object and/or modifiers that serves as a noun, adjective, or adverb [See **Phrases, Verbals.**] 136

INTENSIVE PRONOUN: a pronoun, usually ending in *-self* or *-selves*, that merely emphasizes its antecedent and could be dropped without changing the meaning of a sentence [See **Pronouns.**] 137

INTERJECTIONS

An **interjection** is a word or group of words that expresses emotion.

IDENTIFYING AN INTERJECTION

A strong interjection is followed by an exclamation point. A mild interjection is followed by a comma.

> **Wow!** What a beautiful day!
> **Yikes!** The water feels like ice!
> **Oh my goodness,** I think I left my sunglasses at the beach.
> **Well,** we'll just have to go back and get them.

◆ WHEN YOU WRITE ◆

Interjections help to breathe life into your writing. However, do not overuse them. Too many interjections will give your writing a jerky, breathless quality.

---

139 **INTERROGATIVE PRONOUN:** a pronoun used to ask a question [See **Pronouns.**]

140 **INTERROGATIVE SENTENCE:** a sentence that asks a question and ends with a question mark [See **Sentences: Structures and Types.**]

141 **INTERRUPTER:** a phrase or clause that interrupts a sentence to add information not essential to a sentence's meaning [See **Comma.**]

142 **INTRANSITIVE VERB:** a verb that does not have an object [See **Verbs.**]

143 **INVERTED SENTENCE:** a sentence in which the subject follows the verb [See **Sentences: Structures and Types, Problem Solver #57B.**]

144 **IRREGULAR VERB:** a verb that does not form its past and past participle by adding *-ed* or *-d* to the present form [See **Verbs.**]

ITALICS: slanted type used in printed material to indicate the title of full-length works, movies, words used as words, and so on
[See **Underlining/Italics.**]

145

LINKING VERB: a verb that expresses state of being rather than action and links the subject to a noun, pronoun, or adjective in the predicate
[See **Verbs.**]

146

MAIN CLAUSE: a clause that is not introduced by a relative pronoun or subordinating conjunction and that can stand alone as a sentence
[See **Clauses.**]

147

MISPLACED MODIFIER: a phrase, a clause, or another modifier placed so far away from the word it modifies that it seems to modify something else
[See **Phrases, Problem Solver #60A, B.**]

148

MODIFIER: any word, phrase, or clause serving as an adjective or adverb to describe or limit the meaning of another word, phrase, or clause
[See **Adjectives, Adverbs, Clauses, Phrases, Prepositions, Verbals.**]

149

NAMES
[See **Capitalization, Nouns.**]

150

NEGATIVE: a word, word part, or expression that denies or means "no"
[See **Adverbs, Double Negatives.**]

151

NONRESTRICTIVE CLAUSE: a clause that interrupts a sentence to add information that is not essential to the sentence's meaning
[See **Clauses, Comma.**]

152

NOUN CLAUSE: a subordinate clause that functions in a sentence as a subject, object, or predicate noun
[See **Clauses.**]

153

NOUNS

154

Nouns are among the very first words that humans learn to use. In fact, your own name is a noun. Nouns, or name words, are basic building blocks of every language.

A **noun** is a word naming a person, place, thing, or idea.

IDENTIFYING NOUNS

Types of Nouns

TYPE:	**Common Nouns**
FUNCTION:	to name any person, place, thing, or idea
EXAMPLES:	dog, city, woman, day, team, show
TYPE:	**Proper Nouns**
FUNCTION:	to name a particular person, place, thing, or idea
EXAMPLES:	Rover, Chicago, Samantha, Friday, Houston Astros, *Sesame Street* [Note that proper nouns are capitalized.]
TYPE:	**Collective Nouns**
FUNCTION:	to name a group
EXAMPLES:	team, group, crew, herd, flock, class, congregation, crowd, swarm, pile, gaggle, pride

	Concrete Nouns	**Abstract Nouns**
TYPE:		
FUNCTION:	to refer to things that can be seen, heard, smelled, tasted, or touched	to refer to ideas—things that can't be seen, heard, smelled, tasted, or touched
EXAMPLES:	**apple** **zebra** **sulfur** **roses** **spaghetti** **velvet** **firecracker**	**peace** **hope** **life** **shyness** **bravery** **evil** **health**

Notice that these categories may overlap. For example, a common noun like *team* may also be collective and concrete.

SINGULAR AND PLURAL NOUNS

A **singular noun** refers to one of something:

cow	pickle
nose	train

A **plural** noun refers to more than one:

cows	pickles
noses	trains

Spelling Plurals of Nouns

In many cases, simply adding an *s* to the end of a noun will create its plural form: *cat/cats, fence/fences, muffin/muffins*.

Making nouns plural isn't always that easy, however. Some nouns with certain endings form the plural in special ways. Follow the rules in this chart as a guide.

Nouns with Certain Endings	Rules for Forming the Plural	Singular/Plural
Nouns that end in *ch, s, sh, x,* and *z*	Add *es* to the singular form of the noun.	batch/batches bus/buses wish/wishes box/boxes buzz/buzzes
Nouns that end in *f* or *fe*	Say the plural form of the word aloud.	
	If you hear the *f* sound in the plural form, just add *s*.	reef/reefs cliff/cliffs fife/fifes
	If you hear a *v* sound, change the *f* or *fe* to *ve* and add *s*.	wolf/wolves leaf/leaves knife/knives
Nouns that end in *o*	If there is a vowel just before the final *o*, simply add *s*.	radio/radios cameo/cameos tattoo/tattoos
	If there is a consonant before the final *o*, add *es*	potato/potatoes hero/heroes

		Exceptions: —words borrowed from foreign languages such as **taco/tacos** —musical terms such as **piano/pianos**
Nouns that end in *y*	If there is a vowel just before the final *y*, simply add *s*.	**turkey/turkeys** **donkey/donkeys**
	If there is a consonant before the final *y*, change *y* to *i* and add *es*.	**glory/glories** **candy/candies**

The plural forms of some nouns don't seem to follow any rules at all, and these must simply be memorized.

mouse/mice	**child/children**
woman/women	**louse/lice**
goose/geese	**foot/feet**
man/men	**tooth/teeth**

Spelling Plurals of Compound Nouns

A **compound noun** is made up of two words. If a compound noun is written as one word, make the last of the two nouns plural.

cupcake/cupcak**es**
mailbox/mailbox**es**
racehorse/racehors**es**
salesperson/sales**people**

Some compound nouns are hyphenated. To make a hyphenated compound noun plural, simply use the plural form of the most important noun.

father-in-law/father**s**-in-law
runner-up/runner**s**-up

NOUNS IN SENTENCES

A noun can function as the **subject (S)** of a sentence when it is the doer of the action or when it is the person, place, thing, or idea being discussed in a sentence.

The **bison** lowered its head and charged.
<small>S</small>

A **bison** can be fierce.
<small>S</small>

A noun can also function as the **object** in a sentence. The noun is a **direct object (DO)** when it is acted on in some way by the subject of the sentence.

The **bison** tossed the **photographer** in the air.

A noun functioning as an **indirect object (IO)** receives the action of a verb indirectly.

The **ranger** sent the **photographer** a **get-well card**.

A noun can also function as an **object of a preposition (OP)** such as *for, of, from, at,* and other prepositions.

The **ranger** gave the **bison piles** of **hay**.

Finally, **a predicate noun** further identifies the subject. It follows a linking verb such as one of the forms of the verb *be*.

DEVELOPING YOUR STYLE: NOUNS

CHOOSING SPECIFIC NOUNS

To avoid vagueness, use specific nouns as often as possible. A **specific noun** refers to a particular type of person, place, thing, or idea. A **general noun** refers to a person, place, thing, or idea in a broad, less easy to imagine way. Study the following chart of progressively more specific nouns.

General	Specific	More Specific
animal	horse	racehorse
rodent	squirrel	ground squirrel
bird	songbird	cardinal
food	bread	pumpernickel
vehicle	car	minivan
music	classics	symphony
clothing	shoes	sneakers
technology	computer	laptop

Now read these sentences:

A **bird** flew into the kitchen.
The **dog** knocked me down and licked my nose.
I couldn't wait to get my new **instrument.**

These statements are vague because the general nouns don't help readers picture what the writer is describing. Note how the sentences have been improved by substituting more specific nouns.

A **bald eagle** flew into the kitchen.
The **Great Dane** knocked me down and licked my nose.
I couldn't wait to get my new **clarinet.**

Notice how one writer made the following paragraph more interesting by replacing general nouns with more specific ones.

M O D E L

As the ~~train~~ ^{Broadway Limited} sped through western Pennsylvania, Tom stared out at the ~~scenery~~ ^{landscape}. Fenced, green ~~spaces~~ ^{pastures} alternated with ugly, gray piles from the coal ~~mines~~ ^{slag heaps}. Tidy-looking ~~dwellings~~ ^{farmhouses} yielded regularly to factories resembling ~~castles~~ ^{walled fortresses} that belched smoke into the crisp, blue air. Every so often when they passed a level crossing, a ~~person~~ ^{boy} on a bike would be right up front against the ~~bar~~ ^{trestle}, waving all the while as the train rumbled past the flashing signal lights.

NUMBER: the expression of a noun, pronoun, or verb as **155**
singular (one) or **plural** (more than one)
[See **Nouns, Pronouns, Verbs.**]

NUMBERS 156

There are two kinds of numbers.

Cardinal numbers tell how many: one (1), ten (10), one million (1,000,000).

Ordinal numbers rank items in a series: first (1st), tenth (10th), one millionth ($\frac{1}{1,000,000}$).

Numbers can be spelled out (fifteen) or expressed in numerals (15). As a general rule, numbers from one through one hundred should be spelled out. Use numerals for all numbers above one hundred.

We ran **five miles** today.
We ran **113 miles** this month.

There are some special cases:

1. Spell out numbers that begin a sentence, or rewrite the sentence to change the position of the number.

Six-hundred fifty-eight miles is the farthest anyone has run in a race.
The farthest anyone has run in a race is **658 miles.**

2. Use numerals for house and apartment numbers in addresses.

She lives at **1154 Elm Street, Apartment #5.**

3. Use numerals for exact times expressed with A.M. or P.M. and exact dates.

The marathon will be held on **November 3** at **11:00 A.M.**

4. Use a combination of numerals and words for large round numbers ending in millions, billions, or more.

> More than **100 million** people around the world will see the race on television.

> Probably **200 million** fans will listen to newcasts about the race on the radio.

5. If numbers above and below one hundred appear in the same sentence or paragraph, be consistent and use numerals for all of them.

> Only about **50** of the runners will be seen on television crossing the finish line, although there are over **24,500** participants.

> Only **75** runners among the **24,500** participants will have times under **3** hours.

---

157 **OBJECT:** a noun or pronoun that receives the action, directly or indirectly, of an action verb or verbal, or that a preposition relates to the rest of the sentence
[See **Prepositions, Sentences: Structures and Types, Verbals, Verbs.**]

158 **OBJECT FORM OF A PRONOUN:** the form of a pronoun used as a direct object, an indirect object, an object of a preposition, or any other object [See **Pronouns.**]

159 **OBJECT OF A PREPOSITION:** the noun or pronoun that a preposition relates to the rest of the sentence
[See **Prepositions.**]

160 **PARALLEL STRUCTURE:** expressing similar ideas in similar grammatical structures
[See **Sentence Problems** in Section Two of the book.]

USING PARENTHESES

The first half of a parentheses is called an **open parenthesis** and the second a **closed parenthesis.**

> **Parentheses ( )** are used to enclose information that is useful or interesting but "extra."

> Seven flies **(large ones)** buzzed around the tailor.

1. If parentheses enclose one sentence within another sentence, do not capitalize the first letter of the enclosed sentence or insert a period after it.

> Picking up a rag **(he'd had quite enough)**, he stood up.

2. If the sentence inside parentheses stands alone, capitalize and punctuate it as you would any other sentence.

> The tailor struck hard. **("Take that!" he was thinking.)**

◆ WHEN YOU WRITE ◆

Using parentheses is like telling readers, "Here's another thing, just in case you wanted to know." Therefore, use parentheses when you want to avoid interrupting the flow of the sentence. However, use dashes when you want to call attention to "extra" information. Dashes send a signal: "This makes a difference."

The flies (seven of them) lay dead. [The use of parentheses suggests that the number of flies killed is an interesting extra fact.]

The flies—seven of them—lay dead. [The use of dashes calls attention to the number of flies killed.]

162 **PARTICIPIAL PHRASE:** a group of words consisting of a participle and its object and/or modifiers that serves as an adjective   [See **Phrases, Verbals.**]

163 **PARTICIPLE:** a verb form, usually ending in *-ed* or *-ing*, that is sometimes used as an adjective and sometimes as the main verb after a form of the helping verb *have* or *be*   [See **Verbals, Verbs.**]

164 **PASSIVE VOICE:** a verb form in which the subject receives the action, created by using a form of the helping verb *be* plus the past participle of the main verb   [See **Verbs.**]

165 **PAST PARTICIPLE:** a verb form, usually ending in *-ed*, that is sometimes used as an adjective and sometimes as the main verb after a form of the helping verb *have* (creating a perfect tense) or *be* (creating the passive voice)   [See **Verbals, Verbs.**]

166 **PAST TENSE:** a verb form showing an action or condition that began and ended at a given time in the past, usually created by adding *-ed* or *-d* to the base form of the verb   [See **Verbs.**]

167 **PERFECT TENSE:** one of three verb forms showing an action completed when another action begins or one that began in the past and continues into the present. These tenses are created by using a form of the helping verb *have* and the past participle of the main verb.   [See **Verbs.**]

168 **PERIOD**

IDENTIFYING A PERIOD

A **period (.)** at the end of a sentence signals a complete thought.

For more about types of sentences, see p. 387.

1. Use periods to end both declarative sentences (those that make statements) and imperative sentences (those that give commands or make requests).

> Mrs. Sujimoto teaches people to read faster. (declarative sentence)
> Try her techniques. (imperative sentence—command)
> Please borrow this videotape. (imperative sentence—request)

2. Use a period or periods to show that a letter or group of letters is an abbreviation.

R.N.—registered nurse

For more about abbreviations, see p. 1.

If a sentence ends with an abbreviation, use only one period.

This story was written around 1500 B.C.

3. Some countries often are referred to by their initials. All capitals and periods are required.

U.S.A. (United States of America)
U.K. (United Kingdom of Great Britain and Northern Ireland)

4. Use a period at the end of a single letter to show that the letter is an initial, the first letter of a name.

Victor **H.** Cruz (**H.** stands for Hernandez.)
N. Scott Momaday (**N.** stands for Navarre.)

5. Use a period to end a direct quotation. Put the period *inside* the quotation marks.

Mrs. Sujimoto said, "Read this page."

N. Scott Momaday

If the quoted sentence is not the end of the whole sentence, use a comma, not a period, after it.

"Read this page," she said.

6. Use a period to mark decimals and to separate dollars from cents.

She finished the race with a time of **15.6** seconds.
It costs only **$299.45** a month.

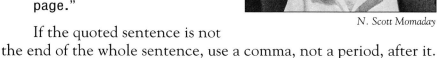

PERSON: a property of nouns and pronouns that indicates who is speaking or writing **(first person)**, the person being addressed **(second person)**, or the person or thing being discussed **(third person)**.

All nouns are in the third person; personal pronouns change form to indicate person, and some verbs change form to agree with their subjects: *I am, you are, he/she/it is,* and so on. [See **Pronouns, Verbs.**]

169

170 **PERSONAL PRONOUN:** one of the pronouns in which the form indicates the person speaking or writing **(first person)**, the person being addressed **(second person)**, or the person or thing being discussed **(third person)**   [See **Pronouns**.]

171 **PHRASES**

A **phrase** is a group of words that acts as a unit without a subject and predicate.

The astronaut and ground crew in the illustration below are speaking in phrases. Perhaps, like these scientists, you use phrases when you want to get your meaning across quickly. In writing, however, phrases serve another purpose. When included in written sentences, phrases add information and elaborate on your meaning.

IDENTIFYING PHRASES

A good way to identify phrases in a sentence is to look for words that form natural clusters or groups. Those clusters that do *not* have subjects or predicates are phrases.

```
not a phrase     phrase
Luis climbed onto a bench.

not a phrase  phrase           not a phrase
He reached for a box that he could barely see.
```

TYPES OF PHRASES

The chart that follows defines each type of phrase and gives examples showing how each type of phrase can be used.

Type of Phrase	Definition	Examples
Prepositional Phrase	A group of related words that begins with a preposition and ends with a noun or pronoun, called the object of the preposition. The two types of prepositional phrases appear below:	There were some mechanical wings **inside the box**. The wings felt light **as clouds**.
ADJECTIVE PHRASE	A prepositional phrase that modifies a noun or pronoun.	The label **on the box** read "One size fits all."
ADVERB PHRASE	A prepositional phrase that modifies a verb, an adjective, or an adverb.	Luis moved his fingers **over gears, springs, and metal feathers.**
Verb Phrase	A group of words that is made up of a main verb and its helping verb or verbs.	Soon Luis **was laughing** joyfully. For more on verb phrases, see p. 407.
Verbal Phrase	A group of words that includes a verbal and all its modifiers and objects. There are three types of verbal phrases:	For more on verbals, see p. 398.
PARTICIPIAL PHRASE	A group of words, made up of a participle and all its objects and modifiers, that modifies a noun or pronoun.	The boy **flying up there like a large pigeon** is Luis.
GERUND PHRASE	A group of words, made up of a gerund and all its objects and modifiers, that acts as a noun.	**Flying like a bird** has always been Luis's dream.
INFINITIVE PHRASE	A group of words, made up of an infinitive and all its objects and modifiers, that acts as a noun, an adjective, or an adverb.	**To see his town from the sky** is thrilling for Luis.
Appositive Phrase	A group of words that acts as a noun and identifies or provides extra information about another noun.	Luis's grandfather, **a cranky, shy postal clerk,** was secretly an inventor.

COMMON USAGE PROBLEMS

Here are some common errors writers make with phrases.

Error	How to Correct
Letting a phrase stand alone as a sentence fragment:	Add a subject and predicate to form a complete sentence:
Plunging into the lake.	**Plunging into the lake,** Luis shrieked.
Misplacing a phrase used as a modifier:	Move the phrase closer to the word or words it modifies, and add words if necessary:
Searchers spotted Luis's shoes **with keen eyes.**	Searchers **with keen eyes** spotted Luis's shoes.
Leaving out the word that the phrase modifies, resulting in a dangling modifier:	Add the word that the phrase modifies and any other necessary words:
To stay afloat, the wings had to be detached.	**To stay afloat,** Luis had to detach the wings.

DEVELOPING YOUR STYLE: PHRASES

Use phrases to provide variety and add interest to your writing. Notice how each of the following phrases enriches this basic sentence:

BASIC SENTENCE: The townspeople saw Luis.

PREPOSITIONAL PHRASE: The townspeople saw Luis **in the lake.**

PARTICIPIAL PHRASE: **Peering through the bushes,** the townspeople saw Luis in the lake.

APPOSITIVE PHRASE: Peering through the bushes, the townspeople saw Luis, **the boy who flew,** in the lake.

Good writers carefully decide when to use phrases and where to place them in sentences for maximum effect.

172 PLURAL: indicating more than one

Nouns, verbs, pronouns, and a few adjectives change form to indicate the plural. [See **Adjectives, Nouns, Number, Pronouns, Verbs.**]

173 PLURAL NOUN: a noun that indicates more than one person, place, thing, or idea and usually ends in *-s* [See **Nouns.**]

POSSESSIVE FORMS

IDENTIFYING POSSESSIVE FORMS

Possessive forms do not always show true possession. For example, although ***Julie's*** *coat* means "a coat that Julie possesses," ***Julie's*** *school* merely means "the school that Julie attends."

> The **possessive form** of a noun or pronoun shows ownership, belonging, or another close relationship.

POSSESSIVE FORMS OF NOUNS

Most singular nouns form the possessive by adding an apostrophe and *s*:

Julie → Julie**'s** dog
dog → the dog**'s** fleas

Most singular nouns ending in *s* form the possessive in the same way:

Gladys → Gladys**'s** boss
boss → the boss**'s** decisions

Plural nouns ending in *s* add just an apostrophe to form the possessive:

fleas → the fleas**'** bites
bosses → the bosses**'** meeting

Plural nouns not ending in *s* form the possessive by adding an apostrophe and *s*:

people → people**'s** pets
geese → geese**'s** squawks

The possessive form of a noun is the same whether it comes before the word it possesses or stands alone:

Julie**'s** dog has fleas.
That old fleabag is Julie**'s**.

POSSESSIVE FORMS OF PRONOUNS

Personal pronouns have possessive forms that do not use apostrophes. In addition, most have two possible forms, depending on whether the possessive comes before the word it possesses or stands alone.

COMMON USAGE PROBLEMS

JOINT VERSUS SEPARATE POSSESSION

By using possessives correctly, you can specify whether you are talking about joint possession of the same thing or separate possession of different things. If two or more nouns jointly possess the same thing, use the possessive form only for the last noun:

> Did you find Aunt Gladys
> and Uncle Pat's dog?

If two or more nouns possess separate things, use the possessive form for each noun:

> Julie's and Mae's dogs are both very old.

POSSESSIVES VERSUS CONTRACTIONS

For more on contractions, see p. 330. The possessive forms of some pronouns are homonyms for contractions of the pronoun with *is* or *has*. Do not mix up the following words. Remember that the possessive forms of personal pronouns and *who* do not use apostrophes.

Possessive Pronoun	Contraction
Whose dog is this?	**Who's** going to claim it?
The dog is **theirs.**	**There's** the name on the license.
The dog eats **its** food.	**It's** as hungry as a horse.

DEVELOPING YOUR STYLE: POSSESSIVE FORMS

STREAMLINING SENTENCES WITH POSSESSIVES

In the following example, notice how a writer used possessive forms to shorten part of a personal narrative.

MODEL	
<u>Our</u> ~~The~~ dog ~~we own~~ has been in the family since I was very young. The ^{dog's}⋀ name ~~of the dog~~ is Mutt, and he is certainly no beauty. Despite all ~~the~~ ^{Mom and Dad's} training ~~Mom and Dad gave him~~, he remains ~~a~~ creature ^{nature's} ~~of nature~~, always ready to fight with ^{neighbors'}⋀ dogs ~~owned by neighbors~~ or take a roll in the mud. Despite ~~the~~ ^{this rough-and-ready pet's} ungainly appearance ~~of this rough and ready pet~~,⋀ we all love him very much. That's why ~~the~~ sudden ^{Mutt's} disappearance ~~of Mutt~~ disturbed ~~the~~ peace of mind ^{everyone's} ~~of everyone~~ and why the whole family went down to the pound to beg ~~the~~ workers ^{its} ~~in the pound~~ to help search for him.	The writer stream-lines the first few sentences by using possessive forms of pronouns and nouns. The writer punctu-ates *Mom and Dad's* to show joint possession and uses an apos-trophe after *s* to form the posses-sive of *neighbors*. The writer also uses an apostro-phe in *everyone's*, and does not use one in *its*, the pos-sessive form of a personal pronoun.

POSSESSIVE NOUN: a noun form that shows owner-ship or belonging and ends in an apostrophe or an apostrophe plus *s*
[See **Possessive Forms, Problem Solver #61 A–D.**]

`175`

POSSESSIVE PRONOUN: a pronoun form that shows ownership or belonging
[See **Possessive Forms, Pronouns, Problem Solver #61E.**]

`176`

PREDICATE: the part of a sentence that tells what the subject does or is
[See **Sentences: Structures and Types.**]

`177`

PREDICATE ADJECTIVE: an adjective that follows a linking verb and modifies the subject
[See **Adjectives, Sentences: Structures and Types.**]

`178`

179 **PREDICATE NOUN:** a noun that follows a linking verb and further identifies the subject
[See **Nouns, Sentences: Structures and Types.**]

180 **PREFIX:** a word part added to the beginning of a base word; for example, *pre-*, a prefix meaning "before," as in *pretest* and *precede*
[See **Spelling.**]

181 **PREPOSITIONAL PHRASE:** a phrase that serves as an adjective or adverb and consists of a preposition (at the beginning), its object (usually at the end), and any words that modify the object
[See **Phrases, Prepositions.**]

182 **PREPOSITIONS**

IDENTIFYING PREPOSITIONS

A **preposition** relates the noun or pronoun that appears with it to another word in the sentence.

Have you ever seen a diagram—perhaps of a hookup of two electronics components—that used arrows to indicate where plugs and wires go? In writing, prepositions serve the same function as arrows in a diagram. They show the relationship between one person, place, thing, or idea and another word in the sentence. These relationships are often ones of time (*before*, *after*) or space (*beyond*, *behind*). In the following sentences, the prepositions in bold type show various types of relationships:

The leopard cubs played **after** their meal. [*After* relates the noun *meal* to the word *played,* showing the order in which they occurred.]

Suddenly, a pack **of** hyenas moved closer. [*Of* relates the noun *hyenas* to the word *pack.*]

Fortunately, the cubs already were **up** a tree. [*Up* relates the noun *tree* to the word *cubs.*]

The following chart shows the most common prepositions:

about	against	as	below	beyond	except
above	along	at	beneath	by	for
across	among	before	beside	down	from
after	around	behind	between	during	in

inside	of	outside	till	until
into	off	over	to	up
like	on	since	toward	upon
near	out	through	under	with

Some prepositions, such as *along with* and *up to*, contain more than one word.

IDENTIFYING PREPOSITIONAL PHRASES

A **prepositional phrase** is a group of words that begins with a preposition **(PREP)** and ends with the noun or pronoun that appears with it. This noun or pronoun is called the **object of the preposition (OP)**. The object of the preposition may have one or more modifiers, or words that describe it. Thus a prepositional phrase usually consists of the following elements:

Preposition + Modifier(s) of the Object + Object of Preposition

In the sentences that follow, notice the modifiers between the prepositions and their objects.

PREP   OP
The mother leopard disappeared **into the thick bush.**

      PREP OP   PREP   OP
The pack **of hyenas** stopped **by the tall tree.**

        PREP   OP
They stared upward **at the now-frightened cubs.**

PREP   OP
In the acacia tree's high branches, the cubs were safe.

A single sentence can have several prepositional phrases. These phrases can appear anywhere in the sentence.

Unlike many other species, leopards can adapt easily **to different environments. In Africa** some **of these remarkable cats** live close **to major towns.**

Prepositional phrases can be used as adjectives or adverbs.

Prepositional Phrases Used as Adjectives and Adverbs

Adjective phrases, which are prepositional phrases used as adjectives, modify, or tell more about, nouns or pronouns.

DESCRIBES A NOUN: The whiskers **of the mother leopard** quivered.

DESCRIBES A PRONOUN: Who **in the world** likes to see its young in danger?

Adverb phrases, which are prepositional phrases used as adverbs, modify, or describe, verbs, adjectives, or adverbs. When they modify verbs, they tell *when,* where, or *how* an action takes place.

DESCRIBES A VERB: When the hyenas left, the mother meowed **to the cubs.**

DESCRIBES AN ADJECTIVE: Leopards are wary **of danger.**

DESCRIBES AN ADVERB: The mother begins hunting soon **after nightfall.**

PREPOSITION OR ADVERB?

Some words such as *up, down, in, out,* and *beyond* can be used either as prepositions or as adverbs. Remember that a preposition is usually followed by a noun or pronoun that is the object of the preposition and that an adverb is a single word that modifies a verb, adjective, or adverb. Therefore, a word that appears alone is usually an adverb. Compare and contrast the following sample sentences:

The mother leopard looked **beyond** the river. [preposition + object of the preposition]

A reedbuck, which is a medium-sized antelope, grazed **beyond**. [adverb modifying the verb *grazed*]

The leopard inched silently **down** the riverbank. [preposition + object of the preposition]

Suddenly she brought the reedbuck **down**. [adverb modifying the verb *brought*]

COMMON USAGE PROBLEMS

ENDING A SENTENCE WITH A PREPOSITION

In the past, formal use discouraged ending a sentence with a preposition. The rule existed to discourage awkward sentences such as the one that follows:

INCORRECT: A preposition is no word to end a sentence **with!**

Certain expressions, however, sound less awkward when you violate the rule. Here is an example.

FORMAL: **About** what are you talking?

BETTER: What are you talking **about?**

You might try to reword a sentence to avoid these situations.

REWORDED SENTENCE: What are you **discussing?**

More and more, though, you will notice that reputable writers use certain idiomatic expressions that end with prepositions.

AVOIDING <u>WHERE . . . AT</u>

Do not use the preposition *at* with questions beginning with *Where*.

CORRECT: **Where** do leopards live? [not Where do leopards live at?]

USING <u>DIFFERENT FROM</u>

Use *different from, not different than,* before a word or phrase.

CORRECT: A cheetah is **different from** a leopard; the first has spots, whereas the second has groups of spots called rosettes.

DEVELOPING YOUR STYLE: PREPOSITIONAL PHRASES

USING PREPOSITIONAL PHRASES IN DESCRIPTION

Prepositional phrases are useful when writing descriptions because they help make spatial and other relationships clear. In addition, you can use prepositional phrases to add details to most sentences.

MODEL

The cubs played joyfully ^at the foot of the tree.^ Their favorite game was to jump ^on their mother's back.^

---

183 **PRESENT PARTICIPLE:** a verb form ending in *-ing* that is sometimes used as an adjective and sometimes as the main verb after a form of the helping verb *be* (creating a progressive form)
[See **Verbals, Verbs.**]

184 **PRESENT TENSE:** a verb form showing an action or condition that exists at the present time, usually consisting of the base form of the verb except when *-s* or *-es* is added to agree with a third-person singular subject
[See **Verbs.**]

185 **PRINCIPAL PARTS OF A VERB:** the four main forms of a verb, from which all other tenses and forms are created
[See **Verbs.**]

186 **PROGRESSIVE FORM:** one of six verb forms showing an ongoing action or condition, created by using a form of the helping verb *be* plus the present participle of the main verb
[See **Verbs.**]

187 **PRONOUN-ANTECEDENT AGREEMENT:** using a pronoun of the same gender, person, and number as its antecedent
[See **Pronouns, Problem Solver #59.**]

188 **PRONOUNS**

IDENTIFYING PRONOUNS

A **pronoun** is a word that takes the place of a noun or another pronoun.

Just as one basketball player substitutes for another who leaves the game, pronouns replace nouns or other pronouns that appear frequently in a passage. The word or group of words that a pronoun replaces is called its **antecedent.**

TYPES OF PRONOUNS

Personal Pronouns

Form:	Subject Pronouns		
	First Person	**Second Person**	**Third Person**
SINGULAR:	I	you	he, she, it
PLURAL:	we	you	they

For more on subjects and objects, see p. 396 and p. 348.

Form:	Object Pronouns		
	First Person	**Second Person**	**Third Person**
SINGULAR:	me	you	him, her, it
PLURAL:	us	you	them

Form:	Possessive Pronouns		
	First Person	**Second Person**	**Third Person**
SINGULAR:	my, mine	you, yours	his, her, hers, its
PLURAL:	our, ours	you, yours	their, theirs

Function:	to refer to people or things
Examples in Sentences:	**She** showed **us** the photographs of the game. **We** like **them**. **They** were better than **ours**. **You** should compare **mine** to **hers**.

Interrogative Pronouns

Forms:	**Referring to People**	**Referring to Things**
	who [subject]	which
	whom [object]	what
	whose [possessive]	

Function:	to ask questions

Examples in Sentences:	**Who** scored the most points?
	Whom did the ref charge with a foul?
	Whose were the most fouls?
	Which is my best shot?
	What was your season average?

Relative Pronouns

Forms:	who [subject]	whom [object]	whose [possession]
Function:	to show the relationship of a subordinate clause [that is, a clause that cannot stand alone] to a noun in the main clause; the form of the relative pronoun depends on its use in the subordinate clause		

Examples in Sentences:	I was guarding Paul, **who *towered over me.*** [***Who*** refers to Paul.]

(superscripts: S V over "who towered")

He is a player **whom *I respect.*** [***Whom*** refers to Paul.]

(superscripts: O S V over "whom I respect")

They have a forward **whose *arms are long.*** [***Whose*** refers to forward.]

(superscripts: POSS S V over "whose arms are")

Demonstrative Pronouns

Forms:	Singular	Plural
	this, that	these, those

Function:	to point out a specific person or thing

Examples in Sentences:	**This** is the best game I ever played.
	Those are my sneakers.

Indefinite Pronouns

Forms:	Singular	Plural	Singular or Plural
	another, anyone,	both, few	all, any, most
	anything, each,	several, many	none, some
	either, everyone,		
	everything, much,		
	neither, no one,		
	nothing, one,		
	someone, something		

Function:	to refer to a noun or pronoun that is not specifically named

Examples in Sentences:

SINGULAR:

Anyone *is* welcome at a home game.

The players are ready, and **each *has*** a chance to play.

Everyone *has* a good view of the court.

Much of the fun ***is*** cheering for your team.

No one *is* able to ignore the excitement.

Something unexpected often ***happens.***

PLURAL:	Few of the fans *leave* early.
	Many of us *go* together to the victory party.
SINGULAR OR PLURAL:	Most of the players *like* to celebrate. [plural]
	None of their joy *is* hidden. [singular]

Reflexive Pronouns

Forms:	First Person	Second Person	Third Person
SINGULAR:	myself	yourself	himself, herself, itself
PLURAL:	ourselves	yourselves	themselves

Function:	to add meaning to the sentence by throwing the action back on the subject [A reflexive pronoun cannot be deleted from a sentence without changing the meaning.]

Examples in Sentences:	I taught **myself** to dribble. [reflexive pronoun as direct object]
	We bought **ourselves** tickets to a pro game. [as indirect object]
	My teammates tried harder and asked more of **themselves,** and so we won the championship. [as object of preposition]

Intensive Pronouns

Forms:	First Person	Second Person	Third Person
SINGULAR:	myself	yourself	himself, herself, itself
PLURAL:	ourselves	yourselves	themselves

Function:	to emphasize or call attention to a noun or another pronoun [An intensive pronoun can be deleted from a sentence without changing the meaning.]

Examples in Sentences:	We **ourselves** raised the money for new uniforms.
	Darryl sent the coach **himself** a letter.
	The players **themselves** led the fund drive.

PRONOUN USAGE

PERSONAL PRONOUN USAGE

Because personal pronouns change form depending on their use in a sentence, you sometimes may have trouble knowing whether to use *I* or *me*, *he* or *him*, *she* or *her*, *we* or *us*, or *they* or *them*.

I, he, she, we, and *they* are **subject pronouns** and are used when the pronoun is the subject of a verb or follows a linking verb.

For more on linking verbs, see p. 403.

> **She** is a star forward and the team captain. [pronoun as subject]
> It is **they** on the court. [subject pronoun following a linking verb]

Me, him, her, us, and *them* are **object pronouns** and are used when the pronoun is a direct or indirect object of a verb or the object of a preposition.

For more on objects of verbs, see p. 403.

> The players' skill amazed **me.** [pronoun as direct object of verb]
> The ref gave **them** possession of the ball. [as indirect object of verb]
> Theoni handed off the ball to **her.** [as object of preposition]

For more on possessive pronouns, see possessive forms, p. 356.

INTERROGATIVE PRONOUN USAGE

The interrogative pronouns *which* and *what* ask questions about things:

> **Which** is the team in first place?
> **What** is the schedule of home games this season?

Who, whom, and *whose* refer to people. The form you choose depends on whether the pronoun is being used as a **subject**, an **object**, the object of a **preposition**, or to show **possession**.

> *Who* is a subject pronoun: **Who** has the tickets?
> *Whom* is an object pronoun: **Whom** did the coach pick?
> To **whom** was the trophy awarded?
> *Whose* is a possessive pronoun: **Whose** uniform is that?

RELATIVE PRONOUN USAGE

In the following sentences, the relative pronouns are in bold type, and the subordinate clauses they introduce are in bold type and italics. In each sentence, an arrow indicates the noun the relative clause modifies.

James Naismith, **who *invented basketball,*** was a Canadian working in Springfield, Massachusetts. [*Who* refers to James Naismith and is the subject of the subordinate clause.]

James Naismith

Naismith, **whom *Springfield College employed as an instructor,*** originally designed the game for nine players. [*Whom* refers to Naismith and is the direct object of the verb *employed* in the subordinate clause.]

The pocket **that *Naismith fixed to the wall in December 1891*** was not a net but a wooden peach basket. [*That* refers to pocket.]

In World War II servicemen **whose *duty took them overseas*** brought basketball to many foreign countries. [*Whose* refers to servicemen.]

Women's basketball, **which *has been growing steadily more popular,*** became an Olympic sport in 1976. [*Which* refers to basketball.]

♦ **WHEN YOU WRITE** ♦

Use the relative pronoun **who** to refer to people and animal characters only. Use **which** to refer to things only. Use **that** to refer to either people or things.

INDEFINITE PRONOUN USAGE

When an indefinite pronoun is the antecedent of a possessive pronoun, make sure that the possessive pronoun agrees in number (singular or plural) and gender (masculine, feminine, or neuter) with the indefinite pronoun. In the following examples, the indefinite pronoun and the personal pronoun that agrees with it are in bold type.

SINGULAR/FEMININE: **Each** of the girls took **her** practice shots.
PLURAL/FEMININE: **Both** want to improve **their** records at the foul line.

With indefinite pronoun antecedents that may be singular or plural, use the context, or the surrounding words and sentences, to decide how to make a personal pronoun agree with its antecedent. You can often tell whether an indefinite pronoun has a singular or plural meaning by looking at the noun in a prepositional phrase that follows the indefinite pronoun. If the object of the preposition is singular, the pronoun is singular. If the object of the preposition is plural, the pronoun is plural.

Some of a game's excitement has **its** effect on the spectators. [*Excitement* is singular; therefore, *some* is singular in this context, and the singular pronoun *its* is correct.]
Some of the fans leap from **their** seats at tense moments. [*Fans* is plural; therefore, *some* is plural in this context, and the plural pronoun *their* is correct.]

COMMON USAGE PROBLEMS

PERSONAL PRONOUN PROBLEMS

It is me versus *It is I*

Sometimes in informal speech or written dialogue, it is acceptable to use an object pronoun after a linking verb, but this usage should be avoided in formal speech or writing.

INFORMAL: Who is taking the shot? It is **me** [or **her, him**].
FORMAL: Who is taking the shot? It is **I** [or **she, he**].

Pronoun Problems in Compound Constructions

You may also have difficulty choosing the correct pronoun in compound constructions in which a noun and a pronoun or more than one pronoun appears.

Yolanda and I [not me] are guards. [*I* is part of the compound subject, *Yolanda and I*.]

I asked **my brother and him** [not he] for tickets to the game. [*Him* is part of the compound direct object, *my brother and him*.]

Pat always sits next to **Hussein and me** [not I] at the games. [*Me* is one of the objects of the preposition *to*.]

Hint: When you are unsure whether to choose a subject or an object pronoun in a compound construction, try dropping one of the parts of the compound and saying the sentence aloud.

CORRECT:	**Our coach and we** are preparing for the game. **We** are preparing for the game.
INCORRECT:	**Our coach and us** are preparing for the game. **Us** are preparing for the game.
CORRECT:	**Yong and I** will be starting in Friday's game. **I** will be starting.
INCORRECT:	**Yong and me** will be starting in Friday's game. **Me** will be starting.

♦ **WHEN YOU WRITE** ♦

In compound constructions, put any first-person pronouns last: Give your suggestions to *Ally and* **me.**

Remember to use an object pronoun in compound constructions after the prepositions *between, except, for,* and *with.*

For more on prepositions, see p. 358.

CORRECT: between **him** and **me**	INCORRECT: between **he** and **I**
CORRECT: except **you** and **her**	INCORRECT: except **you** and **she**
CORRECT: for **her** and **me**	INCORRECT: for **she** and **I**
CORRECT: with Dad and **them**	INCORRECT: with Dad and **they**

To find out which pronoun to use when a noun and a pronoun are used together in a single construction, you can use the strategy of dropping the noun, as in the following sample sentences:

CORRECT: **We** students are starting a club. **We** are starting a club.
INCORRECT: Us students are starting a club. Us are starting a club.

CORRECT: Our coach has given **us** players a pep talk. Our coach has given **us** a pep talk.

For more on usage errors with personal pronouns, see Problem Solver, p. 275.

INCORRECT: Our coach has given we players a pep talk. Our coach has given we a pep talk.

Pronoun Problems After than or as

Another difficulty in choosing the correct personal pronoun occurs in certain sentences using *than* or *as*.

Tamara played less *than* I [or me?].
The coach didn't use her *as* much as me [or I?].

In this kind of sentence, certain words are not stated directly but are implied. If you fill in the missing words, it will be easier to decide which pronoun sounds correct.

Tamara played less than **I** [played]. [*I* is a subject.]
The coach didn't use her as much as [she used] **me**. [*Me* is an object.]

INTERROGATIVE PRONOUN PROBLEM

Be careful not to confuse the possessive pronoun **whose** with the contraction **who's,** a shortened form of *who is* or *who has*.

Whose sneaker is this?
Who's [Who is] ready for the game?

REFLEXIVE PRONOUN PROBLEMS

Be careful not to use the following nonstandard forms:

NONSTANDARD: meself	STANDARD: myself
NONSTANDARD: hisself	STANDARD: himself
NONSTANDARD: theirselves	STANDARD: themselves

Do not use a reflexive pronoun as a subject, direct object, indirect object, or object of a preposition in compound constructions when a form of a personal pronoun is needed.

CORRECT: Juanita and **I** practice after school. [subject]
INCORRECT: Juanita and myself practice after school.

CORRECT: Juanita often outplays Kara and **me**. [direct object]
INCORRECT: Juanita often outplays Kara and myself.

CORRECT: LaKeesha gave Jenna and **me** some pointers. [indirect object]
INCORRECT: LaKeesha gave Jenna and myself some pointers.

CORRECT: Cheryl asked me to go with Brent and **her** to the Celtics game. [object of preposition]
INCORRECT: Cheryl asked me to go with Brent and herself to the Celtics game.

DEVELOPING YOUR STYLE: PRONOUNS

Pronouns can help you avoid repeating the same words over and over in a piece of writing. Pronouns can also function as transition words, making connections between ideas and sentences. To use pronouns effectively, remember to make their antecedents clear.

Notice how a student writer has avoided repetition and connected sentences by inserting pronouns into the following paragraph:

Michael Jordan

MODEL

Michael Jordan was born and raised in Wilmington, North Carolina. ~~Michael Jordan~~ ^{He} was one of five children. The children's parents taught ~~the children~~ ^{them} to strive for excellence. As a young-

Personal pronouns are used to avoid repetition.

The possessive pronoun adds clarity.

ster, Michael was not a born basketball player,

and so ~~Michael~~ (he) had to work hard to achieve ~~the~~ (his)

goals. He won a scholarship to the University of

North Carolina at Chapel Hill, ~~The University of~~ (, which)

~~North Carolina at Chapel Hill~~ is famous both for

~~the~~ (its) academic excellence ~~of the college~~ and for ~~the~~ (its)

basketball team. ~~It~~ (This) is the place where Michael won

two admiring nicknames from fans and team-

mates: "Superman" and "Last Shot."

The relative pro-
noun clause
eliminates unnec-
essary words and
combines two sen-
tences.

The demonstrative
pronoun *this* cre-
ates a transition
between the last
two sentences.

---

189 **PROPER ADJECTIVE:** an adjective that is formed
from a proper noun and begins with a capital letter
[See **Adjectives, Capitalization.**]

190 **PROPER NOUN:** a noun that names one specific person,
place, thing, or idea and begins with a capital letter
[See **Capitalization, Nouns.**]

191 **PUNCTUATION:** the standardized marks used to separate
sentences and sentence parts
[See entries for individual punctuation marks.]

192 **QUESTION MARK**

USING A QUESTION MARK

When you speak, your tone of voice shows that you are asking a question. In writing, you achieve the same effect with a
question mark (?)

1. Put a question mark at the end of any direct question.

What is that noise**?**

Do not put a question mark at the end of an indirect
question.

She asked what was causing the noise.

2. Sometimes a sentence reports that someone has asked a question. If the sentence contains the speaker's exact words, put a question mark at the end of the question, inside the quotation marks.

> She said, "Is that what you call music?"

If a sentence continues after a directly quoted question, put a question mark after the question and an appropriate end mark—usually a period—at the end of the whole sentence.

> "Uh, . . . may I borrow those tapes?" she asked.
> "How can you listen to that stuff?" she queried.

3. Sometimes a sentence asks whether somebody said certain exact words. If the entire sentence is a question, the question mark goes outside the quotation marks.

> Did she say, "It sounds like noise to me"?
> Who said, "Music is the universal language of mankind"?

QUOTATION MARKS

193

QUOTATION MARKS WITH DIRECT QUOTATIONS

1. Use quotation marks to show where direct quotations, or a person's exact words, begin and end.

> Coach Andrews announced, "Tryouts for the track and field team begin at three o'clock this afternoon."

Be careful to enclose in quotation marks only the exact words the person says, not explanatory words such as *Jaime replied* that identify the speaker. Notice the explanatory words, also called speaker tags, that appear in the sample sentences that follow.

> **Quotation marks ("")** are marks of punctuation that set off a speaker's exact words, show words taken from another writer, signal nicknames and slang expressions, and indicate the title of a short work.

For more on quotations, see p. 376.

"Are you going to try out?" **Winona asked Jaime.**

Jaime replied, "I don't think I'm good enough."

◆ **WHEN YOU WRITE** ◆

When you are writing dialogue, try to choose verbs such as *shouted, called, responded,* and *muttered* when they accurately describe the speaker's tone of voice and situation.

For more on dialogue, see p. 142.

COMMAS WITH QUOTATION MARKS

2. When a speaker tag appears before a direct quotation, place a comma after the tag.

Winona cried, "Jaime, you're great on the hurdles. I've seen you!"

3. When a speaker tag comes after a line of dialogue, place a comma after the quotation, inside the quotation marks.

"Well, I practice a lot," Jaime admitted modestly.

4. A **divided quotation** includes an explanatory phrase that interrupts someone's exact words. A pair of commas separates the quoted words from the interrupting words. Notice that the first comma falls inside the quotation marks. The second comma follows the last word of the speaker tag.

"I'm sure you'll get on the team," Winona assured him, "if you try out."

OTHER PUNCTUATION WITH QUOTATION MARKS

5. Place periods inside closing quotation marks.

> Jaime mused, "Maybe I should try out."

6. If a question mark or an exclamation point is part of the quotation itself, place it inside the quotation marks. If a quotation ends with a question mark or an exclamation point, drop the comma before a speaker tag.

> "Where are the tryouts?" Jaime inquired.
> "They're on the playing field. I'm so glad you'll be there!" Winona cried.

7. If a question mark or an exclamation point is not part of the quotation, place it outside the quotation marks.

> Did the coach say, "Tryouts for the team begin at three o'clock"?
> How proud Jaime will be when the coach says, "You're on the team"!

USING SINGLE QUOTATION MARKS

8. Use single quotation marks to show a quotation within a quotation.

> Winona said, "I'm sure I heard the coach shout, 'Nice job!' when you cleared that last hurdle."

USING QUOTATION MARKS WITH NICKNAMES AND SLANG

9. Use quotation marks around special nicknames or unfamiliar slang expressions. (Use slang expressions sparingly.)

> Jaime won so many medals that the team members called him "Champ."
> The coach said he could really "turn on the afterburner," meaning speed up at the end of a race.

USING QUOTATION MARKS WITH TITLES OF SHORT WORKS

10. Use quotation marks to enclose the titles of short works.

SHORT STORY:	"Raymond's Run"
SHORT POEM:	"Oranges"
ESSAY:	"The Strange Geometry of Stonehenge"
CHAPTER TITLE:	"Childhood and Youth"
SONG:	"Mae Swept Me Away"
EPISODE IN TV SERIES:	"New Deal, New York"

194 QUOTATIONS

IDENTIFYING QUOTATIONS

A **quotation** is an exact record of someone's words. You can quote from the spoken or written words of an actual person, or you can make up a speech or dialogue for a fictional character in a story.

"Ask not what your country can do for you; ask what you can do for your country."
—President John F. Kennedy, Inaugural Address

Imagine that you were writing an article on the importance of volunteering for community service. To help make your point, you might choose to include President John F. Kennedy's famous words. In that case, you would put the quoted words in quotation marks and identify the speaker.

DIRECT AND INDIRECT QUOTATIONS

When you repeat a person's exact words, you are making a **direct quotation**. Place quotation marks around all the words of the speaker.

In her speech, the governor said, "Our young volunteers are the backbone of community service programs all over the state." For more on quotation marks, see p. 373.

In an **indirect quotation,** you summarize or restate someone's words in your own way. Do not use quotation marks with indirect quotations.

The governor said that young volunteers are the backbone of the state's community service programs.

QUOTATIONS IN ESSAYS AND I-SEARCH PAPERS

Direct quotations are useful in essays and I-Search papers to support your central idea, give an example, or define a concept or term. The opinion of a respected authority can add weight to your own opinion and strengthen your evidence. Follow these guidelines when using a quotation. For more on documenting sources, see Research Report p. 224.

GUIDELINES FOR USING QUOTATIONS

▶ Be sure the quotation clearly illustrates, explains, or defines the point you want to make.

▶ Check that the person you are quoting is knowledgeable about your topic.

▶ Record the quotation accurately, word for word.

▶ Identify the speaker of the quotation and the written work from which the quotation comes.

LENGTHY QUOTATIONS

When you directly quote a passage of four lines or more in a long piece of writing, start the quotation on a new line and indent it. Lengthy quotations are usually introduced by a colon and do not require quotation marks.

INCORPORATING QUOTATIONS SMOOTHLY

When you include a quotation in a sentence, make the quotation fit grammatically into the sentence so that it reads smoothly.

INCORRECT: The governor described teen volunteers "caring, thoughtful, and considerate."

CORRECT: The governor described teen volunteers as "caring, thoughtful, and considerate."

USING DIALOGUE

Dialogue is a conversation between two or more people. When you write dialogue for a story or personal narrative, you are quoting a speaker's words. Begin a new paragraph every time the speaker changes. Punctuate dialogue the same way as direct quotations. Notice how dialogue appears in a fictional story about the governor's speech to the volunteers.

For more on dialogue, see p. 142.

MODEL

"Where did you get the idea for volunteering at a nursing home, Luella?" the governor asked.

"Actually," Luella admitted, blushing, "it was from you."

DEVELOPING YOUR STYLE

USING QUOTATIONS EFFECTIVELY

Using quotations effectively to support your ideas in an essay or I-Search paper is a skill that takes some practice. Good writers use a balance of their own original ideas, short, embedded quotations to support their views, and a few longer quotations, when necessary, to illustrate a point.

Make sure your quotations come from respected authorities on your subject or from your own carefully conducted questionnaires or interviews. Before you use a quotation, ask yourself it if strengthens your argument or pads it. Try to weave the quotations skillfully into your own sentences so that they do not break the flow of your writing. When you are considering using a long quotation, ask yourself whether the information could be presented more effectively as a summary in your own words.

MODEL FROM LITERATURE

For most of us it's too easy to allow daily problems and failures, large and small, to erode our sense of self-worth continually. Helping someone makes our bodies feel good and gives us back the healthier view of ourselves as good and valuable people. It is a buffer against the daily irritations that are so damaging to health and to self-image.

Another researcher puts it very well. Lowell Levin, professor of public health at Yale University, says that "when you're a helper, your self-concept improves. You are somebody. You are worthwhile. And there's nothing more exhilarating than that."

A skillfully embedded quotation from a respected authority supports the authors' main idea.

When the volunteer questionnaire responses came in, they were astonishing. People's comments on not just the psychological benefits but also the physical effects added to the powerful testimonials about helping's healing potential . . .

I got very excited for the individuals I helped. I felt very in control of myself and my body. I am a runner, and I felt I ran better than ever before. I felt very strong physically. Almost like nothing could conquer me. You want so much to help others, and when you do and see their reactions, you feel so good inside that it makes you explode with energy.

A longer quotation from an actual volunteer supports the idea and adds a more personal touch.

—Allan Luks with Peggy Payne, *The Healing Power of Doing Good*

REFLEXIVE PRONOUN: a pronoun ending in *-self* or *-selves* that refers to an earlier noun or pronoun and is essential to a sentence's meaning   [See **Pronouns.**]   195

REGULAR VERB: a verb that forms its principal parts in the typical way   [See **Verbs.**]   196

RELATIVE CLAUSE: another term for **Adjective Clause**   197

198   **RELATIVE PRONOUN:** a pronoun that introduces a subordinate clause and also stands in for a noun, often serving as a subject or object in the subordinate clause   [See **Pronouns.**]

199   **RESTRICTIVE CLAUSE:** a clause that limits the meaning of a word it modifies and is essential to a sentence's meaning   [See **Clauses, Comma.**]

200   **RUN-ON SENTENCE:** two or more sentences incorrectly punctuated as one

[See **Sentence Problems** in Section Two of the book, **Problem Solver #55.**]

201   ## SEMICOLON

A **semicolon (;)** is like a period and a comma combined.

1. Use a semicolon between two main clauses in a compound sentence. Since main clauses can stand by themselves, the semicolon takes the place of a coordinating conjunction.

> Daniel Hale Williams performed the first open-heart surgery; [in place of *and*] Louis T. Wright led research on antibiotics.

2. Use a semicolon between main clauses joined by conjunctive adverbs and transitional expressions:

> The organic chemist Percy L. Julian was honored for his scientific work; **nevertheless,** he suffered injustice because of racial hatred.

3. Use a semicolon to separate items in a series when the items already contain commas.

> Other black pioneers of science include Lloyd A. Hall, who discovered new ways to sterilize medical supplies; Charles R. Drew, who helped start blood banks; and Garrett A. Morgan, who invented the gas mask.

202   **SENTENCE FRAGMENT:** an incomplete thought incorrectly capitalized and punctuated as a sentence

[See **Problem Solver #56.**]

IDENTIFYING SENTENCES

The **subject** tells whom or what the sentence is about. The **predicate** tells what the subject does or is. Usually the subject comes before the predicate, as in the sample sentences that follow.

> A **sentence** is a group of words that expresses a complete thought and contains a subject and a predicate.

Subject	Predicate
A crowd	parades down a New Orleans street.
The parade of revelers	is celebrating Mardi Gras.
They	wear colorful masks and costumes.

IDENTIFYING SENTENCE PARTS: SUBJECTS

The **complete subject** usually consists of a key noun or pronoun and other words that describe it. The key noun or pronoun is called the **simple subject**. In the complete subjects of the following sentences, the simple subjects are in bold type.

> The **subject** of a sentence tells whom or what the sentence is about.

Complete Subject	Complete Predicate	
Many local **musicians**	perform during Mardi Gras.	*For more on nouns and pronouns, see p. 341 and p. 362.*
Everyone in the crowd	loves the Dixieland bands.	
The **celebration**	lasts for days.	

Sometimes the simple subject is the only word in the complete subject, as in the following sentences.

Complete Subject	Complete Predicate
Musicians	perform during Mardi Gras.
Everyone	loves the Dixieland bans.

For more on proper nouns, see p. 341.

When the simple subject is a **proper noun**, it may contain more than one word. In the following sentence, the simple subject is **New Orleans**.

Complete Subject	Complete Predicate
Festive **New Orleans**	is famous for its music.

For more on prepositional phrases, see p. 352.

Sometimes the complete subject contains a prepositional phrase that describes the simple subject. The simple subject itself is never part of a prepositional phrase. In the following sentences, the simple subjects are in bold type.

Complete Subject	Complete Predicate
The **city** of New Orleans	is the home of many fine restaurants.
Everyone in the city	praises Cajun cuisine.

For more on conjunctions, see p. 323.

Sometimes the complete subject contains two or more main nouns or pronouns linked by a conjunction such as *and* or *or*. These nouns or pronouns make up a **compound subject**. In the complete subjects of the following sentences, the compound subjects are in bold type.

Complete Subject	Complete Predicate
A **king** and a **queen**	lead the Mardi Gras revelers.
She or **he**	is a central Mardi Gras figure.
Jazz, blues, and Cajun **music**	are all Mardi Gras highlights.

IDENTIFYING SENTENCE PARTS: PREDICATES/VERBS

The **predicate** of a sentence tells or asks something about the subject.

The **complete predicate** usually consists of a verb and words that describe it or complete its meaning. The verb is called the **simple predicate** or, more often, the **verb.** In the complete predicates of the following sentences, the verbs are in bold type.

Complete Subject	Complete Predicate
Night clubs	**hum** with music during Mardi Gras.
Cajun musicians	usually **play** catchy dance tunes.

Sometimes the verb is the only word in the complete predicate, as in the following sentences.

For more on verbs, see p. 403.

Complete Subject	Complete Predicate
Night clubs	**hum**.
Cajun musicians	**play**.

The verb, or simple predicate, may also be a **verb phrase,** a main verb with one or more helping verbs, such as a form of *have* or *be*. In the following sentences, the verbs are in bold type. Notice that both simple predicates are verb phrases and that the second one is interrupted by another word, in this case, the adverb *now*.

For more on verb phrases, see p. 403.

Complete Subject	Complete Predicate
A jazz musician	**will perform** at a club.
A blues artist	**is** now **playing** around the corner.

Sometimes the complete predicate contains two or more verbs linked by a conjunction such as *and, but,* or *or*. Verbs linked in this way make up a **compound verb** or **compound predicate.** In the complete predicates of the following sentences, the compound verbs are in bold type. Notice that the compound verb in the first sentence in the following chart includes a verb phrase.

Complete Subject	Complete Predicate
Night clubs	**hum** with music and **may attract** huge crowds.
Singers	sometimes **croon** or **shout**.
Dancers	**shake**, **rattle**, and **roll**.

IDENTIFYING SENTENCE PARTS: OBJECTS, PREDICATE NOUNS, PREDICATE ADJECTIVES

Some action verbs and all linking verbs require other words to complete their meaning. These words may be **direct objects, indirect objects, predicate nouns and pronouns,** or **predicate adjectives.**

A **direct object** is a noun or pronoun that answers the question *what?* or *whom?* after an action verb.

> Many New Orleans restaurants serve spicy **crawfish**.
> Hungry crowds devour **them**.

An **indirect object** is a noun or pronoun that answers the question *to what?, for what?, to whom?,* or *for whom?* after an action verb. Almost all sentences with indirect objects also have direct objects. The indirect object comes between the verb and the direct object.

> Many New Orleans restaurants serve **customers** spicy crawfish.
> Others offer **you** gumbo and jambalaya.

A **predicate noun** is a noun that follows a linking verb and further identifies the subject. A **predicate pronoun** is a pronoun that does the same thing as a predicate noun.

> Crab City is a popular New Orleans **restaurant**.
> Those Cajun recipes are **hers**.

A **predicate adjective** is an adjective that follows a linking verb and describes the subject.

> The food at Anthony's tastes **delicious**.

For more on adjectives, see p. 284.

Like other sentence parts, objects and predicate nouns and predicate adjectives can have compound forms linked by conjunctions such as *and, but,* or *or.*

COMPOUND DIRECT OBJECT:	Many restaurants serve **shrimp, gumbo,** and **jambalaya**.
COMPOUND INDIRECT OBJECT:	Some offer **tourists** and **others** stuffed crawfish.
COMPOUND PREDICATE ADJECTIVE:	That gumbo recipe is **nutritious** and **filling**.

For more on linking verbs, see p. 403.

SENTENCE PATTERNS

A sentence must express a complete thought. In order to do that, it needs a subject and a verb and any object or predicate noun or adjective that the verb requires. The subject, the verb, and these "completer" words are the bare bones of a sentence. When only these bare bones are considered, sentences often fall into one of the four patterns shown on this chart.

Common Sentence Pattern	Sample Sentences
subject—action verb **(S V)**	S V Tourists wait.
subject—action verb—direct object **(S V DO)**	S V DO The groundhog makes his appearance.
subject—action verb—indirect object—direct object **(S V IO DO)**	S V IO DO The crowd gives him a hand.
subject—linking verb—predicate noun, pronoun, or adjective **(S LV PN/PA)**	S LV PN The groundhog is Punxsutawney Pete.

By adding adjectives, adverbs, and prepositional phrases to the key words, you can expand sentences while still maintaining the pattern. Notice how both of the following sentences, despite their differences in length, have the same S V pattern.

ORIGINAL:	S V **Tourists wait**.
EXPANDED:	S V Many **tourists** from all over the country **wait** anxiously on Groundhog Day for the emergence of Punxsutawney Pete from his hole in Punxsutawney, Pennsylvania.

You can also expand a sentence by making one or more of the key words a compound term.

ORIGINAL:	S V Tourists wait.
COMPOUND SUBJECT:	**Tourists** and local **residents** wait.
COMPOUND VERB:	Tourists **watch** and **wait**.

INVERTED WORD ORDER

Most sentences follow one of the four common patterns discussed in the previous section. Sometimes, however, writers change the order of words to add emphasis to an idea or to give variety to their writing. For example, the subject need not always start a sentence.

Sometimes a sentence uses **inverted order,** in which the subject follows the verb. In the following examples, notice how the sentence using inverted order builds suspense by saving the subject for last. It also has a more poetic effect since inverted order was once used a great deal in poetry.

REGULAR ORDER:	S V The daring balloonists fly across the New Mexico skies.
INVERTED ORDER:	V Across the New Mexico skies fly the daring S balloonists.

MODEL FROM LITERATURE

Note the inverted order of subject and verb.

V   S
So through the night rode Paul Revere;

V   S
And so through the night went his cry of alarm

To every Middlesex village and farm.

—Henry Wadsworth Longfellow, "Paul Revere's Ride"

Some sentences using inverted order open with the words *Here is* (or *Here's*), *Here are*, *There is* (or *There's*) or *There are*.

Here are hot-air balloons in all shapes and sizes.

There is also a special competition for helium balloons.

SENTENCE TYPES

A **declarative sentence** makes a statement and ends with a period. It is the most common type of sentence.

Sentences may be classified into one of four types: **declarative, interrogative, imperative,** or **exclamatory.**

A parade of cars streams down a Manhattan street.
Down a Manhattan street streams a parade of cars.

An **interrogative sentence** asks a question and ends with a question mark.

Are the astronauts in New York City today**?**

An **imperative sentence** makes a request or gives a command and ends with a period. Its subject is always *you*. Often *you* is understood and is dropped from the sentence.

[You] Look at the shower of ticker tape.
[You] Do not block the intersection.

An **exclamatory sentence** expresses strong feeling and ends with an exclamation point. Usually it begins with *How* or *What*.

How much litter a ticker tape parade makes!
What a tribute the city gives the honored visitors!

A declarative, interrogative, or imperative sentence becomes exclamatory when it expresses strong emotion. An imperative sentence ends with an exclamation point.

◆ **WHEN YOU WRITE** ◆

Vary sentence types to make your writing more interesting.
■ Use mainly declarative sentences.
■ Use an occasional interrogative sentence to arouse the readers' interest, especially at the start of a composition or section.
■ Use imperative sentences when appropriate, especially to make directions or instructions clear.
■ Use exclamatory sentences when appropriate to the tone and audience of your writing. Avoid overusing exclamation points in sentences that would otherwise be declarative, interrogative, or imperative.

SENTENCE STRUCTURES AND CLAUSES

A **clause** is a group of words that contains one subject and its verb. A **main clause** can stand alone as a sentence. A **subordinate clause** cannot stand alone because it does not express a complete thought.

A sentence's structure may be **simple, compound, complex,** or **compound-complex**, depending on the number and kinds of clauses it contains.

MAIN CLAUSE: Many tourists visit Hannibal, Missouri.

SUBORDINATE CLAUSE: When tourists visit Hannibal

A **simple sentence** is a main clause that stands alone.

For more on clauses, see p. 304.

Hannibal lies on the banks of the Mississippi River.

A **compound sentence** is two or more main clauses, or simple sentences, that are joined together. The clauses are linked by a semicolon or by a coordinating conjunction.

For more on coordinating conjunctions, see p. 323.

Mark Twain grew up in Hannibal; his books often feature the town.

Hannibal was a river port, **and** steamboats stopped there daily.

Hint: Do not confuse compound sentences with simple sentences that have compound subjects or compound verbs.

> **COMPOUND SUBJECT:** **Steamboats** and other **craft** stopped there daily.
>
> **COMPOUND VERB:** Twain's books **feature** the town but **rename** it.

A **complex sentence** contains one main clause and one or more subordinate clauses. In the following sentences, subordinate clauses are in bold type. Notice that a subordinate clause may interrupt a main clause.

> The Tom Sawyer cave, **which tourists visit,** is two miles from town.

> **Though Twain created many characters,** Tom may be the most famous.

Hint: The relative pronoun that begins some subordinate clauses may be the subject of the clause.

> The home of Becky Thatcher, **who was Tom's friend,** draws crowds.

For more on relative pronouns, see p. 380.

Mark Twain

A **compound-complex sentence** contains at least one subordinate clause and at least two main clauses.

> Many visitors come to Hannibal in July, **when the town celebrates National Tom Sawyer Days,** but the town is a year-round attraction.

204 **SERIES:** three or more words, phrases, or clauses in a row, usually with a conjunction before the last item
[See **Comma, Semicolon, Problem Solver #62A.**]

205 **SIMPLE PREDICATE:** the verb or verbs constituting the key word or words in the complete predicate
[See **Sentences: Structures and Types.**]

206 **SIMPLE SENTENCE:** a sentence that consists of just one main clause [See **Sentences: Structures and Types.**]

207 **SIMPLE SUBJECT:** the one or more nouns or pronouns constituting the key word or words in the complete subject
[See **Sentences: Structures and Types.**]

208 **SINGULAR:** indicating one.
Nouns, verbs, pronouns, and a few adjectives change form to indicate whether they refer to one or more than one. [See **Number.**]

209 **SINGULAR NOUN:** a noun that indicates one person, place, thing, or idea [See **Nouns.**]

IMPROVING SPELLING

The good news is that misspelling words does *not* indicate a lack of intelligence. Some of the words most frequently misspelled by freshmen at a leading university (besides *then, there, their, to, too,* and *two*) are *quiet, quit, speak, speech,* and *paid.* The bad news is that misspelling words doesn't look very smart.

SPELLING STRATEGIES

Here are seven strategies for learning spellings that give you trouble:

1. Keep a list of the words that trip you the most often.

2. Concentrate on memorizing one word a day.

3. Pronounce the word. Exaggerate every sound—even silent letters.

4. Trace the word in the air or on a flat surface.

5. Visualize the word in writing ("see" it spelled out in lights on a blimp).

6. Write the word on paper in pencil and then in ink. If possible, type it, too.

7. Use memory devices such as the rhyme "*i* before *e*" on page 392. Pronounce unvoiced letters in odd spellings such as *foreign*. Make up silly associations (the sillier the better): My a**unt runs**; this **ant can't**. W**eird** is too w**eird** to follow the rule. I'm **all** for par**all**el. Take atten**dance** at the **dance**. Hit the b**rake** for goodness **sake**.

While writing a first draft, invent reasonable spellings for tricky words and keep writing. When you revise, refer to a dictionary.

The Dictionary

Keep a dictionary handy and use it often. You don't need to know how to spell a word to look it up. Just begin by sounding out the first part of the word. If a word isn't where you expect it to be, try different spellings for the same sound. For example, an *f* sound can be spelled *f* (**fl**uff) or *ph* (**ph**onogra**ph**). The long *i* can be spelled as in *site* and *sky*.

SPELLING RULES AND TIPS

Here are some tips to improve your spelling.

Ie *and* ei *Words*

Memorizing this rhyme can help you to spell words with **ie** or **ei** combinations.

Put **i** before **e**,	[bel**ie**ve, br**ie**f, p**ie**ce]
Except after **c**,	[rec**ei**ve, conc**ei**t]
Or when sounded like **a**,	
As in n**ei**ghbor and w**ei**gh.	[**ei**ght, v**ei**n, w**ei**ght]

Some exceptions to this rhyming rule are *either, neither, seize, height, leisure, species, caffeine,* and *weird.*

"Seed" *Words*

Many words end with the sound *seed,* which is usually spelled *-cede,* as in *concede* and *precede.* There are four common exceptions: *exceed, proceed, succeed,* and *supersede.* It is useful to memorize frequently used exceptions.

Adding Prefixes and Suffixes

A base word is a word that is complete in itself, such as *fire*. **Prefixes** are syllables or word parts added at the beginning of a base word. **Suffixes** are syllables or word parts added at the end of a base word.

Adding a prefix to a base word is simple. Do not drop any letters from either element, even if the combination results in a double letter.

For example:

mis + fire = misfire
mis + spell = mi**ss**pell
il + logical = i**ll**ogical
co + ordinate = co**o**rdinate

Adding a suffix to a base word often changes the spelling. Remembering the following rules can help you avoid embarrassing spelling errors when adding a suffix to a base word.

Base Words with Final *e*	Examples
If a suffix begins with a **vowel** *(a, e, i, o, u,* or *y)*, drop the final *e*.	giv**e** + **i**ng = giving
	creat**e** + **i**ve = creative
	fam**e** + **o**us = famous
	bon**e** + **y** = bony
	ban**e** + **a**l = banal
	EXCEPTIONS: fle**e**ing, ey**e**ing
If a suffix begins with a **consonant** (any letter that is *not* a vowel), the base word keeps the final *e*.	sens**e** + **l**ess = senseless
	wid**e** + **l**y = widely
	plac**e** + **m**ent = placement
	whit**e** + **n**ess = whiteness
	EXCEPTIONS: aw**e** + **f**ul = awful
	argu**e** + **m**ent = argument

E and *i* make a preceding *c* or *g* soft, as in *dance* and *change*. Keep the final *e* when adding a suffix that begins with *a* in order to keep the *c* or *g* soft.

chang**e** + **i**ng = changing

chang**e** + **a**ble = chang**ea**ble

danc**e** + **i**ng = dancing

danc**e** + **a**ble = danc**ea**ble

peac**e** + **a**ble = peac**ea**ble

Words Ending in y

The following rules apply when adding suffixes to words that end in y.

Base Words with Final *y*	Examples
Keep the final *y* if the base word ends in a vowel plus *y*.	empl**oy** + ed = employed
	st**ay** + ing = staying
	enj**oy** + able = enjoyable
Change the final *y* to *i* if the base word ends in a consonant plus *y*.	rea**dy** + ly = readily
	app**ly** + ed = applied
	EXCEPTIONS: Keep the *y* before *-ing:* applying, readying, flying

Doubling Final Consonants

Which words double their final consonant when a suffix is added? The following rules will help you decide.

Rules	Examples
Remember **1 + 1 + 1**: In words of **one** syllable that end in **one** consonant preceded by **one** vowel, double the final consonant when a suffix begins with a vowel.	**hit** + ing = hitting
	hop + ing = hopping
	run + er = runner
	tap + ed = tapped
	NOTICE: This rule does *not* apply when *two* vowels precede the final consonant.
	h**ea**l + ing = healing r**ai**n + ed = rained

In words of two or more syllables, double the final consonant when these three conditions exist: • the suffix begins with a vowel • the accent is on the last syllable • the suffix does not cause the accent to shift	begin + ing = begi**nn**ing occur + occu**rr**ing rebut + al = rebu**tt**al prefer + ed = prefe**rr**ed **NOTICE:** benefit + ing = benefiting [accent is not on the last syllable] prefer + ence = preference [accent shifts to the first syllable]
Keep the final *l* of a base word when adding *ly*. Keep the final *n* when adding *ness*.	real + ly = rea**ll**y mean + ness = mea**nn**ess **EXCEPTION:** When a word ends in double *l*, drop one *l*: full + ly = fu**ll**y hill + ly = hi**ll**y

For rules on spelling plurals, see nouns, p. 341, and apostrophe, p. 293.

Sound-Alikes

Words that sound alike or almost alike but have different meanings can trip the best of writers. These sentences say very different things.

"I am ending my meal with a little dessert."

"I am ending my meal with a little desert."

In the first sentence, the speaker is enjoying a sweet treat. In the second, the speaker winds up in a dry region. It's useful to memorize the spellings of the sound-alikes you often use.

For more on sound-alike words, see commonly confused or misused words, p. 315.

COMMONLY MISSPELLED WORDS

The list that follows has sixty-eight commonly misspelled words. Try saying each word aloud, slowly and carefully, one syllable at a time. Then close your eyes, and try to "see" the word spelled correctly.

absence	essential	judgment	pharmacy
adviser	existence	laboratory	physical
all right	February	library	physician
answer	foreign	license	privilege
appoint	forty	lightning	receipt
believe	fulfill	liquefy	recognize
benefit	genius	mischievous	recommend
business	government	misspell	resistance
canister	grief	necessary	restaurant
cemetery	gypsy	neighborhood	rhythm
convenient	harass	nickel	separate
definite	height	niece	sincerely
describe	humorous	occasion	technology
disease	incidentally	occur	theory
ecstasy	inoculate	pamphlet	truly
embarrass	irrelevant	performance	variety
environment	jewelry	permanent	Wednesday

211 **SPLIT INFINITIVE:** the use, frowned on in formal English, of an infinitive interrupted by one or more words between the *to* and the base form of the verb [See **Verbals.**]

212 **STRINGY SENTENCE:** a sentence containing too many ideas connected by *and, so, then, and so,* or *and then* [See **Sentence Problems** in Section Two of the book.]

213 **SUBJECT:** the part of a sentence that tells what or whom the sentence is about; also, the key word or words in that part **(simple subject)** [See **Sentences: Structures and Types.**]

214 **SUBJECT FORM OF A PRONOUN:** the form of a pronoun used as a subject or after a linking verb [See **Pronouns.**]

215 **SUBJECT-VERB AGREEMENT:** using a verb with the same number and person as its subject [See **Problem Solver #57.**]

SUBORDINATE CLAUSE: a clause that serves as an adjective, adverb, or noun and cannot stand alone as a complete sentence   [See **Clauses.**]

216

SUBORDINATING CONJUNCTION: a conjunction that introduces a subordinate clause and also links or relates the clause to the rest of the sentence   [See **Clauses, Conjunctions.**]

217

SUFFIX: a word part added to the base form of a word; for example, *-er* is a suffix meaning "one who does," as in *baker* and *faker*   [See **Spelling.**]

218

SUPERLATIVE FORM: an adjective or adverb form used to compare more than two things, usually created by adding *-est* or using *most*   [See **Adjectives, Adverbs.**]

219

TENSE: one of six verb forms indicating time   [See **Verbs.**]

220

THIRD PERSON: the person or thing spoken about; the third-person pronouns are *he, him, his, himself, she, her, hers, herself, it, its, itself, they, them, their, theirs,* and *themselves*   [See **Pronouns, Verbs.**]

221

TITLES: [See **Capitalization, Quotation Marks, Underlining/Italics.**]

222

TRANSITIVE VERB: an action verb with a direct object   [See **Verbs.**]

223

UNDERLINING/ITALICS

224

1. Use italics or underlining to indicate foreign words and phrases.

One well-known national motto is *E pluribus unum,* which means "one out of many" in Latin.

2. Use italics or underlining for words, letters, or numbers referred to as such.

Have you remembered to dot all your *i*'s?
Is *17* really your lucky number?

> **Italics** are printed letters that slant to the right. When you write or type, use underlining to indicate italics.

3. Use italics or underlining for the titles of books, plays, long poems, movies, television series, works of art, long musical compositions, newspapers, magazines, ships, trains, airplanes, and spacecraft. Study the chart below.

TYPE OF NAME	EXAMPLE
Book	*Tuck Everlasting*
Play	*The Flying Tortilla Man*
Long Poem	*The Odyssey*
Movie	*Star Wars*
Television Series	*St. Elsewhere*
Work of Art	*Watching the Flock*
Long Musical Composition	*Grand Canyon Suite*
Newspaper	*The Atlanta Journal*
Magazine	*Newsweek*
Ship	*Queen Elizabeth II*
Train	*Denver Zephyr*
Airplane	*Air Force One*
Spacecraft	*Challenger*

Do not use underlining or italics with titles of your own works.

---

225   **USAGE:** the customary way in which words and phrases are written or spoken   [See **Commonly Confused or Misused Words** as well as entries for individual parts of speech.]

---

226   **VERBAL PHRASE:** a group of words that contains a participle, gerund, or infinitive along with its object and/or modifiers and is used in a sentence as an adjective, an adverb, or a noun
[See **Phrases, Verbals.**]

---

227   **VERBALS**

IDENTIFYING VERBALS

A **verbal** is a verb form used as a part of speech other than a verb.

Since they come from verbs, verbals convey a sense of action even though they are used as nouns, adjectives, and adverbs. Consider the effects of the italicized verbals in the following passage.

MODEL FROM LITERATURE

Even my own cousin Ben was there—*riding* away, in the *ringing* of bicycle bells down the road. Every time I came to *watch* them—[*to*] *see* them *riding* round and round *enjoying* themselves—they scooted off like crazy on their bikes.

—James Berry, "Becky and the Wheels-and-Brake Boys"

The repeated verbal riding stresses the action performed by Ben and his friends.

The verbal ringing appeals to our sense of hearing and shows another activity.

TYPES OF VERBALS

The three kinds of verbals are **participles, gerunds,** and **infinitives.** All three can be used alone or in phrases.

Participles and Participial Phrases

A **participle** is a verb form that can be used as an adjective. There are two kinds of participles, **present** and **past.**

Type	Form	Examples
PRESENT PARTICIPLE:	ends in *-ing*	Megan's old bicycle had **creaking** wheels.
PAST PARTICIPLE:	usually ends in *-ed* or *-d* but may be irregular	Its **rusted** handlebars needed new paint. Its **worn** tires were no longer safe.

A participle that acts as a modifier may occupy one of several positions in a sentence.

For more on adjectives, see p. 284.

Position	Examples
AT THE START OF A SENTENCE OR CLAUSE:	**Laughing,** Megan eyed her huge Christmas present.
JUST BEFORE THE WORD IT MODIFIES:	The **laughing** girl eyed her huge Christmas present.
AFTER THE WORD IT MODIFIES:	"I wonder what it can be?" said Megan, **laughing.**

For more on the past participles of irregular verbs, see p. 403.

A participle may occur in a **participial phrase,** which consists of the participle plus any objects or modifiers. The entire participial phrase then serves as an adjective to modify a noun or a pronoun.

The present, ***wrapped* in yards of gift paper,** had a telltale shape. ***Pretending* ignorance**, Megan tore open the mountain of gift paper. "A new bicycle. What a surprise!" she said, ***laughing* gleefully.**

For more on verb phrases, see p. 403.

A participle can also be used along with one or more **helping verbs (HV)** as part of a verb phrase. In such a case, it is not a verbal; it is a **verb (V).**

Participle as Adjective (Verbal)	Participle as Verb
Laughing, Megan opened the present.	HV V She **was laughing** at the gift's size.

Gerunds and Gerund Phrases

For more on nouns, see p. 341. For subjects, objects, and predicate nouns, see p. 396, p. 157, and p. 358. For objects of prepositions, see p. 359.

A **gerund** is a verb form that is used as a noun. Gerunds always end in *-ing*. Like nouns, they function in sentences as subjects, as direct objects, as predicate nouns, and as objects of prepositions.

Noun Function	Examples
SUBJECT:	**Cycling** is a popular form of recreation.
DIRECT OBJECT:	Many bicycle riders enjoy **racing.**
PREDICATE NOUN:	One of the best forms of exercise is **cycling.**
OBJECT OF A PREPOSITION:	A bicycle is an inexpensive way of **traveling.**

A gerund may occur in a **gerund phrase,** which consists of the gerund plus any objects or modifiers.

> ***Riding* her new bicycle** gives Megan a sense of freedom.
> She dreams of ***racing* in the Tour de France.**

Don't confuse gerunds and present participles, which both end in *-ing*. Remember that gerunds function as nouns, which serve as **subjects (S), objects, (O), predicate nouns (PN),** or **objects of prepositions (OP)**. Present participles function as **adjectives (AD)**, describing nouns or pronouns, or as the **main verbs (V)** in verb phrases, expressing the action that the subject performs.

Gerund	Present Participle
S **Pedaling** supplies a bike's power.	**AD** **Pedaling,** Megan took off on her bike.
S LV PN Her favorite *activity is* **riding.**	**S HV V** *She* **is riding** her new bicycle.

Infinitives and Infinitive Phrases

An **infinitive** is the base form of a verb, usually preceded by *to*. It is used as a noun, an adjective, or an adverb. When used as nouns, infinitives may function as subjects, objects, or predicate nouns.

For more on adverbs, see p. 289.

Function	Examples
SUBJECT (NOUN):	**To race** is one of Megan's dreams.
DIRECT OBJECT (NOUN):	Before the next race, she needs **to practice.**
PREDICATE NOUN:	Her goal is **to qualify.**
ADJECTIVE:	She has the ambition **to succeed.**
ADVERB:	Nevertheless, the race will be hard **to win.**

An infinitive may occur in an **infinitive phrase,** which consists of the infinitive plus any objects or modifiers. Like an infinitive, an infinitive phrase can function as a noun, an adjective, or an adverb.

Function	Examples
SUBJECT (NOUN):	*To race* in France is one of Megan's dreams.
DIRECT OBJECT (NOUN):	She plans *to enter* a local charity race.
PREDICATE NOUN:	Her goal is *to qualify* in the junior division.
ADJECTIVE:	She has the drive *to become* a champion cyclist.
ADVERB:	*To improve* her time, she practices for hours.

Don't confuse infinitives with prepositional phrases that begin with *to*. Remember that an infinitive combines *to* with the base form of a verb; the **preposition (PREP)** *to* links a noun or pronoun, called the **object of the preposition (OP)**, to another part of the sentence.

For more on prepositions, see p. 358.

Infinitive	Prepositional Phrase
Megan wants **to race**.	Hundreds of people will go **to the race**.

COMMON USAGE PROBLEMS

AVOIDING MISPLACED AND DANGLING PARTICIPLES

A participle or participial phrase is **misplaced** when it is placed so far away from the noun or pronoun it modifies that it seems to modify another word. To avoid the problem, place participles and participial phrases as close as possible to the words they modify.

MISPLACED: Megan lost seven pounds **riding** her bicycle daily.

CORRECT: **Riding** her bicycle daily, Megan lost seven pounds.

Also be sure to avoid a **dangling participle,** a participle or participial phrase that seems to modify the wrong word, because the word it really modifies is missing from the sentence.

MISPLACED: **Cycling** in the park, the lanes were peaceful.

CORRECT: **Cycling** in the park, Megan enjoyed the peaceful lanes.

VERB PHRASE: a main verb and all its helping verbs.

[See **Phrases, Verbs.**]

228

VERBS

229

IDENTIFYING VERBS

Every sentence must contain a verb. The verb tells what the subject does or is. To find a verb in a sentence, ask yourself:

> A **verb** is a word that shows an action or the fact that something exists.

1. Which word shows an action?
A strange student **sits** in the third row of our class.
[The verb *sits* shows an action.]

If no word in the sentence shows an action, ask yourself:

2. Which word says that something exists?
This unusual student **is** a teenage werewolf.
[The verb *is* says something exists.]

To be sure you have found a verb, ask yourself one more question:

3. Can the form be changed to show differences in time?
In the examples, since you can change *sit* to *sat* and *is* to *was* to show differences in time, *sit* and *is* are both verbs.

TYPES OF VERBS

Action Verbs and Linking Verbs
The two main categories of verbs are **action verbs** and **linking verbs**.

Action Verb	An **action verb (V)** expresses physical or mental action.
RELATIONSHIP TO SUBJECT:	tells what the subject (S) does
SAMPLE SENTENCES:	S V The werewolf **grins** at his classmates. [physical action] S V Some people **fear** his large teeth. [mental action]

For more on subjects and predicates, see p. 381.

Linking Verb	A **linking verb (LV)** expresses state of being.
RELATIONSHIP TO SUBJECT:	tells what the subject is by linking it to one or more words in the predicate that describe or name it
COMMON EXAMPLES:	be (including the forms *am*, *is*, *are*, *was*, and *were*) seem, appear, feel, look, taste, smell, sound, stay, remain, grow
SAMPLE SENTENCES:	**S** **LV** The werewolf's grin **seems** friendly to me. [links *grin* with *friendly*, which describes the grin] **S** **LV** His favorite book **is** *The Call of the Wild*. [links *book* with its title *The Call of the Wild*]

Some verbs used as linking verbs can also be used as action verbs. Usually, if you can replace the verb with a form of *be* (such as *am*, *is*, *are*, *was*, or *were*) and the sentence still makes sense, the verb is a linking verb.

ACTION VERB:	The teacher **looks** warily at the werewolf.
LINKING VERB:	The werewolf **looks** hungry. [Replacing *looks* with *is* makes sense: The werewolf **is** hungry.]

Transitive Verbs and Intransitive Verbs

Action verbs may be classified as either **transitive** or **intransitive**.

For more on objects, see p. 348.

Transitive Verb	A **transitive verb (TV)** is used with a **direct object (DO)**, the receiver of the action the subject performs.
SAMPLE SENTENCE:	**S** **TV** -----> **DO** The werewolf **scratches** his ear. [Ear receives the action.]

Intransitive Verb	An **intransitive verb (IV)** is a verb used without a direct object.
SAMPLE SENTENCES:	**S** **IV** In flea season, the werewolf **scratches** often. **S** **IV** **IV** Some of his classmates **mutter** and **complain**. [This sentence has a **compound verb**, two separate verbs joined by a conjunction such as *and*.]

For more on conjunctions, see p. 323.

Main Verbs and Helping Verbs

Sometimes two or more verbs work together in a **verb phrase**. The most important verb in the verb phrase is called the **main verb**. The other verb or verbs are called **helping verbs**.

> The werewolf *has been* **practicing** for the swim team.
>
> He *can* **perform** only one stroke, the dog paddle.

The main verb and any helping verbs may be separated by words or contractions that are not part of the verb phrase.

> He definitely *does*n't **swim** like anybody else.
>
> The coach *has* never **seen** a swimmer quite like him.
>
> *Do* any other swimmers **shake** themselves dry?

Common Helping Verbs

FORMS OF *HAVE*:	has, have, having, had
FORMS OF *BE*:	am, is, are, was, were, being, been
OTHER HELPING VERBS:	do, does, did, may, might, must, can, could, will, would, shall, should

VERB FORMS, NUMBER, AND PERSON

Verbs may change form to agree with a subject in **number** and **person**. In the first person, the subject is the speaker. In the second person, the subject is the person spoken to, and in the third person, the subject is the person or thing spoken about.

	Singular	Plural
FIRST PERSON:	I **scratch**	we **scratch**
SECOND PERSON:	you **scratch**	you **scratch**
THIRD PERSON:	he, she, it [or any singular noun] **scratches**	they [or any plural noun] **scratch**

VERB TENSES AND PRINCIPAL PARTS

Verbs also change form to show time. The six main forms that show time are called the **tenses** of the verb. Four **principal parts** of the verb help to create these tenses. The following chart shows principal parts formed in the regular way; you'll learn about irregular ones later in the lesson.

Principal Part	Examples	Description
BASE FORM:	howl, hop, whine	basic form of the verb
PAST FORM:	howled, hopped, whined	adds -ed or -d
PRESENT PARTICIPLE:	howling, hopping, whining	adds -ing
PAST PARTICIPLE:	howled, hopped, whined	adds -ed or -d

The principal parts are used, sometimes along with helping verbs, to form the six main tenses of the verb:

1. present tense
2. past tense
3. future tense
4. present perfect tense
5. past perfect tense
6. future perfect tense

1. The **present tense** shows an action or condition that exists at the present time. It uses the base form of the verb without any helping verbs and adds -s or -es to agree with a third-person singular subject. Two exceptions are the verbs *have* and *be*.

Present Tense (Regular)

You can also express a present action or condition by using a form of be plus the present participle: I am howling.

FIRST PERSON:	I **howl**	we **howl**
SECOND PERSON:	you **howl**	you **howl**
THIRD PERSON:	he, she, it [or any singular noun] **howls**	they [or any plural noun] **howl**

Present Tense of the Verb Have (Irregular)

FIRST PERSON:	I **have**	we **have**
SECOND PERSON:	you **have**	you **have**
THIRD PERSON:	he, she, it [or any singular noun] **has**	they [or any plural noun] **have**

Present Tense of the Verb Be (Irregular)

FIRST PERSON:	I **am**	we **are**
SECOND PERSON:	you **are**	you **are**
THIRD PERSON:	he, she, it [or any singular noun] **is**	they [or any plural noun] **are**

2. The **past tense** shows an action or condition that began and ended at a given time in the past. It uses the past form of the verb without any helping verbs. Usually it does not change form to agree with its subject. The only exception is the verb *be*.

Past Tense (Regular)

FIRST PERSON:	I **howled**	we **howled**
SECOND PERSON:	you **howled**	you **howled**
THIRD PERSON:	he, she, it [or any singular noun] **howled**	they [or any plural noun] **howled**

Past Tense of the Verb Be (Irregular)

FIRST PERSON:	I **was**	we **were**
SECOND PERSON:	you **were**	you **were**
THIRD PERSON:	he, she, it [or any singular noun] **was**	they [or any plural noun] **were**

3. The **future tense** shows an action or condition that has not yet occurred. It is formed by using the helping verb *will* before the base form of the main verb.

Future Tense

FIRST PERSON:	I **will howl**	we **will howl**
SECOND PERSON:	you **will howl**	you **will howl**
THIRD PERSON:	he, she, it [or any singular noun] **will howl**	they [or any plural noun] **will howl**

You can also express future time by saying I am going to howl, using the infinitive to howl.

4. The **present perfect tense** shows an action or condition that already has occurred at an unnamed, indefinite time in the past or one that began in the past and has continued into the present. It is formed by using the helping verb *have* or *has* before the past participle of the main verb.

Present Perfect Tense

FIRST PERSON:	I **have howled**	we **have howled**
SECOND PERSON:	you **have howled**	you **have howled**
THIRD PERSON:	he, she, it [or any singular noun] **has howled**	they [or any plural noun] **have howled**

For more on contractions, see p. 330

Sometimes the helping verb *have* or *has* is contracted to *'ve* or *'s*: *I've howled, you've howled, she's howled, it's howled,* and so on.

5. The **past perfect tense** shows a past action or condition that ended before another past action began. It uses the helping verb *had* before the past participle of the main verb.

Past Perfect Tense

FIRST PERSON:	we **had howled**
SECOND PERSON:	you **had howled**
THIRD PERSON:	they [or any plural noun] **had howled**

Sometimes the helping verb *had* is contracted to *'d*: *I'd howled, he'd howled, we'd howled,* and so on.

6. The **future perfect tense** shows a future action or condition that will have ended before another begins. It uses the helping verbs *will* and *have* before the past participle of the main

Future Perfect Tense

FIRST PERSON:	I **will have howled**	we **will have howled**
SECOND PERSON:	you **will have howled**	you **will have howled**
THIRD PERSON:	he, she, it [or any singular noun] **will have howled**	they [or any plural noun] **will have howled**

Progressive Forms of Verb Tenses

Each of the six tenses has a **progressive form** that is often used to show an action or condition in progress. It uses a form of the helping verb *be* before the present participle of the main verb.

PRESENT PROGRESSIVE:	They **are howling**.
PAST PROGRESSIVE:	They **were howling**.
FUTURE PROGRESSIVE:	They **will be howling**.
PRESENT PERFECT PROGRESSIVE:	They **have been howling**.
PAST PERFECT PROGRESSIVE:	They **had been howling**.
FUTURE PERFECT PROGRESSIVE:	They **will have been howling**.

The present progressive form is commonly used to show a single action in progress now, at the present time. The simple present tense is usually used for an action that occurs in general in the present.

PRESENT PROGRESSIVE: The werewolf **is howling**. [in progress right now]

PRESENT: A werewolf **howls** at night. [in general]

IRREGULAR VERBS

Regular verbs, such as *howl*, form their past tense and past participles by adding *-ed* or *-d*. **Irregular verbs**, such as *bite*, form their past tense and/or past participles in different ways. The following chart lists common verbs that are irregular.

Common Irregular Verbs

BASE	PAST	PAST PARTICIPLE	BASE	PAST	PAST PARTICIPLE
be	been	been	keep	kept	kept
become	became	become	know	knew	known
begin	began	begun	lay	laid	laid
bite	bit	bitten	lead	led	led
blow	blew	blown	leave	left	left
break	broke	broken	lend	lent	lent
bring	brought	brought	let	let	let
buy	bought	bought	lie	lay	lain
catch	caught	caught	lose	lost	lost
choose	chose	chosen	put	put	put
come	came	come	ride	rode	ridden
do	did	done	ring	rang	rung
draw	drew	drawn	rise	rose	risen
drink	drank	drunk	run	ran	run
drive	drove	driven	say	said	said
eat	ate	eaten	see	saw	seen
fall	fell	fallen	set	set	set
feel	felt	felt	sing	sang	sung
find	found	found	sit	sat	sat
fly	flew	flown	speak	spoke	spoken
freeze	froze	frozen	steal	stole	stolen
get	got	got *or* gotten	sting	stung	stung
			swim	swam	swum
give	gave	given	take	took	taken
go	went	gone	tell	told	told
grow	grew	grown	think	thought	thought
have	had	had	wear	wore	worn
hear	heard	heard	win	won	won
hit	hit	hit	write	wrote	written

ACTIVE AND PASSIVE VOICE

Verbs also change form to indicate **voice**. An action verb is in the **active voice** when the subject of the sentence performs the action. It is in the **passive voice** when the subject receives the action—that is, has something done to it. The passive voice uses a form of the helping verb *be* before the past participle of the main verb.

ACTIVE VOICE:	The werewolf **chews** the teacher's desk to splinters.
PASSIVE VOICE:	The teacher's desk **is chewed** to splinters by the werewolf.

The passive voice can conceal the performer of the action or be used when the performer is uncertain.

PERFORMER CONCEALED:	The teacher's desk **is chewed** to splinters.
PERFORMER UNCERTAIN:	The werewolf's secret **was discovered** after many months.

The passive voice can be used in the perfect and future tenses.

PAST PERFECT PASSIVE:	He **had been observed** at several pet shops.
PRESENT PERFECT PASSIVE:	Many flea powder purchases **have been noted**.
FUTURE PASSIVE:	His future behavior **will be monitored**.

COMMON USAGE PROBLEMS

EASILY CONFUSED VERBS

The following pairs of verbs may seem alike, since their principal parts sound similar. Be careful not to confuse them.

Lie and Lay

Lie

MEANING:	rest; recline
TYPE OF VERB:	intransitive verb; never has a direct object

Lay

MEANING:	put; place
TYPE OF VERB:	transitive verb; always has a direct object

Leave and Let

Leave

MEANING: depart; go away from; cause to remain behind

Let

MEANING: allow; permit

USING PRINCIPAL PARTS CORRECTLY

Using the wrong form of a verb can spoil the effect of what you write or suggest careless thinking on your part. Remember that irregular verbs do not form their past tense or past participles in the usual way.

INCORRECT: My brother **lended** the werewolf a secret hair gel formula.

CORRECT: My brother **lent** the werewolf a secret hair gel formula.

When you use irregular verbs in perfect tenses after forms of the helping verb *have*, remember to use their past participles.

INCORRECT: The werewolf's hair **has grew** in a very odd way.

CORRECT: The werewolf's hair **has grown** in a very odd way.

Be especially alert to the use of the contractions *'ve* for the helping verb *have*, *'s* for the helping verb *has*, and *'d* for the helping verb *had*.

INCORRECT: We**'ve saw** an improvement since he**'s ate** the hair gel.

CORRECT: We**'ve seen** an improvement since he**'s eaten** the hair gel.

KEEPING TENSES COMPATIBLE

Avoid changing tenses when events occur at the same time.

INCORRECT: During the track meet with Lobo Middle School, the werewolf's hair gel **itches** like crazy, so he **ran** like the wind.

CORRECT: During the track meet with Lobo Middle School, the werewolf's hair gel **itched** like crazy, so he **ran** like the wind.

On the other hand, change tenses to show that events did not occur at the same time. For example, to show that one event in the past finished before another event in the past began, use the past perfect tense for the first event and the past tense for the second.

INCORRECT: By the time his opponents **crossed** the finish line, the werewolf **was** in the shower.

CORRECT: By the time his opponents **had crossed** the finish line, the werewolf **was** in the shower.

DEVELOPING YOUR STYLE: VERBS

USING PRECISE, VIVID VERBS

Precise, vivid verbs wake up your writing—and your readers too. Often they appeal to one or more of the five senses. In the following excerpt, a girl on a favorite horse is pursuing an African antelope called a *kongoni*. Consider the effects of the precise, vivid verbs that appear in bold type.

 MODEL FROM LITERATURE

Bursts and shatters help us perceive the effect of one word on the stillness.

The verbs describe a variety of movements.

"Now!"

The word **bursts** from my lips because I **can** no longer **contain** it: it **shatters** the stillness. Frightened birds **dart** into the air, the kongoni **leaps** high and **whirls**. . . . We **run**, we **race**. The kongoni **streaks** for the open plain.

—Beryl Markham, "The Captain and His Horse"

Vague verbs like *be, do, come, get, go, have, make,* and *put* can weaken your writing if you overuse them. Use such verbs only when you really need them. Otherwise, replace them with more precise, vivid verbs.

STUDENT MODEL

Trudged, slouched, and slipped are more precise than came, went, and put. They also appeal to our senses. Whined and groaned are much stronger than made whining and groaning sounds.

The werewolf ~~came~~ [trudged] home. ~~He was sad and tired.~~ He ~~went~~ [slouched] into the kitchen and ~~made~~ [concocted] a sandwich. He ~~made whining~~ [whined] and ~~groaning sounds~~ [groaned] until finally he ~~got~~ [removed] a movie from his video library and ~~put~~ [slipped] it into his VCR. It was his favorite film, <u>Dances with Wolves.</u>

—Michael Eisenberg, Darien, Connecticut

CHOOSING THE ACTIVE VOICE

The active voice is usually more straightforward, concise, and lively than the passive voice. Using the active voice makes writing more forceful and easier to understand. For this reason, choose the active voice in most cases.

AVOID:	Cases of pet food **are ordered** by the werewolf's parents.
BETTER:	The werewolf's parents **order** cases of pet food.

Use the passive voice only if the performer of the action is unclear, unimportant, or too obvious or complicated to be worth mentioning.

AWKWARD:	Each week a delivery boy **delivers** five cases of pet food.
BETTER:	Each week five cases of pet food **are delivered**. [The performer of the action, the delivery boy, is unimportant and obvious.]
AWKWARD:	Everybody in school and indeed in the whole neighborhood **views** the werewolf as unusual.
BETTER:	The werewolf **is viewed** as unusual. [The performer of the action is too obvious to be worth mentioning and too complicated to describe.]

VOICE: any verb form indicating whether the subject performs the action **(active voice)** or has the action performed on it **(passive voice)**
[See **Verbs**.]

230

WORDY SENTENCE: a sentence containing words that do not add to its meaning
[See **Sentence Problems** in Section Two of the book.]

231

Guide to Learning

■ ■ ■

Taking Charge of How You Learn

Poster for the Book-of-the-Month Club, 1987, Milton Glaser
Courtesy of the artist

How can the library help me with my research?

Imagine that you have a writing assignment. You have an idea for your paper, and you need information. That's when the library can help. Here is an example of how following your thoughts can lead you to different parts of a library:

Assignment: Essay about an endangered species
Idea: "I'd like to write about the California condor."

"Where does it live?"
"What are its characteristics?"
"How did it become endangered?"

"I need really in-depth information about how it became endangered."

"Well, how is the California condor doing right now?"

   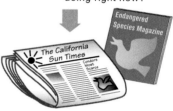  

encyclopedias   special dictionaries   nonfiction works   articles in recent periodicals

"Where do I find these at the Library?"

reference shelves   nonfiction shelves   Readers' Guide   vertical files

WHERE CAN I FIND WHAT I NEED?

A MAP OF THE LIBRARY

The map on pages 416–417 shows the layout, or floor plan, of a typical library. Books are grouped into five main categories: fiction, nonfiction, biography, reference, and periodicals (magazines and newspapers). Books in the adults', young adults', and children's areas of a library all follow the same plan.

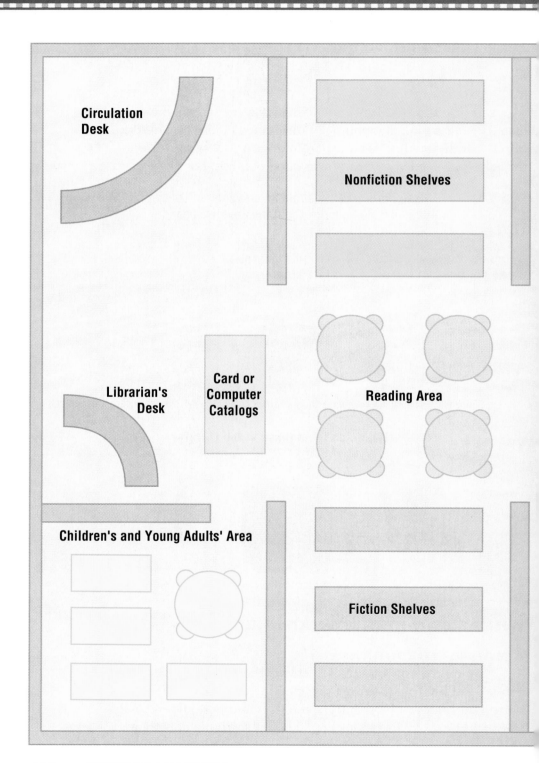

Circulation Desk

Nonfiction Shelves

Librarian's Desk

Card or Computer Catalogs

Reading Area

Children's and Young Adults' Area

Fiction Shelves

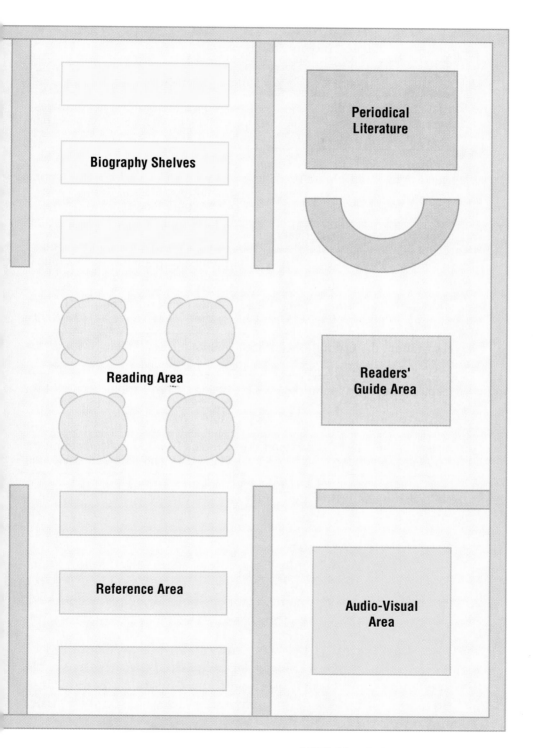

Biography Shelves

Periodical Literature

Reading Area

Readers' Guide Area

Reference Area

Audio-Visual Area

This chart shows how assignments can be researched. Each source is discussed in this chapter.

ASSIGNMENT	SOURCES OF INFORMATION
brief biography of a famous person	biographies and autobiographies, encyclopedias and almanacs, periodicals
comparison/contrast of two characters created by a famous writer	works of fiction containing the characters, critical essays in nonfiction books about the writer's work, periodicals
research report on historical and recent changes in a group's way of life	nonfiction works, encyclopedias and special dictionaries, recent population statistics in an almanac, recent articles in periodicals
short story about immigrants traveling by ship to the United States	nonfiction works about U.S. immigration, encyclopedias, world atlas
essay about the history of a phrase or saying	dictionaries, nonfiction works about language
magazine article about a children's author	articles from periodicals about the author and his/her work, children's books by the author
review of the latest CD released by a popular rock band	articles from periodicals about the band, CD, and listening equipment

Using the following library research tools at the library will save you a lot of work:

LIBRARY CATALOGS

Catalogs contain information that will help you follow your leads. They will help you find a book even if all you know is part of its title or the author's name. Catalogs can also help you choose a subject because the titles they list may suggest books to browse in.

THE CARD CATALOG The card catalog is a cabinet of long, narrow trays, or file drawers, designed to hold three-by-five cards. Every nonfiction book is listed on three kinds of cards: **subject, title,** and **author.** Works of fiction are usually listed only on title and author cards.

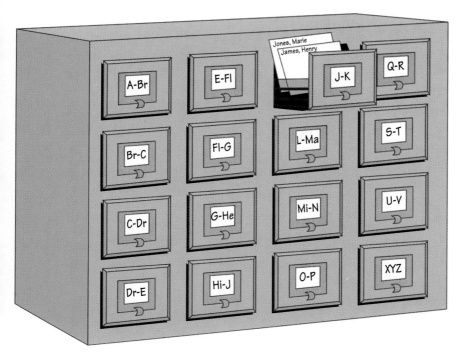

Suppose you want to research how kids your age live in China. Because subject cards tell you about books relating to your subject, you can begin with file drawer C, for China.

call number	**305.23 R**
subject	**China**
author	Rau, Margaret
title	Holding up the sky: young people in China, by Margaret Rau.
publisher	New York: Dutton, 1983.
copyright date	1st ed
number of pages	136 p.: ill; 24 cm.

When you look at a subject card, ask yourself questions to try to determine whether the book is right for you. Does the title capture your interest? Do you know and like the author's work? Is the book recent enough to contain relatively current information?

This is an **author card:**

```
305.23 R



Rau, Margaret
Holding up the sky: young people
in China, by Margaret Rau.
New York: Dutton, 1983.
1st ed
136 p.: ill; 24 cm.
```

You might find several cards in the card catalog under the same author's name, each giving the title of a different book. This information will enable you to browse through an author's works.

This is a **title card:**

```
305.23 R



Holding up the sky: young people
in China
Rau, Margaret.
New York: Dutton, 1983.
1st ed
136 p.: ill; 24 cm.
```

Sometimes a title card will give you clues about new places to look for information. Did you notice the phrase "young people" in this title? If you check Y for "young people" in the subject and title catalogs, you might find other helpful books.

THE COMPUTER CATALOG Many libraries catalog all materials on a computer database. As with the card catalog, a computer database is organized so that you can look up books by subject, title, and author. A computer catalog, however, asks you what you want and digs up the information for you. It also helps you use bits of information to piece together an accurate description of what you need and then find the information. Brainstorming words and phrases that relate to the information you need can help the computer help you.

The way a computer catalog works may differ from library to library. The following is a computer search for a book by title:

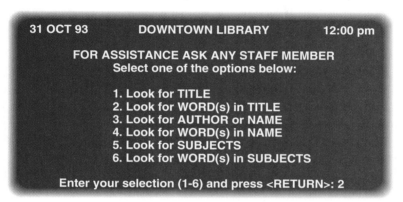

```
31 OCT 93          DOWNTOWN LIBRARY          12:00 pm

        FOR ASSISTANCE ASK ANY STAFF MEMBER
              Select one of the options below:

              1. Look for TITLE
              2. Look for WORD(s) in TITLE
              3. Look for AUTHOR or NAME
              4. Look for WORD(s) in NAME
              5. Look for SUBJECTS
              6. Look for WORD(s) in SUBJECTS

        Enter your selection (1-6) and press <RETURN>: 2
```

After you make your choice from this menu, the next screen will ask you to enter the title, author, or subject. The screen after that will provide information you need to locate the book such as the call number, author, publisher, edition, or a brief description. One of the most important facts you will see is whether the book is on the shelf or has been checked out.

If you typed some key words rather than a complete title, the computer would supply several possible titles. Suppose you wanted to find Margaret Rau's book *Holding Up the Sky: Young People in China.* If you typed the key words *holding sky China,* the computer might supply these titles: *Holding Steady, Holding the Fort with Daniel Boone,* and *Holding Up the Sky.*

HOW DO I GET A BOOK FROM THE SHELVES?

Libraries have systems that help you go straight from the catalog to the shelf on which your book is stored.

CLASSIFICATION SYSTEMS

The **Dewey Decimal System** organizes nonfiction books into ten main categories based on general content areas. Each category is identified by a number. Those ten broad categories are then divided into subcategories.

Most school and public libraries use the Dewey Decimal System. Very big libraries may use a different system, the **Library of Congress System,** because it can be expanded easily. Many college and university libraries, large public libraries, and the Library of Congress in Washington, D.C., use the Library of Congress System.

There are two main differences between the Dewey Decimal and Library of Congress systems.

Dewey Decimal System

- Fiction is separated from nonfiction.

- A biography is shelved alphabetically by the last name of the person the book is about.

Library of Congress System

- Novels are shelved with nonfiction books about their author's life and work.

- A biography is shelved with books in the field in which the subject earned a reputation. (For example, a biography of Booker T. Washington, the educator, is shelved with education books.)

USING CALL NUMBERS

A book's call number contains numbers and letters that identify it. In a library catalog, look for the call number in the upper left corner of the card or the computer screen. That number is on the spine of the book. Here's how the letters in a call number help you locate a book in the Dewey Decimal System:

A call number begins with	The book is shelved with
B	Biographies
F (or *Fic*)	Fiction
J (or *Juv*)	Children's or juvenile literature
M (or *Mys*)	Mystery
R (or *Ref*)	Reference books
YA (or *YAD*)	Young adults' literature
SF (or *Sci F*)	Science fiction

HOW CAN I FIND BITS OF INFORMATION?

THE REFERENCE SHELVES

You may be surprised to learn how much information you can find in a dictionary, an atlas, a set of encyclopedias, and in a small library, which offers many other reference books. The following chart shows a few of the available reference books:

REFERENCE BOOKS	EXAMPLES
Dictionaries	*Thorndike Barnhart Advanced Junior Dictionary* *Random House Webster's Collegiate Dictionary for Children*
Special Dictionaries	*Webster's New Dictionary of Synonyms* *Dictionary of Animals* *A Concise Dictionary of Indian Tribes of North America*
Encyclopedias	*World Book Encyclopedia* *Compton's Encyclopedia* *Encyclopaedia Britannica*
Special Encyclopedias	*International Wildlife Encyclopedia* *The Golden Encyclopedia of Music*
Almanacs	*The World Almanac and Book of Facts* *Almanac of Famous People* *1994 Baseball Almanac*
Atlases	*World Book Atlas* *The Atlas of the Living World* *National Geographic Picture Atlas of Our Fifty States*

VERTICAL FILES

Vertical files are file cabinets that hold hard-to-shelve booklets, brochures, and articles from magazines and newspapers. The documents are usually placed in alphabetized folders.

Before you use vertical files, think about the words under which your topic could be found. For example, articles about urban vegetable gardens could be filed under "cities," "gardens," "urban life," or the names of individual cities such as "Los Angeles, California."

PERIODICALS: MAGAZINES AND NEWSPAPERS

If you want up-to-date information, check the latest magazines and newspapers. They often present unusual situations, local events, interesting people, and viewpoints not found in books.

For more information on periodicals on CD-ROM, see Technological Resources, p. 425.

With microfilm and microfiche, a small library can store hundreds of back issues of magazines and newspapers. Microfilm and microfiche contain miniature photographs of magazines and newspapers. Microfilm consists of long rolls of film; microfiche consists of sheets of film about the size of index cards. Special machines in the library show magnified pages on a screen so that you can read them.

Your librarian can help you use indexes to news sources such as the *Readers' Guide to Periodical Literature*. You can look up articles by subject and author.

This is a **subject entry:**

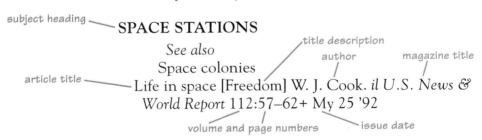

233

RESEARCH:
TECHNOLOGICAL RESOURCES

How do I find information?

What if you could visit a zoo and see and hear the animals any time you wanted? Imagine you could go back in time and listen to Rev. Martin Luther King, Jr., deliver his "I have a dream" speech! How would you like to find people around the world who share your interests and exchange thoughts with them? You can do all this, and much more, thanks to technology.

More and more libraries are making technological resources, as well as books, available. Many of these resources can even be used at home. Here are some resources you can use:

Audio Resources 	These include audiocassette tapes, compact disks (CDs), and records. Many libraries have audiotapes, CD players, and record players available. Your school may also provide these resources for student use.
WHAT'S AVAILABLE:	recordings of live concerts and speeches, instructions for learning foreign languages, tales and music from cultures around the world, interviews with important people, and authors reading their works aloud
Visual Resources 	These include prints, slides, filmstrips, and videotapes. Slide projectors and viewers, film projectors, and VCRs (videocassette recorders) are available in many libraries, offices, museums, schools, and in some homes.
WHAT'S AVAILABLE:	fine art prints of masterpieces from the world's museums; slides of cells, molecules, and atoms photographed through microscopes; filmstrips on science or history; videotapes of plays with the world's best actors; and videotaped interviews with celebrities

Microform Resources

To keep all the newspapers, magazines, catalogs, and indexes that libraries get would take up too much space. Instead, the pages are photographed, reduced to postage-stamp size, and kept on film. **Microfilm readers** and **microfiche readers** are magnifying viewers, used to read the pages. Most libraries have these viewers.

WHAT'S AVAILABLE: newspapers, magazines, catalogs, and indexes

---

Computer Resources

These include **software,** sets of electronic codes or programs directing the computer; **online services,** one kind of network that offers information and search services; and **CD-ROM,** compact disks that can hold large amounts of information, such as all the volumes of an encyclopedia. Many libraries and schools have computers and software you can use. Personal computers in homes can access much of the same information through software and online services.

WHAT'S AVAILABLE: writing, graphics, and educational computer programs; online encyclopedias and reference works; and interactive, multimedia CD-ROM programs

---

◆ WHEN YOU SEARCH ◆

Technological resources vary widely from library to library. Keep in mind that the equipment required for these resources varies. For example, microfilm readers may work differently from place to place.

USING COMPUTERS

From the machines you use to play video games to advanced machines that contain whole libraries' worth of information, computers are changing the way we gather, use, and present information. To make computers work for you, you need to know their basic parts and understand what those parts can do.

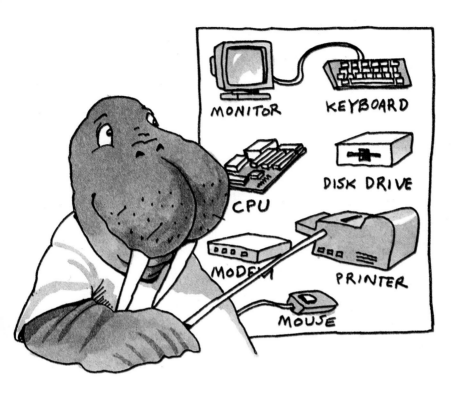

The **monitor** is the screen on which words and graphics are displayed. The **keyboard** is used to type commands to the computer. The **CPU (Central Processing Unit)** is the electronic circuitry of the computer. The **disk drive** is the mechanism that runs computer programs. The **printer** prints out **hard copy,** text or graphics from the computer. The **mouse** is a hand-held device with buttons to press to give the computer commands. The **modem** connects computers with telephone lines.

USING SOFTWARE

The "brain" of a computer is its **software,** disks or cartridges that are put into a computer to tell it what to do. Software is created by writing **programs**—sets of electronic codes. Software can be used to get a computer to do everything from writing to drawing to playing games. Here are some types of software available for computers:

- **Word processing** These programs turn your computer into a magical writing machine. You can type and then edit your work, moving words, sentences, and paragraphs. Some programs help you check spelling and grammar.
- **Graphics** These programs let you create graphs, charts, maps, drawings, and even cartoons.
- **Page layout** You can create your own leaflets, newsletters, and brochures with these programs.
- **Educational** You can learn a foreign language, practice your math, explore history, do science experiments, or learn about whatever interests you.
- **Reference** Dictionaries, encyclopedias, almanacs, and many other reference works now come on computer disks.

USING ONLINE RESOURCES

Online resources are computer resources you access by using a **modem** and your computer to call up other computers. Since you are using telephone lines to call another computer, you are "on line." Online services operate large central computers that store reference materials, newspaper and magazine articles, advice, games, and other resources and also allow computer users to communicate directly with one another.

Some libraries subscribe to online services, and these services are also available to people with personal or "home" computers. Keep in mind, however, that many online services charge a fee. Here are some resources offered by three popular online services:

Online Service	Examples of Information Available	Examples of Services Available
CompuServe:	Associated Press Online, *Grolier's Encyclopedia, Consumer Reports*	Shopping, news, games, discussion groups, messages, travel
Prodigy:	*Sports Illustrated, Consumer Reports, Grolier's Encyclopedia, USA Today*	Shopping, news, education information, messages, advertising
America Online:	*Compton's Encyclopedia, National Geographic, USA Today*	Shopping, news, games, education information, discussion groups, messages, travel

USING CD-ROM RESOURCES

Would it surprise you to learn that CDs—the compact disks that make music sound so great—are also excellent for storing information? **CD-ROMs** are compact disks used to store information. CD-ROM stands for **C**ompact **D**isk-**R**ead **O**nly **M**emory, which means you can only read the memory, not change it. Many of these programs contain music, detailed graphics, and even motion pictures.

◆ WHEN YOU SEARCH ◆

For printed listings of available CD-ROMs, check these reference books:
- *CD-ROMs in Print*
- *CD-ROMs for Librarians and Educators*

ELECTRONIC NEWSPAPERS

Extra! Read all about it—on your computer! Electronic newspapers can bring you the very latest information. Online newspapers are much more than copies of what the newsstands sell. Electronic editions offer extras that newsstand editions don't have space for. These extras include background on many articles, related articles from past editions, and local items like school lunch menus. Some offer computer users a chance to talk with the newspaper reporters and editors via modem.

◆ WHEN YOU SEARCH ◆

To learn which electronic newspapers are available to you,
- phone your local newspaper.
- ask at your library.
- check with any online service you use.

As technology becomes increasingly sophisticated, you will need to keep your eyes open for new developments. Check with librarians to find out about the latest innovations.

234

STUDY SKILLS:
GENERAL STUDY SKILLS

 How can I study more effectively?

Learning how to study effectively is one of the most useful skills you can master. When you study effectively, you use time efficiently, get good results, and may even reduce the overall amount of time you spend studying. A regular study routine can improve your performance in school. Establish a regular routine by choosing a place and time to study.

WHERE WILL I BE ABLE TO WORK?

Your study area can be a room or corner at home, a school or neighborhood study hall, or a table at the library. A desk, a chair, good lighting, and peace and quiet can turn almost any place into a good study spot. Having a permanent study area where you can leave your materials is convenient but not essential. You can easily set up a study area with a few basics that you carry in a book bag or knapsack.

Notebook: This basic organizational tool enables you to keep track of assignments.

Writing tools: A pencil is good for notetaking, writing rough drafts, and brainstorming. You may need a pen with dark ink for formal papers. Typewriters and word processors are also excellent writing tools, but they are not essential.

Paper: Have a supply of lined paper for written assignments and unlined paper for maps, sketches, and typed work.

Textbooks: Make sure you have the appropriate textbooks. (Use the assignment page in your notebook to list the textbooks you need.)

Dictionary: In addition to definitions and spellings, a good abridged dictionary contains historical names, geographical places, math symbols, a metric table, and more.

Handy items: These include a pocket calculator, a ruler, a high-lighting marker, a pencil sharpener, an eraser, correction fluid, paper clips, a hole punch, scissors, and tape.

WHEN SHOULD I STUDY?

A study schedule has to fit in with the rest of your life, or you will not stay with it. As you plan a study schedule, ask yourself these questions:

- When am I the most alert? Have I scheduled my work during that period of time?

- Does my schedule allow me time for my other activities?

- Does my schedule allow me enough time to finish my work?

- When is my study area quiet and free of distractions?

HOW TO STUDY

YOUR LEARNING STYLE Do you know that everyone has seven forms of intelligence, or ways of thinking and learning? Although you can think and learn with each of these forms of intelligence, you probably use one or two forms more often. These represent your **learning style.**

Your learning style is the way you learn best. For example, you may *hear* detailed directions to your friend's house and get completely lost. Perhaps if you *saw* a map or *wrote down* the directions, you would easily find the house. *Listening, seeing,* and *writing* are different styles of learning. Even though you do all three, one may be an especially effective way for you to learn.

You should study in the ways that work best for you. The following chart suggests learning methods that you can explore. Try one or more of these styles, depending on the particular assignment.

STYLE	SKILLS	LEARNING METHODS AND MATERIALS
Language Readers, writers, storytellers	Speaking, hearing, reading, writing	Study guides, writing workshops, audiotapes, textbooks, lectures, class discussions
Logic and math Problem solvers, questioners	Hands-on exploring, classifying, working with numbers	Laboratory equipment, games, machines (to take apart and build)
Visualization Artists, puzzle solvers	Drawing, organizing data, visualizing or imagining outcomes	Graphic organizers such as charts, sketches, maps, diagrams
Music Instrumentalists, vocalists, music fans	Listening for all aspects of sound: melody, tone, pitch, rhythm	Musical instruments, audio equipment, recordings
Physical action Athletes, builders, performers	Moving, touching, handling, talking, physical sensing	Manipulatives such as math objects, art and building materials
Social interaction Leaders, peacemakers, negotiators, socializers	Discussing, debating, interviewing, organizing, teamwork, setting group goals	Study groups, flash cards and games for two or more players, role-playing
Independent effort Individualists, dreamers, original thinkers	Following personal interests, expressing originality, setting own goals	Independent projects, "permission" to be unique

MANAGING YOUR ASSIGNMENTS

Do you remember how you felt when some particularly large project was assigned? Do you recall times when it seemed you had big assignments due in every one of your classes, all on the same day? It's difficult to avoid feeling overwhelmed by assignments at such times, but there are strategies you can use to keep your workload manageable. Take charge of your workload by setting up a section in a notebook to keep track of assignments. Include these two sections in your assignment notebook:

- an assignment log to jot down an assignment the minute you get one
- a weekly planner on which to write your study goals for the week

Here is a way to set up an assignment log:

When you complete an assignment, record the date in your assignment log. Keeping good records helps you be organized. Records can also protect you if an assignment is lost after you hand it in.

ASSIGNMENT LOG

Date Due	Subject	Assignment	Date Done
Oct. 8	Science	Observe/take notes on lunar eclipse.	
Oct. 12	Social Studies	Write letter advising Lincoln on any issue in Chap. 2 of textbook.	
Oct. 20	English	Have *Bearstone* read.	

Your weekly planner represents a specific strategy for getting your work completed. Estimate the days you will need for an assignment. Break down every assignment into daily goals you can manage. If necessary, decide on the order of importance of particular tasks, but try to balance your time among subjects. Also, use a monthly assignment calendar, which provides a quick overview of upcoming due dates for assignments and test dates. It helps you plan your time so you can stay current in all your subjects.

Keep returned papers and tests in manila file folders, one for each subject. These folders make up your personal portfolio.

How can I improve my reading?

The "magic" formula that helps athletes improve their performance can also work for readers: practice plus strategy.

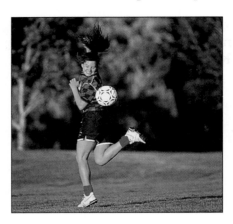

TYPES OF READING

Before you read any material, ask yourself, "What is my purpose for reading?" Are you going to read a novel for pleasure or a textbook to prepare for a test? Depending on your answer, you may need to skim, scan, or use silent sustained reading.

TYPE	METHOD	OCCASION
Skimming is looking over a text to get a quick overview of the contents.	Look for highlighted text, headings, and topic sentences.	Skim a library book to see if it interests you before you read or study it.
Scanning is looking over a text for particular information. You scan to see whether a source will be useful.	Look for specific words that relate to your topic or purpose for reading.	Before a test, scan your notes and textbook to review major ideas and key words. When doing research, scan a book for useful information.
Silent Sustained Reading is reading for thorough understanding.	Ask questions and evaluate information and ideas.	Use this method to help you understand both fiction and nonfiction.

READING NONFICTION

Except for the literature you read in English class, most of your reading in school is nonfiction. Your textbooks for science, math, and social studies, for example, are nonfiction. Two strategies that work well for reading nonfiction are KWL and SQ3R.

KWL STRATEGY

KWL is a way of focusing your reading to help you find and remember the information you really need to know. The letters *KWL* stand for **K**now, **W**ant to know, and **L**earned.

Before you begin reading, create a KWL chart to help you focus your research. Fill in what you know about your topic in the first column and what you want to know in the second column. In the third column you will eventually fill in the information you find. Here is how a KWL chart on the topic of space probes might look.

SPACE PROBES

What I know	What I want to know	What I have learned
Space probes can reach and explore other planets.	How do space probes carry enough fuel to get to other planets?	
They are scientific instruments that study the planet's surface and atmosphere.	How do they send information back to Earth?	

Before you do the research necessary to fill in the third column, you may want to add a column to list likely places to look for answers.

SQ3R STRATEGY

SQ3R stands for **S**urvey, **Q**uestion, **R**ead, **R**ecord, **R**eview. (The number *3* is shorthand for the "three Rs"—Read, Record, and Review.) The SQ3R strategy is helpful in two situations you often face as a student. One situation is searching for information on a specific topic or for answers to questions listed in the Want-to-Know column on a KWL chart. Another situation is doing assigned reading on an unfamiliar subject.

SURVEY. Survey means "to preview." Skim and scan the text to get an idea of what it is about. Read titles and other headings. Notice any highlighting used to catch your eye such as bold type, enlarged type, or color. If you are surveying an entire book rather than a chapter, be sure to read the table of contents and to scan the index.

QUESTION. Ask questions about what the material contains. Preview questions that may be listed at the end of the chapter. Use charts, illustrations, and chapter or section titles to raise new questions about your topic.

READ. Read the material. Look for answers to your questions. Look for key terms and mentally restate the main ideas in your own words as you read.

RECORD. Take notes on main ideas, definitions, and key concepts and write answers to your questions. If you are using a KWL chart, record answers under the heading "What I Have Learned."

REVIEW. Look over your notes to make sure you have recorded all key points. Skim the material to review headings and highlighted information. Try to summarize what you have learned. Research shows that summarizing increases your understanding and your ability to recall and integrate information.

A graphic organizer is a good tool to use to summarize or review information. It provides a quick overview of a subject. Creating a graphic organizer requires you to consider how the various parts of a subject are related. The format you choose depends on those relationships.

TRY THIS

You can review by
- telling someone what you learned.
- making flash cards.
- making up a song.
- drawing a picture.

For more on graphic organizers, see p. 15.

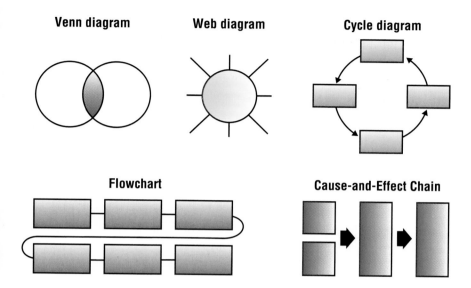

Venn diagram

Web diagram

Cycle diagram

Flowchart

Cause-and-Effect Chain

READING FICTION

Fiction is any work of literature in which characters and events have been imagined by the author. Novels, novellas, and short stories are works of fiction. For most people, reading fiction is usually a more personal experience than reading nonfiction. Reading fiction is just as active and engaging a process as reading nonfiction, but it requires a few different skills. A good fiction reader has developed the imagination to visualize a story and to make a personal connection to its characters. Use the following steps to enhance your enjoyment of reading fiction:

QUESTION. As you read, react to the characters as if they were people you know. Ask yourself why they behave the way they do and why events are happening in certain ways. Also, ask yourself questions about why the author chose to tell the story the way he or she did. For example, why did the author choose a first-person or a third-person point of view? In other words, why did he or she reveal one character's thoughts and not another's? Does the narrator's point of view lead you to empathize with or distance yourself from one or more of the characters?

VISUALIZE. To deepen your involvement in a story or novel, try to picture the characters and the action in your mind. People who really enjoy reading can "see" the whole story unfolding in their imaginations as they read. They know what all the main characters look like and are sometimes even disappointed when they see the movie version of a favorite book because it does not look the way they imagined it. If you can't visualize a certain character or part of the story, try going back and rereading that part until you can "see" it clearly.

PREDICT. This is another way to really get involved in a story. Keep trying to guess what will happen next, whether a certain character will change, or how things will turn out in the end. As you read on, check to see if your predictions are correct. It can be fun to guess right, but it's just as fun to be surprised by unexpected twists in the plot that you weren't able to guess.

CONNECT. As you read, look for connections between the people in the story and your own life. Do you know people similar to the characters in the story? Have you faced a situation similar to the one faced by the main character? Also notice how all the events of the story are connected to one another.

SUMMARIZE. At appropriate points in the story, pause to summarize or review what has happened so far. Then keep this summary in mind as you read the next segment of the story.

RESPOND. Notice how you are feeling about the characters and their situations as you read. Afterward, think about what the story means to you and whether it has helped you gain a better understanding of people and of life. Did you enjoy reading the story? Why or why not?

ANALYZE. At the end of the story, pull all the details together. What do you think is the author's central point? What is the main insight you have gained from reading the story?

How do I interpret information in graphic aids?

You probably have heard the expression "a picture is worth a thousand words." A **graphic aid** such as a **chart, graph, flowchart,** or **timeline** is a good example of such a picture. A lot of information can be packed into a graphic aid and organized so that it can be read quickly and easily. You're most likely to find graphic aids in nonfiction materials where facts and figures would take up a lot of space if they were explained in page after page of writing. Use these tips when reading a graphic aid:

> A **graphic aid** is a diagram or picture that presents a great deal of information.

- **Read the title.** It will tell you what kind of information to expect.

- **Next, read any small titles, or subheads.** These subheads appear in columns or along the top, bottom, and sides. They categorize and show relationships among the items of information presented in the graphic aid.

- **Decode any symbols within the graphic aid.** Sometimes graphic aids contain symbols such as abbreviations. Look for a footnote or key that explains the meaning of these symbols.

- **Finally, link the information presented.** Read across and down a chart to interpret, compare, or contrast information. Look at the numbers presented in a line graph to find trends and make predictions. Follow the arrows in a flowchart to understand a process. Read along a timeline to find out what happened when.

READING A CHART

A **chart** is a graphic aid organized into columns with clearly labeled headings. The purpose of a chart is to display information clearly so that readers can compare and contrast or analyze it easily. For instance, the following chart lists different birds, their habitats, and their feeding habits. You could use the chart to compare and contrast types of birds or to find a specific piece of information about one type quickly.

ENDANGERED WESTERN BIRDS
Where They Live, What They Eat

TYPE OF BIRD	HABITAT	MAIN FOOD
Spotted owl	Old-growth forests	Rodents
Bald eagle	Seacoasts, rivers, lakes	Fish
Peregrine falcon	Open country	Birds
California condor	Mountains, open country*	Dead animals
Marbled murrelet	Old-growth forests, seacoasts	Fish
Trumpeter swan	Wetlands	Vegetation

*The entire remaining population is now in captivity.

From this chart, you can draw such conclusions as these:

• Among the birds on the chart, the marbled murrelet and the bald eagle share the most in common: a habitat (seacoasts) and main food (fish).

• Spotted owls can exist only in a forest of centuries-old trees.

• The California condor is the most endangered bird listed on the chart.

READING A GRAPH

A **graph** is a diagram that presents facts and figures. You might read a graph to find out, for example, the record high temperatures in U.S. cities. Another graph might show an increase in a city's population over time. Different kinds of graphs are used to show certain kinds of information.

There are four main types of graphs:

• the **circle graph** (also known as a **pie chart**)

• the **line graph**

• the **bar graph**

• the **picture graph**

THE CIRCLE GRAPH

A **circle graph,** sometimes called a **pie chart,** is a circle that is divided into sections. The circle stands for 100 percent of something. Each section stands for a certain portion, or percentage, of the whole.

The following circle graph represents one class's preferences for different pizza toppings. Each section of the circle is shown in various ways to make it easier to read.

Here are some steps for reading a circle graph:

1. Look at the numbers that go with the sections.

2. Match the sections with the key.

3. Use the numbers and sections to make comparisons.

MS. PERON'S CLASS: FAVORITE PIZZA TOPPINGS

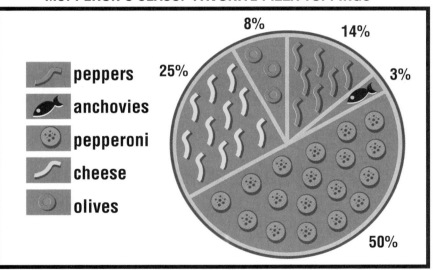

peppers 25%   8%   14%   3%

anchovies

pepperoni

cheese

olives

50%

Here are some conclusions you can draw from studying this circle graph:

• Half the students like pepperoni on their pizza.

• Plain cheese is second in popularity; 25% of students chose it.

• Very few students like anchovies on their pizza.

After seeing an example of a circle graph, you can understand why it is sometimes called a pie chart. Like a pie (or a pizza), a circle graph can be cut into pieces.

THE LINE GRAPH

A **line graph** features a line that connects points. The points represent numbers or amounts of something. To make the graph easier to read, the points may appear as actual dots. You can read a line graph in two ways.

- **To find specific information** Locate a point on the line. Read the text that relates to that point along the side and bottom of the graph.

- **To find a trend** Look at the graph as a whole before analyzing specific points. Does the line go up and down in a regular pattern? Does it seem to be heading up even if it occasionally goes down? If you extended the line on the graph, where would you predict the next point on the line would be?

The following is an example of a line graph. It tracks the number of movie theaters operating in one county over the course of eight years.

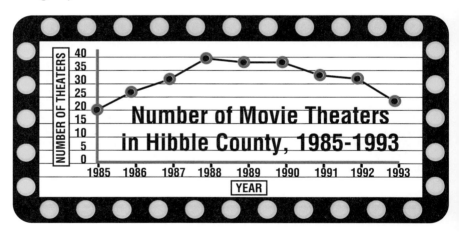

Reading this line graph tells you that the number of movie theaters doubled in the course of three years—1985–1988, but that many had gone out of business by 1993. You might use this graph in various ways, including the following:

- **Use it to formulate questions for analysis.** What happened that might have affected the increase or decrease in the number of movie theaters each year?

- **Use it to make predictions.** How successful or unsuccessful might new movie theaters be in the future in Hibble County?

THE BAR GRAPH

A **bar graph** is similar to a line graph, but instead of reading points on a line, you read the "heights" or "lengths" of bars to see what numbers they represent.

Like a line graph, a bar graph can show changes over time and help you make predictions. A bar graph, however, is more often used to compare and contrast information.

Here are some steps for reading a bar graph:

1. Look at the heights or lengths of the bars.

2. Match the subject that goes with the bar to the number the bar reaches.

3. Compare and contrast the heights or lengths of the bars with one another. This can reveal interesting similarities and differences among the items compared.

The following bar graph shows the results of a class survey in which students were asked what career they want to follow when they grow up.

MR. WALDRON'S CLASS: "WHAT WE WANT TO BE WHEN WE GROW UP"

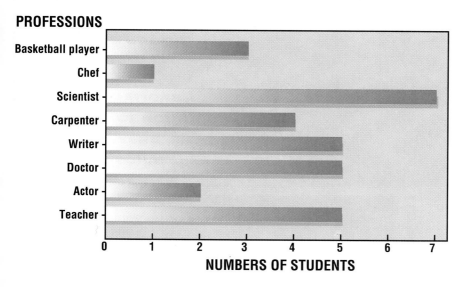

Reading this graph tells you that seven students want to be scientists—the most popular goal in the class. Becoming a chef is the dream of only one student. Equal numbers of students want to be writers, doctors, and teachers. More students want to be carpenters than actors.

THE PICTURE GRAPH

Circle, line, and bar graphs are usually straightforward diagrams. Sometimes, however, pictures are used instead of sections, lines, and bars. **Picture graphs** are eye-catching and fun to read. For example, the following graph uses actual pictures of buildings instead of bars to show the various heights of structures. Read the picture graph just as you would a bar graph.

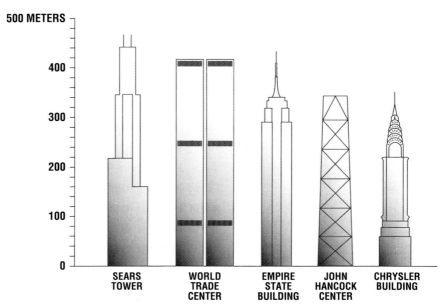

HEIGHTS OF TALL BUILDINGS*

* Heights do not include towers or antennas

READING A FLOWCHART

A **flowchart** is a diagram that shows the steps involved in making or doing something. Here are some suggestions for reading a flowchart:

- **Boxes or circles** in a flowchart show the steps in the process in the order in which they should occur.

- **Arrows** link the boxes or circles and guide readers to follow the sequence correctly. They also point out alternate steps or routes in the "flow" of action.

The following flowchart shows the steps involved in baking a batch of cookies.

MAKING COOKIES

READING A TIMELINE

A **timeline** is a line that connects points that stand for different events or circumstances. These items are placed in the order in which they occurred in history—that is, in **chronological order.**

A timeline can run up, down, or sideways. To read a timeline, follow these steps:

1. Find the earliest date on the timeline.

2. Start reading at that end of the timeline.

3. If you are looking for events that happened within a specific period, read the information between the two points on the timeline representing the beginning and the end of the period you are interested in.

The following timeline illustrates important events in the history of the television set:

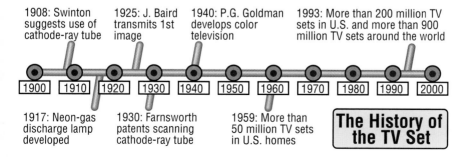

1908: Swinton suggests use of cathode-ray tube

1925: J. Baird transmits 1st image

1940: P.G. Goldman develops color television

1993: More than 200 million TV sets in U.S. and more than 900 million TV sets around the world

1900 1910 1920 1930 1940 1950 1960 1970 1980 1990 2000

1917: Neon-gas discharge lamp developed

1930: Farnsworth patents scanning cathode-ray tube

1959: More than 50 million TV sets in U.S. homes

The History of the TV Set

STUDY SKILLS: ASSESSMENT

 How can I become a better test-taker?

Tests and assessments are part of school life. They help you and your teachers measure how much you have learned. Although you will probably never look forward to taking tests, these strategies can make you a better test-taker:

CLASSROOM TESTS

Classroom tests check how well you know the subjects you are studying. To do better on tests, try these strategies:

1. Start studying several days ahead of time. Don't wait until the night before to cram. If you feel tired, you will not do as well.

2. When you review, look at the big picture. What main events or concepts are likely to be covered on the test? Why are they important? How do they relate to other concepts you have already learned? Where and how do the specific details fit in?

3. Identify key data—facts, terms, formulas, or dates. Write or say them repeatedly until you have them memorized.

4. Predict questions. What questions would you ask if you were the teacher? Write answers to these questions. If you study with a friend, take turns asking and answering likely test questions.

5. Skim the test first. Do all questions count equally, or are some worth more points than others? Which parts of the test can you do quickly, and which parts will take you more time? (A good strategy is to do the easier parts first and then use the time remaining to complete the more difficult sections.)

6. Read the directions carefully. Then read each question carefully, paying attention to all its parts.

OBJECTIVE TESTS

Objective tests require a short, specific answer to each question. There are usually five types of questions on objective tests:

True-False
- Mark a statement false when you know any part of it is false.

- Watch for generalizations—words like *every*, *all*, *always*, *never*, or *none*. These may signal a false statement since there are usually exceptions to every rule.

- Check for qualifiers—words such as *often*, *usually*, *sometimes*, *many*, *most*, and *some*. These may signal a true statement since they provide for some exceptions.

Example: Ⓣ F Most plants contain chlorophyll.
(Not all plants contain chlorophyll—but the majority do. The qualifier *most* makes the statement true.)

Multiple Choice
- Look at every choice before selecting the correct answer since one may seem correct, but if you keep reading, you will see that another is actually correct.

- Rule out any choices that are clearly wrong. Then choose the answer from those remaining.

Example: The nine justices of the Supreme Court
    A. are appointed, not elected.   C. serve for life.
    B. interpret laws.   Ⓓ. all of the above.
(A is correct. However, B and C are also correct. Therefore, D is the best choice.)

Matching
- Double-check the directions. Must every answer item in a column be matched with an item in the other column? Can the same answer be matched more than once?

- Don't start at the top of a column and work down. Instead, scan both columns, and begin matching the items that you are certain about.

Example: Match names in the second column with titles in the first. You may use a name more than once.

D 1. *The Red Pony*   A. Ann Petry
C 2. *A Wind in the Door*   B. Esther Forbes
D 3. *The Pearl*   C. Madeleine l'Engle
A 4. *Tituba of Salem Village*   D. John Steinbeck
B 5. *Johnny Tremain*

Sentence Completion • First, fill in the words you are sure of.

• Notice the structure of each sentence. It may give you a clue to the word you need to complete the sentence.

Example: In art, <u>perspective</u> , or the illusion of depth and distance, is created by using tints and shades.

(The verb *is* is singular, so you know that a singular noun is needed. *Perspective* is a singular noun.)

Short Answer • Double-check the directions. Should your answers be in sentences, or are lists acceptable?

• Make your answers as specific as you can.

Example: In one or two sentences, explain the meaning of the following formula: c = πd
<u>The formula means that you can find the circumfer-</u>
<u>ence (c) of a circle by multiplying pi (3.1416) by the</u>
<u>diameter (d).</u>

ESSAY TESTS

In an essay test, write one or more paragraphs for each answer. Here are a few tips that can help you take essay tests:

1. Check the clock. Decide how much time you'll give to answering each question. Allow a little time to plan or prewrite each response. Leave three to five minutes at the end to revise and proofread each response.

2. Scan the questions. Look for terms that tell you what process to perform. For example, should you *describe, explain, define, compare and contrast,* or *summarize?* Should you discuss a *process, causes and effects,* or a *chain of events?*

3. Plan your response. Make a list, a cluster, or a brief outline. Include important terms, dates, numbers, and names.

4. Save Margin Space. Leave space in the margins for changes.

5. Revise and proofread. Go over each response; add information; and check grammar, punctuation, and spelling.

STANDARDIZED TESTS

Standardized tests measure a person's general knowledge or ability. Reviewing and memorizing usually aren't needed to prepare for standardized tests. However, it will help to learn which types of questions you will encounter.

READING-COMPREHENSION QUESTIONS

These questions, based on content, measure your understanding of written passages. You might be tested on *finding the main idea*, *locating details*, *making inferences* (informed guesses), and *drawing conclusions*.

• Skim the questions before you read the passage.

• As you read, be alert for the answers to the questions.

• If more than one answer seems right, rereading quickly will help you decide which answer is correct.

Example: Read the paragraph and answer the question.

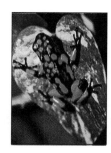

If you looked at Earth from space, you might see tropical rain forests like green jewels, dotting the regions near the equator. Zooming in for a close-up, you might pick out brightly colored flowers gleaming in the lush rain-forest growth. In these low-lying areas, over 100 inches of rain falls throughout the year. Rain forests are as beautiful and as valuable as jewels. They shelter up to 40 percent of Earth's plant and animal species. Rain forests play a key role in keeping Earth's climate stable.

The paragraph is mostly about
A. seeing Earth from space.   B. why rain forests are valuable.
C. rain forests.   D. climate.

VOCABULARY QUESTIONS

These questions give a specific word and ask you to identify a **synonym** (a word similar in meaning) or an **antonym** (a word opposite in meaning).

- Read the directions carefully.

- As you check your answers, recall what you know about word roots and prefixes and suffixes.

Example: Choose the word closest in meaning to the underlined word.

1. the <u>site</u> of the building
A. looks   B. place
C. view   D. size

Choose the word opposite in meaning to the underlined word.

2. a <u>dauntless</u> leader
A. fearless   B. fearful
C. careless   D. excellent

ANALOGY QUESTIONS

Analogies show relationships between ideas. An analogy question usually requires that you complete a sentence or some type of equation consisting of two pairs of words.

Example: The following is an analogy question:
Ear : hear :: eye : _____
The question includes a pair of terms, *ear* and *hear;* a third term, *eye;* and a blank. Decide what word *eye* relates to in the same way that *ear* relates to *hear.*
- Notice how the words in the first pair are related: What an *ear* does is *hear.*
- Next, try using the third term in the same way: What an *eye* does is . . . .
- Choose the word that best completes your sentence: What an *eye* does is *see.*

Here are four common relationships expressed in analogies:
- function (*Ear* is to *hear* as *eye* is to *see.*)
- part to whole (*Hen* is to *flock* as *cow* is to *herd.*)
- opposites (*Hot* is to *cold* as *high* is to *low.*)
- similar meanings (*Grin* is to *smile* as *sprint* is to *run.*)

GRAMMAR, USAGE, AND MECHANICS QUESTIONS

These test items measure your knowledge of standard English. They consist of a sentence with underlined sections. Your task is to decide whether the underlined sections contain any errors in grammar, usage, or mechanics and to choose the letter indicating the correct answer.

- Be alert for small errors in capitalization, punctuation, and spelling, as well as for major grammatical errors.

- Remember that in some sentences, the underlined sections contain no errors and therefore you must choose *D*, indicating this.

Example: Here is the pizzas that Marie ordered an hour ago.
       Ⓐ   B   C

No error.
  D

(There is an error in part A. The verb should be *are*, not *is*, to agree with the plural noun *pizzas*.)

WRITING ASSESSMENTS

Writing assessments measure your ability to compose written passages in response to specific directions. The prompts (the writing tasks given) ask you to write from your own experiences and observations rather than to supply or identify data you have learned in school. Here are some useful strategies:

- **Write only one draft.** Allow yourself about five minutes for quick prewriting. Leave five to ten minutes to revise and proofread your draft at the end.

- **Analyze the writing prompt.** Notice what topic, purpose, audience, and form it specifies. If the prompt doesn't mention a specific audience, assume that teachers will be reading your response. If the prompt doesn't mention a specific form, assume an essay is expected.

- **Attach your notes to your answer sheet.** If you don't have time to finish writing your final draft, at least your readers will see what you planned.

- **Show, don't just tell.** Instead of writing *I felt nervous*, for example, use details that show exactly what you felt: *My hands felt wet and cold, my heart thumped in my ears, and my throat went dry.*

PORTFOLIO ASSESSMENT

A **portfolio** is a collection of the work you have done during a set period of time. At assessment time, select from your portfolio the assignments to be evaluated. Prepare for portfolio assessment in the following ways:

- Reflect on each assignment. Write down your thoughts about each one. Think about questions such as this: What was hard or surprising about the assignment?

- Develop standards for recognizing good work. Trust your own judgment. Also, use your teacher's guidelines. Have peer readers help: ask which of your written assignments seem strongest to them, and why.

- Talk with your teacher about what you hoped to accomplish.

PERFORMANCE ASSESSMENT

In a performance assessment, you are graded on the way you complete an assigned project. Your goals should be to

- Locate resources in your school and your community.

Tips   Read encyclopedia articles for an overview.
Interview teachers, friends, or other community members.
Visit appropriate museums or businesses.
Use computer online services to expand your search.

- Add depth to your findings by using skills you have learned in math, social studies, science, art, and music classes.

Tips   Math skills can help you create charts and graphs and calculate survey results.
Use what you have learned in social studies to create a timeline or a diorama.
Science classes can be sources of observations and data.
Skills learned in art and music classes can help you present your findings visually or with sound effects.

- Choose the most effective way to present your project.

Tips   Include photos, illustrations, or objects with your project.
Get friends to help. Your group presentation can take the form of a TV newscast or a choral reading.

For more on multimedia activities, see p. 261.

238

HUMANITIES: LOOKING AT ART

The elements of the visual arts—content, medium, color, line, and composition—all contribute to the emotional impact and meaning of a work of art. This is true for graphic art, such as posters, and for fine art, such as paintings and drawings. When you look at art, consider how each element affects your response. The chart below suggests questions to help you clarify your thoughts and feelings. Exploring the world of art may show you new ways of seeing—or it may reveal that you and an artist share a similar vision.

ELEMENT	EXPLANATION	QUESTIONS TO ASK
Content	the subject of a work of art	What is the subject of the work? Is it realistic? Abstract? What does it suggest about the artist's purpose?
Medium	the material that makes up a work of art	What materials has the artist used? How do these materials relate to the artist's purpose?
Color	Colors evoke certain moods and emotions: **Neutral:** black, white, gray **Cool:** blues, greens **Warm:** reds, oranges, yellows, some browns	What colors has the artist used? Which moods and emotions do these colors evoke? How do the colors reflect the artist's feelings about the subject?
Line	the marks that define the shape of an object and show the touch of the artist's hand	What kinds of lines does the artist emphasize—horizontal, vertical, diagonal, curved? Where do the lines lead my eye?
Composition	the arrangement of lines, colors, and space in a work of art	Does the work of art look balanced? What is its center of interest and how does that center relate to the artist's subject and purpose?

The Boating Party, 1893–1894, Mary Cassatt, The National Gallery of Art, Washington, D.C.

How does Mary Cassatt use the five elements of art?

Three people in a boat are the subject, or content, of this picture. The sunlight, the green shore, and the expressions, postures, and clothing of the people all suggest a relaxed summer outing. Cassatt may have wanted to preserve the memory of an event. She may also have wanted to capture colors, shapes, and lighting that attracted her.

The medium of *The Boating Party* is oil on canvas. When dry, oil paint retains brushmarks and looks glossy. Mary Cassatt might have chosen her medium for its texture or for the way it reflects light.

The colors in *The Boating Party* suggest Cassatt's feelings about her subject. Greenish shadows, the deep green shore, and the blue sky and water generally fill much of the canvas. In the boat, the man in one corner dressed in cool indigo blue accentuates the warmth of the mother and baby, whose dresses glow with delicate lavender and pink.

The direction of lines in a work of art can create specific effects. Horizontal lines can create a sense of calmness; vertical lines, a feeling of energy. In *The Boating Party*, the shoreline and boat seat are horizontal, and the painting itself has a horizontal format. This is in keeping with the calm, relaxed feelings suggested by the painting's content.

The composition of *The Boating Party* reinforces a sense of ease and openness by surrounding the adults with open space.

For more information on looking at art, consult *History of Art for Young People*, by H. W. Janson and Anthony F. Janson, © 1987, Harry W. Abrams, New York.

When was the last time you hummed along with a tune or tapped your foot to a beat? Learning about the five elements of music can add to your enjoyment and deepen your understanding of what you hear. Look at the chart that follows.

ELEMENT	EXPLANATION	QUESTIONS TO ASK
Rhythm	a pattern of strong and weak stresses, or *beats,* and their *tempo,* or speed	Is the rhythm predictable or is it full of surprises? How does it make me feel?
Melody	*tune:* a pattern of sounds, called *tones. theme:* a brief melody repeated with variations.	What patterns do I hear in the melody? What feelings does the melody suggest?
Harmony	the sound of two or more tones together	Where do I hear harmonies? Do they sound soothing or jolting?
Form	the structure of a musical work	Does the melody, rhythm, or harmony change greatly? Do certain parts repeat?
Content	the subject matter of a musical work	What content clues does the title give? Does the music tell a story or does the composer just want to explore pure sound?

Try to hum the song "Yankee Doodle." Notice that every other beat is stressed, as shown:

YAN-kee DOO-dle WENT to TOWN, a RID-ing ON a PO-ny . . .

The simple, predictable **rhythm** makes "Yankee Doodle" sound spirited—you can understand why the song was a favorite during the Revolutionary War. Now try humming "Yankee Doodle" slowly. With a slower tempo, the beat and melody sound serious, even sad.

Now ask one friend to sing "Row, Row, Row Your Boat." What you hear is the **melody.** Then have two friends sing this song together in a round—in other words, when one singer completes the phrase "Row, row, row your boat" and is just about to sing "gently down the stream," the second person starts singing "Row, row, row your boat." What you hear is the **harmony** created by the two singers. If melody is like a line of notes continuing in time, harmony is the interaction of two tones occurring at the same time.

The form of a musical work gives you some idea of what to expect. A **song,** for example, has words meant to be sung. When you hear a song, you listen not only to the melody, rhythm, and harmony, but also to the emotion expressed in the lyrics.

Longer, more complex works are often divided into parts. For example, a **symphony** is a work written for the musical instruments of a full orchestra. It usually has four parts, or **movements.** The first movement is usually fast and exciting, the second slow and serious, the third moderately fast, and the fourth very fast, building up to a dramatic ending. The movements may be tied together by one or more brief melodies that are repeated, with variations, throughout the symphony. These are called **themes.**

All musical works are explorations of sound patterns. Some works, however, have nonmusical content. They are linked to experiences or stories beyond the world of music. For example, in Prokofiev's short piece *Peter and the Wolf,* a different melodic theme and instrument represents each character.

All five elements—rhythm, melody, harmony, form, and content—work together to create the overall effect of each musical work.

For more on listening to music, consult *The Wonderful World of Music* by Benjamin Britten, ©1968, Doubleday, Garden City, New York.

ACKNOWLEDGMENTS (continued)

unpublished work.) Reprinted by permission.

Luke Newman
Excerpt from "What is Courage" by Luke Newman. (An unpublished work.) Reprinted by permission.

The New York Times
Excerpt from "A Damage Report: The World's Oceans are Sending an S.O.S.," by Michael Specter, 5/3/92. Copyright © 1992 by The New York Times Company. Reprinted by permission.

Harold Ober Associates, Inc.
Excerpt from "The Old Demon" by Pearl S. Buck. Reprinted by permission of Harold Ober Associates, Inc. Copyright © 1939 by Pearl S. Buck; copyright renewed 1966 by Pearl S. Buck.

Orchard Books, New York
From "Becky and the Wheels-and-Brake Boys" in A Thief in the Village and Other Stories by James Berry. Copyright © 1987 by James Berry. Reprinted by permission of Orchard Books, New York.

Paramount Publishing
Excerpt from Wonders in Words by Maxwell Nurnberg. Copyright © 1968. Reprinted by permission of the publisher, Prentice Hall/A Division of Simon & Schuster, Englewood Cliffs, NJ.

John Pempek
Excerpt from "Drug Abuse" by John Pempek. (An unpublished work.) Reprinted by permission.

Mary Jane Perna
Excerpt from "The Wise Old Woman from Japan" from The Sea of Gold and Other Tales from Japan by Yoshiko Uchida. By permission of The Estate of Yoshiko Uchida.

Putnam Publishing Group, Inc.
Excerpt from The Joy Luck Club by Amy Tan. Copyright © 1989 by Amy Tan. "Everybody Says" by Dorothy Aldis from Everything and Anything. Copyright © 1925–1927, 1953–1955 by Dorothy Aldis. Reprinted by permission of G.P. Putnam's Sons.

Leslie Randolph
Excerpt from "Ecology" by Leslie Randolph. (An unpublished work.) Reprinted by permission.

Random House, Inc.
Excerpt from The Sound of Flutes and Other Indian Legends, edited by Richard Erdoes. Copyright © 1976 by Richard Erdoes. Excerpt from Saving the Earth by Jon Bowermaster and Will Steger. Copyright © 1990 by Byron Preiss Visual Publications. Excerpt from "April Rain Song" and "Dreams" from The Dream Keeper and Other Poems by Langston Hughes. Copyright © 1932 by Alfred A. Knopf, Inc. Excerpt from I Know Why the Caged Bird Sings by Maya Angelou. Copyright © 1969 by Maya Angelou. Excerpt from The Healing Power of Doing Good by Allen Luks with Peggy Payne. Copyright © 1991 by Allen Luks and Peggy Payne. Reprinted by permission of Random House, Inc.

Reader's Digest
Excerpted with permission from "The Indian All Around Us" by Bernard DeVoto, Reader's Digest, April 1953. Copyright © 1953 by The Reader's Digest Association, Inc.

Marian Reiner
Excerpt from "Simile: Willow and Gingko" from A Sky Full of Poems by Eve Merriam. Copyright © 1964, 1979, 1973, 1986 by Eve Merriam. Reprinted by permission of Marian Reiner.

Scholastic Inc.
Excerpt from "Seven Styles of Learning"

from "Different Child, Different Style" by Kathy Fagella and Janet Horowitz, in Instructor, September 1990. Copyright © 1990 by Scholastic Inc. Reprinted by permission.

St. Martin's Press, Inc. and Harold Ober Associates Inc.
Excerpt from "Debbie" from All Things Wise and Wonderful by James Herriott. Copyright © 1976, 1977 by James Herriott. Reprinted by permission.

Elisa Smith
Excerpt from "Campfire" by Elisa Smith. (An unpublished work.) Reprinted by permission.

Jane Stockman
Excerpt by Jane Stockman. (An unpublished work.) Reprinted by permission.

Brady Tabor
Excerpt from "Debbie" by Brady Tabor. (An unpublished work.) Reprinted by permission.

Rosemary A. Thurber
Drawing and text from "The Pet Department" from The Owl in the Attic. Copyright © 1931, 1959 by James Thurber. Drawing and text from My Life and Hard Times. Copyright © 1933, 1961 by James Thurber. Published by Harper & Row. Reprinted by permission.

Ralph M. Vicinanza, Ltd.
"Hallucination" by Isaac Asimov, published in Boys Life. Copyright © 1985 by the Boys Scouts of America. Published by permission of the Estate of Isaac Asimov, c/o Ralph M. Vicinanza, Ltd.

Washington Speakers Bureau
"Single Room, Earth View" by Sally Ride, published in the Apr./May 1986 issue of Air & Space/Smithsonian Magazine, published by The Smithsonian Institution. Reprinted by permission of the author.

Nancy Yearling
Excerpt from "What I Prize Most" by Nancy Yearling. (An unpublished work.) Reprinted by permission.

Lynn Yen
Excerpt from Lynn Yen's work on conjunctions. (An unpublished work.) Reprinted by permission of her teacher, Ms. Sandra Blackman, Marston Middle School, San Diego.

Note: Every effort has been made to locate the copyright owner of material reprinted in this book. Omissions brought to our attention will be corrected in subsequent editions.

ART CREDITS

1 Section I Opener: The Mather School, 1988, Jonathan Green, Courtesy of the artist; **54** The Thinker, Auguste Rodin, © The Rodin Museum, Jules E. Mastbaum Gift; **56** Section II Opener: E, 1915, Marsden Hartley, oil on canvas, The University of Iowa Museum of Art, Mark Ranney Memorial Fund; **98** Section III Opener: Laurence Typing, 1952, Fairfield Porter, oil on canvas, Courtesy of the Parrish Art Museum, Southampton, NY, Gift of the Estate of Fairfield Porter, photo, Noel Rowe; **112** Family Supper, Ralph Fasanella, 1972, Courtesy of the artist; **118** Handball, Ben Shahn, Museum of Modern Art; **267** Section IV Opener: Incident in the Library I, 1983, Julian Opie, Courtesy Hal Bromm Gallery; **297** The Outlier, Frederic Remington, 1909, © The Brooklyn Museum; **303** Midnight Ride of Paul Revere, Grant Wood, 1950, Arthur Hoppock Hearn Fund, Metropolitan Museum of Art; **321** Landscape, Maurice de Vlaminck,

Nimatallah, Art Resource, NY; **414** Section V Opener: Poster for the Book-of-the-Month Club, Milton Glaser, Courtesy of the artist; **453** The Boating Party, Mary Cassatt, National Gallery of Art, Chester Dale Collection, Washington, DC

PHOTOGRAPH CREDITS

3 Pressens Bild/Photofest; **6** © Michael Heron/The Stock Market; **28** © Arthur Tilley/FPG International; **31** © Jerome Wexler/Photo Researchers, Inc.; © Ray Coleman/Photo Researchers, Inc.; **37** © FPG International; **42** © Josef Pelaez/The Stock Market; **53** © Jeff Isaac Greenberg/Photo Researchers, Inc.; **63** Jacques M. Chenet/Gamma-Liaison; **87** Lawrence Migdale; **96** © A&J Verkaik/The Stock Market; **100** © Charles Krebs/The Stock Market; **102** © Ken Lax/Photo Researchers, Inc.; Richard Hutchings; © Gabe Palmer/The Stock Market; **111** Andrew Wyeth, Collection of Mr. & Mrs. Frank E. Fowler; **123** Giraudon/Art Resource; **133** The Bettmann Archive; **135** Drawing and text from My Life and Hard Times, copyright © 1933, 1961 by James Thurber. Published by Harper & Row; **151** © The Bettmann Archive; **167** © Flip Chalfant/The Image Bank; **176** Bas Van Beek/Leo deWys, Inc.; **179** The Stock Market; **185** © Stephen Green-Armytage/The Stock Market; **190** © DiMaggio-Kalish/The Stock Market; **193** The Signing of the Declaration of Independence, Edward Hicks, Art Resource; **222** The Bettmann Archive; **224** Drawing and text from "The Pet Department" from The Owl in the Attic. Copyright © 1931, 1959 James Thurber. Published by Harper & Row; **233** Art Resource/Werner Forman Archive; **245** © Jeffrey W. Meyers/The Stock Market; **250** © NASA/Starlight; **253** George Rose/Gamma-Liaison; **266** © Mary Allen; **298** Mark Reinstein (bottom), John Scowen (top)/FPG International; **301** © Brownie Harris/The Stock Market; **305** © San Francisco Mime Troup; **318** © Mark Rollo/Photo Researchers, Inc.; **360** Juan Rios/Wide World Photos; **367** © UPI/Bettmann; **369, 371** Focus on Sports, Inc.; **374** © Ed Bock/The Stock Market; **377** © Bettmann Newphotos; **389** Portrait of Samuel Clemens/The Bettmann Archive; **434** Anne-Marie Weber/The Stock Market; **435** NASA/Starlight; **449** © J.T. Collins/Photo Researchers, Inc.

ILLUSTRATION CREDITS

Cover illustration by Theo Rudnak/Renard Represents
Eldon Doty/HK Portfolio: 4, 11, 15, 18, 22, 23, 30, 44, 48, 50, 51, 57, 59, 60, 66, 67, 72, 75, 78, 79, 81, 84, 92, 95, 107, 108, 120, 122, 131, 137, 138, 140, 146, 147, 149, 157, 171, 172, 186, 217, 235, 239, 240, 257, 259, 261, 274, 278, 281, 288, 290, 294, 299, 306, 310, 316, 323, 330, 335, 342, 344, 345, 348, 349, 352, 355, 356, 359, 376, 377, 380, 381, 383, 385, 391, 392, 393, 395, 399, 403, 406, 408, 425, 426, 427, 430, 431, 455
Tara Framer: 3, 12, 24, 47, 55, 100, 101, 118, 189, 191, 193, 226, 228, 301, 415, 433, 444
Saki Mafundikwa: 113, 228
Maria Pia Marrella: 201
Steve Sullivan: 2, 16, 18, 64–65, 91, 139, 168, 170, 205, 206, 210, 211, 212, 220, 258, 416, 417, 421, 435, 437, 441, 442, 443, 445

INDEX

in sentences, 76–77, 336, 348
for speeches, 242–243
Paraphrasing, for reports, 229
Parentheses, 333, 349
Participial phrases, 311–312, 350, 353, 354, 400
Participles, 274, 350, 362, 399–400, 401, 402
    dangling, 333, 402
    introductory, 311–312
    misplaced, 402
    past, 274, 350, 399
    present, 362, 399, 401
passed, past, 319
Passive voice, 175, 350, 410, 413
Past form, of verbs, 274
Past participle, 274, 350, 399
Past perfect progressive, 408
Past perfect tense, 406, 408, 411
Past progressive, 408
Past tense, 274, 350, 406–407, 411
peace, piece, 319
Peer response, 41–44
Perfect tense, 350
Performance assessment, 452
Period, 282, 335, 350–351
Person, 351
    first, 140, 336, 351, 352
    second, 351, 352
    third, 140, 351, 352, 397
    of verbs, 405
Personal essay, 37–38, 105–110
Personal feelings, 32, 34
Personal interest inventory, 3
Personal journal, 100
Personal letters, 39, 102–104, 313, 314
Personal narrative, 38, 106, 126–132
Personal pronouns, 352, 356, 362, 366, 368–370
Personification, 97
Persuasive essay, 38–40, 183, 203–209
Phrases, 352–354
    adjective, 284, 353, 360
    adverb, 289, 353, 360
    appositive, 296, 353, 354
    gerund, 337, 353, 362, 401
    infinitive, 339, 353, 401–402

participial, 311–312, 350, 353, 354, 400
prepositional, 284, 289, 311–312, 353, 354, 358, 359–360, 361
verb, 353, 400, 403, 405
verbal, 353, 398
Picture graph, 444
Pie chart, *see* Circle graph
Plagiarism, 230–231
Plot, in story, 139, 142–144
Plural nouns, 279–280, 294, 343–344, 354, 355
Poems, 145–152, 303
Point of view, for story, 140
Portfolio, 55, 452
Possessive forms, 317, 355–357
    apostrophes for, 268, 279–280, 293–295, 366
    contractions vs., 356
    joint vs. separate possession, 356
    of nouns, 279–280, 293–295, 355, 357
    of pronouns, 280, 331, 356, 357, 363
Possessive pronouns, 280, 331, 356, 357, 363
Predicate, 70, 322, 357, 390
Predicate adjectives, 287, 292, 357
Predicate nouns, 358
Prefixes, 338, 358, 393
Prepositional phrases, 284, 289, 311–312, 353, 354, 358, 359–360, 361, 374
Prepositions, 358–361
    adverbs vs., 290–291, 360
    conjunctions vs., 325
    object of the, 325, 345, 348, 359, 402
Present participle, 362, 399, 401
Present perfect progressive, 408
Present perfect tense, 406, 407–408
Present progressive, 408
Present tense, 362, 406
Prewriting techniques, 2, 3–10, 12–14, 22
principal, principle, 319
Problem-and-solution essay, 38–39, 177–182
Prodigy, 428

S

indefinite pronoun as, 273
sentences combined by
    joining, 80
    simple, 390
    verb agreeing with, 268,
        271–273, 293, 396
Subject card, 418, 419
Subject pronouns, 362, 366
Subordinate clauses, 86, 284,
        288, 304–308, 311, 341,
        388–389, 397
Subordinating conjunctions,
        79–80, 311, 324–325,
        327–328, 330, 397
Suffixes, 338, 393–395, 397
Superlative form, 397
    of adjectives, 286, 287, 397
    of adverbs, 291, 397
Supporting sentences, 57,
        59–60
Syllabication, 338–339
Symbols, 97, 295
Symphony, 456
Synonyms, 67

T
take, bring, 316
teach, learn, 318
Technological resources,
        425–429
    see also Computer resources
Telling, showing vs., 119
Tests, 446–451
    classroom, 446–449
    standardized, 449–451
    see also Assessments
Textbooks, for studying, 430
Thank you letter, 104
than, then, 320
that, word groups with, 85
their, there, they're, 320
theirs, there's, 320, 356
Theme
    of story, 140
    of symphony, 456
Thesaurus, 30, 347
Thesis statement, 229
they, antecedent for, 277
Third person, 140, 351–352,
        397
Time, possessive form with, 295
Timeline, 439, 445
Time of day
    abbreviations for, 282

colon with, 309
    numbers in, 347
Title card, 418, 420
Titles, italics or underlining
    for, 398
Topic
    finding and developing, 2,
        3–10, 12–14, 22
    narrowing, 5–6, 12–14
Topic sentence, 57–59, 60–61
to, two, too, 320
Traditional verse, 152
Transitional words, 64–65,
        68–69, 160–161
Transitive verbs, 397, 404
True-false questions, 447
two, to, too, 320

U
Underlining, 397–398
Unity, in writing, 62–63
Usage, 52, 398, 451

V
Variety
    for sentences, 82–88, 388
    for speeches, 241
Venn diagram, for essays,
        157–158
Verbal phrases, 353, 398
Verbals, 398–402
    gerunds, 337, 400–401
    infinitives, 339, 401–402
    participles, 274, 350, 362,
        399–400, 401, 402
    past participle, 274, 350,
        399
    present participle, 362,
        399, 401
Verb phrases, 353, 400, 403,
        405
Verbs, 403–415
    action, 283, 403, 404
    active voice, 175, 283, 410,
        412–413
    adverbs modifying, 289, 292
    compound, 323
    confused, 410–411
    helping, 337, 400, 405
    intransitive, 340, 404
    irregular, 25, 273–274, 340,
        409, 411
    linking, 287, 292, 341, 368,